THE INSIDERS' GUIDE®

TO

Atlanta Greater

Co-published and marketed by:
Macon Telegraph Publishing Co.
120 Broadway
Macon, GA 31201
(912) 744-4200

Co-published and distributed by:
The Insiders' Guides Inc.
The Waterfront • Suites 12 &13
P.O. 2057
Manteo, NC 27954
(919) 473-6100

•

FIRST EDITION
1st printing

•

ISBN 0-912367-68-7

The Macon Telegraph Speciality Publications

Project Manager
Harry Davis

Advertising/Production Manager
Ed Campbell

Advertising Creative Services Manager
Kay Beasley

Advertising Representative
Ed Willard

Artist
Jennifer Shermer

Photography
Chuck Morgan

The Insiders' Guides® Inc.

Publisher/Managing Editor
Beth P. Storie

President/General Manager
Michael McOwen

Vice President/Advertising
Murray Kasmenn

Creative Services Director
Mike Lay

Partnership Services Director
Giles Bissonnette

New Technology Products Director
David Haynes

Project Editor
Theresa Shea Chavez

Project Artist
Mel Dorsey

Fulfillment Director
Gina Twiford

Sales and Marketing Director
Julie Ross

Controller
Claudette Forney

Preface

Welcome to Atlanta!

No matter how you know our city — by one of its historical names: Terminus, for the end of the rail line; Marthasville, after a governor's daughter; Whitehall, after the first tavern and store — or by one of its nicknames: Gate City, as in "Gateway to the South;" L.A., for Lovely Atlanta; Hotlanta, as in the Allman Brothers' song — or as a sports mecca that's home of the 1991 and 1992 National League Champion Atlanta Braves, the 1994 Super Bowl and the 1996 Olympics — we're very glad you're here.

In fact, though you may not know it, it's people like you who have made Atlanta what it is: the social, cultural and economic capital of the South.

That's because since its earliest days, Atlanta's soundtrack has been the music of motion: unceasing change has been its one constant. Its chief product has always been a service — transportation — that, by its nature, provokes endless renewal.

From the day in 1835 when the Whitehall Tavern opened at a wagon crossroads near what became Five Points, Atlantans have looked toward the future, excited about the arrival of the next stagecoach, train, automobile or jet plane. Though humbled and broken by the Civil War, Atlanta got on with life and rose, like the mythical Phoenix whose image graces the city's seal, from its own ashes.

Ongoing upheaval and continuous infusions of new people, money and ideas have created an environment unique among Southern cities. Here the focus is the future, not the past. Here what is old may be respected, but what is new is adored.

This attitude has created an intellectual and economic environment where bold innovations flourish. An Atlanta pharmacist invented the world's most popular soft drink. An Atlanta journalist wrote the world's most popular novel. And an Atlanta minister led the South and the United States away from the cruel vestiges of slavery and toward the true realization of the ideals of the Declaration of Independence: "that all men are created equal."

Today Atlanta has become a new kind of crossroads, this time on the information superhighway. Satellites carry news, weather, sports and entertainment programming from Atlanta to the rest of the world 24 hours a day. Atlanta is home base for a plethora of services offered by media mogul Ted Turner: Cable News Network (CNN), CNN International, Headline News, Cartoon Network, Cartoon Network - Latin America, Cartoon Network - Europe, Turner Network Television (TNT), TNT - Latin America, TNT - Europe, Turner Classic Movies, SportSouth, SuperStation TBS and the CNN Airport Network. The 24-hour Weather Channel also beams up-to-the-minute world weather forecasts from Atlanta.

Modern Atlanta is composed of many parts. There's downtown, with its soaring skyscrapers and big-city pace. Atlanta is home to Atlanta University Center, the nation's largest consortium of historically African-American colleges. Along the tree-lined streets of Midtown, Virginia-Highlands and Inman Park, renovators have breathed new life into grand old homes. In the shops and clubs of eclectic Little Five Points and fashionable Buckhead, trendsetters are ever on the prowl for the new and different.

Atlanta just keeps right on growing, with new residential areas popping up farther and farther from the city proper. Tens of thousands of Atlanta workers commute from homes so remote they once would have been a long day's buggy ride away.

Atlanta's reputation as a "party town" is as old as the city itself, and today few will deny it. Here you'll find a huge variety of nightclubs, including everything from booming 24-hour discos to intimate jazz clubs to cozy neighborhood bars. Your restaurant choices here include the world's largest drive-in, classic home cooking places, exquisite five-star dining rooms and everything in between. And with attractions such as Six Flags Over Georgia, White Water, Zoo Atlanta, Fernbank Science Center, SciTrek and the World of Coca-Cola, there's plenty of excitement for younger visitors too.

Almost everything about Atlanta has changed in the 160 years since the first drink was poured in the old Whitehall Tavern. Little Terminus went from the end of the line to the center of the South, and from a smouldering, war-ravaged ruin to one of the premiere cities of the United States.

But one thing that lives on — and that we hope always will — is the adventurous spirit of that spunky little rail crossroads. This is no place to sit still or to dwell endlessly on days gone by. Of course Atlantans are proud of our city's past, and we jealously guard our old landmarks. But we're quite pragmatic too. There's no room here for empty, ritualized traditionalism: What's of no use is simply swept away.

That adventurous spirit — and the ability to attract people who share it — remains Atlanta's abiding strength. Whether you're a longtime resident, a new Atlantan, a first-time visitor or a frequent guest in town, we're glad to see you. And just like our 19th-century predecessors watching the trains pull in, we're eager to hear your news and ideas, for they help us keep our city fresh and exciting and ready for the future.

Thank you for coming — and welcome to Atlanta!

About the Authors

David Goldman is a native of Greenwood, South Carolina, where he graduated from Lander College in 1979 after being named outstanding English major. He moved to Atlanta in 1981 and, though the economy was deep in recession, quickly found work as an assistant editor on a trade magazine. In 1986 he was promoted to editor-in-chief of the national trade monthly *Professional Furniture Merchant*. A freelance writer since 1989, he has written more than 250 articles for a variety of publications.

David has lived in several Atlanta neighborhoods (always in-town). He now resides in Inman Park, the historic district that was at the center of the Civil War Battle of Atlanta.

After 20 years of regular visits to family and friends in Atlanta, **Terry Hunter** decided to make her enjoyment of the city permanent in 1992. With a convert's fresh-eyed appreciation, she revels in Atlanta's four distinct seasons and special brand of hospitality.

A writer and editor for 15 years, she's headed magazines devoted to architectural design, real estate, development, city style, health, business and graphic design. Forming her own company, Special Publication Inc., in 1987, Hunter provides editorial services including new publication start-ups, newsletters, scripts and marketing projects. A graduate student at Georgia State University, she works from her in-town office in south Buckhead.

Exploration of the city's hilly terrain and the exotic variety of its multicultural population are Hunter's avocation. In researching this book, a real pleasure emerged for the writer in the willingness of Atlantans to share their city, its treasures and its stories. She's found the prevailing evidence of Southern influence wedded to an international flavor to be an unbeatable combination.

Acknowledgments

Writing a book about the city I love and have called home for most my adult life has been a thoroughly amazing project. I've seen places that I never had a chance to visit in my more than a dozen years as an Atlantan, and I've learned fascinating facts about our past that explain much about life today.

But most of all, I've been reminded of what I love in the spirit of the people of Atlanta. Here, at this nexus of roads, rails and air routes, the newcomer is the rule, not the exception. Here you really can start over — and people do, every day.

In an exclusive interview for this book, former Mayor Sam Massell put it this way: "In Atlanta, we work at it. We invite people, we welcome them and we encourage them." That's certainly the Atlanta attitude that brought me here in 1981. I hope that spirit comes through on every page of this book, and I hope you experience it in all your encounters with Atlantans.

This book would not have been possible without the help of many people. My deep and grateful thanks to:

My coauthor Terry Hunter, our editor Theresa Chavez and our publisher Beth Storie for their patience and valued input; and to Harry Davis of the Macon Telegraph Co.

The many organizations and individuals who offered me valuable information: the Atlanta Chamber of Commerce, the Atlanta Convention and Visitors Bureau, the Atlanta History Center, the Atlanta Preservation Center, Metropolitan Atlanta Rapid Transit Authority, AAA of Georgia, Julia W. Bond, Sam Massell, Kirk Melhuish and Mike Malloy at WSB-AM 750, the office of U.S. Representative John Lewis, the office of Atlanta City Council Member Mary Davis, Michael Malone of Midtown Travel, Carole Mumford of the Wren's Nest, Barry Steig of Hartsfield Atlanta Airport, Janet Marie Smith of the Atlanta Braves, Stephen Januseski of Tall Tales Books, Philip Mooney of the Coca-Cola Co., James Taylor of the Atlanta-Fulton Public Library and all the friendly, brainy bookworms who answer the library's telephone reference lines.

My other editors and employers for helping me rearrange my schedule to accommodate this project.

All my teachers, both in and out of the academic world.

My parents, Margie and the late John Wesley Goldman.

The many wonderful friends who offered ideas and insights on this book, all the while helping keep my hectic life sane and amusing, most especially to Potsy Duncan and Paul Burke, Pam Perry and Craig Fine, Holly and Robert Lowry III, Jon Baker, Bob Beverly, James Bond, Angela Bowie, Charles Dodson, Jon

Goldman, Kathryn Kelly, Joe Kelly, Chuck Morgan, Bobby Nealis, Keita Nishitani, Sue and James F. Ouzts, Jack Pelham and David Moore, Henrietta Richards, Joe Roman and Paula Gately Tillman, Ted Rubenstein, RuPaul, Susan and Lee Rush, Vala and Perry Schwartz, Steve Shipman and Mike Pellegrinon, Rosser Shymanski, Gail Walker, Randy and Ronnie Wilder and Rose-Marie Williams. Also, to my dogs and cats, who insisted that I take time to play.

Thanks most of all to Dick Richards, best friend and toughest editor, for his ideas, inspiration, patience, good humor and unfailing kindness throughout this project.

For Margie Ouzts Goldman
and for Dick Richards

— David Goldman

Daunting doesn't begin to describe the task of presenting Atlanta's ambiance. Without the help of many kindhearted people, this book could not have been accomplished. Though a mere thank you seems inadequate for the services rendered, I offer my gratitude.

The Atlanta Chamber of Commerce always seemed to have answers or direction to them. Other area chambers of commerce provided invaluable facts on their localities. Reliable maps from AAA Tour Guides helped orient information for the formidable Daytrips chapter. Particularly helpful were the convention and visitors bureaus' comprehensive printed materials shared so willingly. I highly recommend *Georgia At Its Best* by Jeanne Perkins Harman and Harry E. Harman III for its friendly tone and thorough detail on the entire state of Georgia.

The Georgia Department of Natural Resources, the Georgia State Parks and Historic Sites, the Georgia Department of Industry, Trade and Tourism, and The Atlanta Preservation Center all contributed useful data.

Several chapters required specialized knowledge: For the Green Atlanta chapter Ed Macie, regional urban forestry coordinator with the USDA Forest Service - Southern Region, gave both direct and indirect aid as a conduit to related sources. Other valuable input came from Trees Atlanta, Georgia's Stone Mountain Park and the Atlanta Botanical Gardens. Thanks to Terry Morris, vice president with Northside Realty for insight into Atlanta's real estate scene. The Service Directory, as well as others, benefited from librarian extraordinaire, writer and editor Cal Gough of the Atlanta-Fulton Public Library. Jim Cashin of Georgia Radio Reading Service and the Georgia Blind Adventures provided much needed resources. Thanks to the parks and recreation departments of the City of Atlanta and Cobb, DeKalb, Fulton and Gwinnett counties for their assistance with the Recreational Sports chapter. Of course, the Atlanta Track Club was a helpful source many times over. A reliable and entertaining source on the outdoors is *Atlanta Walks* by Ren and Helen Davis. For the lowdown on education, I consulted the various school boards, the Georgia Department of Education, the Atlanta Area Association of Independent Schools as well as the *Economic Overview of Secondary Education in the Atlanta Area* compiled by Georgia Power Company. The Atlanta History Center proved a good source for insight into the metro area's places of worship with such books as *Ebenezer: A Centennial Time Capsule* and

Gloria Sampson's artistic *Historic Churches and Temples of Georgia.*

For his support and encouragement, I thank my co-author David Goldman.

Completing such a task as this book requires the patience of a writer's family and friends as they take a back seat to an editorial schedule. For her understanding, I thank my mother, Ruth Christian, to whom my visits can now once again become more regular. For my dear father's support from my first story written, I am thankful. To John and Amy, to my sister, my brother and to all my friends, especially Ann, Kevin and Sharon, who thought (correctly) I could discuss nothing but this project: I am blessed you are in my life — thanks so much for hanging in there with me.

— Terry Christian Hunter

Table of Contents

Directory of Maps

Atlanta

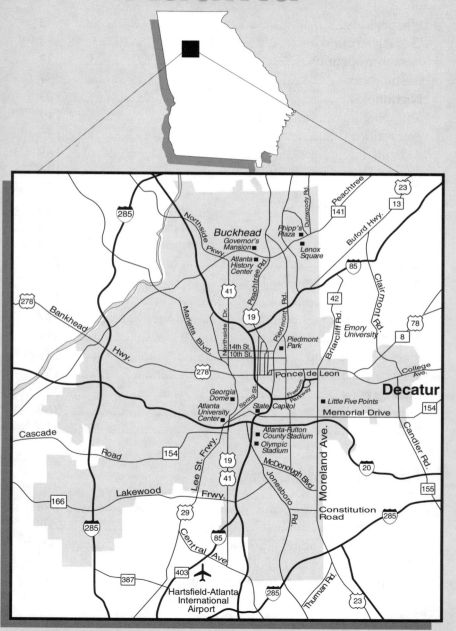

Greater Atlanta

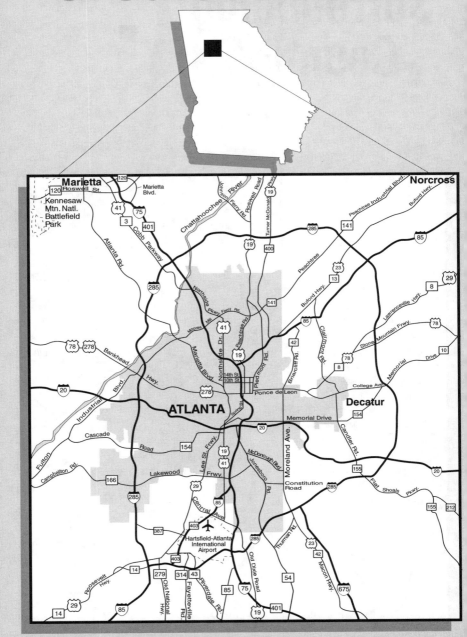

Atlanta's Surrounding Counties

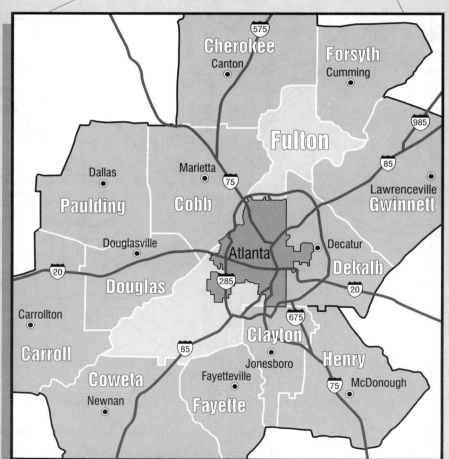

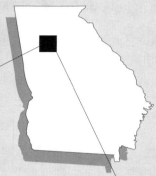

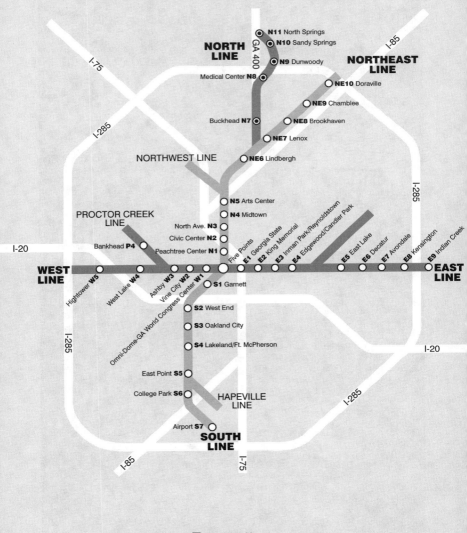

N11 North Springs
N10 Sandy Springs
N9 Dunwoody

NORTH LINE
GA 400

NORTHEAST LINE
I-85

Medical Center **N8**

NE10 Doraville

NE9 Chamblee

Buckhead **N7**
NE8 Brookhaven

NE7 Lenox

NORTHWEST LINE
NE6 Lindbergh

I-285

I-75

I-285

N5 Arts Center
N4 Midtown

PROCTOR CREEK LINE

North Ave. **N3**
Civic Center **N2**
Bankhead **P4**
Peachtree Center **N1**

Five Points
E1 Georgia State
E2 King Memorial
E3 Inman Park/Reynoldstown
E4 Edgewood/Candler Park
E5 East Lake
E6 Decatur
E7 Avondale
E8 Kensington
E9 Indian Creek

I-285

I-20

WEST LINE

Hightower **W5**
West Lake **W4**
Ashby **W3**
Vine City **W2**
Omni-Dome-GA World Congress Center **W1**

S1 Garnett

EAST LINE

I-285

I-20

S2 West End

S3 Oakland City

S4 Lakeland/Ft. McPherson

East Point **S5**

College Park **S6**

HAPEVILLE LINE

I-285

Airport **S7**

SOUTH LINE

I-85

I-75

■ East-West Line
■ North-South Line
□ Interstate Highways
◉ Under Construction

marta®

Photo: Georgia Tourist Division

Unceasing change has made Atlanta the social, cultural, and economic capital of the South.

How To Use This Book

We've planned this book so that it gives you quick and easy access to everyday, practical information. All chapters are independent and can be read in any order: If you're starving and your first priority is finding a place to eat, you can turn immediately to our Restaurants chapter. If you're reading this on an Atlanta-bound flight and need to know how to get out of the airport and into town, flip right to our Getting Around chapter and read the sections on Hartsfield Atlanta Airport and MARTA.

We've tried to organize our information in a way that makes it easy for you to explore areas that interest you and breeze by those that don't. But we hope you'll find time to look over those chapters you might initially skip. You don't have to be a history buff to be enthralled by the story of Atlanta's birth, destruction and rebirth, which you'll find in our History chapter. And even if you're not shopping for a home, our chapter on neighborhoods will help you understand the locations and characteristics of city districts you'll hear people talking about everyday.

This is no coffee table book: It's designed to be used. Don't leave it in your hotel room! Keep it in your glove compartment, briefcase or backpack; make notes in it. No matter where you travel in the Atlanta area, take this book with you to find the best food, entertainment, lodging, attractions and things to do.

While we have made every effort to ensure accuracy and to include all of the best of Atlanta, we're only human. Atlanta is a city built on constant change, and no one can keep up with every single aspect of life here. If you find mistakes in our book, if you disagree with something we've said or if you'd like to see additions or changes in future editions, we would appreciate your taking time to write to us in care of The Insiders' Guides corporate offices:

The Insiders' Guide to Greater Atlanta
The Waterfront, Suites 12 and 13 — P.O. Box 2057
Manteo, North Carolina 27954

How This Book is Organized

Atlanta's city limits have not been revised since 1952, when they were expanded to take in another 92 square miles and more than 100,000 people. About 400,000 people now live in the 136-square mile city.

Several city and county governments share authority over the central part of the Atlanta metro area. In a practical sense, Atlanta's "real" boundary is defined by I-285 — what we call "the Perimeter." Within the Perimeter are contained large portions of Fulton and DeKalb counties and small slices of Cobb and Clayton counties. This can get confusing: One person may live in Atlanta city and DeKalb County, another in Decatur city in DeKalb County and another in College

Park in Fulton County. But to avoid confusion, all three people would probably give the short answer "Atlanta" when asked where they're from.

So, to help keep life simple, we've organized our book along the following lines: We've used "Atlanta" and "Beyond Atlanta" to geographically arrange many chapters and categories within chapters. Any restaurant, shop, theater, etcetera that falls under "Atlanta" lies within the I-285 Perimeter. Anything under "Beyond Atlanta" lies outside the I-285 Perimeter, and we've often organized those attractions and businesses by county. When helpful, we also refer to the neighborhood of a location.

Two small portions of the city of Atlanta are actually outside the Perimeter: The Ben Hill section in the southwest and the Adamsville section in the west. Consistent with our use of the Perimeter as Atlanta's practical boundary, we will consider these areas to be "Beyond Atlanta."

Atlanta enjoys the world's largest toll-free dialing area. All telephone numbers are within the 404 area code unless otherwise noted. A few 404 numbers are long distance from Atlanta.

Inside
History

Insightful Beginnings

It was, indeed, a curious spot to build a town.

Deep in the northwest Georgia woods, more than 1,000 feet above sea level, near no commercially navigable waterway, on land of marginal agricultural value in an area only recently held by the Cherokee and Creek — the location that was to become Atlanta had little to recommend it.

But in the early 1800s, Georgia, the largest state east of the Mississippi River, badly needed a better transportation corridor to the prosperous north. Acting on the results of a forward-looking land survey, the state Legislature voted to build the Western & Atlantic railroad from the Tennessee state line southward, ending at a point where three tall granite ridges converged. Here, the new line was to link with extensions of railroads from other parts of the state. The tiny railroad settlement had a humble beginning: Even its name —Terminus — said this was the end of the line. "The terminus," declared W&A engineer Stephen Long in 1837, "will be a good location for one tavern, a blacksmith shop, a grocery store and nothing else."

In fact, as unbelievable as it would have seemed at the time, little Terminus (briefly called Marthasville, then Atlanta) was already on its way to becoming the economic and cultural center of the southern United States. Just 20 years after regular train service began, Atlanta was linked by rail to Chattanooga, Augusta, Macon, Mobile and many points beyond.

Because the tracks made it a crossroads in the quickly booming overland transportation industry, Atlanta evolved

Photo: Chuck Morgan

Many Civil War monuments may be found throughout the Atlanta area.

from the start as a new kind of town: an inland port. People, goods, money and news were always moving through. The constant flow of travelers and rough-and-ready railroad men gave the town a bawdy flavor. The first tavern opened in 1835; the first church-and-schoolhouse had to wait until 1845. In the first mayoral election in 1848, the temperance candidate was defeated by a Decatur Street tinsmith and still-maker backed by the Free and Rowdy Party.

From the very beginning, Atlanta promoted itself as modern city, different from the tradition-bound South. Atlanta's bustling, forward-looking spirit is well evidenced in the following two items quoted by Norman Shavin and Bruce Galphin in their excellent illustrated history, *Atlanta: Triumph of a People*.

An educator who arrived in 1847 found the citizens quite welcoming, noting that they "bow and shake hands with everybody they meet, as there are so many coming in all the time that they cannot remember with whom they are acquainted." And an 1859 city directory boasted, "Our people show their democratic impulses by each allowing his neighbor to attend to his own business, and our ladies are even allowed to attend to their domestic and household affairs without being ruled out of respectable society." Between 1850 and 1860, Atlanta's population swelled from 2,500 to nearly 10,000.

The Civil War

But proud Atlanta's shining rails were about to be twisted into its noose. The U.S. Civil War was the first war in history in which railroads played a major role, and Atlanta beat as the iron heart of the Confederacy, pumping soldiers and supplies to battlefronts across the South. In the unsentimental eyes of U.S. Gen.

William Tecumseh Sherman, the railroad hub was a key military target — even though it sat at the center of a city of more than 20,000.

In the spring of 1864, Atlantans knew Sherman was on the march from the Tennessee border and that he had set his sights on their city, but most were confident that Confederate troops would halt the advance. Besides, they believed that the city, ringed by 10 miles of sharpened stakes, rifle pits and forts with cannons, would never fall. In fact, the fortifications did hold: Not a single Union soldier fought his way across them. (Ironically, a Yankee designed them: Col. Lemuel P. Grant was a brilliant civil engineer who moved South in the railroad-building prewar years. Today Grant Park, home to Zoo Atlanta and the Cyclorama, bears his name.)

By summer, the city's bravado was replaced by dread as the booming battles, now within earshot of the city, grew louder daily. After suffering ghastly casualties on July 22 in what became known as the Battle of Atlanta, the Confederate troops were forced to take refuge inside the city's fortifications.

Once their big guns were within range, Union troops mercilessly shelled the city. From July 20, when the shells claimed their first civilian victim (a little girl playing with her dog), until the bombardment ceased on August 25, hell rained down on Atlanta, and terrified residents cowered in makeshift bomb shelters. When Union troops seized the railroad south of the city on September 1, the Confederates realized their hopeless plight and abandoned Atlanta to avoid capture. To prevent their use by enemy forces, the Rebels blew up 81 freight cars full of ammunition and seven locomotives. The enormous fire destroyed the Atlanta rolling mill — one of only two factories in the South that could turn out badly needed iron rails.

After the mayor's formal surrender on September 2, Atlanta became a Union camp. Sherman ordered the remaining civilians evacuated: A total of 1,644 people were forced out to face more hardships further south. On the night of November 14, as his 62,000 men pulled out to march to Savannah, Sherman ordered most of the town's remaining structures set afire. Of the 4,000 buildings in the city at the war's beginning, only 400 survived the conflagration. One month shy of the 17th anniversary of its incorporation as a city, Atlanta lay in ruins.

Rising from the Ashes

Throughout the South for fifty years there would be bitter-eyed women who looked backward, to dead times, to dead men, evoking memories that hurt and were futile, bearing poverty with bitter pride because they had those memories. But Scarlett was never to look back.

— Chapter 25, *Gone With the Wind*

The numbers tell the tragic tale: The Civil War claimed more than 618,000 American lives — more than the combined U.S. casualties of every other war from the Revolution to the Korean War. That bloody spring and summer of 1864, 31,687 Union troops and 34,979 Confederates lost their lives in the Atlanta Campaign, which had more fatalities than the number of Americans killed in battle during all the years of the Vietnam War.

After Confederate Gen. Robert E. Lee's surrender on April 9, 1865, a pall of misery and destitution hung heavy over once-haughty Dixie. But Atlanta — like the spitfire heroine who would symbolize the city in Margaret Mitchell's novel 70 years later — got on with life. The South was split into five military governorships and, as the headquarters of the third Military District under U.S. Gen. John Pope, Atlanta was again at the center of things. Federal troops continued to occupy the city for the better part of 10 years.

The railroads had been wrecked in the war, as Union soldiers ripped up the rails, roasted them over fires and twisted them into what were called "Sherman's neckties." But with help from the Army, liberated slaves and Northern investors, the four rail lines were restored in just two years, and a new line was working its way to Charlotte, North Carolina, by 1869.

Life was tough in the harsh winter of 1864-'65, and a smallpox epidemic swept through in 1866. Even so, the town was struggling its way back to civilization. Theatrical performances resumed in 1865, and by 1866 the reborn city boasted two opera houses. That October, a 75-member touring company presented Italian grand opera on three consecutive nights, although the steep ticket price ($2) kept many Atlantans away.

In 1868, the Georgia capitol was relocated to Atlanta from Milledgeville, a decision that was ratified in a popular referendum in 1877. By 1867, 250 stores were

Insiders' Tips

open in the city. Atlanta was home to 21,000 people in 1870 and to 37,000 in 1880.

Everywhere there were signs of progress: In 1871, the first horse-drawn streetcar began to service a 2-mile route. In the 1870s, the city inaugurated free mail delivery and a downtown garbage collection service.

In 1886 Atlanta produced what remains its most famous export. John Pemberton, a Marietta Street pharmacist, blended a "brain tonic" with a secret recipe of extracts from the coca plant and kola nuts. When a customer happened to order his Coca-Cola syrup with soda instead of plain water, the world's favorite soft drink was born. Dr. Pemberton sold ownership of his product for $2,300 to entrepreneur Asa Candler in 1887. Available only in Atlanta at first, Coca-Cola soon spread across the South and the nation. By 1899 the company was shipping 300,000 gallons of syrup a year and beginning to sell the premixed drink in bottles.

In 1890, the city had 65,000 residents, only 12 percent of whom had called the "first" Atlanta home. In the South, only Richmond, Nashville and New Orleans were larger than Atlanta. By 1894 electricity, not mules, powered the streetcars on their routes.

Foreshadowing the importance of the modern-day convention business, Atlanta hosted large expositions in 1881, 1887 and 1895, attracting international attention and investment. Gen. Sherman himself came to the 1881 exposition; President Grover Cleveland attended the 1887 fair. The Liberty Bell was displayed at the 1895 exposition, which attracted nearly a million visitors in its three-month run and boldly included pavilions celebrating the progress and accomplishments of blacks and women. The latter two fairs were held on the site of the present Piedmont Park, purchased by the city for $93,000.

The Dawning of a New Century

As the 20th century dawned, Atlanta's population stood at 90,000.

Atlanta's African-American population grew rapidly during the war years as slaves were ordered in to aid the Confed-

Photo: Chuck Morgan

You can visit the historic home of Alonzo F. Herndon, a former slave and founder of the Atlanta Life Insurance Company.

eracy, and many of these new citizens returned to make their homes in the city after the war. By 1870, the black community was five times larger than it had been in 1860. By 1890, blacks made up 43 percent of the population and 50 percent of the workforce.

Northern missionaries and other reformers started Freedmen's Schools to educate ex-slaves and their children. (One such school operated in a box car divided into classrooms). This early movement planted the seeds that made Atlanta a center of black higher education, and today, the Atlanta University Center is the largest consortium of historically African-American colleges in the nation.

Even in the days of enforced racial separation, Atlanta prided itself on being a town with the good sense to put business before prejudice — although it was not always successful. On September 22, 1906, a white mob, enraged by inflammatory newspaper reports of numerous "outrages" against white women, attacked and murdered blacks and burned black homes. Order was not fully restored until September 27, and the rioting left at least 20 blacks and several whites dead. The white rampage, reported throughout the nation and in Europe, badly damaged Atlanta's emerging reputation.

In the wake of the riot, much of Atlanta's African-American business community withdrew to Auburn Avenue (then called Wheat Street). Auburn became Atlanta's *other* main street, offering a full range of retail, service and en-tertainment concerns, as well as religious and social organizations. Among its most successful businesses was Atlanta Life Insurance Co., founded by Alonzo Herndon, an ex-slave and sharecropper who built a lucrative barber business and became Atlanta's first African-American millionaire. In 1956, *Fortune Magazine* called Auburn "the richest Negro street in the world."

Civil Rights

It was only natural that Atlanta, long a center of black culture and education, would become a center of civil rights activities in the tumultuous 1960s. And although integration was certainly a contentious issue, forward-thinking black and white leaders helped Atlanta avoid the eruptions of violence that tore apart so many U.S. cities in those years. It was tough, but Atlanta lived up to Mayor William Hartsfield's boast in a 1959 *Newsweek* article: "Atlanta is a city too busy to hate."

At the center of the civil rights movement throughout its most dramatic years was Dr. Martin Luther King Jr. King was born in a modest frame house on Auburn Avenue on January 15, 1929. A gifted student, he was admitted to Morehouse College at age 15, then earned his doctorate from Boston University in 1955. After leading the successful drive to desegregate buses in Montgomery, Alabama, King returned to Atlanta in 1960 as president of the Southern Christian Leader-

Downtown's most convenient full-service post office is at the Atlanta Market Center entrance to Peachtree Center station; take the stairs marked MARTA on the west side of Peachtree.

Insiders' Tips

Headstrong Heroine

She was small, but it's said she enjoyed corn liquor, cigarettes and a good dirty joke. Peggy Mitchell was a popular features writer when she left the *Atlanta Journal* in 1926 to nurse an injured ankle and make a life with her new husband. In response to his persistent suggestions, she began a novel.

Born in a house that had been spared Sherman's torch, Mitchell was fascinated by the Civil War and spent many childhood hours listening to the harrowing tales of its elderly survivors. So vivid were their recollections that Mitchell thought the war had ended just before she was born — and she was utterly astonished at age 10 when some black farm workers broke the news to her that the South had actually lost the war.

Typing at the sewing table she used as a desk, dressed in her husband's baggy clothes and wearing a writer's green eyeshade, Margaret Mitchell spent the next 10 years writing a novel (originally called *Another Day*, then *Tomorrow is Another Day*) about a strong-willed Southern girl of Irish descent (originally named Pansy O'Hara) who came of age in the last days before the war, survived the destruction of Atlanta and grew rich during Reconstruction.

Mitchell began by writing the novel's last chapter. When visitors came calling, she hid the growing stacks of manuscripts under a large towel, for she jealously guarded her privacy and shuddered to think that anyone would find the novel autobiographical. (In fact, the twice-married, headstrong Mitchell had much in common with her plucky heroine.)

Most reluctantly, Mitchell gave the ragtag manuscript to a Macmillian agent scouting the South for new writers in 1935, then immediately panicked and wired him: "Send the manuscript back. I've changed my mind." But it was too late. The agent, like the millions and millions of readers who followed him, was instantly hooked.

Gone With the Wind sold 50,000 copies on the first day it was offered. In the years since, it has sold more than 28 million copies around the world and remains the bestselling novel of all time. David O. Selznick paid $50,000 for the movie rights; the 1939 world premiere in Atlanta was a spectacular event reported around the world; the movie won 10 Academy Awards and, by its 50th anniversary, had grossed more than $840 million.

"In a weak moment, I have written a book . . . . " Mitchell said in a 1935 letter. It was a book that catapulted its author to international celebrity and forever affected the way the world thought of her hometown.

ship Conference and co-pastor (with his father) of Ebenezer Baptist Church.

In October of 1960, King and 51 others were arrested when they staged a sit-in to protest segregation at Rich's department store; in all, some 180 people went to jail. Most refused to post bail in order to attract attention to their demands.

King's arrest was especially problematic because he was on probation for driving without a Georgia license (he possessed one from Alabama). His probation was revoked, and he was sentenced to six month's in the state penitentiary. Presidential candidate John F. Kennedy is said to have intervened personally to secure King's early release.

In Atlanta, as in most Southern communities, the desegregation of public schools was hotly debated. But here integration proceeded far more smoothly than in many cities. On August 30, 1961, nine black students made history by enrolling in formerly all-white high schools. That afternoon, President Kennedy publicly congratulated the city, urging other communities "to look closely at what Atlanta has done and to meet their responsibility, as the officials of Atlanta and Georgia have done, with courage, tolerance and, above all, respect for the law."

To the chagrin of many conservatives, King was awarded the Nobel Prize for Peace in Sweden in 1964. Although still a very controversial figure in his hometown, King was honored with a black-tie banquet staged by city leaders, Coca-Cola magnate Robert W. Woodruff chief among them.

On April 4, 1968, an assassin's bullet stilled King's voice for peace and progress. Gripped by grief and rage, many U.S. cities exploded in violence, but Atlanta, again, was spared. The eyes of the world focused on the city on April 9, when hundreds of thousands watched King's cortege make its way slowly from Ebenezer Baptist Church to Morehouse College, where president emeritus Dr. Benjamin E. Mays said, "To be honored by being requested to give the eulogy at the funeral of Dr. Martin Luther King is like asking one to eulogize his deceased son, so close and so precious was he to me."

Today King's body rests in an elevated marble crypt at the Martin Luther King, Jr. Center for Nonviolent Social Change on Auburn Avenue, near his boyhood home and beside his church. The Center stands on a 23-acre National Historic Site and annually welcomes more visitors (3.5 million) than any other Atlanta attraction.

After King's death, Atlanta continued to make important strides toward social justice for all. In 1974, 35-year-old Maynard Jackson became the youngest mayor in Atlanta's history and the first African American to become mayor of a major southern city. Jackson's aunt, Metropolitan Opera soprano Mattiwilda Dobbs, performed at his inauguration; she had previously refused to sing in Atlanta because audiences here were segregated.

The atmosphere fostered by the coalition of civil rights leaders and white liberals made the city a progressive oasis in conservative Georgia. Even as some affluent whites fled the city for the suburbs in the 1960s and '70s, many more people took their places. Flower children, gays and lesbians, peace activists and a variety of intellectuals and nonconformists made their homes here, eager to live in a harmonious and evolving integrated urban environment.

While the city is hardly the "People's Republic of Atlanta" that its detractors sometimes portray, its politics remain decidedly left-leaning. In the '70s Atlanta was a center of antiwar activity: Presidential candidate Senator George McGovern once led a peace march down Auburn Avenue with Mayor Sam Massell. In the '80s Atlanta was deeply involved in the fight to free South Africa. Recently released political prisoner Nelson Mandela was wildly received by an enormous throng at Georgia Tech's Grant Field when he came here to thank the city in 1990. And each June, the mayor proclaims Lesbian and Gay Pride Week in recognition of that community's contributions to the city's life.·

And then there's the matter of the Georgia state flag, a controversy that may rage right through the Olympics. The Georgia Legislature modified the flag in 1956, in a defiant anti-integration gesture, to include the Confederate battle emblem. After a movement to remove the Stars and Bars failed in the state Legislature, Atlanta City Council acted on its own, banishing the banner from City Hall and replacing it (on February 4, 1993) with the pre-1956 flag.

Ushering in the Jet Age

If Atlanta was born in 1837 on the day the Western & Atlantic surveyors drove in the "zero milepost" that marked the end of the rail line, modern Atlanta was born in 1925 on the day the city took a five-year, rent-free lease on an abandoned auto racetrack in Hapeville, 10 miles south of town, promising to develop the overgrown 287-acre site as an airfield.

Interest in flying built slowly at first. Atlanta was already at the center of a web of tracks and roads; aviation was more of an expensive curiosity than a major factor in transportation. But when young William Hartsfield looked at planes, he saw the future. First as an alderman, then, for 22 years as Atlanta's mayor, Hartsfield pushed for improvements in aviation. By the early 1930s, Atlanta had the second-largest number of air routes in the country.

From the beginning, the demand for aviation services far outstripped Candler Field's capacity. More land was acquired, runways added and better facilities built, but the booming aviation business quickly

outgrew each improvement. In 1955, 2 million passengers passed through the airport, making it the busiest in the nation. A $21-million ultramodern facility (the largest single terminal building in the country) opened in 1961. It, too, was quickly too small. "Whether you're bound for heaven or hell," said the old joke, "you'll have to change planes in Atlanta."

In January 1977, work began on the world's largest terminal building at the airport (now renamed Hartsfield Atlanta International Airport to honor the mayor whose vision had readied Atlanta for the jet age). The project cost half a billion dollars and took three-and-a-half years to complete. Throughout construction, normal operations continued at the world's second busiest airport. The new Hartsfield, built around a space-age, automated people-moving system 40 feet underground, opened to much fanfare on September 21, 1980. Hartsfield is home to Delta Air Lines, one of the world's leading carriers. Delta offers more than 500 domestic and international flights a day out of the airport. In 1993, the airline carried more than 85 million passengers worldwide.

Even huge Hartsfield had its limitations, and in September 1994, the city unveiled the new Concourse E for international travel. It is, predictably, the largest concourse in the nation, and airport planners are betting it will adequately meet demand into the next century. But with the way Atlanta keeps growing, you never know . . . .

Accommodating Atlantans and the World

Throughout recent decades, Atlanta has continued to acquire the high-visibility accessories of a world-class city and to host events of international interest.

The city built an arts center with the largest regional theater in the Southeast and a symphony hall; a 4,591-seat civic center that hosted the Metropolitan Opera; a 16,000-seat coliseum; a baseball/football stadium; a 2.5 million-square foot convention center; and the world's largest cable-supported domed stadium. Atlantans even pulled together to prevent the destruction of the lavish, 4,678-seat Fox Theatre, now one of the nation's few surviving grand movie palaces.

In 1966 Atlanta became the first city ever to acquire professional baseball and football teams in the same year. Professional basketball followed in 1968. Atlanta's Omni complex was the site of the 1988 National Democratic Convention, which was watched worldwide. The city's new Georgia Dome hosted Super Bowl XXVIII in 1994, attracting sports fans and media from around the world.

But modern Atlanta's biggest challenge lies ahead. In 1990 the city surprised the world when it overcame stiff competition and was awarded the 1996 Olympics, the 100th anniversary of the modern Olympic games. This enormous event will have a tremendous impact on the city and its people, and there's much work yet to be done. But Olympic officials and citizen volunteers are working hard to make sure that Atlanta will be ready to welcome everyone when the world comes calling in the summer of 1996.

Now that you understand a bit about Atlanta's past, we'll bet you're ready to start exploring the modern city. So put on your Braves cap and some comfortable shoes, grab your sunglasses and/or your umbrella (more about the weather later), and let's have some fun in Atlanta!

Photo: Chuck Morgan

Historic Oakland Cemetary was on the outskirts of Atlanta when it was established in 1850.

Inside
Getting Around

Atlanta was a transportation nexus long before the advent of modern transportation. Located in the foothills of the Appalachian Mountains, this is a hilly region where giant granite ridges form natural transportation corridors. The granite ridges upon which Atlanta rests were used by Native Americans as land bridges between the coastal, piedmont and mountain areas of southeastern North America. Railroads, then highways, followed those same routes.

Today Atlanta is at the center of a web of rails, roads and air routes. Getting to Atlanta is easy . . . much easier, in fact, than avoiding Atlanta — not that you'd want to!

Roadways

Interstates and Highways

Atlanta is served by three interstate highways. On radio traffic reports, these are frequently identified by their location relative to downtown instead of by number.

I-85 N. (the Northeast Expressway) connects Atlanta with Greenville, South Carolina, and Charlotte, North Carolina, before merging with I-95 at Richmond, Virginia. South of the city, I-85 S. (the Southwest Expressway) continues to Montgomery, Alabama.

I-75 N. (the Northwest Expressway) extends from Atlanta to Chattanooga and Knoxville in Tennessee, Cincinnati, Detroit and the Canadian border. Below Atlanta (the Southeast Expressway) I-75 is the route to Florida via the Georgia cities of Macon and Valdosta.

I-20 W. (the West Expressway) goes from Atlanta to Birmingham; Jackson, Mississippi; Dallas and beyond. I-20 E. (the East Expressway) continues to Augusta, Georgia, and Columbia, South Carolina, connecting with I-95 in Florence, South Carolina.

There are two connecting interstate highways that are important to understand:

I-285 (the Perimeter) is the 62.77-mile ring road encircling Atlanta.

I-75 and **I-85** merge just north of Georgia Tech and become the same road, curving around the downtown business district. This section is called the Downtown Connector and is marked on maps as 75/85. The interchange connecting the combined 75/85 with I-20 is near Atlanta-Fulton County Stadium. 75 and 85 go their separate ways just north of Hartsfield Atlanta Airport; I-85 goes to the airport and on to Montgomery, and I-75 continues south to Macon and Florida.

Another bit of shorthand you're likely to hear on radio reports is **Spaghetti Junction**. This is not a favorite spot for pasta, but rather the looping, futuristic interchange that connects the Northeast Expressway with I-285.

I-675 is a short, new stretch of interstate that connects the southeast side of I-285 with I-75 about 10 miles south of town. It's hard to find — some maps cover it up with ads or a street index — but a real time-saver. If you're heading south from the east side of town, take Moreland Avenue south until it crosses I-285; I-675 is on your left. It's handy for hooking up with I-75 S. during rush hour, since it lets you steer clear of the downtown connector and the congested section of I-285 between the interchanges for I-75 and I-85.

North of the city, **Georgia 400** travels toward Lake Lanier. Southbound 400 once ended at I-285, but a newly completed extension now connects it to the Northeast Expressway near Lindbergh Plaza. Georgia 400's extension inside I-285 to I-85 is a toll road (50¢). The toll plaza is located just north of the Buckhead/Lenox Road Exit.

On the toll portion of Georgia 400, have your 50¢ ready. As you drive north, the booths on the right have attendants to make change; the center lanes take exact change only; the left lanes are for "cruise card" holders only. (A cruise card is an electronic device attached to your sun visor; it automatically debits your account each time you pass through the toll plaza. A camera photographs the license plate of anyone who zips through the cruise lanes without a card; freeway freeloaders will shortly receive a ticket and a fine by mail.)

Atlanta's newest road is the **Freedom Parkway**, which opened in the fall of 1994. The 3.1-mile parkway begins at the downtown connector at International Boulevard and leads north to Ponce de Leon (just east of Midtown) and east to Moreland Avenue

(just south of North Avenue) after dividing at the Carter Presidential Center. For years, the road was at the center of a legal battle between the Georgia Department of Transportation and area residents, who did not like the initially proposed larger highway's potential impact on their neighborhoods. In the end, the neighbors won significant changes in the parkway: It has jogging trails, bike paths and a 35 mph speed limit.

INTERSTATE TIPS

Driving north on the downtown connector, I-75 and I-85 split just after you pass downtown: You must take one or the other. The division comes up only 1.25 miles after the first sign announcing it, so you have to be prepared to act fast. This seemingly straightforward stretch of interstate has confused many a driver, and it's easy to see why. The three lanes for I-85 (the North*east* Expressway) are on the *left*; the three lanes for I-75 (the North*west* Expressway) are on the *right* — exactly backwards from what you'd instinctively expect. Begin to move into the appropriate lanes as soon as you safely can after seeing the first signs for the upcoming split, or you may get caught on the wrong side. And, even if you've paid attention and found your lane early, be alert for other drivers frantically switching sides at the last minute.

As you approach Atlanta by interstate, be particularly cautious at I-285, as its interchanges with the expressways are frequently the sites of accidents. I-285 is nearly always crowded: All 18-wheel vehicles traveling the interstates are required by law to take the Perimeter unless their destination is inside Atlanta. Many a trucker has jackknifed on I-285's ramps after failing to slow down.

Traffic on the north side of I-285 has swamped its capacity. Morning and after-

The MARTA Rail System provides convenient transportation from Hartsfield Atlanta Airport.

noon rush hours on this highway are when Atlanta most resembles Los Angeles. East of I-75 across the top of the Perimeter, past I-85, through Spaghetti Junction and sometimes all the way over to I-20 E., the northside Perimeter at rush hour can be totally maddening. It often seems there are only two speeds on this highway: 65 mph and stopped.

Drivers who have driven I-285 for years have watched its traffic get worse and worse as northside office and retail developments mushroomed. A smooth, fast rush hour ride on I-285 is definitely the exception, not the rule. If you must travel to or from the north/northeast Perimeter area on a daily basis, it's worth your while to investigate alternate routes or travel times. Unless you like inching along surrounded by thousands of other frustrated commuters, you're better off finding another path to your rush hour destination.

As part of the preparations for the 1996 Olympics, car-pool lanes are being added to many Atlanta interstates. Only vehicles with two or more persons may use these lanes.

The Georgia 400 extension has won raves from those commuting from Roswell, Alpharetta and Lake Lanier. It's also very popular with Atlantans who never travel that far north. The reason has to do with the location of the toll plaza: It's just north of the exit for Lenox Road/Buckhead. This is a real break for in-towners: It means you can ride for free from the beginning of 400 directly up to mega-malls Lenox Square and Phipps Plaza. From downtown, take I-85N. to the Georgia 400-Cumming-Buckhead toll road Exit 29; get off at Exit 2 "Lenox Road Buckhead last exit before toll." Turn right at the "To Peachtree Road" sign: Phipps Plaza will be on your left; the Ritz-Carlton Buckhead will be on your right; Lenox Square is just across Peachtree.

Surface Streets

Something like 55 streets in Atlanta have the word "Peachtree" in their name. How did this mania begin?

The first Peachtree was a Creek Indian village on the Chattahoochee River called Standing Peachtree. An army out-post built nearby took the name Fort Peachtree. The road that linked it to Fort Daniel in Gwinnett County was the first Peachtree Road. (The Old Peachtree Road exit on the Northeast Expressway has confused many a traveler heading into Atlanta, since it's more than 30 minutes outside town.)

From this has come a forest of Peachtrees. But even if you could keep this jumble straight, there are more hazards ahead.

It's not uncommon for the same street to have two, three or even more names in different locations. You're driving on Juniper Street and suddenly it's Courtland; you head south on Charles Allen Drive, which becomes Parkway Drive and finally Jackson Street before it ends at DeKalb Avenue.

This is sometimes the result of the way the city developed, block by block. In other places, it dates from the days of racial segregation, when it was meant to convey an unsubtle message of divided territory. This was the case at Ponce de Leon Avenue, once a racial dividing line. South of Ponce, Monroe becomes Boulevard; Briarcliff becomes Moreland.

A favorite city hall activity is renaming streets — or sections of streets — to honor civic leaders or to recognize social changes. Although a noble gesture in itself, this too causes confusion. Consider the route that begins in Little Five Points as Austin Av-

enue, then changes to Irwin before ending at Peachtree as John Wesley Dobbs Avenue. Before it was renamed for the distinguished businessman and activist in 1994, the final stretch was called Houston (pronounced "house-ton" in Atlanta-speak). Such changes typically take years to show up on most maps.

Here's one example of how difficult it can be to keep up with all of Atlanta's changes. Let's say you want to attend services at West Hunter Street Baptist Church, where civil rights leader and Southern Christian Leadership Conference president Dr. Ralph David Abernathy was pastor. First off, you will find that Hunter Street no longer exists — it was renamed to honor Dr. Martin Luther King Jr. Upon arriving at M.L. King Jr. Drive, you will find that another church, Grace Covenant Baptist, now holds services in the building formerly occupied by West Hunter Street Baptist. The latter church relocated in 1973 to Gordon Street, which was later renamed to honor Dr. Abernathy. So to find West Hunter Street Baptist, you would go to Ralph David Abernathy Boulevard, which still appears on many maps as Gordon Street.

Furthermore, terms like "street" and "avenue" and "boulevard" are often used without apparent rhyme or reason. Peachtree Street runs north and south, but 10th Street runs east and west. North Avenue runs east and west, but Piedmont Avenue runs north and south. Ralph McGill

Insiders' Tips

If you're picking up arriving friends at Hartsfield, ask them to wait on the covered median that runs the length of the baggage claim/ticketing area. It's much easier to stop and collect your friends and their bags there than in the crowded lanes closest to the terminal building.

Boulevard runs east and west, but Boulevard (south Monroe Drive) runs north and south. (Before it was renamed as a tribute to the progressive newspaper editor, Ralph McGill Boulevard was called Forrest Avenue, honoring a father of the Ku Klux Klan.)

In driving around Atlanta, you'll find you have more options when traveling north and south than when traveling east and west. In the afternoon rush hour, you may move south along Peachtree at a brisk clip — then turn left onto Ponce de Leon to find traffic crawling east toward Decatur. Commuters trying to avoid crosstown traffic often work out curious diagonal routes through neighborhoods, keeping off the clogged main streets. This may not save time, but some folks prefer it to sitting still.

There's no overnight way to learn your way around Atlanta's streets, but here are a few suggestions that should help.

Concentrate on learning the main roads first. About Peachtree's various forms: It is both street and road (and eventually boulevard, as you'll see later). It is Peachtree Street from downtown to a point just north of the Midtown district where it becomes Peachtree Road. We're told that decades ago, this is where the paved road ended and a country dirt road began. Atlanta is a hilly town, and **Peachtree Street** runs along its highest ridge. Peachtree begins downtown (its short, southernmost stretch is called Whitehall, after Atlanta's first store and bar) then passes through the hotel district, Midtown, Peachtree Battle and Buckhead. There the street forks: To the right, Peachtree Road continues on past Lenox Square, Phipps Plaza, Oglethorpe University and on to I-285, which it crosses as Peachtree Industrial Boulevard. The left fork in Buckhead becomes Roswell Road: It travels north to Sandy Springs, Roswell and Alpharetta. Peachtree is Atlanta's main street and though often crowded is always a dependable north/south route.

Piedmont Avenue can be a good alternative to Peachtree for traveling between downtown, Midtown and Buckhead.

Ponce de Leon Avenue is an easy route to Decatur and to Stone Mountain. Eastbound, Ponce forks just after the stone railroad overpass: To the left, Scott Boulevard continues out to the Lawrenceville Highway; to the right, East

Ponce de Leon goes to downtown Decatur (where the speed limit is strictly enforced) and Stone Mountain.

Martin Luther King Jr. Drive is the direct route between downtown and the Atlanta University Center area. Within the AU district, James P. Brawley Drive runs north and south between ML King Drive and Spelman College, near I-20.

U.S. Highway 41 (also known at different locations as Northside Drive, Northside Parkway and Cobb Parkway) is a non-interstate route out to the Cumberland Mall/Galleria area and on to Dobbins Air Force Base and Marietta.

Here are a few general pointers for getting your bearings on Atlanta's streets:

• Start by studying the maps we've included in our book. Spend a little time getting to know the major streets and highways. Once you understand just a few of the main north/south and crosstown routes, you'll feel more confident and find your knowledge of Atlanta's roads increasing rapidly.

• Then graduate to a good, larger street map. They're inexpensive, widely available and always come in handy.

• Take MARTA. Riding MARTA's buses and trains (whose tracks are usually always above-ground) is a great way to get your bearings and study the lay of the city without having to fight traffic.

• When you're riding with friends (or a knowledgeable cabbie), ask the driver what route he or she is taking. You'll find you're on the same streets again and

again, though you may not always recognize them at first.

• Ask veteran Atlantans for their favorite shortcuts. Most newcomers understandably stick to the busy main roads. Friends or co-workers may be able to give you tips about routes that bypass the worst jams.

• For goodness sake, don't be shy about asking directions. You'll frequently hear longtime Atlantans having involved conversations about main routes and alternates, street openings and closings. Many a conversation begins with "What's the best way to get from ____ to ____ now?" There's definitely no stigma here attached to asking directions; it may even make you seem more like a native.

• In Atlanta, it's always hard to say today what route will be best tomorrow. This city's rebuilding began in 1865 and shows no sign of letting up, so road construction and utility work are always a part of life. Back in the 1980s, the popular Wit's End Players comedy troupe even had a song about it in their act, "They're Tearing Up Peachtree Street Again."

This is especially true now as the city spruces to welcome the world in 1996. In 1994 Atlanta city voters approved a huge bond issue that will finance millions of dollars in infrastructure improvements before the summer of '96. Watch for crews repairing roads, rebuilding bridges and laying new pipes for sewers and storm runoff. There are sure to be plenty of tie-ups and detours as this work progresses.

Insiders' Tips

Even horses get first-class treatment at Hartsfield. The airport's Atlanta Equine Center cares for horses and domesticated animals en route to points around the globe.

Rules of the Road

Because traffic laws differ from state to state, take a moment to look over the following rules. You may obtain a free copy of *Georgia Driver*, the official state handbook, at any driver's license renewal location. Call 657-9300 for more information.

• The driver and all front-seat passengers of every car must wear a seat belt. Persons between the ages of 4 and 18 must wear a seat belt in the car at all times.

• Children younger than age 4 must ride in an approved child safety seat. (This law has exceptions: A seat belt is sufficient for kids between 3 and 4, and the law does not apply to nonresidents of Georgia.)

• After coming to a complete stop at an intersection, you may make a right turn on red, traffic permitting. Some intersections, however, are posted "no turn on red."

• A left turn on red is permissible only when turning from the left lane of a one-way street on to another one-way street on which traffic is moving to the driver's left.

• Your headlights must be on (day or night) when you are driving through rain, fog, snow or smoke.

• You must stop when approaching (from either direction) a school bus with its stop sign out and its lights flashing. On a highway divided by a median, you are required to stop when you are behind a stopped bus but not when you're coming from the opposite direction.

• You must pull to the right and stop to yield to official vehicles answering an emergency call. Police cars have blue emergency lights; ambulances and fire trucks have red lights.

• You must yield to pedestrians at marked and unmarked crosswalks without traffic signals, in intersections, at stop signs, when turning and when entering the street from a driveway. You must yield to a blind person with a white cane or guide dog.

• The maximum speed limit in Georgia typically is 55 mph. On rural interstates, where posted, the speed limit is 65 mph. In all business and residential districts, the speed limit is 30 mph unless otherwise posted.

• If you can steer it, clear it. Drivers involved in a minor accident are required to remove the accident vehicles from the roadway immediately.

• Drivers are considered drunk in Georgia when they register 0.08gm percent or more. Penalties are severe; don't get caught driving drunk in Georgia.

• Motorcycle drivers and passengers must wear a helmet.

• Bicycle riders younger than age 16 must wear a bicycle helmet.

• If you are moving to the state, you are required to get a Georgia license and to register your car in your county within 30 days.

It's Customary

From the moment you notice the interstate traffic speeding up (although the speed limit decreases) as you motor into Atlanta, you may find driving here a tad intimidating. Rush hour never seems to end on some of our main roads. And the 55 streets named Peachtree don't exactly help you get your bearings, either.

But for most people, driving around Atlanta gets easier fast. The best drivers seem to develop an alert yet laid-back attitude. The alert part is essential, since traffic here is often quick and close and the streets are curvy and hilly. But the laid-back part, though harder to develop, is essential, too. (It explains why some people never get speeding tickets and others get them over and over.) The worst thing is to take the traffic personally. Confrontational people are miserable driving in Atlanta.

Given that many of our thoroughfares are carrying far more cars than they were built to handle, Atlanta traffic would be an ongoing disaster were it not for our secret weapon: Most Atlanta drivers are really quite courteous.

We're not suggesting for a moment that there are no hot-head speed demons on the streets of Atlanta — there are some — but happily they're the exception, outnumbered by drivers who realize that a little neighborliness and cooperation can help get everybody home on time.

Here are a couple of other pointers along these lines:

• Blowing your horn when you're stuck in traffic is not a custom here — and won't help you make friends, either. During a recent visit to Manhattan, we heard more horns in one hour than we hear in a month here. In Atlanta, excessive horn blowing is considered downright rude.

• Use your turn signals. Most drivers will be happy to let you maneuver through traffic — if you give them a clue as to what you're trying to do.

• Don't tailgate. Rear-ending someone is a terrible way to meet.

• Don't run red lights, and don't speed. Going almost anywhere in Atlanta involves traveling through residential areas filled with kids, dogs, bicyclists and people backing out of driveways. Zooming around neighborhoods at 55 mph can lead to a ticket or a tragedy.

• Never proceed into an intersection, even when you have the green light, until you've checked to make sure oncoming traffic has actually stopped.

• Call ahead for directions when you're going somewhere unfamiliar; don't rely on a map alone to find a strange address. Two streets may have similar names but be an hour apart on opposite sides of town.

• MARTA buses make their way through many streets that are not really wide enough for them — this is especially a problem at sharp turns. When a bus is trying to turn a corner and its way is blocked by cars waiting at the light, all the cars must back up to make way for the bus. This is less likely to happen if you observe the stopline at intersections.

• Having cautioned you against excessive horn-blowing, we should note that judicious use of your horn can definitely help prevent accidents. Keep one hand close to your horn, especially when you're driving in tight, fast-moving traffic. If your reaction time is quick, you can "beep" weaving drivers back into their lane before they bump into you.

• When driving downtown at night on big one-way streets like Piedmont and Courtland, it's a good idea to keep to the right lanes: It's not uncommon to meet someone calmly going the wrong way on these wide streets if there's not enough traffic to warn them away.

Insiders' Tips

If you're taking MARTA to the airport and someone is driving you to the train, ask them to drop you off at a station on the north/south line. You'll save time and avoid hassles by not hauling your luggage through Five Points station to change trains.

"Now I'm *really* confused . . . "

- Five Points is the center of downtown Atlanta. It's formed by the intersection of Peachtree, Decatur/Marietta streets and Edgewood Avenue.
- *Little* Five Points is 2.5 miles east of downtown at the convergence of Moreland, McLendon and Euclid avenues. It's Atlanta's most eclectic shopping area and a multicultural mecca, a scaled-down version of New York's East Village.
- *Downtown* is the area around Five Points. *Midtown* is the area around Piedmont Park; it's the first neighborhood bordering Peachtree north of downtown. *Uptown* is Buckhead, filled with lots of upscale clubs, restaurants and boutiques; it's populated with shoppers by day and bar-hoppers by night.
- *Brookwood* station is Amtrak's Atlanta terminal; it's on Peachtree Street near the north end of the downtown connector. *Brookhaven* station is the MARTA station serving the Brookhaven community in northeast Atlanta.
- The "L" in DeKalb is silent: Say "de-CAB."

Cruising and Freaknik

We freely admit Atlanta's worst shortcoming: no beaches. Deprived of an oceanside main drag, lots of young people have taken to cruising Peachtree between downtown and Midtown on warm weekend nights. The resulting traffic tie-ups are annoying but concentrated on and around Peachtree, (especially near Five Points and Underground Atlanta). Just get off Peachtree and pick up one of the other north/south streets, such as Piedmont, Courtland, West Peachtree, Spring or Techwood.

Much harder to avoid is the commotion associated with the spring break festival Freaknik, which brings in about 200,000 African-American college students. It's a weekend-long party with lots of music, cruising and flirting, and the kids seem to have a blast. But many Atlantans find the noise and round-the-clock traffic jams a nuisance, since travel around downtown, Midtown and Piedmont Park can become gridlocked. To put it mildly, Freaknik, held in the latter half of April, is the worst traffic weekend of the year.

MARTA

Atlanta's mass transit system is called MARTA (Metropolitan Atlanta Rapid Transit Authority). MARTA is one of the most advanced rapid transit systems in the United States.

Though approved by referendum in 1965, MARTA lacked money until 1971, when voters agreed to fund the system with a sales tax. To win approval of the tax, an arrangement was made to cut bus fares from 40¢ to 15¢ and to hold them there for seven years. The tax passed; the promise was kept; and MARTA was on its way.

Today MARTA serves the 800-

square-mile district at the heart of the metro area. The first MARTA rail stations opened in June 1979. When the Airport station opened in June 1988, Atlanta became one of the few U.S. cities to offer direct rail service from the airport to downtown. Five additional northside rail stations are currently under design or construction; two will be ready by 1996.

MARTA operates 240 electric rail cars on 40 miles of track with regular service to 33 rapid rail stations. In addition, 678 buses traverse 150 routes covering 1,545 miles. On an average weekday, the system records 450,000 passenger boardings.

Weekdays, trains run every 8 minutes between 5 AM and 7 PM; from 7 PM until 1 AM they run every 15 minutes. Saturdays, trains run every 10 minutes between 5 AM and 7 PM; from 7 PM until 1 AM they run every 15 minutes. On Sundays and holidays, trains run every 15 minutes from 5:30 to 12:30 AM. Extra trains are typically called into service during big downtown events.

Bus schedules vary, but there's a printed timetable for every route. You can get free schedules at Five Points station and at MARTA information kiosks. Each bus usually has a supply of its own schedule; ask your driver.

A single MARTA fare (required for each passenger older than 3) is currently $1.25, including two free transfers. (This means you can take a bus to the train, change at Five Points to a train on the other line, ride to another station, then take a bus from the station to your destination — all for a single fare. You can't, however, use a transfer as your return fare in a round trip.)

All buses and train stations accept the MARTA TransCard. For a flat fee ($11 for the Monday through Sunday weekly card, $43 for the monthly card) patrons get unlimited use of the entire system. TransCard users do not need transfers. Token value packs (10 for $12) and TransCards are sold at RideStore locations (at Five Points, Airport and Lenox stations, at MARTA headquarters, beside Lindbergh station, and in many grocery and convenience stores throughout the service area.)

The weekly TransCard is good for a calendar week (not for unlimited travel on any seven days); the monthly card is good for a calendar month. Weekly and monthly cards are both available before the date they take effect; you can buy your next week's card before you start your weekend if you like.

MARTA route and schedule information is available by phone from 6 AM to 10 PM Monday through Friday and from 8 AM to 4 PM Saturdays, Sundays and holidays; call 848-4711. Tell the operator your location and destination; she or he will tell you which bus to take, where to catch it, whether you need to transfer and when the bus runs.

(Please note: Every effort has been made to ensure accuracy, but MARTA's services, schedules and fares are subject to change.)

Riding the Train

MARTA's rapid rail system is easy and fun to use: The two lines go the length and width of Atlanta. The 22-mile north/south "orange" line goes from the Airport to Five Points, Midtown, Lenox Square and ends at the northeast Perimeter. The 15-mile east/west "blue" line goes from Hightower station in the west to Indian Creek station in the east.

Classical music plays softly in the background at rail stations; each station is architecturally different, and some are quite attractive. Most spectacular is

Peachtree Center station, which was blasted out of the solid-granite ridge under Peachtree Street. Getting here is half the fun! Access is by the steep 192-foot escalators. (Of course, you may take the elevator if you prefer.) Exposed rock forms a natural cave around the platforms, where you'll wait for your train some 12 stories below Peachtree Street!

The north/south and east/west lines intersect at the huge Five Points station, and that's the only place to change lines. You don't need a transfer to go from one train line to the other, as they're both inside the station. Five Points station has its own entrance to Underground Atlanta via a tunnel under Peachtree Street; it's on your right just before you exit the station on the Peachtree side.

Rail station turnstiles accept exact change in coin (but not pennies, half-dollars or dollar bills) and MARTA tokens, which are sold in vending machines at all stations. Token machines take $1, $5, $10 and $20 bills; and, although generally reliable, these machines can sometimes be excessively picky about wrinkled money. If this happens, try another machine. If no machine will cooperate (or if one eats your money) don't panic. Pick up the nearby white courtesy phone and tell your troubles to the MARTA employee who answers. She or he will give you permission to enter through the "Handicapped" gate (just ignore that loud alarm!).

Take the appropriate escalator to the train boarding area. In stations where the platform is between the tracks, the escalator is marked, "To All Trains." Other stations have two platforms with the tracks between them. In these, you must use the escalator marked with the direction in which you're traveling.

The front of each train is labeled with the name of its final stop: "Airport" for southbound trains; "Doraville" for northbound trains; "Indian Creek" for eastbound trains; and "Hightower" for westbound trains.

Wait well behind the white granite strip at the edge of the platform until the arriving train has come to a complete stop. When the doors open, allow departing passengers to exit the train before you board. MARTA's electric trains are speedy: As soon as you board, sit down or grab the nearest handrail to avoid losing your balance as the train whisks away.

When the train begins slowing down for your stop, gather up your belongings and your group and prepare to disembark. Atlanta is not Tokyo, but the trains are fast-paced. If you're in the middle of a crowded rail car and take your time getting to the exit, the doors may close before you have a chance to get off.

Signs inside all MARTA stations indicate bus stops, surrounding streets and major buildings.

(Note: If you're going to the end of the west line, make sure to board a westbound train marked "Hightower," not "Bankhead." The latter goes to Bankhead station on a spur that turns northwest off the main line. If you board this train in error, just return to Ashby station and catch the next Hightower train. During rush hour some trains shuttle between close-in [to Five Points] stations without going to the end of the line. If the train you're on goes out of service before reaching your stop, get off at the station and board the next train going your way.)

Riding the Bus

To board a MARTA bus, wait at a bus stop (indicated by either a white concrete obelisk or a tricolor pole-mounted MARTA sign). The front of each bus is marked with

What's with the weather?

Sooner or later, someone will say to you: "If you don't like the weather in Atlanta . . . just wait a half-hour!"

It's a corny old joke, but there's a lot of truth to it. With an elevation of just more than 1,000 feet above sea level, Atlanta is among the highest major U.S. cities. Changes in our weather often roll in with the speed and power of a locomotive. Huge swings in temperature, sudden, violent thunderstorms, even the occasional single-digit deep-freeze accompanied by a foot of snow — all these and more can materialize with very little warning.

Kirk Melhuish, meteorologist for WSB AM-750, knows that Atlanta's weather — though sometimes extreme — is more often quite pleasant.

So what's the deal with Atlanta's weather? We asked meteorologist Kirk Melhuish (pronounced MEL-ish), an eight-year veteran with WSB AM-750. WSB has been on the air since 1922, when it became Georgia's first commercial radio station. (Its call letters, by the way, stand for "Welcome South, Brother.")

"The North and South may have clashed here in the 1860s, but Sherman had nothing on Mother Nature: Weather-wise, North and South struggle for control here all the time," Melhuish says.

"The weather we get here in Atlanta is sometimes the weather of the southern Appalachians, sometimes the weather of the Atlantic seaboard and sometimes the weather of the bayou. Every week, all year long, all three of these seem to be fighting for control. Occasionally, we'll get a taste of southern Florida, or even of northern Illinois."

Natural defenses usually spare Atlanta the worst winter weather. "The mountain barrier in Tennessee, northeast Alabama and the northwest part of Georgia is just tall enough so that most of the time, it can prevent the really bitter cold from making it into Atlanta. Because of that barrier, colder temperatures can reach Houston and New Orleans more readily than they can reach Atlanta — even though we're farther north."

But why the sudden weather shifts? "We are at a specific point which can be influenced by strong weather of conflicting types. Most of the time, the mountains keep the severe cold out and prevent the rain from changing to snow. But we're also very close to the Gulf Stream; occasionally, that will brew up a big storm that will pull down the cold, give us a major cold wave and change rain to snow. There's always just a little bit of a balance; will it stay up in Tennessee, or will it come pouring through?"

"In the summertime, we've got the humidity off the Atlantic and the Gulf, and we've got the hot sunshine, both of those are working together. In July or August, we can go from an almost blue sky to a severe thunderstorm producing hail, high winds and all the fireworks in 20 minutes or even less."

But, Melhuish adds, "The good news about Atlanta is that comfortable days are possible any time of the year, and you can't say that about many places in the world."

What should you pack for a trip to Atlanta? "Lightweight cottons are a must all through the summer months. In July, bring an umbrella. In the winter, bring a few layers and a couple of sweaters. No matter how cold it gets, it's probably going to be two or three days at the longest before it warms back up to comfortable levels. Never pack for a severe winter," Melhuish says.

Excellent advice — to which we'll simply add the following weather facts:

- Average highs in the three hottest months (degrees Fahrenheit) — June: 86. July: 88. August: 88.
- Average lows in the three coldest months — December: 35. January: 33. February: 35.
- Normal amount of rain in the three rainiest months (in inches): January: 4.91. March: 5.91. July: 4.73.
- Highest temperature on record: 105 in July 1980.
- Lowest temperature on record: -8 in January 1985.

the route number and the route name. Different bus routes use the same bus stops — make sure to board the right bus. (Express bus routes include stretches along which passengers are neither picked up nor discharged. Before boarding a bus marked "express," ask the driver whether you'll be able to disembark at your desired stop.) When you see your bus approaching, raise your hand to signal to the driver that you wish to board.

Enter through the front door. Drop your fare into the fare box, hand your transfer to the driver, or pass your TransCard through the card reader. Fare boxes accept cash (including dollar bills and any combination of coins) and MARTA tokens, but drivers do not carry change. If you'd like a transfer, you must request it when you pay your fare. Using the local shorthand,

just say "train" if you'd like a rail transfer or "bus" if you're changing buses. Some bus routes terminate inside stations, where you won't need a transfer to board the train. Your driver will let you know if this is the case.

If you're unsure about directions, tell the driver your destination as you board; sit up front and you'll be let off at the closest stop. Pressing the yellow "stop request" strip or pulling the cord will signal the driver that you want off at the next scheduled stop. Use the rear door when exiting.

Special Events

Shuttle service from the West End station to Atlanta-Fulton County Stadium begins 90 minutes before the start of Braves games and runs continuously until an hour after the game. You'll need a transfer to board the shuttle, so remember to get one when you pay your fare at the rail station.

Especially if the weather is nice, lots of Braves fans take the train to the Georgia State station and walk to the stadium; it's less than three-quarters of a mile. The extra effort really pays off after the game: If you take the train from Georgia State, you'll be back in your car and on your way home long before traffic clears out around the stadium.

Postgame only, MARTA operates a downtown hotel shuttle. These buses park farthest north of the stadium and have flashing blue lights. The fare is $1.25, and they begin leaving at the top of the eighth inning.

During the summer concert season, shuttle service from the Lakewood/Ft. McPherson station to the Lakewood Amphitheater begins 90 minutes before showtime and continues after the show until the venue is empty.

Special Services

For MARTA schedule information, call 848-4711. Call anytime for recorded information on airport service, 848-3454; rail service, 848-3450; stadium shuttle, 848-3457; and elderly and handicapped services, 848-3452.

To make a suggestion or report a problem, call 848-5115.

All MARTA buses and trains have seats designated as "reserved" for any eld-erly or handicapped persons onboard. Disabled persons and those 65 and older are eligible for a special reduced fare of 60¢. The required half-fare card may be obtained free of charge at any RideStore. All MARTA stations have at least one entrance that is fully accessible to the elderly and those with disabilities.

For physically challenged riders, MARTA operates specially equipped buses along routes based on service requests. A single fare on lift-equipped buses is $2.50. For more information, call 848-4180 or 848-3304.

Deaf persons may use MARTA's TTY schedule information line, 848-5665.

Parking

MARTA has thousands of parking spaces for use by system passengers, including 22,000 spaces at rail stations and 2,800 spaces at park and ride lots. Parking is free at all times in all MARTA lots except for the following.

Parking is $1 weekdays between 5 AM and 6 PM at the Lenox and Lindbergh stations. For airport patrons, Brookhaven station offers a fenced parking lot with 24-hour security. Parking is $2 per day, payable upon exiting the lot. Brookhaven is just 1.5 miles north of Lenox Square.

MARTA to the Airport

Hartsfield Atlanta Airport is the last stop on the south rail line; board the train marked "Airport." North/south train cars

Photo: MARTA

The MARTA system provides both bus and rail transportation.

have a designated space where you may stow your luggage; of course, you should keep an eye on it at all times. The ride from Five Points to the airport is about 15 minutes. As you exit Airport station, follow the signs to your airline's ticketing area. South terminal is to your right; north terminal is to your left. There is no extra charge for the trip to the airport; the fare is $1.25. Taking MARTA back to the city after your trip is a breeze: The station is adjacent to baggage claim.

Security

MARTA maintains its own 290-member police force. Armed uniformed and plain-clothes officers heavily patrol the system. Surveillance cameras are also used to deter vandals, gate-jumpers and other criminals.

All stations include white-colored passenger-assistance telephones, which connect riders with helpful MARTA operators, and blue police emergency telephones, which connect callers to the MARTA police. Both are located near the fare gates and on the platforms. Every rail car has an intercom that connects passengers with the train conductor.

One word of caution: In spite of the vigilance of the MARTA police, crime does occur in the system. Especially when traveling alone or at night, keep your guard up. Access to many stations is by long stairways and pedestrian overpasses, which can be scary. If you feel you're being followed, avoid walking alone into these areas. If you're frightened, stay in the main part of the station, in plain view of the security cameras, and use the blue telephone to request assistance from the MARTA police. Avoid strangers in the parking lot; have your keys ready and walk briskly to your car.

Rules

Be sure to observe the following rules.

• On all buses and in all trains and rail stations, it is illegal to smoke, eat, drink, litter or play radios or stereos without earphones.

• Moving between train cars, unless directed to do so by MARTA personnel in an emergency, is forbidden.

• MARTA's high-voltage tracks are extremely dangerous. Passengers must never climb onto the tracks or attempt to cross them.

Cobb County Transit

Atlanta's northwest neighbor Cobb County operates its own bus system on local and express routes around Cobb and to Atlanta. CCT buses access MARTA at Lenox, Arts Center and Five Points stations. The system operates both local (adult fare $1) and express (adult fare $2.50) routes. Kids less than 42 inches tall ride free; youth through high school fare is 50¢; senior citizen and handicapped fare is also 50¢.

For information on schedules and monthly passes, call 427-4444.

Hartsfield Atlanta International Airport

Hartsfield Atlanta International Airport is located 10 miles south of downtown on I-85. It compares in size and population to a small city. Including airline employees, some 36,000 people earn their livelihood at 3,750-acre Hartsfield, which has an $8 billion-a-year impact on the Atlanta economy — making it the largest employer in Georgia. More than 47 million passengers pass through Hartsfield each year.

For three-and-a-half years in the late 1970s, the Atlanta airport was the biggest construction project in the South; throughout the work, operations continued normally at the second-busiest airport in the world. When the new Hartsfield opened in 1980, it was the largest airport on earth. But before long, Atlanta's growth began to test its capacity.

In 1991, the city broke ground on the airport's fifth concourse, E, which opened in September 1994. Dedicated exclusively to international travel, the 1.2-million-square foot, five-story addition is the largest concourse in the nation. It has 24 gates (expandable to 34) and can handle 18 of those humongous 747-400s simultaneously, processing 6,000 passengers an hour through customs and immigration.

Because of all the necessary security, international concourses can sometimes look more like detention facilities than airports. By contrast, Concourse E is filled with natural light from skylights and decorated in a corporate yet vibrant burgundy and gray scheme. Marble floors and columns complete the affluent effect.

By fall 1995, work should be completed on another big improvement at Hartsfield: a 225,000-square-foot, four-story renovation that will triple the size of the terminal and link the north and south ticketing and baggage claim areas around an enclosed atrium. The remodeled terminal will feature many amenities, including meeting space, a business center, a food court, additional concessions and a premium restaurant. The goal is to make the airport — long considered one of the world's most efficient — more aesthetically appealing.

With the opening of Concourse E, many of Hartsfield's basic procedures changed, especially as they affect international passengers. Here's a brief walk-through of Hartsfield for arriving, departing and international passengers.

Domestic Arrivals

Your domestic flight will taxi in to concourse A, B, C or D. (A small minority of domestic flights now use the T gates — downstairs in the north terminal — which were used for international flights before the opening of Concourse E.) In welcoming you to Atlanta, your flight attendant will probably tell you the number of the carousel where the flight's checked baggage will be delivered. A flashing sign at your gate in the concourse will also show the carousel number.

Follow the signs for Terminal/Baggage Claim. You'll go down an escalator or elevator to the transportation mall, Hartsfield's mile-long backbone that connects all five concourses to the terminal. Computer-operated trains run (free of charge) about every 2 minutes, traveling between all concourses and the terminal. Automated announcements will direct you onboard. Blocking the doors will elicit a scolding from a futuristic robotic voice.

If you like, you may walk through the transportation mall or take the moving sidewalk, but we don't recommend this

Hartsfield Airport is completely accessible to physically challenged persons; to arrange for special assistance at the airport, call your airline.

Insiders' Tips

except for traveling between concourses. If your plane comes in at the last gate on Concourse D and you take the train, you'll be at baggage claim in less than 15 minutes. The moving sidewalk route, which also involves long stretches of stationary sidewalk, will take closer to 30 minutes.

Airport Advice

• Both departing and arriving planes can be delayed by the weather or other problems here or in other cities. It's always advisable to call the airline before heading to the airport.

• Here's the easiest way to arrange to pick up arriving airport passengers: Have them call you when their plane lands and arrange to meet them at their airline's curbside baggage claim area. You'll likely arrive at about the same time they've claimed their bags, and you'll avoid the hassle of a long wait at the crowded curbside.

• Driving up to the south terminal, you'll first find ticketing, then baggage claim. If you're picking someone up at the south terminal, keep to the left lanes to steer clear of the congestion around ticketing. This is reversed at the north terminal: Here you'll first encounter baggage claim, then ticketing. If you're dropping someone off at the north terminal, keep to the left to avoid the congestion around baggage claim.

• It's much easier to pick up or drop off passengers at the large covered median that runs down the middle of the curbside areas of both north and south terminals instead of in the lane closest to the terminal itself — that one is always crowded.

• Yield to all pedestrians in the wide yellow crosswalks. Of course, there's no parking in the crosswalks.

• Stopping briefly to drop off or pick up a passenger is OK, but don't even think of parking at curbside, as you'll quickly get a ticket.

• Many hotels have free courtesy phones; these are located on the east end of both baggage claim areas.

• As you enter a concourse from the transportation mall, you may hear someone noisily calling to get your attention. This is one of those "free speech" areas, where religious and other groups have the right to campaign. Keep moving, and don't give it a second thought; the airport is required to let these folks talk, but you are certainly not required to listen.

• Finally, here's some airport trivia about the no-nonsense robot voice of Hartsfield's trains. Years ago, the train's invisible conductor had the pleasant voice of a human female. But because too many passengers were disregarding the train's instructions, a new, more robotic voice was developed: still quite courteous, yet slightly more authoritative. If you find yourself especially eager to obey the train's voice, perhaps you're psychologically responding to the one that inspired it — that of HAL the computer in the movie *2001: A Space Odyssey.*

Hartsfield Atlanta International Airport Terminal Map

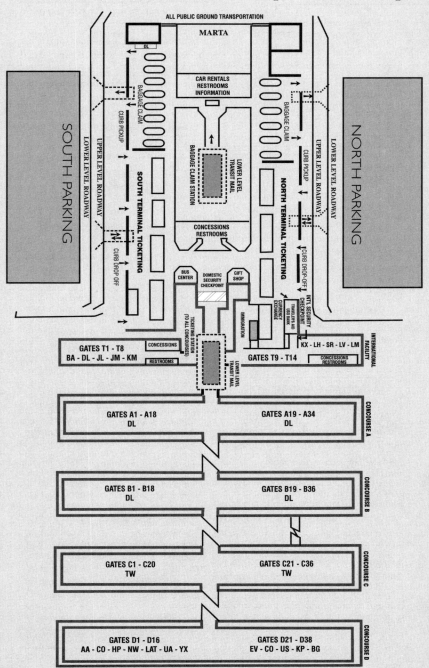

At the terminal, you'll be directed up the escalator or elevator to baggage claim and all ground transportation. Here you'll also find the rental car offices. Signs will further direct you to the appropriate baggage area for your airline. Flight numbers flash over the various baggage carousels as the bags roll up the conveyor belt. Delta requires its passengers to present their half of the baggage check ticket for each checked bag before leaving south terminal baggage claim; uniformed employees near the exits will ask for your check tickets.

If you're being picked up by a friend, exit through the glass doors to the curbside area. Since there are two baggage claim areas (one on either side of the terminal), it's important to let your friend know what airline you're flying.

For all other transportation — taxi, limo, shuttle bus or MARTA train — follow the signs to "Ground Transportation" at the west curb.

Domestic Departures

As you approach Hartsfield from I-85, large signs will direct to either the north or south terminal, depending on your airline. (All Delta flights use the south terminal.)

Most airlines have curbside check-in for ticketed passengers, and all have ticket agents inside the terminal. If you have your boarding pass and no luggage to check, you can learn your concourse and gate from one of the TV monitors located near the ticket counters (and also in the transportation mall). After passing through security, take the train or sidewalk to your concourse.

International Departures

International ticketing for Delta, Sabena, Varig, Caymen and ALM Antillean is in the south terminal; ticketing for all other international flights is in the north terminal. Check your bags at your airline's counter and proceed through security and the transportation mall to Concourse E, where signs will direct you to your gate.

Airlines

Planning your trip to Atlanta? The following is a list of the airlines that serve Hartsfield Atlanta Airport. An * indicates that Atlanta is the airline's hub.

Aero Costa Rica	(800)237-6274
Aeromexico	(800)237-6639
Air Jamaica	(800)523-5585
Air South	(800)247-7688
ALM Antillean Airlines	(800)327-7230
American Airlines	(800)433-7300
American West	(800)235-9292
Atlantic Southeast Airlines*	765-5000
British Airways	(800)247-9297
Cayman Airways	(800)422-9626
Continental Airlines	(800)525-0280
Delta Airlines*	(800)221-1212
Japan Airlines	(800)525-3663
Kiwi Airlines	(800)538-5494
KLM Royal Dutch Airlines	(800)374-7747
Korean Air	(800)438-5000
Lufthansa	(800)645-3880
Mark Air	(800)627-5247
Midwest Express Airlines	(800)452-2022
National Airlines*	(800)949-9400
Northwest Airlines	(800)225-2525
Sabena	(800)955-2000
Swissair	(800)221-4750
Trans World Airlines	(800)221-2000
United Airlines	(800)241-6522
USAir	(800)428-4322
ValuJet*	(800)825-8538
VARIG Brazilian Airlines	(800)468-2744

International Arrivals

Here's where some major changes have recently taken effect. As your international flight arrives at Concourse E, you'll first be directed upstairs to pass through immigration. From there you'll go downstairs to claim your bags and pass through customs.

Once you've cleared customs, you *must* recheck your bags at your airline's counter. If you're continuing to another city, they will be checked through to your final destination. But, even if your travel terminates in Atlanta, you are still *required* to recheck your bags — they will then be delivered to the terminal, where you can pick them up at baggage claim. This policy is designed to alleviate overcrowding on the underground trains, but it seems certain to cause confusion until everyone gets used to it.

Airport Parking

Hartsfield has about 20,000 parking spaces. Lots near the terminal are for short-term parking ($1 an hour for 12 hours maximum). The economy lots are for long-term parking ($4 a day). In addition, satellite lots around the airport have thousands more parking spaces. These lots run vans or buses to the airline curbsides and pick up returning passengers at ground transportation — eliminating that long walk back to the car when you're dead-tired from your trip. (If you do have to lug your luggage very far, you may wish to rent a cart for $1.50 from the stands in baggage claim.)

Hartsfield's lots can fill up at peak travel times such as holidays, some weekends and whenever the airlines slash fares to whip up business. If all the airport lots

are filled, you'll have to backtrack and park at one of the satellites. To avoid this delay, call the airport parking office, 530-6725, before you leave and ask whether parking is tight.

Here are some satellite lots; call for directions. Ask about return procedures: Some companies note your returning flight and meet you outside ground transportation; others require you to call when you arrive.

Airport Valet Parking, $6/day	761-4133
Park Air Express, $5/day	762-0966
Park N Fly, $7.25/day	763-3185
Park N Fly Plus, daily rates: valet, covered: $12; valet, uncovered: $10; self-park: $5	
	761-6220
Park N Go, daily rates: covered: $7.25; uncovered: $5.25	669-9300
Park N Ticket, $6.50/day	669-3800
Prestige Parking, $6/day	559-4475
Value Rent-a-Car, $5/day	763-0220

Rental Cars

Rental car offices are located in the corridor between north and south baggage claim. The numbers given are for the airport offices unless otherwise noted. From left to right, you'll find Value, 763-0220, in College Park; Alamo, 768-4161; Dollar, 766-0244, in College Park; Budget, 530-3000; Hertz, 530-2925; Avis, 530-2725; and National, 530-2800. Check with individual companies for car rental policies and procedures.

Ground-Transportation Directory

A lighted directory listing ground transportation alternatives is located at the west curb, just before you exit the terminal. As you exit at west curb and walk away from the terminal, you'll encounter the following types of vehicles in this order: taxis, rental car shuttles, downtown and metro area buses, non-metro area buses, courtesy vehicles and prearranged limousines.

MARTA

The easiest, fastest and cheapest transportation into the city is the MARTA train. The station entrance is located near baggage claim at the west curb, just before you reach the outside doors. MARTA trains run from early in the morning until past midnight. The fare is $1.25, and an attendant is on hand to answer your questions. (For detailed information, please see the MARTA section of this chapter.)

TAXIS

Taxis line up in the first lane at the west curb at Hartsfield. Follow the ground transportation signs. If you like, an agent outside will arrange for you to share a cab into the city.

Atlanta's 1,594 cabs operate under a limited flat rate structure. From the airport to the downtown business and convention district, the fare is $15 for one passenger; $8 each for two; and $6 each for three or more passengers. From the airport to the Buckhead business district, the fare is $25 for one passenger; $13 each for two; and $9 per person for three or more.

Fares for travel within the downtown and Buckhead business districts are $4 for one passenger and $2 per person for two or more. For all other destinations,

rates are $1.50 for the first sixth of a mile, 20¢ for each additional sixth of a mile and $1 per each extra passenger. Per hour waiting time is $12; use of additional space for luggage is $5.

The downtown business and convention district is bounded by Boulevard, 14th Street, Northside Drive and Memorial Drive (extended to Atlanta-Fulton County Stadium during Braves games). The Buckhead business district is harder to explain, but it's basically the heart of Buckhead, from Pharr Road up to Wieuca Road (that's just north of Lenox Square and Phipps Plaza).

For more information on Atlanta's taxis or to report a problem, call 658-7600. Some cab company numbers follow.

Atlanta Yellow Cab	521-0200
Buckhead Safety Cab	233-1152
Checker Cab	351-1111
Classic Taxi	438-1040
Style Taxi	455-8294

HOTEL COURTESY VEHICLES

Some 30 Atlanta hotels provide airport transportation for their guests. These hotels and their phone numbers are listed on the ground transportation directory.

LIMOUSINES AND HIRED CARS

If you'd prefer to arrive at your Atlanta destination in high style, you may wish to hire a limousine or sedan; some 127 limo companies serve Hartsfield Airport. Although it's best to reserve your car a day before your arrival, companies can often accommodate you with less notice.

Rates vary by company and by destination. Rates for a sedan to downtown are in the $40-to-$50 range; for a stretch limo, expect to pay about $60 to $70. Rates do not include tax and gratuity.

When you make your reservation, ask about pick-up arrangements. Most drivers meet their arriving passengers outside in the ground transportation area. There's typically an additional charge of around $10 to be met at your arrival gate; international gate service may add $30 to $60. Some companies include domestic gate service in their basic rates.

Following are some Atlanta hired car companies; all accept most major credit cards. Check the Yellow Pages for a complete listing.

Atlanta Limousine	*351-LIMO*
Carey Limousine	*223-2000*
Superior Limo Service	*532-3115*
VIP Limousine	*587-3828, 536-7660*

(Basic rate includes domestic gate pick-up.)

METRO AREA SHUTTLES

Here's a partial listing of airport shuttle services. Reservations may be required; call for complete information. When two rates are shown, the second is for a round trip.

AAA Airport Express offers scheduled service to Northlake-Tucker $15 one-way, $25 round-trip; Norcross, Gwinett, Suwanee and Lawrenceville, $18, $30; Lake Lanier, Gainesville, Chateau Elan, Braselton and Athens, $25, $45. Call for departure times and reservations, (800)354-7874; local 767-2000.

Airport Connection offers scheduled service: from the airport (6 AM to 11:30 PM); to the airport (6 AM to 5 PM; later by reservation). Routes to Perimeter Center hotels $17 one-way, $25 round-trip; Galleria $17, $25; and Peachtree Corners $18, $30. Call for schedule and reservations, 457-5757.

Atlanta Airport Shuttle offers scheduled service to all downtown hotels $8 one-way, $14 round-trip; Buckhead, $12, $20; and Emory, $12, $20. Hours are 7 AM to 11 PM. Call for departure times and reservations, 524-3400.

Dunwoody Airport Express departs at the top of the hour from 6 AM to 11:30 PM. Fares for service to Perimeter Center are as follows: $17 one-way, $25 round-trip; Windy Hill, $15, $25; Roswell, $18, $30; Alpharetta, $25, $45; Smyrna, $15, $25; and Norcross, $18, $30; 804-1812.

Interstate Airport Jitney departs 15 minutes past the hour from 8 AM to 11 PM to Perimeter Center, Windy Hill, Delk Road. By reservation to Lake Lanier and other destinations, 967-0044.

Perimeter Connection provides service to Windy Hill, Galleria, Perimeter Center, Marietta, Dunwoody, Norcross and Roswell. Hours are 8:30 AM to midnight. Rates are $15 to $17. Reservations recommended. Call 202-8736.

NON-METRO SHUTTLES

These firms transport passengers out of town or out of state.

Alabama Limousine departs for Anniston, Alabama, and Ft. McClellan weekdays 11 AM and 9:30 PM; Satur-

Be sure to keep an Atlanta road map in your car.

Insiders' Tips

days 5 PM; Sundays 8:30 PM. One-way fare is $23. Reservations are required, (800)824-6463.

Airport Shuttle Service offers door-to-door service between the Atlanta airport, hotels and Montgomery, Alabama. Costs are — round-trip: $90 first passenger, $60 each additional; one-way: $60 first passenger, $40 each additional. Reservations are required, (205)279-6662.

Dixie Excursions provides regular service to La Grange, Georgia, $24; Valley, Alabama, $28; Auburn, Alabama, $35 one-way, $65 round-trip; and Tuskegee, $45, $90. For service to hotels and homes, add $4. Reservations are required at least 24 hours in advance, (205)887-6294 or 887-6295.

Groome Transportation offers service to Macon, $20; Warner Robins $24; Byron, $43; Ft. Valley, $43; Perry, $43; and Milledgeville, $38. On weekdays shuttles depart on the hour from 9 AM to 9 PM. On Saturdays they depart every 2 hours between 9 AM and 9 PM. On Sundays shuttles depart every 2 hours between 9 AM and 3 PM and depart every hour from 3 PM to 9 PM. Reservations are not accepted. Shuttles departs from Space 5, (912)741-3636.

VIP Limousine and Shuttle Service provides service by reservation only to hotels in Macon, $20; Warner Robins, $20; Perry, $39; and Ft. Valley, $39. For home service, add $5. Call (912)788-3232 or 781-0000.

Other Area Airports

DeKalb-Peachtree Airport
3915 Clairmont Rd.   936-5440

DeKalb Peachtree is a general aviation airport near I-85 in DeKalb County. Known by the initials PDK, the airport, built on the site of a World War I training base, is the second busiest in Georgia. The airport has no commercial or scheduled flights; most users are corporate aircraft. More than 1,000 people work at PDK, which contributes some $75 million annually to the local economy.

Fulton County Airport - Brown Field
3952 Aviation Cr.   699-4200

This 600-acre general aviation facility, known locally as Charlie Brown, is owned by Fulton County. It has three active runways and is adding a 7,000-foot fourth runway as part of an $86 million expansion. The airport is used by many domestic and international corporate aircraft and also by state and federal government planes. Its location is convenient to I-20, Martin Luther King Jr. Drive and Fulton Industrial Boulevard.

Amtrak

Atlanta's is served by Amtrak's *Crescent*, a long-distance train that travels between New Orleans and New York City.

The eastbound train leaves Atlanta seven days a week at 7:45 PM, arriving in Washington, D.C., at 9:28 AM and in New York at 2:45 PM. The Atlanta-bound train leaves New York seven days a week at 1:42 PM and arrives in Atlanta at 8:30 AM.

As part of the train system's general cut-back, service between Atlanta and New Orleans was reduced in 1995. The New Orleans-bound train leaves Atlanta at 8:45 AM on Sunday, Tuesday and Thursday, arriving in New Orleans at 7:28 PM. The Atlanta-bound train leaves New Orleans at 7:05 AM on Monday, Wednesday and Friday, arriving in Atlanta at 7:20 PM.

Amtrak uses the Brookwood train station, 1688 Peachtree Street N.W., 881-

3060. The station is at the corner of Deering Road, just north of the Peachtree overpass across the downtown connector.

For more information and reservations, call Amtrak, (800) 872-7245.

Greyhound Bus Lines

Greyhound runs some 90 buses a day out of Atlanta. In addition to the main terminal at 81 International Boulevard NW (downtown near the Westin Peachtree Plaza), the company operates six other bus stations in the metro area.

For route and fare information, call (800)231-2222. Tickets may be purchased by phone with a credit card; however, you must allow two weeks to receive them by mail. To travel on shorter notice, you must make your reservations at a Greyhound terminal: For the nearest location, check the business pages of the phone book or call the main terminal, 584-1728.

A Word About Crime

Nobody likes to think about crime. Unfortunately in Atlanta, as in nearly every other American city, crime is a fact of life. Atlanta typically ranks near the top in the FBI's survey of violent crimes. We will not attempt to deny this, but we will try to put it into perspective.

Atlanta's city limits have not been expanded since 1952. The city proper is only 136 square miles; it's home to about 400,000 people. The Atlanta Metropolitan Statistical Area, however, is huge: It's a 20-county, 6,150-square-mile region that's home to more than 3 million.

Crime (again, as is the case in other cities) tends to be more concentrated within the densely populated city. To get a representative picture of the crime problem, city leaders insist it's necessary to look at the numbers for the metro region — not just the city of Atlanta. When metro Atlanta's crime statistics are evaluated against those of other metro areas, a different picture emerges, quite at odds with the 1994 *Money* magazine article that rated Atlanta the most dangerous U.S. city of its size.

When the crime rate per 100,000 inhabitants in the metro Atlanta region is compared to that of 43 other metro areas, Atlanta ranks 20th in violent crimes, 19th in murders and seventh in property crimes. In 1991 and 1992, metro Atlanta's violent crime rate was the lowest of any Southern metro area.

While these numbers are nothing to crow about — we wish they were much, much lower — they are probably more representative of the realities of life here. Further, a shocking amount of crime in Atlanta occurs among family members or acquaintances but not between strangers.

Following are a few tips, gleaned from several sources, on keeping safe in Atlanta.

• We hope you find Atlanta welcoming and friendly — but never forget that you're in a big city. The same commonsense precautions you would take in New York, Chicago or Los Angeles are appropriate here. Keep your guard up. A healthy dose of suspicion is a good crime preventative.

• Travel in a group when possible. Avoid deserted areas.

• Walk with confidence, and keep moving. Don't be lured into conversations with strangers or panhandlers. If you're wearing a conference name tag, remove it before going out on the street to avoid alerting others that you're in unfamiliar surroundings.

• If you feel you are in danger, go to the nearest pay phone and dial 911 (no coin necessary). Tell the operator your situation, and follow his or her instructions.

• When using a telephone calling card, make sure no one is spying to learn your secret code.

• Choose ATMs carefully, especially after dark. Many 24-hour grocery stores have ATMs inside; use one of these instead of a deserted outdoor one.

In the car:

• Keep your doors locked and windows up at all times.

• Don't leave valuables or packages exposed in your parked car.

• Downtown, don't try to save money by parking on the street. Choose a well-lighted, attended lot.

• At red lights, leave enough room to maneuver between other cars, walls, etc.

• If you are harassed at an intersection, blow your horn and run the light (traffic permitting).

• If you are being followed, go to an open business or other well-lighted location and call 911. Never drive directly home if you're being followed.

• When returning to your car, have your keys in your hand. Check the interior of the car; enter quickly and lock all doors.

• Ignore and avoid obnoxious drivers; never get into an argument on the road.

• If you have a traffic accident in a deserted area, you are allowed to drive to a lighted, public area to telephone the police.

Inside
Accommodations

The big cotton expositions of 1881, 1887 and 1895 laid the foundations for the modern-day convention business and helped make Atlanta's hotel trade a vital part of the city's economic fabric.

Atlanta emerged from the booming 1980s with an overbuilt hotel market, and development quickly slacked off. While this has given demand a chance to catch up with supply (area hotels do fill up during big events), there are still slow times when hotels light up the "Vacancy" signs and cut their rates dramatically. And while it's easy to spend a bundle during a deluxe stay in Atlanta's best hotels, the cost of an average night's lodging and food here is surprisingly economical compared to other major U.S. cities.

Every hotel room for miles around, of course, will be occupied during the 1996 Olympics. Some Atlanta hotels (selected at random) will receive a limited number of tickets to key Olympic events, which will be included in special packages for Olympic visitors. Watch for hotels to publicize these package deals as they become available.

In the listing that follows, hotels and motels are arranged by area: Downtown; Midtown; Buckhead; Emory/Northeast Expressway; Northwest Expressway; Airport and the area beyond Atlanta, including Barrow County, Cobb County, DeKalb County, Douglas County, Fulton County, Gwinnett County and Hall County. When a hotel has a toll-free reservations number, it is included in the listing along with its local number.

Each hotel's listing includes a symbol indicating a price range for a one-night stay, midweek, double-occupancy.

$50 or less	**$**
$51 to $100	**$$**
$101 to $150	**$$$**
$151 and more	**$$$$**

Note: Pricing information was provided by the hotels and is presented as a guide to help you approximate likely costs. Rates are often higher during major conventions or other peak travel times. On weekends and whenever business travel slows down, even the best hotels may cut their rates dramatically — it pays to shop around. Look for the lowest rates during the winter months on weeks when no major convention is in town. Off-peak specials can easily take the rate into the next lower price category.

Hotels accept major credit cards unless otherwise noted.

In the city of Atlanta and in Fulton County, hotels charge a 7-percent room tax that is in addition to the usual 6-percent sales tax, for a total tax of 13 percent on the cost of lodging.

Our goal is to present a good cross-section of the various types of hospitality properties available around Atlanta. Due to space limitations, we cannot list every Atlanta location for each national chain. If you prefer to lodge with a particular chain but don't see a hotel listed that's convenient for you, ask the company's central 800-number operator about other Atlanta locations.

At the end of this chapter you'll find bed and breakfast inns and hostels.

Hotels

Downtown

ATLANTA DOWNTOWN TRAVELODGE
311 Courtland St. N.E.   659-4545
$$ (800)255-3050

Two blocks off Peachtree, this family-owned and operated 71-room hotel is near the Marriott Marquis and Atlanta Hilton. Its amenities include a free continental breakfast and daily newspaper, cable TV with HBO, free covered parking and a heated outdoor pool. The hotel is just off the downtown connector at the Courtland Street Exit.

ATLANTA HILTON AND TOWERS
255 Courtland St. N.E.   659-2000
$$$$ (800)HILTONS

The 30-story downtown Hilton has 1,224 rooms (including 40 suites), a health club with an outdoor pool and four outdoor tennis courts. The top three guest floors comprise the private Hilton Towers, whose lounge offers complimentary continental breakfast in the morning and hot hors d'oeuvres in the evening. Atop the hotel are the nightclub Another World and

the renowned fine dining restaurant Nikolai's Roof; downstairs is the South Pacific cuisine of Trader Vic's.

ATLANTA MARRIOTT MARQUIS
265 Peachtree Center Ave.   521-0000
$$$$ (800)228-9290

File this one under "Hotels as Thrill Rides": The John Portman-designed Marquis has an astonishing 50-story open atrium and superfast, bullet-shaped glass elevators. Instead of being aligned, the floors are offset. The effect is rather like a fan unfolding. It's a fun place to explore. Each floor has windows in the corridors offering great views of the city.

The 1,671-room Marquis is Atlanta's largest hotel and has received AAA's Five-Diamond Award. It has 150,000 square feet of function space, five restaurants, a health club (complimentary for guests) with an indoor/outdoor heated swimming pool, a sports bar and two lounges. Via Peachtree Center, the hotel is connected directly to MARTA.

ATLANTA RENAISSANCE HOTEL DOWNTOWN
590 W. Peachtree St.   881-6000
$$$ (800)228-9898

The 25-story Renaissance is just east of the I-75/85 connector in the northern part of the downtown district; it's actually closer to Midtown. The hotel has 504 rooms, two restaurants and an outdoor pool. Guests on the Renaissance Club floors receive deluxe accommodations and amenities, including a complimentary continental breakfast and nightly hors d'oeuvres. The

Insiders' Tips

Look for discounted hotel rates during the winter months (except during major conventions) and on the weekends, especially at major business hotels.

North Avenue MARTA station is just up the street.

COMFORT INN ATLANTA DOWNTOWN
101 International Blvd.   524-5555
$$ (800)535-0707
This 260-room property is convenient to the Apparel, Merchandise and Inforum marts. On-site parking, a restaurant, a lounge and an outdoor pool are among the hotel's amenities.

DAYS INN ATLANTA/DOWNTOWN
300 Spring St.   523-1144
$$$
Across from the Apparel, Inforum and Merchandise Marts, this 215-room hotel offers remote-control cable TV with HBO and an outdoor pool. Kids 17 and younger stay free.

HAMPTON INN ATLANTA FULTON COUNTY STADIUM
759 Washington St.   658-1961
$$ (800)HAMPTON
You can't get much closer to big-league action than this 87-room hotel directly across the street from the home of the Braves. The hotel has an outdoor pool and a weight room and is convenient to downtown, the Georgia Capitol, City Hall and the Georgia State MARTA station.

HYATT REGENCY ATLANTA
265 Peachtree St.   577-1234
$$$ (800)233-1234
Way back in the swinging '60s, the bold blue dome of the Hyatt Regency dominated Atlanta's skyline and symbolized the brash city's enchantment with the futuristic. And, even though it's now overshadowed on several sides by much taller buildings, the John Portman-designed Hyatt Regency and its glowing UFO-shaped top remain among the city's best-known landmarks.

The 23-story open atrium, a stunning architectural first when the hotel opened in 1967, is still beautiful today, with its space-age glass elevators gracefully zipping up and down. In the Avanzare restaurant you can savor Italian cuisine while you gaze at exotic fish in the 1,800-gallon salt water aquarium. Beneath the blue dome atop the Hyatt is the rotating Polaris restaurant and cocktail lounge. The hotel has 1,275 guest rooms and 105,000 square feet of function space; it's served by the Peachtree Center MARTA station.

OMNI HOTEL AT CNN CENTER
Marietta St. at Techwood Dr.   659-0000
$$$$ (800)THE OMNI
The Omni Hotel is inside CNN Center and adjacent to the Omni Coliseum, the Georgia World Congress Center, the Georgia Dome and the Omni MARTA station; it has 465 deluxe rooms and suites and 40,000 square feet of meeting space. Bugatti is a fine dining restaurant serving northern Italian cuisine. Within CNN Center is a variety of restaurants, shops, a six-screen theater and the always-bustling CNN newsrooms. Stay at the Omni, and you'll have celebrity neighbors: Media tycoon Ted Turner and wife Jane Fonda keep a luxury apartment in CNN Center.

PASCHAL'S MOTOR HOTEL
830 Martin Luther King Jr. Dr.   577-3150
$
Five minutes west of downtown near the Georgia Dome and Atlanta University Center, Paschal's is an important part of Atlanta's history. Begun as a modest restaurant opened by brothers James and Robert Paschal, it eventually became a large restaurant and a 120-room hotel. Paschal's is a nerve center of Atlanta's African-American community; it's said that much political history has taken place over the restaurant's famous fried chicken. Many

R&B legends have played its Le Carousel Lounge.

RADISSON HOTEL ATLANTA
165 Courtland St. at International Blvd.
$$ 659-6500, (800)333-3333

One block from Peachtree Center, the 754-room Radisson features an outdoor pool, a business center and a fully equipped health club. The hotel has 60,000 square feet of meeting space and offers two-level hospitality suites for entertaining. Guests in the 32 executive suites receive complimentary continental breakfast and *USA Today*, as well as complimentary cocktails and hors d'oeuvres.

RAMADA HOTEL DOWNTOWN ATLANTA
175 Piedmont Ave. N.E.   659-2727
$$ (800)2-RAMADA

On Piedmont just off the downtown connector, the Ramada has 473 rooms and suites and an outdoor pool. The hotel offers complete convention and banquet services for up to 600 people.

THE RITZ-CARLTON ATLANTA
181 Peachtree St.   659-0400
$$$$ (800)241-3333

Luxury is always the order of the day at the Ritz, which has received the Five-Diamond rating from AAA. Oil paintings and Persian rugs adorn the lobby; each of the 447 rooms and suites has a bay window. This elegant hotel (and its mate, the Ritz-Carlton Atlanta-Buckhead) are favorites of visiting celebrities. Tea is presented each afternoon in The Lobby Lounge and The Bar; The Restaurant serves award-winning French cuisine.

THE SUITE HOTEL AT UNDERGROUND
54 Peachtree St. at Upper Alabama 233-5555
$$$ (800)477-5549

On Peachtree Street at the west end of Underground Atlanta, this is downtown's only all-suite hotel. Each guest room includes a marble bath, two color TVs with cable and movies and three telephones; some suites feature a Jacuzzi. You can't beat the location for convenience: It's adjacent to all the shopping and fun at Underground, directly across Peachtree from the Five Points MARTA station and close to the Capitol and state, county and city office buildings.

THE WESTIN PEACHTREE PLAZA
Peachtree St. at International Blvd.   659-1400
$$$$ (800)228-3000

The amazing John Portman-designed Peachtree Plaza opened in 1976 and for years was the tallest hotel in the world (it's still the tallest hotel in the United States). Within the 73-story glass cylinder are 1,068 rooms including six bilevel super-suites suitable for entertaining up to 150 guests. The hotel includes three restaurants and an indoor/outdoor pool with a complete health club.

Even if you don't stay here, you owe yourself a drink in the rotating Sun Dial Lounge. The ride up — nonstop to the 71st floor inside a glass elevator shaft on the outside of the building — is the closest most people ever come to being fired from a cannon. The drinks are pricey, but the view is priceless. The Peachtree Plaza is served by the Peachtree Center MARTA station.

Midtown

ATLANTA MARRIOTT SUITES MIDTOWN
35 14th St. at W. Peachtree   876-8888
$$$$ (800)228-9290

Each of the 254 suites in this 18-story Marriott has a living room, a king-size bed and a marble bath with separate tub and shower, two remote control TVs, two dual-line telephones, a refrigerator and a wet bar. Complimentary coffee and danish are served each morning. The health club has a whirlpool and an indoor/outdoor pool. The hotel is convenient to Colony Square, Woodruff Arts Center, the IBM and AT&T buildings and numerous restaurants and nightclubs.

COURTYARD BY MARRIOTT MIDTOWN
1132 Techwood Dr. 607-1112
$$$ *(800)321-2211*
The Midtown Courtyard is off 14th Street on the Georgia Tech side of the downtown connector. The hotel has an outdoor pool and cable TV with HBO; it also offers a complimentary shuttle service to the Midtown MARTA station, Georgia Tech and the downtown marts.

MARRIOTT RESIDENCE INN MIDTOWN
1041 W. Peachtree St. at 11th St. 872-8885
$$$ *(800)331-3131*
Here's a convenient location: on West Peachtree (one way, northbound) between the downtown connector and the Midtown MARTA station. West Peachtree and the parallel Spring Street (one-way, southbound) are nearly always quick routes between downtown and Midtown. Every suite has a fully equipped kitchen and cable with HBO; the rooftop has a sun deck and a whirlpool. A complimentary continental breakfast is served daily.

The hotel has a terrific landmark: It's right beside the giant broadcast tower that beams out the signal for WTBS channel 17, the original cable SuperStation.

OCCIDENTAL GRAND HOTEL
75 14th St. 881-9898
$$$$ *(800)952-0702*
"Grand" is the key word: In the three-story lobby, light from the 10-foot-high Baccarat chandelier plays across the rose-colored Spanish marble walls around the broad grand staircase. A lounge on the mezzanine serves cocktails and afternoon high tea. Florencia Restaurant presents gourmet cuisine in an intimate, incredibly plush atmosphere. The Grand Ballroom showcases a skyline view from its 6,000-square-foot open terrace. The health club boasts the latest exercise equipment, and its gorgeous indoor lap pool suggests a Roman bath.

The hotel occupies the first 20 floors of The Grand, a 51-story tower designed by the Atlanta firm Rabun Hatch & Associates. Above the hotel are offices, apartments, luxury condos and an enormous penthouse residence.

REGENCY SUITES HOTEL
975 W. Peachtree St., at 10th St. 876-5003
$$$ *(800)642-3629*
Each of the Regency's 96 suites includes a microwave-equipped kitchen, cable with HBO and a living room with a queen-size sleeper sofa. In addition to a free continental breakfast daily, the hotel serves a complimentary "lite fare" dinner Monday through Thursday evenings. The location is superb: Downtown and Buckhead are just minutes away, and the Midtown MARTA station is right next door.

SHERATON COLONY SQUARE
188 14th St., at Peachtree 892-6000
$$$ *(800)422-7895*
The 461-room Sheraton is part of the Colony Square multiuse complex, whose other features are offices, luxury residences and 160,000 square feet of retail space and restaurants, including a food court and the popular Country Place restaurant. The Sheraton's 18th and 19th floor Colony Club rooms have extra amenities; guests here receive complimentary continental break-

fast and evening cocktails. Piedmont Park and the Woodruff Arts Center are just one block away; there are numerous good restaurants within a couple of blocks.

TRAVELODGE MIDTOWN

1641 Peachtree St. N.E.   873-5731
$ *(800)255-3050*

This 56-room motel is right on Peachtree Street near the Brookwood Amtrak station. It's just south of where Peachtree crosses over the downtown connector — that's about halfway between downtown and Buckhead. It offers a continental breakfast, cable TV and an outdoor pool.

WYNDHAM MIDTOWN ATLANTA

Peachtree St. at 10th St.   873-4800
$$$ *(800)822-4200*

On the busy corner of Peachtree and 10th in the heart of Midtown, the 11-story Wyndham is an easy walk to the Fox Theatre, Woodruff Arts Center, Piedmont Park and numerous Midtown restaurants and clubs. The 191-room Wyndham's 7,000-square-foot Midtown Athletic Club features an indoor lap pool. Hotel amenities include in-room coffee makers and cable TV. The deluxe band buses frequently parked outside attest to the well-located Wyndham's popularity with touring rock and country music stars. (The hotel is across 10th Street from the apartment building where Margaret Mitchell wrote *Gone With the Wind*.)

Buckhead

EMBASSY SUITES ATLANTA/BUCKHEAD

3285 Peachtree Rd. N.E.   261-7733
$$$ *(800)EMBASSY*

On Peachtree Street in Buckhead, each of the Embassy's suites has two remote control TVs, two telephone lines with voice mail for messages, a refrigera-

tor, microwave and coffee maker. There's an indoor pool, and the fine amenities package includes a free cooked-to-order breakfast every morning in the atrium, complimentary cocktails served nightly from 5:30 to 7:30 and free transportation within a 1-mile radius, which includes Phipps Plaza, Lenox Square, Lenox MARTA Station and many restaurants and bars. Arriving guests may telephone from Lenox station for free pickup.

HAMPTON INN/ATLANTA BUCKHEAD

3398 Piedmont Rd. N.E.   233-5656
$$ *(800)HAMPTON*

Here's a moderately priced hotel in the heart of Buckhead. The 154-room Hampton is centrally located between Buckhead's major dining/entertainment area and mega-malls Lenox and Phipps, near the Hotel Nikko and the Tower Place office complex. A free continental breakfast is served daily; there's no charge for local calls; the hotel has an outdoor pool.

HOTEL NIKKO ATLANTA

3300 Peachtree Rd. at Piedmont   365-8100
$$$$ *(800)NIKKO-US*

Atlanta's luxury hotels compete fiercely for the many prestigious charity balls that fill the social calendar during the year. Even before its opening in 1990, the Nikko had begun signing up high-profile affairs. The dramatic, 440-room hotel's lavish lobby overlooks a three-story-tall Japanese garden and waterfall. The Library Bar serves cocktails in a cozy club-like atmosphere. Two separate fine dining restaurants offer Mediterranean (Cassis Restaurant) and Japanese (Kamogawa) cuisine. Guests on the three club-level floors have access to a private lounge with a view of the city. Excellent service is a hallmark of this Japan-based hotel chain.

HOLIDAY INN AT LENOX
3377 Peachtree Rd. N.E.   264-1111
$$ (800)526-0247

It's a shopper's dream come true: The 11-floor, 297-room Holiday Inn at Lenox is beside Lenox Square and just south of Phipps Plaza. Rooms include cable TV with HBO, voice mail, modem hookups and coffee makers. There's an outdoor pool, and the Lenox MARTA station is a short walk away. The rate is quite reasonable, given the prime location.

J.W. MARRIOTT HOTEL AT LENOX
3300 Lenox Rd.   262-3344
$$$$ (800)228-9290

The J.W. Marriott was built literally in the back parking lot of Lenox Square, and it's directly across from the Lenox MARTA station entrance. There are 371 guest rooms including 43 suites and parlors. Special features include a health club with an indoor pool. All rooms are equipped with cable TV (with movies), dedicated modem jacks, two telephones, robes, hair dryers and designer toiletries. Best of all, there's an enclosed walkway to the hotel's biggest amenity: 1.4 million-square-foot Lenox Square.

MARRIOTT RESIDENCE INN BUCKHEAD
2960 Piedmont Rd. N.E.   239-0677
$$$ (800)331-3131

Just south of the intersection of Piedmont and Pharr roads, this hotel's amenities appeal especially to long-term travelers: fully equipped kitchens, complimentary grocery shopping service, complimentary executive breakfast and hospitality hours, newspapers and health club privileges. There's also a pool, where guests are invited to a weekly barbecue. Each suite has curbside parking and a private entrance.

THE RITZ-CARLTON BUCKHEAD
3434 Peachtree Rd. N.E.   237-2700
$$$$ (800)241-3333

Directly across from Lenox Square stands the flagship hotel in the Ritz-Carlton chain. Lavishly appointed with art and antiques, the 553-room Ritz is a favorite of celebrities (everyone from The Grateful Dead to visiting royalty stays here). The Dining Room is one of the city's best-known fine dining restaurants. The fitness center has an indoor pool. Guests on the Club level enjoy greater privacy, an exclusive lounge and five complimentary meal presentations daily. The Ritz-Carlton has received AAA's Five-Diamond award.

SUMMERFIELD SUITES HOTEL ATLANTA BUCKHEAD
505 Pharr Rd.   262-7880
$$$ (800)833-4353

Suites at this hotel include two or three color TVs and a VCR; the larger suites have three beds and two baths. There's a complimentary grocery shopping service Monday through Friday. The hotel hosts a complimentary beer and wine happy hour Monday through Thursday and offers breakfast every day. On weekdays, the hotel's shuttle provides free transportation within a 3-mile radius, which covers all of Buckhead. The exercise facility has a heated pool and whirlpool.

SWISSÔTEL ATLANTA
3391 Peachtree Rd. N.E.   365-0065
$$$ (800)253-1397

To Americans, the phrase "European elegance" typically conjures up images of dark paneling and antiques. The Swissôtel is elegant after the fashion of modern Europe: sleek and smooth, with curving lines and sweeping expanses of glass. The hotel is the site of numerous charity balls during the year. Each of the 363 guest rooms in the 22-floor property features three phones and a modem hookup, voice mail, cable TV with HBO, bathrobes and a hair dryer. The hotel's health club has an indoor pool. A special benefit is a complimentary shuttle service to destinations within 3 miles, which includes all of Buckhead. Lenox Square is next door; the Lenox MARTA station is only half a mile from the hotel. Celebrity visitors to the Swissôtel have included Lilly Tomlin, Whitney Houston, The Judds and Robin Leach.

THE TERRACE GARDEN BUCKHEAD
3405 Lenox Rd.   261-9250
$$$ (800)241-8260

Lenox Square, Phipps Plaza and the Lenox MARTA station are just steps away from the Terrace Garden, where the 360 rooms and suites feature cable TV, voice mail, call-waiting and computer ports. Club level guests get deluxe accommodations and complimentary continental breakfast, hors d'oeuvres and cocktails. The fitness center has an indoor/outdoor pool and two racquetball courts.

Emory/Northeast Expressway

ATLANTA TRAVELODGE HOTEL
2061 N. Druid Hills Rd. N.E.   321-4174
$$ (800)255-3050

Emory University and Buckhead are 5-minute drives from the 180-room Travelodge, a nine-story full-service hotel whose amenities include cable TV with HBO and free parking. Club level guests receive robes, in-room coffee service, a complimentary continental breakfast and a wine and cheese reception.

DAYS INN ATLANTA NORTHLAKE/STONE MOUNTAIN NORTH
2158 Ranchwood Dr.   934-6000
$$ (800)325-2525

The Northlake area is a big retail destination (thanks not only to Northlake Mall but also to the retail developments that have sprung up around it). This 130-room Days Inn is just a minute from the mall, and it operates a complimentary shuttle for guests, who also receive a complimentary deluxe continental breakfast and cable TV with HBO. The Northlake area enjoys easy access to I-285.

EMORY INN
1641 Clifton Rd. N.E.   712-6700
$$ (800)933-6679

Emory Inn is near the center of the Emory University and Hospital area, directly across the street from the U.S. Centers for Disease Control and Prevention. The inn has 107 guest rooms, a lounge and cafe, a pool and a hydrotherapy pool. The inn also manages the nearby D. Abbott Turner Conference Center, an architecturally award-winning, 7,000-square-foot facility that can accommodate groups of up to 250 people.

HAMPTON INN NORTH DRUID HILLS
1975 N. Druid Hills Rd.   320-6600
$$ (800)HAMPTON

With 111 rooms, this Hampton Inn is conveniently situated between the Emory area and Buckhead at Exit 31 off I-85. There's a complimentary continental breakfast daily, and the hotel has a pool and an exercise room. The immediate area offers a range of moderately priced dining choices.

HOLIDAY INN PERIMETER DUNWOODY
4386 Chamblee Dunwoody Rd.   457-6363
$$$ (800)HOLIDAY

This hotel is southwest of the intersection of Chamblee Dunwoody Road and I-285 (Exit 22), convenient to the Perimeter Mall area. Each of the 250 guest rooms has two telephones, and cable TV with HBO. The fitness center has a sauna, whirlpool and outdoor pool. A '20s deco theme inspires the hotel's design.

RED ROOF INN DRUID HILLS
1960 N. Druid Hills Rd.   *321-1653*
I-85 at Exit 31   *(800)THE ROOF*
$

This budget property is convenient to both the Emory area and the attractions of Buckhead. Unlimited free local calls are a bonus, and children 18 and younger stay for free in their parents' room.

SHERATON CENTURY CENTER
2000 Century Center Blvd. N.E.   *325-0000*
$$$ *(800)325-3535*

Alongside I-85, 8 miles northeast of downtown Atlanta, Century Center is a major corporate development that includes the Sheraton hotel. Its 287 rooms surround a 15-story atrium. Guest rooms include in-room movies and a dual-line phone system. With easy access to both the Northeast Expressway and the Perimeter, the hotel is especially well situated for those doing business on the north side and in the counties northeast of Atlanta.

Northwest Expressway

COURTYARD BY MARRIOTT CUMBERLAND CENTER
3000 Cumberland Cr.   *952-2555*
$$ *(800)321-2211*

This 182-room hotel across from Cumberland Mall has a full-service health club with an indoor pool, sauna and spa. Covered parking and in-room coffee are complimentary; rooms include cable TV with HBO. Transportation within a 5-mile radius is free.

HAMPTON INN ATLANTA CUMBERLAND
2775 Cumberland Pkwy.   *333-6006*
$$ *(800)HAMPTON*

One block from Cumberland Mall,

Cobb Galleria Centre and the Galleria Specialty Mall, this inn offers guests free continental breakfasts and free local calls. Rates here are on the lower end of the $50-to-$100 range.

HOLIDAY INN POWERS FERRY
6345 Powers Ferry Rd. N.W.   *955-1700*
$$ *(800)HOLIDAY*

Each of the Holiday Inn's 300 guest rooms includes satellite TV with Showtime and an AM/FM clock radio. The fitness area has an indoor/outdoor heated pool and men's and women's saunas. A courtesy van provides free transportation within a 5-mile radius.

HOMEWOOD SUITES ATLANTA-CUMBERLAND
3200 Cobb Pkwy. S.W.   *988-9449*
$$ *(800)CALL HOME*

Each of the Homewood's 124 luxury suites includes two color TVs, a VCR and a kitchen with a refrigerator, stove, microwave and coffee maker; 28 suites even have fireplaces. Guests receive a free *USA Today* and continental breakfast, plus there's a complimentary evening social hour. Free transportation is provided within a 5-mile radius.

SHERATON SUITES CUMBERLAND
2844 Cobb Pkwy. S.E.   *955-3900*
$$$ *(800)325-3535*

The 17-story, all-suite Sheraton is beside the 1.2 million-square-foot Cumberland Mall and across the street from Cobb Galleria Centre convention facility and the Galleria Specialty Mall. Each suite includes two phones with voice mail, two remote control TVs, a VCR (movies may be checked out free of charge), a refrigerator with an honor bar, a microwave and a coffee maker with free coffee and tea. A complimentary full breakfast buffet is served daily until 10:30 AM. The fitness center has indoor and outdoor pools, and a courtesy van provides free transportation within a 3-mile radius. The business center is available around the clock.

STOUFFER WAVERLY HOTEL

2450 Galleria Pkwy.   *953-4500*
$$$$ *(800)468-3571*

Connected to the new $50 million Cobb Galleria Centre trade show complex, this luxury hotel has 521 rooms arranged around a sunlit, 14-story atrium. Guest rooms have three telephones and cable TV with free HBO and The Disney Channel. Coffee and a newspaper are delivered free of charge with a guest's wake-up call. The Club Floor offers complimentary continental breakfast and evening hors d'oeuvres, plus deluxe accommodations and amenities. On Friday evenings, guests are invited to dance to the Big Band tunes of a live orchestra. Across the street is the 150-store Cumberland Mall. The hotel provides free transportation within a 5-mile radius.

WYNDHAM GARDEN HOTEL - VININGS

2857 Paces Ferry Rd.   *432-5555*
$$$ *(800)822-4200*

The Vinings Wyndham is inside I-285 south of its intersection with U.S. 41. Each of the 159 guest rooms includes remote control cable TV, a hair dryer and a coffee maker with coffee. The athletic center has a heated outdoor pool and two lighted tennis courts. At the center of the project is a landscaped, tree-shaded garden. The Garden Cafe serves breakfast, lunch and dinner daily. Cumberland Mall and Cobb Galleria Centre are 5 minutes away; downtown Atlanta is 15 minutes southeast.

Airport

ATLANTA AIRPORT HILTON AND TOWERS

1031 Virginia Ave.   *767-9000*
$$$ *(800)HILTONS*

North of Hartsfield Airport, this 503-room hotel has in-room coffee makers and a sports bar with a 100-inch TV. Monitors in the lobby display updated flight information for all the major airlines. Children, regardless of age, stay for free in their parents' room.

COURTYARD BY MARRIOTT ATLANTA AIRPORT NORTH/VIRGINIA AVENUE

3399 International Blvd.   *559-1043*
Hapeville   *(800)321-2211*
$$

The world headquarters of Delta Airlines is only a quarter mile from this Courtyard, which operates a complimentary airport shuttle. The hotel has an exercise room and an outdoor pool; guest rooms include coffee and tea service and remote control cable TV with HBO.

COURTYARD BY MARRIOTT ATLANTA AIRPORT SOUTH/SULLIVAN ROAD

2050 Sullivan Rd.   *997-2220*
College Park   *(800)321-2211*
$$

This Courtyard is inside the Perimeter just south of Hartsfield Airport. It has an indoor pool and operates a free airport shuttle service for guests. All rooms feature coffee and tea service and remote control cable TV with HBO.

HAMPTON INN ATLANTA AIRPORT

1888 Sullivan Rd.   *996-2220*
College Park   *(800)HAMPTON*
$$

Rates at this 130-room inn south of Hartsfield Airport are typically on the lower end of the $50-to-$100 range. The hotel has a pool and operates an airport shuttle for guests.

Barrow County

CHATEAU ÉLAN

100 Rue Charlemagne	*932-0900*
Braselton	*(800)233-WINE*

$$$$

Set on 2,400 acres 40 miles northeast of Atlanta off I-85, this unusual resort mixes business with pleasure. The complex includes a 16th century-style French-inspired resort and 16,000-square-foot conference center, a 170-acre golf course, a Stan Smith-designed seven-court tennis center, a European-style spa, an art gallery, horseback and nature trails and more than 200 acres of vineyards producing a variety of fine wines. Each of the resort's 144 deluxe rooms and suites includes an oversize bath with separate garden tub and shower, three dual-line phones, a personal safe and a mini-bar. Golf, tennis and luxurious spa packages are offered. Homes in the resort's residential community start at $250,000. Since it opened in 1984, the Chateau Élan winery has received more than 200 medals of excellence. Today it produces 15 varieties of wine; free tours and wine tastings take place every day except Christmas.

Cobb County

ATLANTA MARRIOTT NORTHWEST

200 Interstate N. Pkwy.	*952-7900*
$$$	*(800)228-9290*

This 400-room hotel was completely renovated in 1994. Each room includes color TV with HBO, two direct dial phones with voice mail, an iron and an ironing board. At the fitness center are three lighted tennis courts, an indoor/outdoor pool and a hydrotherapy pool. This 16-floor hotel has 49 concierge-level rooms.

FRENCH QUARTER SUITES

2780 Whitley Rd.	*980-1900*
$$$	*(800)843-5858*

The French Quarter's 155 suites surround a glass-roofed courtyard with a gazebo bar, exotic plants and a fountain. There's a phone in every room of every suite, and each suite has a large jetted whirlpool bath. Other amenities include in-room coffee service, hair dryers and complimentary breakfast each morning in the courtyard. The Café Orleans serves classic French and New Orleans food; the Bourbon Street Cabaret maintains the jazzy theme. A big brunch is served in the courtyard on Sunday. Ask about the special weekend rate.

HAWTHORN SUITES
HOTEL ATLANTA-NORTHWEST

1500 Parkwood Cr.	*952-9595*
$$$	*(800)338-7812*

The 200-unit, all-suite Hawthorn is nestled on 13 landscaped acres northeast of the I-75/I-285 interchange. A complimentary breakfast buffet is served daily, and the outdoor picnic areas feature gas grills. Each one- or two-bedroom suite includes color TVs and a video cassette player, a fully equipped kitchen plus a balcony or patio. Among recreational amenities are an outdoor pool with waterfalls and a whirlpool, two lighted tennis courts and a basketball court.

NORTHWEST ATLANTA HILTON INN

2055 S. Park Pl.	*953-9300*
$$$	*(800)HILTONS*

Near the Windy Hill Exit off I-75 in Marietta, the Hilton has 222 deluxe guest rooms, an indoor/outdoor pool and a fitness room. Parking is free, and so is the daily paper. A van provides free transportation to attractions within a 5-mile radius, which include the Galleria Centre, Cumberland Mall and the wet, wild thrills of White Water amusement park. There is no charge for children, regardless of age, when they occupy the same room as their parents.

DeKalb County

ATLANTA MARRIOTT PERIMETER CENTER

246 Perimeter Center Pkwy. N.E.   394-6500
$$$ (800)228-9290

The 402-room Marriott is just outside I-285 at Exit 21 about halfway between I-75 and I-85 at the heart of the booming Perimeter Center area. It offers an indoor/outdoor pool, lighted tennis courts and an exercise center. Guest rooms feature two phones and color TV with HBO and The Disney Channel. Concierge-level guests receive a complimentary newspaper, a continental breakfast and hors d'oeuvres. Right across the street is the 1.2-million-square-foot Perimeter Mall; the surrounding area is a booming retail mecca featuring everything from exclusive specialty shops to the large electronics discounter Best Buy.

EMBASSY SUITES PERIMETER CENTER

1030 Crowne Pointe Pkwy.   394-5454
$$$ (800)EMBASSY

Each suite includes a living room with a queen-size sofa bed, a separate bedroom, plus a coffee maker, microwave, wet bar and refrigerator. There's an indoor pool, and guests are invited for a free, cooked-to-order breakfast every morning as well as a 2-hour reception nightly.

HAMPTON INN STONE MOUNTAIN

1737 Mountain Industrial Blvd.   934-0004
$$ (800)HAMPTON

The 129-room Hampton is 15 minutes east of downtown and just 3 miles from all the fun at Georgia's Stone Mountain Park. Amenities include an exercise room and a pool.

THE MARQUE OF ATLANTA PERIMETER CENTER

111 Perimeter Center West   396-6800
$$$$ (800)683-6100

The Marque is a luxury hotel in a parklike setting near Perimeter Mall. All rooms have a balcony and cable TV; suites have fully equipped kitchens. The fitness center includes an exercise room and an outdoor pool.

Douglas County

HAMPTON INN - SIX FLAGS

1100 N. Blairs Bridge Rd., Austell   941-1499
$$ (800)HAMPTON

The 74-room Hampton has a pool and is only 3 miles from all the screams and excitement of Six Flags Over Georgia.

Fulton County

COURTYARD BY MARRIOTT ROSWELL

1500 Market Blvd., Roswell   992-7200
$$ (800)321-2211

This north metro hotel is 5 miles from historic Roswell and 7 miles from Chattahoochee Nature Center. All rooms include coffee and tea service and cable TV with HBO. There's an outdoor pool; ask about special rates for weekends and extended stays.

DOUBLETREE HOTEL ATLANTA

7 Concourse Pkwy.   395-3900
$$$ (800)222-TREE

At The Concourse, a 64-acre wooded, corporate center near Perimeter Mall, the 370-room Doubletree rises 20 stories above a lake. Concierge level rooms include continental breakfasts and evening hors d'oeuvres in a private lounge. Guests pay a small charge to use the adjacent 85,000-square-foot Concourse Athletic Club, which has seven clay tennis courts, indoor and outdoor 25-meter pools, a full-size gym, a cushioned indoor running track and private tanning. From I-285, take Exit 20 and go north on Peachtree Dunwoody Road; you can't miss the twin Concourse office towers on your left.

GUEST QUARTERS SUITE HOTEL
6120 Peachtree Dunwoody Rd.   668-0808
$$$ (800)424-2900
  Two blocks from Perimeter Mall, this 224-suite hotel features an indoor/outdoor pool and a fully equipped health club. Each suite has two color TVs, a coffee maker, wet bar and a patio or balcony.

MASTERS INN ECONOMY SIX FLAGS
4120 Fulton Industrial Blvd.   696-4690
$ (800)633-3434
  This 171-room motel is 7 miles west of downtown and just 3 miles from Six Flags Over Georgia. Local calls are free; rooms include cable TV with HBO.

SUMMERFIELD SUITES
HOTEL ATLANTA/PERIMETER
760 Mt. Vernon Hwy.   250-0110
$$$ (800)833-4353
  The Summerfield is in the Perimeter Mall area; each suite has a full kitchen, a video cassette player and voice mail for messages. A complimentary continental breakfast is served each morning; a beer and wine social is offered Monday through Thursday evenings. An exercise room with a pool and whirlpool is available for guests.

WYNDHAM GARDEN
HOTEL PERIMETER CENTER
800 Hammond Dr. N.E.   252-3344
$$$ (800)WYNDHAM
  Five minutes from Perimeter Mall, the 143-room Wyndham features a landscaped garden, an indoor/outdoor pool and a fully equipped exercise room. Rooms include cable TV, two telephones and coffee makers with coffee. The hotel operates a complimentary shuttle to local offices and attractions.

Gwinnett County

COURTYARD BY MARRIOTT
GWINNETT MALL
3550 Venture Pkwy.
Duluth   476-4666
$$ (800)321-2211
  The shopping excitement of the 1.2-million-square-foot GwinnettPlace Mall is just a quarter mile from this Courtyard, which is 18 miles from downtown and 30 miles from Hartsfield Airport. There's an outdoor pool, and guests enjoy in-room coffee and tea service and cable TV with HBO.

DAYS INN - GWINNETTPLACE MALL
1948 Day Dr.
Duluth   476-1211
$$ (800)DAYS INN
  Complimentary breakfast and cable TV with HBO are amenities at this 131-room high-rise hotel across from GwinnettPlace Mall.

Hall County

COMFORT INN
I-985 at Mundy Mill Rd. (Exit 4)   287-1000
$$ (800) 221-2222

  This 72-room hotel is 5 miles from Gainesville and 4.5 miles from all the action at the Road Atlanta racetrack. There are four king suites and four whirlpool suites. A deluxe complimentary continental breakfast is served each morning. Rates are in the lower end of this range and are sometimes less than $50.

LAKE LANIER ISLANDS HILTON RESORT
7000 Holiday Rd.   945-8787
Lake Lanier Islands   (800)768-LAKE
$$$
  Lake Lanier Islands is a waterfront rec-

Sam Massell: The Mayor Who Brought MARTA to Atlanta

Sam Massell holds a law degree; he's been a travel agent, a trade magazine editor, a real estate broker and the chief booster of the city's Buckhead district. But history will most likely remember him as the mayor who brought MARTA to Atlanta.

Mr. Massell served 22 years in elected office, including eight as vice-mayor. He was elected mayor in 1970, the first Jewish Atlantan to hold that office. Mr. Massell was convinced that a modern rapid-transit system would give Atlanta a critical edge and help secure its place among the ranks of America's great cities, and he set out to convince the voters that mass transit deserved public support — in the form of a 1-percent sales tax increase.

Sam Massell, Mayor of Atlanta from 1970 to 1974, is now president of the Buckhead Coalition.

"We started with the premise that mobility is man's fifth freedom. Large numbers of people don't have a car and cannot afford one: The city loses their input and participation if they are immobile. Public transportation enables everyone to use the whole city, the same way the more fortunate people are able to," Mr. Massell says.

"Once we explained why we need public transportation, we explained why we need to subsidize it." The old, privately owned system of streetcars and buses was nearing bankruptcy, with ridership declining each time fares went up. For the MARTA system, Mr. Massell says, "I lobbied for a free fare, and I still think that would have been best. People are shocked when they hear that, but we have other services that are free, such as parks, libraries and schools. You came up to my 10th floor office on an elevator, and that transportation was free."

Mayor Massell pulled out all the stops to convince Atlantans to fund the ambitious system. "I even went up in a helicopter over the expressway during rush hour with a bullhorn and said, 'If you want to get out of this mess, vote yes!' This being the Bible Belt, people thought God was telling them what to do! I would get on a bus at the front door, give people literature and talk to them while I was walking through, then go out the back door and get on the next bus. I did this day in and day out.

"We did everything we could do, and it passed, but just barely. Any one of those things could have been the swing vote," Mr. Massell says. Once MARTA was funded, the authority took over the private system, slashed the fare to 15¢ and held it there for seven years. Today the system serves the 800-square-mile area at the heart of the metro region. It's generally acknowledged that MARTA, the airport and the freeway system played a crucial role in helping Atlanta capture the 1996 Olympics — not to mention countless meetings, conventions and relocating businesses. "The airport was the single-most important improvement ever made in Atlanta," Mr. Massell says. "Our preeminence is transportation."

Newcomers are a natural byproduct of that advanced transportation network, and lifelong adult Atlantans are a small minority with a fascinating perspective. Mr. Massell was born here in 1928 and graduated from Georgia State University and Atlanta Law School. He's seen many changes in his hometown. "What has changed the most would have to be social reforms, particularly integration. And the growth! I think of my father and what he would say if he could see what's going on now."

Happily, one feature has changed little: "The tree canopy — the tremendous number of trees on rolling land — is unique to Atlanta. When I was Mayor, more visitors would express amazement and pleasure at that than anything else. We should do all in our power to conserve those trees."

It's entirely appropriate in this forward-looking city that Mr. Massell is today best-known not as a former mayor, but rather as president of the Buckhead Coalition, a select group of business people organized "to nurture the quality of life and promote orderly growth in Buckhead." The group's master plan *Buckhead Blueprint*, published in January 1994, is subtitled *Buckhead's Book of Its Future.* Housing is just one of the issues it addresses: "Building high-rise multi-family units encircling the business core of Buckhead will be the real answer: They will create a buffer for the single-family homes and provide a labor market for the businesses here," Mr. Massell says. Buckhead's population is expected to triple by 2007. "If that's only half right, it's awesome.

"And Atlanta continues to grow and expand, with no natural barriers to deter growth in any direction: no mountains, oceans or rivers. We're 1,000 feet above sea level in the center of the Southeast. As long as we have a good network of roads and public transportation, we can keep expanding."

Atlanta's other big advantages — its welcoming spirit and its fascination with the new — are less tangible but not less important. "There's an attitude in Atlanta that says we have to achieve and succeed. Atlanta attaches a lot of importance to developing new leadership. There are many areas — not only in business but also in the political arena, the academic world and the religious community — where our leadership has been sterling. With the six predominantly black colleges here, our African-American leadership, in particular, has been outstanding."

In Atlanta, Mr. Massell says, "We work at it. We invite people, we welcome them and we encourage them."

reational complex 45 minutes northeast of downtown Atlanta on Lake Sidney Lanier. It features a concert amphitheater, campgrounds and a water park with the largest wave pool in Georgia. The Hilton resort offers a par-72 golf course, tennis, water sports and fine dining. Each of its more than 200 guest rooms has a view of the lake or the forest. With 12,500 square feet of meeting space, the hotel can accommodate meetings of up to 350 people. Children, regardless of age, stay for free in their parents' room.

STOUFFER RENAISSANCE PINEISLE RESORT

9000 Holiday Rd. 945-8921
Lake Lanier Islands (800)HOTELS-1
$$$$

Each of the Stouffer's 250 rooms includes cable TV, two robes, a stocked refreshment center and a safe. There's a hot tub on an enclosed patio outside each of the 28 spa rooms. Complimentary coffee and a newspaper are delivered with each guest's wake-up call. Guests can golf on the par-72 course, play tennis on one of the four outdoor lighted courts or three enclosed courts, swim in the indoor/outdoor pool or relax in the three-story elevated outdoor hot tub. In the style of European hotels, the hotel is "tip-free." Gratuities are already included in rates and prices. Rates are lower between late November and late March.

Bed and Breakfasts

BEVERLY HILLS INN

65 Sheridan Dr. N.E. 233-8520
$$

Just 3 minutes from the Atlanta History Center and 5 minutes from Lenox and Phipps, this is Buckhead's only bed and breakfast. Each of the 18 guest rooms has a kitchen, a balcony and a private bath. The inn's common areas include

hardwood floors, Oriental rugs and a garden room where a complimentary breakfast is served daily. Arriving guests receive a welcoming bottle of wine.

THE GASLIGHT INN

1001 St. Charles Ave. N.E. 875-1001
$$$

A 1913 Virginia Highlands home that was completely renovated in 1990, the Gaslight has been featured in numerous magazines, including *Southern Living* and *Better Homes and Gardens*. Rooms, suites and private, detached cottage units are available. All rooms have a private bath, TV and include an elaborate continental breakfast. Some rooms have private decks overlooking the walled garden. By special arrangement, the owner, an avid chef, will prepare your dinner. Smoking is not permitted indoors.

OAKWOOD HOUSE BED & BREAKFAST

951 Edgewood Ave. N.E. 521-9320
$$ (800)388-4403

This 1911 home is in charming Inman Park, Atlanta's first suburb. Nearby are the Inman Park/Reynoldstown MARTA station and the bohemian shopping village Little Five Points. The surrounding area was the site of the decisive Battle of Atlanta on July 22, 1864, and features many historical markers. Nearby Burton's Grill, at the corner of Edgewood and Hurt, 658-9452, serves breakfast and lunch on weekdays and is the home of the best fried chicken in all Atlanta. Each of Oakwood's rooms has a telephone and a private bath. Continental breakfast is served daily. Oakwood is 2 miles east of downtown. Smoking is not permitted indoors.

SHELLMONT BED & BREAKFAST

821 Piedmont Ave. N.E. at Sixth St. 872-9290
$$

Built in 1890, the Shellmont is listed on

the National Register of Historic Places. It's in the wonderfully wooded Midtown neighborhood and is close to Piedmont Park and the Fox Theatre. All rooms have a private bath; lodging is offered in both the main house and a carriage house. Continental breakfast is served every day; children 12 and younger are allowed only in the carriage house.

THE WOODRUFF BED & BREAKFAST INN
223 Ponce de Leon at Myrtle St. 875-9449
$$

After 30 years as a well-known brothel, this three-story, turn-of-the-century Victorian home was "rehabilitated" into a bed and breakfast in 1989. Named for Miss Bessie Woodruff, the madam of the previous establishment, the inn is near the Fox Theatre and Midtown's restaurants and bars; it's a short stroll away from Piedmont Park. Choose from deluxe suites with private baths, single rooms with private baths or family suites. The special occasion suite has a hot tub. Enjoy a full Southern or continental breakfast daily.

Hostels

ATLANTA DREAM HOSTEL
222 E. Howard Ave.
Decatur   370-0380
$

This rambling, art-filled, dormitory-style hostel offers communal lodging for the young and young at heart. It's wonderfully eclectic: There's a big backyard with rabbits, peacocks and antique cars. Beneath a large awning, the patio is finished in a mosaic of tile fragments. The daily rate is incredibly cheap, so be kind to the owner and act as your own maid. The hostel is convenient to the downtown Decatur MARTA station. Smoking is not allowed indoors, and credit cards are not accepted. The surrounding area offers several dining choices. For lunch (weekdays only), try Our Way Cafe, 373-6665, just across the railroad tracks.

HOSTELING INTERNATIONAL - ATLANTA
223/229 Ponce de Leon Ave.   875-2882
$

On the southern edge of Midtown, this 50-bed, dormitory-style hostel sleeps four to six guests in a room; some private baths are available. Common area amenities include TV, pinball and a pool table. Complimentary doughnuts are served daily. Nonmembers of Hosteling International pay an additional $3 fee. There is a two-night minimum stay for credit card users. Piedmont Park and many Midtown attractions are nearby.

Photo: La Montagne, Inc.

Midtown's Veni Vidi Vici serves authentic Northern Italian cuisine in an elegant cosmopolitan atmosphere.

Inside
Restaurants

Atlantans are a hungry crowd. Consider this statistic: The Georgia Hospitality and Travel Association reports there are some 12,000 restaurants in Georgia (population 6.9 million). Of those, about 8,000 are in metro Atlanta (population 3.3 million)!

The Atlanta restaurant industry has several built-in advantages. The city's advanced transportation network and numerous farmer's markets make fresh food accessible and affordable. Atlanta is a magnet to people from many backgrounds who introduce and create a market for their own particular ethnic cooking. In the same way, economic diversity exerts a demand for good food at practically every price level. Here you may dine in sumptuous luxury atop the Atlanta Hilton at world-class Nikolai's Roof — or, about a mile away, have the world's best onion rings brought right to your car at the Varsity Drive-In.

Such a vibrant marketplace naturally promotes change: For every Atlanta restaurant that makes it, there are many more that don't. With so much competition for the public's dining dollar, customers and critics alike are not long tolerant of bad food or bad service. Less than adequate restaurants — particularly those seen as an overall bad value — don't generally get to celebrate their first anniversary. In nearly every case, we have restricted our restaurant recommendations to places that have been open at least one year; some, in fact, have been in business for decades.

Value is always an issue. Atlanta's advantages and keen restaurant competition keep the average tab significantly lower than the cost of dining out in many other cities. In 1994, using meal prices provided by the Zagat Restaurant Survey, the Atlanta Convention & Visitors Bureau ranked the cost of a typical dinner in Atlanta the lowest of 15 cities. The average cost of a meal, drink, tax and tip here was $18.49, far below other cities such as Miami, $25.13; Washington, $25.72; San Francisco, $27.31; and, the high-price leader, New York, $30.32.

With 8,000 restaurants in metro Atlanta, you could eat at a different one every day for almost 22 years! Clearly, our task — choosing a tiny fraction of those 8,000 to tell you about — is not easy. We've tried to let neither haute cuisine nor hot dog stands hog too much space; there is, as we've said, excellent food at nearly every price in Atlanta. Whether you're looking for an unusual spot for lunch, a place to grab a quick burger, or a special location for an extraordinary occasion, you'll find it among our selections.

Dozens of national restaurant chains are active in the Atlanta market. Because of space limitations, we have generally not included these in our chapter. If you're craving a particular chain's food, check the business or Yellow Pages in the telephone book for various locations around town. We are, however, including a few chain restaurants that either originated here, are based here, or are found here but in few other cities, such as the Hard Rock Cafe and the Zesto Drive-Ins.

The price key symbol in each restaurant listing gives the range for the likely cost of the following: dinner for two, including cocktails, beer or wine, appetizer and dessert, excluding tax and tip. Not all restaurants serve alcohol; the typical cost will be lower at those "dry" establishments than at others. Obviously, your own bill at a given restaurant may be higher or lower, depending on what you order. These symbols are meant only as a guide.

Less than $20	$
$21 to $50	$$
$51 to $100	$$$
$100 plus	$$$$

Most Atlanta restaurants take all major credit cards, but some take no plastic at all. We'll let you know when this is the case. In general, the following is true of reservations. Some of Atlanta's fine dining establishments request (or even require) them; the lower-priced eateries have never heard of them; some mid-priced restaurants will accommodate a reservation for a larger-than-average-size party. It never hurts to ask.

Atlanta restaurants are required to offer nonsmoking sections; some have banned smoking altogether. Whether or not you choose to smoke, most restaurants will have no problem accommodating your seating request.

We've divided this chapter into two major parts: Atlanta and Beyond Atlanta. Restaurants in the Atlanta section are within the I-285 Perimeter. Those in the Beyond Atlanta section are outside the I-285 Perimeter. Within these two major sections we've categorized restaurants by types of cuisine and have arranged these categories alphabetically. The categories are: American, Caribbean and African, Chinese, Continental and Fine Dining, Cross-cultural Favorites, Greek/Mediterranean, Indian, Italian and Pizza, Japanese, Korean, Latin, Seafood, Southern and Barbecue, Thai, Vegetarian and Vietnamese. We've divided some of these categories into subcategories. For example, you'll find Cajun restaurants in their own subcategory under Southern Food and Barbecue, and you'll find steakhouses, as well as many other categories under American. So, take your time, browse through this chapter and join us in our favorite dining spots.

Atlanta

American

Good Basic American Food

AMERICAN ROADHOUSE
842 N. Highland Ave. N.E.   872-2822
$

Serving breakfast all day and blue plate specials, American Roadhouse is big with neighbors in Virginia-Highland. Main dishes include meatloaf and pasta; the vegetables are fresh. The Roadhouse has beer and wine and free parking; it's open until 11 PM nightly and until midnight on weekends.

ATKINS PARK
794 N. Highland Ave. N.E.   876-7249
$$

With a liquor license first issued in 1927, Atkins Park has the distinction of being the oldest bar in Atlanta. It's a perennial neighborhood favorite in Virginia-Highland, offering such American fare as stuffed pork chops, seafood, pasta and burgers. Atkins Park is open nightly until 3:30 AM and serves brunch on Saturday and Sunday; there's free parking in the rear.

EINSTEIN'S
1077 Juniper St. N.E.   876-7925
$$

You don't have to be a genius to see that Einstein's has caught on in a big way since its 1992 opening. Popular munchables include the coconut shrimp, Einstein's Reuben sandwich, the humus dip appetizer and a variety of pastas. Dine indoors or on one of the two outside patios, where gas heat lamps chase away the chill in cooler months. The restaurant serves lunch and dinner daily; it's open late and is a fun place to grab a drink and a snack after the theater.

GOOD OL' DAYS
401 Moreland Ave. N.E.   688-1006
$

This location has been in business only two years, but Good Ol' Days has been an Atlanta favorite for almost two decades. The menu's sandwiches are prepared on flower pot bread: honey wheat bread that is actually fresh-baked in a flower pot (don't ask why, just enjoy). Chicken wings are another specialty. You'll find the only pool tables in Little Five Points at the Moreland location, which serves beer and wine; the Sandy Springs location (below) has a full bar. Each has an outdoor patio and big-screen TV; both locations are open daily for lunch and dinner.

Additional location: 5841 Roswell Road, 257-9183.

HARD ROCK CAFE
215 Peachtree St. N.E.   688-7625
$$

The neon-emblazoned Peachtree location of the famous London-based restaurant chain opened in 1993 and quickly became a tourist favorite. Inside is an array of rock 'n' roll memorabilia, from an Elton John outfit to an Elvis Presley guitar. Menu standouts include hamburgers and the pig sandwich, made from pork shoulder roast. The cafe rocks daily for lunch and dinner.

HOUSTON'S
3321 Lenox Rd. N.E.   231-0161
$$

This Houston's, Atlanta's first, opened in 1978; now the city is home to the corporate headquarters of the 27-location chain company. Houston's menu includes barbecued ribs, grilled fresh fish and prime rib. Lunch and dinner are served daily; Houston's is open until 11 PM Sunday through Thursday and until midnight Friday and Saturday.

Additional locations: 2166 Peachtree Road N.W., 237-7534; 1955 Powers Ferry Road S.E., 563-1180; 3539 Northside Parkway N.W., 262-7130.

MANUEL'S TAVERN
602 N. Highland Ave. N.E.   525-3447
$

Manuel's Tavern has been an in-town gathering place since 1956. The walls are covered with beer signs and pictures of sports heroes and Democratic Party leaders and icons. (President Clinton and Vice President Gore often stop by when they're in town.) Throughout the main barroom and the two dining rooms, regulars roam from bar to booth to table, catching up on all the latest while enjoying Manuel's wings, burgers and salads. It can get hectic — on a busy night, you may have to introduce yourself to your waiter more than once — but the atmosphere is friendly and inviting. It's open daily for lunch and dinner. Additional location: 4877 Memorial Drive, Stone Mountain, 296-6919.

MICK'S

2110 Peachtree Rd.   *351-6425*
$$

This Mick's, at the entrance to the Bennett Street antique shopping district, is part of the Atlanta-based Peasant Restaurants group. The first Mick's opened in 1984, and now there are 11 locations around the metro area. The upbeat, welcoming restaurants are noted for their tasty food and big portions. The big burgers are a favorite; other popular items include chicken with penne pasta, fried chicken salad, fried green tomatoes, corn and tomato linguini — and for dessert, Oreo cheesecake and ice cream Heath bar pie. The wide-ranging menu and good value make Mick's a hit with families and couples alike. All locations have a full bar.

Additional locations: 557 Peachtree Street, 875-6425; Lenox Square, 262-6425; 4540 Ashford Dunwoody Road, 394-6425; 116 E. Ponce de Leon Avenue, Decatur, 373-7797; Underground Atlanta, 525-2825; Peachtree Center, 688-6425; 3525 Mall Boulevard No. 4, Duluth, 623-1855; Town Center, 429-5370; North Point, 667-2330; Cumberland Mall, 431-7190.

PLANET HOLLYWOOD

218 Peachtree St. N.W.

Under construction as we went to press, Planet Hollywood was scheduled to open in the summer of 1995. In February, sledge hammer-wielding co-owner Arnold Schwarzenegger terminated a wall and officially kicked off construction on the 21,000-square-foot, four-level, $6 million restaurant, which will seat about 260 people and include a *Gone With the Wind* diorama. Seventeen other Planet Hollywood locations are open worldwide; each showcases movie and TV memorabilia, such as Judy Garland's dress from *The Wizard of Oz*, and Macaulay Culkin's sled from *Home Alone*. The restaurant will offer classic California cuisine, including pasta, turkey burgers, gourmet

You'll find 17th-century opulence along with fine continental and French cuisine at 103 West.

pizzas and vegetarian items. Movie montage films and coming attraction movie trailers will entertain diners.

ROASTERS ROTISSERIE
2770 Lenox Rd.   *237-1122*
$$

Rotisserie-roasted chicken is the star at Roasters, which offers American and Southern food. Barbecue pork ribs are another specialty, and the menu generally offers 15 to 20 selections of fresh vegetables. For smaller appetites, there are sandwiches and salads. The location listed in the header serves beer and wine only; the following location has a full bar. Parking is free; both locations are open daily for lunch and dinner. Additional location: 2180 Pleasant Hill Road N.W., Duluth, 476-8424.

ST. CHARLES DELI
752 N. Highland Ave. N.E.   *876-3354*
$$

Breakfast, lunch and dinner are served daily in this friendly deli-style restaurant. The artichoke dip and toast-points appetizer is good, and the burgers, vegetable club and Reuben sandwiches are best sellers. The North Highland location is big with neighbors in the Virginia-Highland section. Beer and wine are sold at both restaurants. Additional location: 2470 Briarcliff Road N.E., 636-5201.

R. THOMAS DELUXE GRILL
1812 Peachtree Rd. N.W.   *872-2942*
$$

R. Thomas' year-round outdoor patio has, without a doubt, the best outdoor statuary and ornament collection of any Atlanta restaurant. But those lured in by the yard art end up staying for the eats, such as big hamburgers, penne pasta, Picata chicken and plump wings. Beer and wine are served, and parking is free.

R. Thomas is open 24 hours, and sometimes attracts celebrities: Madonna, Jasmine Guy and Eric Clapton are all said to have munched here.

TACO MAC
1006 N. Highland Ave. N.E.   *873-6529*
$$

Taco Mac has been a laid-back Atlanta party spot since 1979, when this location (the original) opened. The fare is American bar food with a Mexican twang: Favorites include chicken salad, chicken wings, burritos, tacos and salads. Each location is a little different; this one features more than 300 beers. Most locations have a patio for warm weather fun outdoors. Prices are in the low end of this range; two can snack for less than $20.

Additional locations: 375 Pharr Road N.E., 239-0650; 771 Cherokee Avenue S.E., 624-4641; 2615 George Busbee Parkway N.W., Kennesaw, 426-1515; 3281 Highway 5, Douglasville, 942-0499; 3334 Highway 78 S.W., Snellville, 736-1333; 1318 Johnson Ferry Road N.E., Marietta, 977-4467; 2120 Johnson Ferry Road N.E., 454-7676; 2845 Mountain Industrial Boulevard, Tucker, 621-3601; 1444 Oxford Road N.E., 377-2323; 1630 Pleasant Hill Road N.W., Duluth, 717-7169; 5830 Roswell Road N.W., 257-0735; 2359 Windy Hill Road S.E., Marietta, 953-6382.

VICKERY'S CRESCENT AVE. BAR AND GRILL
1106 Crescent Ave. N.E.   *881-1106*
$$

A charming Midtown home converted to a restaurant, Vickery's opened in 1983 and serves American bar and grill food with a Cuban flair. The atmosphere is casual and friendly, and there's a full bar. In addition to daily specials, Vickery's boasts out-of-this-world hamburgers,

Cuban-style roasted chicken and backwater bayou seafood saute. Especially during the spring and fall, the tree-shaded brick patio on Crescent Avenue is a lovely place to relax for a few hours. Vickery's fare is consistently good, the service is excellent, and the eclectic crowd makes for great people-watching. It's open daily for lunch, dinner and late-night snacks.

ZAC'S
820 Woodland Ave. S.E.   627-9266
$$

Zac's is one block off Moreland in the Ormewood Park section of Southeast Atlanta, where pleasant neighborhoods and relatively low home prices are attracting new residents all the time. The fare at Zac's, which is in an old brick trolley station, ranges from standard American (meatloaf, chicken pot pie) to upscale trendy (black and white linguini with salmon and bay scallops in seafood sauce). The owners are catering-industry veterans who opened the restaurant in 1992. Zac's is open for dinner Thursday through Saturday from 6 to 10 PM and for brunch Saturday and Sunday from 10 AM to 3 PM. No alcohol; no credit cards.

Better American and Fine Dining

AZALEA
3167 Peachtree Rd. N.E.   237-9939
$$$

Casual, upscale Azalea serves new American cuisine. The sizzling catfish appetizer and the hot smoked and seared salmon are popular menu items; afterward, cool off with the almond basket with ice cream and seasonal berries. Azalea is open nightly for dinner; reservations are accepted for Sunday through Thursday nights only; you may choose to dine outdoors in the warmer months. There's valet parking.

BLUE RIBBON GRILL
4006 LaVista Rd., Tucker   491-1570
$$

The fare at Blue Ribbon ranges from meatloaf and other Southern favorites to hand-cut steaks, prime rib, chicken pot pie and fresh fish. There's a full bar; the restaurant seats about 156 diners. Large parties may call ahead for reservations, or even fax in their order if they prefer. The restaurant is closed on Sunday; it's open for lunch on weekdays, for brunch on Saturdays and for dinner six nights a week.

BUCKHEAD DINER
3073 Piedmont Rd. N.E.   262-3336
$$$

Rather like the marriage between a retro deco-style diner and the plush dining car from the *Orient Express*, this restaurant's decor provides an environment appropriate to its eclectic modern American cuisine. You might want to start with the salt and pepper calamari, go on to a specialty such as the veal and wild mushroom meatloaf or the grilled smoked pork chop and finish up with the white chocolate banana cream pie. Ever heard of an upscale restaurant serving cheese grits? Well, there's a first time for everything. Part-time Buckhead boy Elton John is said to drop in occasionally. The diner is open daily for lunch and dinner.

CHEESECAKE FACTORY
3024 Peachtree Rd. N.W.   816-2555
$$$

Yes, you'll find plenty of cheesecake (some 50 varieties!) in this large, odd-looking Buckhead eatery, but there's also much more to enjoy. A mixed crowd frequents this casually elegant, eclectic American restaurant, which has a full bar and a wide-ranging menu with pasta, steaks and seafood. The Cheesecake Factory joined the Atlanta restaurant scene in 1993; it's open daily for lunch and dinner; there's valet parking.

CHOW
1026½ N. Highland Ave.   872-0869
$$$

Chow, which opened in 1985, serves contemporary American fare in a casual atmosphere that appeals to its neighbors in laid-back Virginia-Highland. We've heard that Michael Stipe of R.E.M. has been known to chow down here. Specialties include ginger tuna and lemon basil chicken. Lunch and dinner are served daily (except there's no lunch downtown on Saturday). The weekend brunches are festive affairs. The downtown location has secured parking and accepts reservations. Additional location: 303 Peachtree Center Avenue, 222-0210.

CITY GRILL
50 Hurt Plaza   524-2489
$$

This restaurant, in the heart of downtown, is in a former Federal Reserve Bank in a 1913 building, and its decor conveys an appropriate sense of affluence. The cuisine is American regional with a Southern flair: Specialties include Southern-fried quail, barbecued shrimp and crab cakes. The atmosphere is fine dining on the relaxed side. Call for reservations. City Grill is closed on Sunday; it serves lunch on weekdays and dinner Monday through Saturday.

THE COUNTRY PLACE
1197 Peachtree St. (in Colony Square)881-0144
$$

In business since 1978, the casually upscale Country Place offers an American menu that includes maple-basted salmon, New York strip steak, fillets and Montrachet chicken. There's live entertainment beginning at 6 PM

Tuesday through Saturday. Luncheon reservations are accepted; dinner reservations are accepted only for parties of eight or more. Parking in the Colony Square garage is free for patrons; ask for validation.

DAILEY'S RESTAURANT AND BAR
17 International Blvd.   681-3303
$$$

Dailey's opened in 1981; it's a shadowy, noisy and altogether pleasant downtown eatery serving creative American fare. Big sellers are the swordfish au Poivre and the apple brandy duckling. For dessert, try Dailey's famous french fried ice cream. The big portions make Dailey's popular with sports celebrities, politicians and the downtown business and convention crowd. Dinner is served nightly; lunch is served daily, except Sunday.

HORSERADISH GRILL
4320 Powers Ferry Rd. N.W.   255-7277
$$$

This trendy, casual restaurant near Chastain Park opened in 1994 after a major remodelling of its space, the former Red Barn Inn, which was one of Atlanta's oldest restaurants. Its cuisine is in-season Southern fare, and all grilled items are cooked over a hickory fire. Specialty dishes include a basil-stuffed trout fillet wrapped in bacon and grilled, fillet of sauteed grouper, veal chops and strip and fillet steaks. The full bar has a dazzling array of spirits, especially single-malt scotches. In spite of receiving accolades in *Esquire, Bon Apetit* and *Atlanta* magazines, management aspires to preserve the restaurant's reputation for catering to locals: Some 50 percent of patrons are repeat guests. The Horseradish Grill is open daily for lunch and dinner and offers valet parking.

KUDZU CAFE

3215 Peachtree Rd. N.E.   262-0661
$$

The creeping and all-but-indestructible kudzu vine has been the bane of generations of Southern gardeners, but here it is pressed into use as the design motif for a pleasant upscale restaurant. The fare is heavily influenced by Southern favorites, but it's been updated with less fat and a more imaginative presentation. Specialties include fried green tomatoes, hickory-smoked pork chops, the vegetable plate and a diet-destroyer known as the Kudzu Moon Pie. The dining room has lots of booths and artwork by Southern photographers. In business since 1992, the Kudzu Cafe is open daily for lunch and dinner and offers valet parking.

PANO'S & PAUL'S

1232 W. Paces Ferry Rd. N.W.   261-3662
$$$

Since 1979, Pano's and Paul's has been serving modern American cuisine in a luxurious environment of chandeliers and tuxedoed waiters. The restaurant is a regular with locals, who come in for the batter-fried lobster tail, swordfish and veal dishes. It's open for dinner only and closed on Sunday; reservations are accepted; jackets are requested for gentlemen.

PEACHTREE CAFE

268 E. Paces Ferry Rd. N.E.   233-4402
$$$

Peachtree Cafe has been on Atlanta's menu since 1978; its cuisine is American with Italian and other influences. Popular dishes include salmon on flat focaccia bread with herbed goat cheese and roma tomatoes, mesquite-grilled marinated chicken breast with potato cakes and vegetables, and the Oriental salad with greens, grilled chicken and baby corn. The

cafe is open daily for lunch and dinner; reservations are accepted; there's valet parking. Sunday brunch, 11 AM to 4 PM, is a special treat.

THE PEASANT RESTAURANT AND BAR

3402 Piedmont Rd. N.E.   231-8740
$$

The Peasant on Piedmont serves creative American cuisine with Southwestern and Cajun influences. With a greenhouse dining room and wicker furniture, the ambiance is casually elegant; the restaurant draws locals and conventioneers. Herb-crusted grouper, rack of lamb and cappellini pasta are recommended dishes. Lunch is served daily except Saturday; dinner is served nightly; there's valet parking.

THE PEASANT UPTOWN

3500 Peachtree Rd. (in Phipps Plaza) 261-6341
$$$

In 1974, the Peasant Uptown was the first restaurant to spin-off from the Pleasant Peasant downtown (see separate listing). The Peasant Uptown serves lunch and dinner daily in a casually elegant setting that suggests a greenhouse, and the crowd includes Atlantans as well as many out-of-towners who come to shop at Phipps and Lenox Square. The garlic fillet and the sauteed Oriental grouper are two specialties. There's valet parking; reservations are not accepted.

PITTYPAT'S PORCH

25 International Blvd. N.W.   525-8228
$$

This restaurant takes its name from Scarlett O'Hara's aunt by marriage Pittypat Hamilton. Pittypat's presents American Southern cuisine in a casual atmosphere reminiscent of *Gone With the Wind*, complete with rocking chairs and hand fans. Crab cakes, baby back ribs,

Outside dining is enjoyable at this Midtown restaurant.

venison pie, fried chicken and fresh seafood are all on the menu, and your dinner includes vegetables and a salad bar with 10 Southern salads. Pitty's is right across from the Westin Peachtree Plaza Hotel, and it's open daily for dinner only. Reservations are accepted.

PLEASANT PEASANT
555 Peachtree St. N.E.   874-3223
$$$

When the Pleasant Peasant opened in 1973 it immediately became an Atlanta dining favorite. This location is the grand dame of the entire Atlanta-based Peasant Restaurants group, which includes the Mick's chain and other restaurants in the metro area and in Washington, D.C., Maryland, Pennsylvania, Virginia, Tennessee and Florida. Through all this growth, the original New York-style bistro has retained its lively, exciting mood and its sense of humor. Recommended entrees include steak au poivre, plum pork and apple barbecued rack of lamb. The Peasant is open weekdays for lunch and nightly for dinner; valet parking is available at night. Reservations are not ac

cepted, which can mean having several drinks at the bar.

WINFIELD'S
1 Galleria Pkwy. in the Galleria Centre 955-5300
$$$

Winfield's serves creative American cuisine in a restaurant reminiscent of a European grand ballroom. Crab cakes, salmon grill, Thai chicken pasta and Caribbean rack of lamb are all longtime favorites. The restaurant is popular with locals and with conventioneers from the Cobb Galleria Centre. Dinner is served nightly; lunch is served daily except Saturday.

Steakhouses

COACH AND SIX RESTAURANT
1776 Peachtree St. N.W.   872-6666
$$$

This steakhouse has been an Atlanta standard since 1962. From the light spinach puff hors d'oeuvres to steaks, triple-cut lamb chops, chicken or fish and the chocolate mousse, there's lots to enjoy at the Coach, where the atmosphere is el egant but inviting. Speaker of the U.S. House Newt Gingrich reportedly stopped in recently. There's valet parking; the restaurant is open for dinner only and closed on Sunday.

BONE'S

3130 Piedmont Rd. N.E.   237-2663
$$$$

In business since 1979, Bones serves steak and seafood in a fine dining atmosphere that's clubby yet lively. Menu favorites include live Maine lobster (flown in daily), prime rib, steaks and lamb chops. There's valet parking; reservations are accepted. Bone's is open weekdays for lunch and every night for dinner.

CHOPS

70 W. Paces Ferry Rd. N.W.   262-2675
$$$

Chops steakhouse, open since 1989, has received national attention in *Esquire* and elsewhere. The atmosphere is casual chic, suggesting a 1930s-era men's club. On the menu are steaks, lamb chops and swordfish. The wine list is a connoisseur's dream, with selections up to $3,000 a bottle. Reservations are strongly recommended; there's valet parking. Chops is open every night for dinner and is open for lunch on weekdays.

COWTIPPERS

1600 Piedmont Rd.   874-3469
$$

Decked out in a whimsical Western steakhouse theme, Cowtippers is a popular in-town place for hearty fare. Along with steaks and prime rib, Cowtippers whips up beef, chicken, shrimp and veggie kebabs and fresh salmon, tuna and swordfish. With a full bar and a friendly staff, Cowtippers attracts lots of Midtowners with big appetites.

HIGHLAND TAP

1026 N. Highland Ave. N.E.   875-3673
$$$

This popular in-town steakhouse is in a granite-walled cellar below the intersection of N. Highland and Virginia avenues. In a masculine room reminiscent of the 1940s, the restaurant's menu includes steaks, lambchops and duck. Martini aficionados should try the Tap's four-ounce "world-class martini." The restaurant is open every day for lunch and dinner, except there's no lunch on Monday.

MORTON'S OF CHICAGO

245 Peachtree Center Ave. N.E.   577-4366
$$$$

Morton's masculine, clubby decor suggests a Chicago speakeasy. You'll enjoy porterhouse, prime rib and live Maine lobster. Morton's is open nightly for dinner. Reservations are recommended, as are jackets for the gentlemen. There's valet parking. Additional location: 3379 Peachtree Road N.E., 816-6535.

PILGREEN'S RESTAURANT AND LOUNGE

1081 Lee St. S.W.   758-4669
$$

Pilgreen's steakhouse is an Atlanta tradition, still operated by the family that established it in 1932. The atmosphere is casual and friendly, and many customers are regulars. Specialities of the house include fillets, T-bones and the steak for two. Both locations have a full bar; the original Lee Street restaurant has free secured parking.

Additional location: 6335 Jonesboro Road, Morrow, 961-1666.

SUN DIAL RESTAURANT AND LOUNGE

Westin Peachtree Plaza Hotel
210 Peachtree St. N.W.   589-7506
$$$

There's nothing like dining atop the world's second-tallest hotel to make your troubles seem oh-so-small. Seventy-one floors above Peachtree Street, Sun Dial is a room with a dazzling view; and, since the whole place rotates, you'll get to see it all. The three-course dinner begins with a shrimp appetizer, and the entrees include smoked prime rib, filet mignon, chicken, swordfish and salmon. The Sun Dial is open every day for lunch and dinner, including all holidays; reservations are accepted. Even if you only stop by for a cocktail in the upper-level lounge, the Sun Dial (especially the nonstop ride up in a glass-enclosed elevator outside the building!) is always a thrill.

Tasty, Quick and Cheap

EATS
600 Ponce de Leon Ave. N.E.   *888-9149*
$

EATS is a favorite with college kids and other Generation Xers who groove on the friendly atmosphere, eclectic music and terrific food. There are separate counters: One serves pasta (the big seller is cheese tortellini with marinara sauce), and another serves jerk chicken and vegetables (try the collard greens). EATS, right across from the big red brick City Hall East building, has become a Midtown dining staple since it opened in 1993. Beer and wine are sold; no credit cards.

SUSIE'S COFFEE SHOP
1660 McLendon Ave. N.E.   *371-0889*
$

Susie's is an old-fashioned coffee shop and grill that's a regular stop for residents in the Candler Park and Lake Claire neighborhoods. The friendly, cozy shop with a counter and a few tables serves breakfast and lunch daily. Breakfast and burgers are cooked to order by Susie herself in front of a large window on

McLendon. The home-fried potatoes are terrific. No alcohol; no credit cards.

TASTY TOWN RESTAURANT
67 Forsyth St. N.W.   *522-5865*
$

This pleasant, nostalgic little restaurant near the Central Library is a great place to grab lunch downtown. A variety of sandwiches is offered, along with main courses such as fried trout. Nothing shakes off the midday blues like the chopped sirloin steak and a half-dozen cups of Tasty Town's rich coffee. It's open for breakfast and lunch Monday through Saturday; no alcohol; no credit cards.

THE VARSITY
61 North Ave. N.W.   *881-1706*
$

At the corner of Spring Street, the Varsity is just across the North Avenue bridge from Georgia Tech. It opened in 1928 and claims the distinction of being the world's largest drive-in: Every day, this single restaurant serves up to 2 miles of hot dogs, a ton of onion rings and 5,000 pies. Friendly carhops will bring your food to your car, or you can eat inside and watch TV in one of the several large dining rooms. The serving counters inside are a beehive of activity: The slogan here is "Have your money in your hand and your order in your mind." The onion rings may just be the best on the planet. No alcohol; no credit cards.

Additional locations: 1085 Lindbergh Drive N.E., 261-8843; 6045 Dawson Boulevard N.W., Norcross, 840-8519.

WOODY'S FAMOUS PHILADELPHIA CHEESESTEAKS
981 Monroe Dr. N.E. (at Virginia Ave.) 876-1939
$

Woody's is just across from Piedmont Park, and since 1975 Atlantans have been visiting this tiny restaurant for cheesesteak sandwiches and submarines. There's nothing fancy about Woody's — just real good cheesesteaks and a variety of Breyer's ice creams. It's closed Sunday; no alcohol; no credit cards.

ZESTO DRIVE-IN
544 Ponce de Leon Ave. N.E.   607-1118
$

Since 1949, Atlanta has been stopping by Zesto's. The Illinois-based soft ice cream chain was once in 46 states. Today, few restaurants remain, but, with seven locations, Atlanta is still a hotbed of them. Try a Chubby Decker hamburger and a side order of fried okra (if you're in the right Zesto's — each one's menu is quirkily different from the others) and top it off with a Nut Brown Crown. The satiny soft ice cream is the real thing. The Ponce restaurant, a recently built chrome-colored "classic" diner, is the best-looking Zesto's.

Additional locations: 1181 E. Confederate Avenue S.E., 622-4254; 2665 East Point Drive, East Point, 761-9518; 151 Forest Parkway, Forest Park, 366-0564; 3165 Glenwood Road, Decatur, 289-9519; Little Five Points, 523-1973; 2469 Piedmont Road N.E., 237-8689.

Caribbean/African

BRIDGETOWN GRILL
689 Peachtree St. N.E.   873-4705
$$

Some people call it fusion, some call it Jamaican. Whatever you call it, the food is simply delicious. Jerk chicken, guava barbecued ribs, conch fritters and Caribbean gazpacho set the pace on a lively menu. Try a chimale, a corn and ham tamale topped with black bean chili and melted Jack cheese, garnished with sweet Bermuda onions. Service is friendly in this casual, relaxed setting. Brightly painted walls, banners and artwork create an upbeat atmosphere. Lunch and dinner are served seven days a week. A full-service bar is available at the Peachtree location. Other locations are 1156 Euclid Avenue (beer and wine only), 653-0110, and 7285 Roswell Road (full bar), 394-1575.

IMPERIAL FEZ
2285 Peachtree Rd. N.E.   351-0870
$$$

Prepare yourself to enter a world of exotic experiences. Sinuous veiled dancers, tantalizing aromas and colorful decor create a setting that induces relaxation and enjoyment. Feast on authentic Moroccan cuisine, served with smiling hospitality, while you recline on silken cushions. The restaurant guarantees MSG, curry and lard are not used in the dishes. A full vegetarian menu is available. For a fixed price of $30 each person, you'll dine on a five-course meal. This includes soup, five different salads and appetizers, a choice of 34 entrees (such as shish kebab, pheasant, quail), and for dessert, fresh fruits and pastries. The Imperial Fez serves dinner nightly and recommends reservations.

RED ROOSTER
INTERNATIONAL CAFE & BAR
3649 Clairmont Rd.
Chamblee   986-9918
$$

Highly seasoned food in a lively setting is yours in this restaurant/club just 3 miles inside I-285. Open for lunch and dinner every day but Sunday, Red Rooster offers stews, fried collard greens and a wide sampling of rice-based entrees. Beef, shrimp and hen flavor the vegetable-laden dishes. Other favorites are pot roast, chicken curry and the peppers with cayenne. The nightclub features African, Caribbean and pop music on weekends with live bands for dancing.

PATTI HUT
595 Piedmont Ave. N.E.   *892-5133*
$

In the Rio Shopping Center, this small, squeaky clean casual place pleases the palate. Get ready for some tasty treats, such as big juicy chunks of the freshest jerk chicken, tender goat stew and curry chicken in light sauce. The rice and bean dishes are nutritiously filling. Peruse the steam table's bountiful vegetables and spike them with the house-made Scotch Bonnet pepper sauce. You may sop up the greens' juice with Patti Hut's special cornbread. Locals line up for the Monday special, which may be corned beef and cabbage. With your meal, have a Jamaican ginger beer or a fruit-based soda and spicy fries and fried plantains on the side. Low cost and large portions delight the regulars, who dine inside, at the few tables out on the sidewalk or take their goodies home.

THE AFRICAN BROWN BAG
Ford Factory Square Building, Kroger Shopping Center
699 Ponce de Leon Ave. N.E.   *642-3434*
$$

You can eat here for less than this price range, but do yourself a favor and go big. The entrees, turned out by talented hands, combine French sensibilities with African spice. The owner advises bringing a sense of adventure as you approach the daily changing menu. Try the Cuban pork roast, spicy with red pepper salsa, chilies and a sauce based on tequila. Frequent menu items are based on game, fish, chicken, pasta, fresh vegetables and homemade breads, including a special bread cooked in a seasoned clay pot. It's

open for dinner Monday through Saturday. Some Saturday nights you'll find a blues singer or other entertainment at the Brown Bag. Lunch can be arranged in advance for parties of 10 or more. No credit cards are accepted.

Chinese

CHIN CHIN
3887 Peachtree Rd. N.E.   *816-2229*
$$

You can watch mouthwatering authentic Chinese cuisine being prepared in the open-kitchen setting in Cherokee Plaza. Chin Chin's owner/chef John Kuan draws on his 20-plus years of experience in a five-star New York restaurant to create crowd-pleasing entrees. These include tangerine steak, gold coin shrimp patties, honey-glazed spare ribs and steamed vegetables. Open every day for lunch and dinner, Chin Chin offers a full bar and free delivery within a 3-mile radius. Although Chin Chin's dinners may run on the high side of this range, grab a good bargain with the lunch special. For $4.50, choose from a 28-item spread.

GRAND CHINA
2975 Peachtree Rd. N.E.   *231-8690*
$$

Order from a sizable menu for reliable food in this longtime Buckhead fixture. Szechuan, Cantonese and Taiwanese entrees join those originating in Singapore.

The bar, with its lattice motif bamboo shades, offers a pleasant setting. Try the General Tsao Chicken, small chunks of boneless chicken breast lightly fried, then covered with a hot-sour sauce and sesame seeds. Noodle dishes, both hot and cold, are favorites. An outdoor section is open in good weather. Grand China is open every day for lunch and dinner. No reservations are needed.

CHOPSTIX
4279 Roswell Rd. N.E.   255-4868
$$$

For a lovely setting with candlelight, fine china, linen-covered tables and gourmet Chinese food worthy of the upscale atmosphere, join the faithful clientele at Chopstix.

Hot and cold appetizers include stir-fried alligator and mango roasted duck salad. The extensive menu includes many shrimp and scallop dishes as well as seafood, shellfish, pork, chicken and beef entrees. Princess Prawn, Ginger Duck in a crispy rice-bowl, Satay Seafood Hot Pot with eggplant, shrimp, scallops and lobster are among the favorites. Dress casually and relax with cocktails, beer or wine in the piano bar. Reservations are recommended for this restaurant in Chastain Square. Chopstix serves lunch on weekdays and dinner every night.

HAU'S GOURMET CHINESE RESTAURANT
192 Peachtree Center Ave.   659-2788
$$$

For fine dining in downtown Atlanta, visit this charming and picturesque restaurant. The food is new Cantonese cuisine in Hong-Kong style and has won many fans among residents and visitors. Ask about the seafood specials, the Peking duck served in two courses and vegetarian entrees. Hau's offers a full-service bar as well as wines by the glass or bottle.

HONTO
3295 Chamblee-Dunwoody Rd.
Chamblee   458-8088
$$

Excellent food and fast turnover draw crowds to this shopping center location. Ambiance and amenities are best found elsewhere. A faithful clientele, many of whom are Asians, rates favored seating in the inner room. Among the specialties are the barbecue pork rolls and dumplings with shrimp and vegetables. The curry tarts and steamed whole fish also are popular, as are grouper cheeks and salt-and-pepper squid. Lunch and dinner are served every day. Dim sum, which has been described as a kind of smorgasbord on wheels, (or, more delicately, as a Chinese tea lunch) is served midday on Saturday, Sunday and Monday.

LITTLE SZECHUAN
Northwoods Plaza
5091-C Buford Hwy.   451-0192
$

Another of the good Asian restaurants clustered in strip centers on Buford Highway, Little Szechuan concentrates on food, not atmosphere. Opened in 1992, an imminent renovation of this successful restaurant will double its size. Mandarin Chinese with Szechuan spices characterizes the menu. Creative and well-seasoned, the dishes here include stir-fried Szechuan string beans, shredded pork with garlic sauce, chicken in sherry with garlic sauce, steamed fish with black beans and spicy garlic shrimp. Look for sizable portions and fast service. Although in our lowest price category, you'll likely spend more than $20. Beer and wine are offered in a casual atmosphere, and there's lots of free parking outside. Little Szechuan serves lunch and dinner every day except Tuesday. Reservations for parties of six or more are accepted.

UNCLE TAI'S RESTAURANT
3500 Peachtree Rd.   816-8888
$$$

Upscale and sophisticated, this restaurant specializes in authentic Hunan cuisine. Gourmet specialties include sa-chia shrimp, sauteed lobster and lamb cooked with ginger root. You may also order salads, soups and light fare. Uncle Tai's Phipps Plaza setting (across from Lenox Square) makes it a natural for important business gatherings or social events. Gourmet take-out is offered. It's open for lunch and dinner seven days a week.

THE ORIENT AT VININGS
4199 Paces Ferry Rd.   *438-8866*
$$

Cantonese cuisine with modern touches is the specialty here. It's served in a contemporary setting with romantic overtones. Exquisite walnut chicken, firecracker pork and sesame beef are among the favorites. Several fresh fish entrees are featured. Ask about the weekly lunch special. Friendly service is a mainstay of this popular restaurant, which you'll find is at the top end of this price category. Reservations are suggested. The Orient is open for dinner every night and for lunch every day but Saturday. It serves brunch on Sunday.

JYH DONG GOON
5285 Buford Hwy.   *457-7014*
$$

Mandarin-Szechuan cuisine is the specialty here, where you may dine seven days a week and have lunch Monday through Friday. A favorite is the Phoenix and Dragon plate, half chicken and half shrimp with rice and vegetables. Flavorful soups and vegetarian fare are offered. Desserts at no charge include fruit and fortune cookies.

PUNG MIE CHINESE RESTAURANT
5145 Buford Hwy.
Doraville   *455-0435*
$$

Among the popular dishes in this well-recommended place are pot stickers, fried or steamed rice and noodle soups. A range of Chinese specialties keeps customers of all nationalities coming back for more. Beer is offered; fruit desserts are included in the meal. Pung Mie is open for lunch and dinner seven days a week.

Continental and Fine Dining

57TH FIGHTER GROUP RESTAURANT
3829 Clairmont Rd.   *457-7757*
$$

This restaurant, whose decor suggests a World War II French farmhouse, is near DeKalb-Peachtree Airport, which handles much of the small private plane traffic in Atlanta. You can relax at a table with a runway view while you enjoy the continental fare, which includes lemon veal, citrus salmon and prime rib. The music is Big Band; the atmosphere is comfortably casual. Dinner is served nightly; lunch is served on weekdays, brunch on Sunday. Reservations are accepted, and there's a full bar.

THE ABBEY
Piedmont at North Ave.   *876-8532*
$$$

Looking for a dinner that's almost a religious experience? Try The Abbey, a fine dining restaurant serving contemporary continental cuisine in a deconsecrated Methodist church. Rack of lamb in herbed mustard crust and venison loin are two popular entrees. The restaurant has been in business since 1968 and has been at this location since 1978; it draws tourists as well as locals out celebrating that special occasion. It's open daily for dinner only; there's valet parking; reservations are suggested.

ANTHONY'S

3109 Piedmont Rd. N.E.   262-7379
$$$

Continental cuisine with a Southern flair is the specialty at Anthony's, which is just off Piedmont Road in a beautiful 1797 plantation home with seven working fireplaces. The house was originally in Washington, Georgia, where it's said that Gen. Sherman spared it because the family had an infant. An Atlanta restaurant landmark since 1967, Anthony's offers fine dining in a friendly atmosphere. Popular entrees include chateaubriand, rack of lamb and Veal Anthony: grilled medallions of veal topped with lump crabmeat and lemon/garlic hollandaise sauce. Anthony's is open for dinner only and is closed on Sunday; reservations are recommended; there's valet parking.

BABETTE'S CAFE

471 N. Highland Ave.   523-9121
$$

In a Greenwich Village-style setting, Babette's presents European provincial fare that includes a fried oyster appetizer on dill biscuits with cucumber sauce, artichoke and olive ravioli, coq au vin and the French stew or cassoulet. There's a full bar; dinner is served nightly Tuesday through Sunday; brunch is served on Sunday.

CAPO'S CAFE

992 Virginia Ave. N.E.   876-5655
$$

Rumor has it that an inordinate number of wedding proposals take place in little, romantic Capo's. The fare is continental; fettuccine Alfredo, stuffed rainbow trout and crab cakes are all recommended. The owner stresses that the friendly, attitude-free servers are a big part of the restaurant's appeal. Beer and wine are served; reservations are not accepted,

and there's nearly always a wait. Capo's is open Tuesday through Sunday for dinner and on Sunday for brunch.

DANTE'S DOWN THE HATCH

3380 Peachtree Rd. N.E.   266-1600
$$$

How about a place with live jazz and Swiss fondue that looks like a big ship tied to a wharf? That's Dante's, an Atlanta original with two locations. The original Dante's was one of the best-known spots in the first Underground Atlanta, and when the attraction was re-invented, Dante's owner eagerly returned. The second location is right across from Lenox Square in Buckhead. The design of both restaurants does indeed suggest a sailing ship at dock, and there's live jazz on the ship seven nights a week. The fare is fondue — the mandarin fondue is popular — and your server will be happy to instruct you in the basics. The full bar boasts more than 300 wines. Both Dante's serve dinner nightly; reservations are recommended.

Additional location: Underground Atlanta, 577-1800.

THE DINING ROOM

The Ritz-Carlton, Buckhead
3434 Peachtree Rd. N.E.   237-2700
$$$$

In 1994, for the sixth consecutive year, the Dining Room earned AAA's 5-Diamond award. Seating just 78 people, the intimate room is elegantly appointed with art and antiques. A four-course prix fixe dinner is served nightly except Sunday, with or without special wines from the master sommelier. The menu changes continually, but popular items include the veal carpaccio with pomegranate and tarragon appetizer, the pumpkin soup with crab cake and sea urchin, and the sika venison escalope. Reservations are strongly encouraged; jackets are requested for the gentlemen; there's valet parking.

FLORENCIA
Occidental Grand Hotel
75 14th St. 881-9898
$$$

In the opulent Occidental Grand Hotel, the intimate Florencia seats only 60 guests. The fine dining room is elegantly appointed with silk wall coverings and a fireplace and is known as a special occasion restaurant. Menu standouts include grilled Gulf shrimp with squid ink spatzle, foie gras, smoked duck fricassee, rack of lamb and Maine lobster. There's valet parking; reservations are encouraged.

THE HEDGEROSE HEIGHTS INN
490 E. Paces Ferry Rd. N.E. 233-7673
$$$

In business since 1981, Hedgerose Heights has earned quite a reputation among fine-dining devotees. It's in a charming house-turned-restaurant, and the cuisine is entirely seasonal, with an emphasis on game. Reservations are requested; the restaurant is open for dinner only and closed on Sunday and Monday.

LA TOUR RESTAURANT
3209 Paces Ferry Pl. 233-8833
$$$

La Tour serves continental cuisine in an atmosphere of lavish European elegance, complete with original oil paintings, marble, chandeliers and live piano entertainment each evening. Specialties include Dover sole and lobster. La Tour opened in 1986 and serves dinner Monday through Saturday evenings. Reservations are requested, as are jackets for the gentlemen.

THE MANSION
179 Ponce de Leon Ave. N.E. 876-0727
$$

A grand 1885 home on a hill is the setting for The Mansion, a continental restaurant that opened in 1976. In surroundings rich with period furnishings and antiques, The Mansion serves lunch and dinner daily; specialties include the Georgia peach chicken and filet mignon. The Mansion's elegant walled pool area is a popular spot for weddings. Dress is smart; reservations are accepted. The entrance to the parking area is on Piedmont (northbound) just above North Avenue.

NIKOLAI'S ROOF
The Atlanta Hilton and Towers
255 Courtland St. 221-6362
$$$$

When nothing less than total extravagance will do, there's Nikolai's Roof — if you planned ahead, that is. Advance reservations are nearly always necessary at this famous fine dining restaurant atop the Atlanta Hilton, which specializes in French and Russian cuisine. A six-course prix fixe dinner is served nightly, with seatings at 6:30 and 9:30; the menu changes with the availability of game and other specialty items. There's an extensive wine list. Coat and tie are requested for the gentlemen. Nikolai's, which also provides stupendous views of Atlanta north of downtown, has been dazzling diners since 1976.

103 WEST
103 W. Paces Ferry Rd. N.W. 233-5993
$$$

In the heart of Buckhead, 103 West serves continental and French cuisine in an atmosphere of fine dining. Reservations are recommended at this elegant eatery, whose interior suggests 17th-century opulence. Popular menu items include the mushroom pastry puff appetizer and the fried lobster tail. There's valet parking; 103 West serves dinner only and is closed on Sunday.

THE RESTAURANT
The Ritz-Carlton, Atlanta
181 Peachtree St. N.E.   659-0400
$$$

Seating only 85 guests in an intimate, English hunt club atmosphere, The Restaurant offers Mediterranean-influenced French cuisine. Specialties include foie gras, souffles and a variety of game and fish. Reservations are recommended; jackets are requested for gentlemen; there's valet parking. The Restaurant is open for dinner only and is closed on Sunday.

English

REGGIE'S BRITISH PUB AND RESTAURANT
CNN Center (Techwood at Marietta) 525-1437
$$

Cheerio, old chap, there'll always be a Reggie's — at least there has been since 1976, when this casual Victorian pub poured its first ale. The menu spotlights American fare and British specialties, such as scotch eggs, bangers and mash, and steak and kidney pie. The full bar features more than 40 beers, with eight on draft. Reggie's hosts the Grand Losers Party every July 4th and is honored to be the Atlanta venue for Veterans of the Royal Air Force, who gather each September to commemorate the Battle of Britain.

French

ANIS
2974 Grandview Ave. N.E.   233-9889
$$

Anis has built a good reputation quickly since opening in 1994 and is quite popular. The fare is French Provencale, and it's good. The seafood escabeché appetizer, shrimp a la Anis with saffron rice, and lamb Corsica are all popular. The restaurant is in a brick house on a quiet Buckhead street, and there's a patio for outdoor dining. Inside can get a little crowded, but the mainly French staff knows its business, and everyone gets taken care of. Beer and wine are available; there's live entertainment on Tuesday, Thursday and Sunday. Anis is open Tuesday through Sunday for lunch and dinner.

BRASSERIE AU BAR
1049 Juniper St. N.E.   875-5976
$$

In a large Midtown house converted to a restaurant, Brasserie Au Bar serves French fare with continental influences. Grilled lamb chops with pesto sauce, grilled fresh salmon on lentil salad and coq au vin are popular with patrons, who typically include Atlantans and conventioneers. There's a full bar; reservations are accepted. It's open nightly for dinner and weekdays for lunch.

BRASSERIE LE COZE
3393 Peachtree Rd. N.E.
In Lenox Square   266-1440
$$

Designed as a reproduction of a turn-of-the-century Parisian brasserie, this restaurant serves French and other cuisines. Signature dishes include mussels marieniere, coq au vin and roast monkfish. Le Coze has its own pastry chef. There's a full bar; an outdoor patio is open in warm weather. Lunch and dinner are served Monday through Saturday; reservations are accepted.

CIBOULETTE

1529 Piedmont Rd. N.E.   874-7600
$$$

There's an upscale, relaxed attitude at Ciboulette, where local folks make up about 80 percent of the diners. The modern French menu includes foie gras du jour and duet of brandade and crab cakes appetizers, plus hot smoked salmon with wild mushrooms, ginger and soy, and roast squab with cabbage au jus. Reservations are accepted; there's a full bar and an extensive wine list. The open kitchen lets you watch the chef at work.

PETITE AUBERGE RESTAURANT

2935 N. Druid Hills Rd. N.E.
Toco Hills Shopping Center   634-6268
$$

This French continental restaurant opened in 1974. It's cozy and romantic with an expert staff; three of the four original waiters are still on duty. Standout entrees include grouper Marguery, filet mignon and beef Wellington. It's open Monday through Saturday for dinner and on weekdays only for lunch. Dinner reservations are accepted.

SOUTH OF FRANCE

2345 Cheshire Bridge Rd.
In Cheshire Square   325-6963
$$$

South of France opened in 1977; it serves country French cuisine in the intimate atmosphere of a French inn. Specialties include quail with port wine and dishes featuring rabbit, duckling and seafood. Dinner is served Monday through Saturday; lunch is served on weekdays. There's a full bar, and reservations are accepted.

Cross-cultural Favorites

BISTANGO RESTAURANT

1100 Peachtree St. N.E.   724-0901
$$$

This fashionable Midtown spot draws a cross section of patrons to its elegant setting. Popular with theater-goers, the restaurant is just two blocks south of Woodruff Arts Center, where many cultural events are staged. A varied menu ranges from beef and pasta dishes to spicy seafood paella. This mixture of fresh fish

Award-winning Nikolai's Roof offers an outstanding view of Atlanta's environs.

Photo: E. Alan McGee

and shrimp over a bed of zesty rice tingles and pleases the palate. Enjoy a cocktail or your choice from the outstanding wine list either in the elegant bar or on the outdoor patio. Bistango is open for lunch Monday through Thursday and for dinner every night but Sunday. The restaurant accepts reservations, and valet parking is available.

CAFE TU TU TANGO

220 Pharr Rd.   *841-6222*
$$

This Buckhead restaurant combines the air of an artist's loft with light and color used in a most creative fashion. The setting includes a painter at work before an easel. Called multi-ethnic in influence, the tapas-style menu consists of appetizer portions intended for sharing. The choices are invariably delicious and highly original. Barcelona stir-fry, Cajun chicken egg rolls, wild mushroom raviolis — see what we mean about multi-ethnic? The cafe's full-service bar is a popular meeting spot. The restaurant is open every day for lunch and dinner and till the wee hours on the weekend.

CASSIS

3300 Peachtree Rd.   *365-8100*
$$$

With sophisticated decor and a menu to match, Cassis resides in the snazzy Hotel Nikko in Atlanta's Buckhead area. The cuisine shows influence of the south of France, the wider Mediterranean and Japan. The mixed seafood grill with Mediterranean salsa is popular, as is the grilled shrimp with eggplant and roasted tomato. Or try the luscious rack of lamb with raisin cous cous. It's easy to spend more than $100 on dinner for two here. Cassis serves dinner nightly. Reservations are suggested; your call will be routed through the hotel desk.

Greek/Mediterranean

BASIL'S MEDITERRANEAN CAFE

2985 Grandview Ave. N.E.   *233-9755*
$$

Right in the center of Atlanta's Buckhead district, enjoy Basil's exotic specialties in an elegantly casual setting. A favorite with many diners is the grilled lamp chop in wine sauce served with rosemary-scented mashed potatoes and beans. Another is the grilled salmon on ratatouille with basil pesto and steamed potatoes. Your aperitif in the full bar will prepare your appetite for the delicious entrees, which have drawn a crowd since the restaurant's opening in 1990. Basil's accepts reservations for lunch and dinner every day but Sunday.

PARTNERS — A MORNINGSIDE CAFE

1399 N. Highland Ave. N.E.   *876-8104*
$$$

This lively bistro serving Mediterranean and regional American favorites has been delighting Atlantans — particularly its neighbors in Morningside and Virginia-Highland — since 1985. The fare includes fresh pasta, seafood and free-range chicken dishes. The full bar spotlights an array of single-malt scotches. Partners is open nightly for dinner. Large parties may call for reservations.

LAWRENCE'S CAFE

2888 Buford Hwy.   *320-7756*
$$

Enjoy the belly dancing, on weekends only, amidst delicious humus and tahini-based dishes. The vegetarian platter is a popular choice, as is the shish kebab. Another favorite is the grilled lamb steak with shrimp, served with rice, green peppers and onions. You may choose wine and beer to go with your meal. Dinner is served every day, lunch every day but Sunday.

OASIS CAFE

618 Ponce de Leon Ave. N.E.   *881-0815*
$$

This restaurant business with three locations is family owned and prides itself on fresh, made-to-order food right down to the yogurt used in the featured Middle Eastern specialties. These include all kinds of kebabs, vegetarian stuffed grape leaves and a dish called mjadra, which is made with lentils, rice, onions, fresh tomato, yogurt and cucumber. The menu also offers Spanish entrees, such as paella, and vegetarian selections. All entrees include soup and salad; three daily lunch and dinner specials are available. Beer and wine are served; desserts are Middle Eastern pastries. A belly dancer performs on Saturday nights at the Ponce de Leon and Sandy Springs locations. Other locations are: 1799 Briarcliff Road N.E., 876-0003; 5975 Roswell Road N.E., Sandy Springs, 847-0901.

SHIPFEIFER ON PEACHTREE

1814 Peachtree Rd.   *875-1106*
$$

Specializing in Mediterranean and vegetarian food since 1974, this cozy place is popular with patrons from nearby office buildings and residents of the in-town area. You could eat for less than the price range shown by choosing from the menu's sandwich and sandwich wrap sections. The menu aims to please many tastes with a variety of dishes. Choices range from Greek favorites to jerk chicken to a Philly cheesesteak. Try the filling moussaka, a casserole of ground beef blended with herbs, spices and eggplant, topped with feta cheese and a creamy Bechamel sauce. A puff pastry filled with mushrooms, calamata olives, artichokes, peppers, on-

ions, tomatoes and cheese will satisfy a craving for vegetables. Children's meals are offered. Baklava, the famous Greek honey nut pastry, is the star dessert. For a beverage, you may choose from domestic or imported beers and specialty coffees. Free parking is provided behind the restaurant, which is open for lunch and dinner seven days a week.

PARTHENON GREEK RESTAURANT

6125 Roswell Rd. N.E.   *256-1686*
$$

Besides the lamb specials, look for the Parthenon Special, a combination of gyro, sausage and grilled onions with a special homemade sauce. Or try the chef's special, a type of Greek lasagna with stuffed grape leaves and vegetables. All entrees come with a Greek salad; beer and Greek wines are available. Desserts include rice pudding and baklava. It's open for lunch and dinner every day but Sunday.

Indian

CALCUTTA

1138 Euclid Ave.   *681-1838*
$$

Set in the Little Five Points district, Calcutta is known for high-quality dishes. Chicken curry with prawns is a favorite with many diners here. Lunch and dinner are served seven days a week. Wine and Indian beers are available. Parking behind the restaurant is available.

INDIAN DELIGHTS

1707 Church St.
Decatur   *296-2965*
$

Low on atmosphere but high on food quality, this restaurant features dishes from the southern part of India. The spotlight is on creatively seasoned grains and vegetables at inexpensive prices. Masala dosa, a large crepe filled with curried potatoes, is a favorite. Spicy soups, homemade noodles and hot sauces will bring you back for more. Both restaurants are open for lunch and dinner every day but Monday. Additional location: 3675 Satellite Boulevard, Suite 100, Duluth, 813-8212.

JEWEL OF INDIA
1529-B Piedmont Ave.   873-0009
$$

With the standards covered, this menu branches out to offer some unusual dishes, such as a dinner for two combining chicken, lamb and rice, which includes appetizers and bread. Tandoori style barbecue and shrimp are other favorites. Open for dinner every night, the Jewel offers lunch every day but Sunday.

RAJA INDIAN RESTAURANT
2919 Peachtree Rd. N.E.   237-2661
$$

This small restaurant has developed a following of residents by serving an assortment of fine entrees. Tandoori mixed platters, chicken and lamb specialties and a pleasing range of vegetarian dishes are among the offerings. Rice entrees include the tasty Shrimp Biryani, pilau rice cooked with shrimp, raisins, nuts and peas. For your beverage, choose from American and Indian beers, plus Indian herbal teas. It's open for dinner seven nights a week and every day but Sunday for lunch.

Italian and Pizza

ABRUZZI RISTORANTE
2355 Peachtree Rd. N.E.   261-8186
$$$$

Tucked away in the upscale Peachtree Battle Shopping Center, Abruzzi has been a favorite of Buckhead area residents and their guests since 1989. Combining low-key elegance with superior service, this coat-and-tie restaurant offers many specialties, such as superb homemade pasta, seasonal game dishes, risotto with salmon, sea bass, and vegetable ravioli. From October through December, Abruzzi serves fresh white truffles over rice or pasta, a delicacy the owner believes is available only here. A daily selection of homemade gelato and other desserts tempts even the most steadfast dieter. The restaurant offers a full bar and ample parking in front. Abruzzi is open every day except Sunday for dinner and Monday through Friday for lunch. Reservations are required.

ALFREDO'S
1989 Cheshire Bride Rd. N.E.   876-1380
$$

Since 1974 Alfredo's has been winning devotees to its regional Italian cuisine, featuring dishes from both northern and southern Italy. Come for a romantic dinner by candlelight and leave satisfied by fine food and good service. Among the entrees are veal scaloppine with three different sauces, veal saltimbocca, scampi Alfredo with garlic and broiled snapper with wine sauce. Alfredo's is open for dinner seven nights a week. A full bar and an extensive wine list are provided for your enjoyment. Reservations are accepted. For your convenience, there's parking right in front of the restaurant.

AZIO PIZZA AND PASTA
220 Pharr Rd. N.E.   233-7626
$$

This popular pizza and pasta place is in the heart of the Buckhead entertainment district. A stylish, casual bistro, Azio specializes in thin crust, brick oven pizzas. Also on the menu you'll find antipasto, grilled fish and chicken and a variety of homemade pastas. You'll also find the cost near the top of this price range. It's open for lunch and dinner daily. A second location on International Boulevard at Peachtree Center is scheduled to open in spring 1995.

BERTOLINI'S AUTHENTIC TRATTORIA
3500 Peachtree Rd. N.E.   *233-2333*
$$

In the upscale Phipps Plaza, Bertolini's opened in 1992. Offering authentic northern Italian food at affordable prices, the restaurant recommends reservations. Lunch and dinner are served seven days a week. It draws a mixed crowd, from upscale dressers to jeans wearers. For an unusual dining experience, Mr. Bertolini suggests tagliolini al fruiti di mare with lobster, shrimp, scallops, scallions, tomatoes and cream. Or perhaps the sausage with polenta and roasted peppers. A full-service bar and complimentary valet parking are offered.

CALIFORNIA PIZZA KITCHEN-MIDTOWN
181 14th St.   *892-4343*
$$

Imaginative pizzas, pastas and salads for both lunch and dinner are served in a casual contemporary atmosphere. Snazzy entrees from the impressive menu include a mind-boggling array of pizzas with nearly 30 gourmet toppings including barbecue chicken, Peking duck and Southwestern burrito. Among other entrees are chicken tequila pasta, grilled meats and sandwiches on the luscious focaccia bread. Hours of operation and availability of alcohol vary by location, of which there are five. You'll enjoy al fresco dining in some locations. Additional locations: 3393 Peachtree Road N.E. (in Lenox Square), 262-9221; 1949 Powers Ferry Road S.E., Marietta, 956-8956; 4600 Ashford Dunwoody Road N.E., 393-

0390; 6301 North Point Parkway, Alpharetta, 664-8246.

LA GROTTA BUCKHEAD
2637 Peachtree Rd.   *231-1368*
$$$

Fine Italian cuisine here includes "pasta come piace a noi in Italia" — pasta as we like it in Italy. Treat yourself to the scaloppine of swordfish or fettuccine with shrimp as you dine overlooking a lovely garden scene.

Among the menu selections are meals approved by the American Heart Association; the pastry cart selections, alas, are not among them. Dinner only is served Monday through Saturday; reservations are recommended. A second location, La Grotta Ravinia, 4355 Ashford Dunwoody Road at I-285, 395-9925, has a special garden setting and serves lunch and dinner Monday through Friday. Dress is formal.

LA STRADA GRILLE
3101 Piedmont Rd.   *233-2565*
$$$

Offering some of the metro area's most delicious Italian food, La Strada's menu covers all the bases. Feast on the fettuccine shrimp and scallops with fresh leeks and cherry tomatoes in a white wine garlic lemon sauce. Or try the Chicken Sorrentino, whole chicken breast with prosciutto, mozzarella and parmesan in lemon butter. Among the daily specials are seafood dishes in addition to stuffed shrimp and softshell crab. You'll find a casual, welcoming atmosphere here plus a full-service bar. La Strada serves lunch on weekdays and dinner every night.

ROCKY'S BRICK OVEN PIZZERIA
1770 Peachtree St. N.E.   *876-1111*
$$

This source of delectable pizzas, pasta and other authentic treats is so well

Julia Washington Bond Reflects on a Life in Atlanta

Julia Washington Bond moved to Atlanta in 1957 with her husband, Dr. Horace Mann Bond, and their children Jane, Julian and James. Dr. Bond, author of the landmark scholarly work *Negro Education in Alabama: A Study in Cotton and Steel*, had recently completed 11 years as the first African-American president of his historically black alma mater, Lincoln University near Oxford, Pennsylvania. He was named dean of Atlanta University's School of Education, then became director of its Bureau of Educational Research until his retirement in 1971. Bond's life and work are chronicled in *Black Scholar: Horace Mann Bond, 1904-1972* by Wayne J. Urban.

Julia W. Bond and Dr. Horace Mann Bond moved to Atlanta with their family in 1957.

When the Bonds moved to Atlanta, Mrs. Bond, who had earned an English degree from Fisk University in Nashville in 1929, took the opportunity to return to graduate school; she received a master's degree in library sciences from Atlanta University at age 56 and was circulation librarian at the university's Treavor Arnett Library for seven years. She continues to work as a part-time reference librarian at the university's Robert W. Woodruff Library.

Dr. Bond died in 1972; today Mrs. Bond and their younger son James manage the family's small apartment building near the Atlanta University Center. Sitting in her living room surrounded by books, newspaper clippings, knitting and correspondence, Mrs. Bond looks far younger than her 86 years. Hers is a bibliographer's mind: Her remarks on practically any topic are supported with references from her voracious reading. In her 37 years as an Atlantan, Julia Bond has seen many changes, but one stands clearly above the others.

"Desegregation is the most prominent change. When we moved here, our children were very frightened. We went to the courthouse to register our cars, and they had a rope dividing the white people from the black. If anyone in the white line needed attention, all the blacks had to wait. That really terrified my children; they had never seen anything like it. Julian was so afraid that he wouldn't go downtown to shop for clothes. But they soon got over it."

The cruelties of segregation were particularly ironic for black intellectuals such as the Bonds. Highly regarded in the insular world of black higher education, they were nonetheless subject to racist mistreatment in society at large.

"There was a lot of conflict and a lot of worry. When Horace worked for the Rosenwald Fund — which awarded scholarships and helped build some 5,000 black schools — he traveled the South a lot, and I was always afraid something would happen. He was stopped one time by some white people, and when he reached for his handkerchief to sneeze there was a tense moment until they realized he wasn't reaching for a gun. Anything could happen with just a little provocation. You always traveled in the daytime, and you stopped where you knew someone."

Then came the tumultuous '60s, and suddenly the Bonds' son Julian was thrust into the spotlight as the spokesperson of the Student Nonviolent Coordinating Committee. "I can remember when Julian was arrested the first time they had a sit-in at Rich's. He came home and was so excited — then he changed his clothes to go to Paschal's (Restaurant and Motor Hotel) because Mr. Paschal was giving a dinner for all the people who had participated."

In 1968, Julian Bond headed for the Democratic Convention in Chicago as part of a progressive delegation challenging the credentials of the 93-percent-white Lester Maddox-led Georgia delegation. Julian not only made it to the floor; he heard thousands chant his name as he was nominated for U.S. Vice President. He was seven years too young to qualify and so withdrew, but he still received the second-highest vote total after the victorious Edmund Muskie. "It was all very unexpected," says Mrs. Bond. "My husband was in a meeting, and I called him and said, 'Julian's on national television!'"

Julian Bond served 20 years in the Georgia House of Representatives and Senate, but only after initially being denied his elected seat due to his opposition to the Vietnam War. He lost his bid for a Congressional seat in a close 1986 race against longtime friend John Lewis. Julian continues to write, lecture and teach, most recently at the University of Virginia. He lives in Washington, D.C., where he hosts the nationally syndicated TV program *America's Black Forum*. His son, Michael Julian Bond, is a member of Atlanta City Council (as Julian's brother James had been from 1974 to 1982).

Retired but always occupied, Mrs. Bond's busy life includes her library work and membership in the Chautauqua Circle, a literary study club founded in 1913 whose membership includes some of Atlanta's leading African-American women. She takes time occasionally to visit the High Museum of Art and to attend matinees at the Alliance Theatre, where she is a subscriber.

The Bonds traveled extensively during their working years; Mrs. Bond says she is happy that she and her husband chose Atlanta as their retirement destination. "When we moved here," Mrs. Bond recalls, "Atlanta was just a sleepy little town. It has changed, but I never really felt a great sense of change. It's been so gradual, day by day. I really wouldn't want to live anywhere else now — would you?" she smiles. "I think this is an ideal city."

known you'll rarely see it reviewed. As you enter the homey, bustling restaurant, mouthwatering aromas escape the kitchen and opera music fills the air — sometimes inspiring a duet from the local celebs, musicians, including Mick Jagger, and media people who dine here. Pizza baked in hickory- and oakwood-burning ovens made in Milan plus Rocky's homegrown herbs and tomatoes make most anything on the menu memorable. Try the pasta balsamico with wine, on the open-air patio. Or indulge in the Rudolph Valentino pizza, complete with sweet-onion sauce and rosemary-seasoned roasted new potatoes. Two could squeak by for less than $20, but don't deprive yourself of a creamy tricolor tortoloni for dessert. Beer and wine accompany dinners, which are served seven nights a week.

VENI VIDI VICI
41 14th St.   875-8424
$$$

If authentic northern Italian cuisine in a cosmopolitan, elegant atmosphere suits you, this is your kind of restaurant. Smack in the middle of the Midtown scene, Veni Vidi Vici rarely disappoints. Peruse the extensive hot and cold antipasti piccoli, which are small appetizers well designed to pique, not squash, your appetite. Among the restaurant's specialties are suckling pig, hunter-style chicken with wild mushrooms, various beef and veal dishes and a variety of imaginative pasta entrees. Visit the bocce ball court next to the patio. Lunch is served on weekdays, and dinner is served every night. There's a full-service bar on the premises. Reservations are recommended.

FELLINI'S PIZZA
2809 Peachtree Rd. N.E.   266-0082
$

Wacky decor, loud music and classic-style pizza in a casual, high-energy setting — that's Fellini's in all five locations. Don't expect finesse, just good eats. Made with the freshest ingredients, the pizzas are regular or Sicilian. Besides the traditional toppings, try the white pizza, which is especially good here. Plump calzones

stuffed with sausage and cheese will fill you with satisfaction, as will the salads. They serve beer and wine. The Fellini's are open seven days a week for lunch and dinner.

Other locations: 1991 Howell Mill Road N.W., 352-0799; 923 Ponce de Leon Avenue N.E., 873-3088; 4429 Roswell Road N.E., 303-8248; 422 Seminole Avenue N.E., 525-2530.

LUNA SI
1931 Peachtree Rd. N.E.   355-5993
$$

Trendy and irreverent, the setting, service and menu are in perfect sync here. Place yourself under the able guidance of stellar chef/owner Paul Luna for delicious food. The Luna Si menu and decor show what can be done with high-level creativity on a budget. A tongue-in-cheek code of behavior beside the front door — ending with a warning against whining — prepares you for the out of the ordinary. Contemporary Italian cuisine firmly based on healthful principles characterizes the menu, which changes monthly. Treat yourself to Luna's unique take on pastas, meats and seafood. Dinner is served seven nights a week. Cooking classes take place on Saturdays. The restaurant offers several prix fixe items, such as the two-course choice or three courses for $17.

PRICCI
500 Pharr Rd.   237-2941
$$$

Even amidst the Buckhead district's estimated 200-plus restaurants, Pricci's glamorous setting makes it a standout. Delicacies await you in a chic interior where upscale informality reigns. Among the house specialties are regional dishes, homemade pastas and pizzas from wood-burning ovens. A favorite with diners is the large roasted lobster tail with linguine, crushed red pepper and fresh oregano. Specialty desserts include zucotto tuscano, Tuscan style zucotto cake filled with chocolate cream, pistachio and candied orange.

A full-service bar and extensive wine list will meet high expectations. Pricci's recommends reservations. Lunch is served on weekdays and dinner every night.

Japanese

HASHIGUCHI JR.
3400 Wooddale Dr. 841-9229

In Lenox Shopping Center near Lenox Square on Peachtree Road, this Japanese restaurant is a popular spot with sushi fanatics. Good service is yours at the full sushi counter. The spicy tuna roll is sure to awaken your taste buds, as will the clams steamed over sake. Check out the traditional tempura dishes, one of which features bass. Tofu, crisply fried and dressed with shredded ginger, shows the culinary imagination. For beverages, try Japanese beer or sake, and finish your meal with a dish of green tea ice cream. Closed on Monday, Hashiguchi Jr. serves lunch Tuesdays through Saturday; dinner dates are Tuesday through Sunday. A second location, the original, is at 3000 Windy Hill Road S.W. in Marietta, 955-2337.

RESTAURANT SUNTORY
3847 Roswell Rd. N.E. 261-3737
$$$

Light, airy and spacious, Suntory's streamlined interiors promote a relaxed dining experience. House specialties include sukiyaki, sushi and prime beef shabu-shabu. Traditional tempura dishes, with a creative assortment of vegetables, are cooked at your table. Combination platters, such as Chicken Teriyaki and Shrimp Tempura, are favorites here. Intriguing appetizers include such choices as Asparagus Beef Maki, a thinly sliced beef and asparagus roll. A full-service bar is available. Suntory is open for lunch on weekdays and dinner every night but Sunday. The restaurant recommends reservations.

RU SANS
1529 Piedmont Ave. N.E. 875-7042
$$

California-style sushi and Japanese fusion entrees fill the menu of this casual restaurant. The friendly, upbeat atmosphere earned it a "place to meet people" rating from *Singles* magazine. Opened in 1993, Ru San is open for dinner every night and for lunch every day but Sunday. Specialties include soft shell crab rolls, eel and avocado-filled Rock 'N' Roll and a spicy pasta dish called Yakiudon. Sushi, tempura and yakitori bargains for $1 each are wildly popular. Beer and wine are available.

Korean

ASIAN GARDEN
5150 Buford Hwy.
Doraville 452-1677
$$

Here you'll find a combination of Korean and Japanese cuisine. The Korean-style barbecue is a favorite. So is the sushi-shasimi, prepared at your table. Five lunch specials are offered. Up to 10 different vegetable dishes are popular. It's open for lunch Monday through Friday and for dinner seven nights a week.

KANG SUN RESTAURANT
5181 Buford Hwy.
Doraville 451-8989
$$

When your cook is the owner, generally you can count on a good meal and prompt service. This friendly place is no exception. Thirty years of experience produces a varied menu of delicious dishes. Seafood and barbecue dishes are a specialty of the house. And for entertainment, Kang Sun provides a karaoke room. In Pinetree Plaza, the restaurant welcomes reservations.

KOREAN MIRROR RESTAURANT
1047 Ponce de Leon Ave. N.E.   874-6243
$$

Two miles from downtown, you'll find authentic Korean cuisine and more. In addition to Korean specialties, such as bool go ghi, a barbecue beef rib-eye dish, and the beef short ribs entree called gahl bee, you may choose Chinese dishes, seafood and vegetarian delights. Open since 1980, the Korean Mirror is open for dinner every day and for lunch all but Sunday.

Latin

CARAMBA CAFE
1409-D N. Highland Ave.   874-1343
$$

The food at this family-owned Mexican restaurant is prepared using vegetable oil. In addition to burritos, tacos, quesadillas and chalupas, the menu features a number of meat-free and cheese-free dishes. Mia's Margaritas are a crowd-pleaser, and so is the homemade flan. Dinner is served nightly; parties of six or more may call for reservations.

COCO LOCO
2625 Piedmont Rd. N.E.   364-0212
$$

This small restaurant in a shopping center prepares delicious Cuban and Caribbean dishes such as jerk chicken, conch fritters, paella, arroz con pollo and Cuban sandwiches. There's a full bar, and live entertainment is featured on Saturday night. Coco Loco, where the attitude is fun and tropical, is open for lunch and dinner everyday.

DON JUAN'S
1927 Piedmont Cr. N.E.   874-4285
$$

This Spanish continental restaurant opened in 1977. Specialties of the house include paella, veal, a variety of fresh fish and black bean soup. Dinner is served Monday through Saturday; reservations are accepted; parking is free, and there's a full bar.

EL AZTECA
3424 Piedmont Rd. N.E.   266-3787
$

As you roam around Atlanta, you'll often find yourself close to a friendly, colorful El Azteca restaurant. The local chain has been serving spicy, reasonably priced Mexican food since 1981. All locations have a full bar; all except the Auburn Avenue location have an outside patio. The menu offers cheap lunch specials, an array of combination plates and specialty entrees such as beef and chicken fajitas and quesadillas.

Additional locations: 25 Auburn Avenue, 521-2584; 939 Ponce de Leon Avenue, 881-6040; 6078 Roswell Road, 255-9807; 6100 Roswell Road, 256-9930; 5800 Buford Highway, 452-7192; 235 S. Main Street, Alpharetta, 664-4868; 880 Atlanta Street, Roswell, 998-6553.

EL TORO
5899 Roswell Rd.   257-9951
$

El Toro prepares all your Mexican favorites; the food is deliciously flavored and served quickly. Choose from an almost endless variety of combination platters and specialties. All locations have a full bar and are open daily for lunch and dinner.

Additional locations: 1775 Lawrenceville Highway, Decatur, 321-9881; 4300 Buford Highway, 636-7090; 2973-B Cobb Parkway, 955-9873; 1085 Holcomb Bridge Road, Roswell, 641-8127; 4805 Lawrenceville Highway, Lilburn, 925-9411; 5288 Buford Highway, 455-6884; 5071 Peachtree Industrial Boulevard, Chamblee, 455-8811; 1255 Johnson Ferry Road, Marietta, 977-9906; 1060 E. Piedmont Road, Marietta, 973-3173; 10945 State Bridge Road, Alpharetta, 442-8474.

FRIJOLEROS
1031 Peachtree St. N.E.   892-8226
$

Big burritos and quesadillas made fresh to order are what's cooking at Frijoleros on Peachtree near the corner of 11th Street. You can eat in the dining room , which is decorated with countless band posters, or outside on Peachtree. The atmosphere is hip and collegiate, and the delicious food is served in whopping portions. Credit cards are not accepted; beer is sold; Frijoleros is open daily for lunch and dinner.

LA BAMBA RESTAURANTE MEXICANO
1139 W. Peachtree St. N.E.   892-8888
$

In a brightly painted house in the shadow of the IBM building at W. Peachtree and 14th Street, La Bamba serves up big portions of traditional Mexican favorites, such as fajitas, quesadillas,

pepper steak and more. Margaritas are a specialty, and the best place to enjoy them (weather permitting) is the big outdoor deck. La Bamba is open daily for lunch and dinner; parking is free. Parties of six or more may call for reservations. We hear that this spot is popular with local TV newspeople and that wrestling superstar Rick "Nature Boy" Flair popped in recently to party.

LA FONDA LATINA
1150 Euclid Ave. N.E.   577-8317
$

Noisy, gaudily painted La Fonda is the place to go in Little Five Points for spicy Latin-influenced food. The paella, served in a sizzling iron skillet, is offered as a vegetarian dish or loaded with chicken, seafood and sausage. The quesadillas come with big portions of black beans and yellow rice. Beer, wine and a delicious homemade sangria are poured at La Fonda. It's open daily for lunch and dinner; credit cards are not accepted.

Additional locations: 2813 Peachtree Road N.E., 816-8311; 4427 Roswell Road N.E., 303-8201.

MAMBO RESTAURANTE CUBANO
1402 N. Highland Ave. N.E.   876-2626
$$

Mambo, which features a nine-foot-tall mural of Carmen Miranda, serves Cuban cuisine nightly for dinner. Crowd-pleasers include paella, Chino-Latino (a Cuban-Chinese fish dish) and ropa vieja

For the time, temperature and Atlanta forecast, call 603-3333. This is a free call.

Insiders' Tips

(a dish of shredded beef, garlic, tomatoes and peppers). Beer and wine are served; lively Latin music is featured; reservations are accepted.

MEXICO CITY GOURMET
2134 N. Decatur Rd.   634-1128
$$

Upscale but friendly, this restaurant delivers what its name suggests: imaginatively prepared Mexican food. Fish dishes and other specials are offered with favorites such as shrimp fajitas and chile rellenos. Both locations have a full bar; try the Perfect Margarita, made with Gran Mariner instead of triple sec. Additional location: 5500 Chamblee Dunwoody Road, Dunwoody, 396-1111.

RIO BRAVO MEXICAN RESTAURANTS
3172 Roswell Rd. N.W.   262-7431
$$

Rio Bravo started serving its Tex-Mex fare in Buckhead in 1984 and since has expanded to the suburbs, Tennessee and Florida: Now there are 16 in all. Crowd-pleasers include the fajitas, quesadillas and cheese dip. Free valet parking is offered on weekends, and there's a large patio. Rio Bravo is open every day for lunch and dinner. All locations have a full bar.

Additional locations: 5565 New Northside Drive N.W., 952-3241; 440 Ernest W. Barrett Parkway N.W., Kennesaw, 429-0602; 1570 Holcomb Bridge Road, Roswell, 642-0838; 2250 Pleasant Hill Road, Duluth, 623-1096.

SUNDOWN CAFE
2165 Cheshire Bridge Rd. N.E.   321-1118
$$

Creative Mexican and Southwestern food is the attraction at Sundown. The menu changes frequently to showcase various appetizers and entrees. Eddie's

pork, grilled and served with jalapeno gravy, is popular. Try the spicy Mexican turnip greens. There's a full bar. Lunch is served weekdays; dinner is served Monday through Saturday.

TORTILLAS
774 Ponce de Leon Ave. N.E.   892-3493
$

This fun, noisy California-style burrito place is big with students and everyone who likes spicy food cheap. These fat burritos are bursting with beans and rice, and the sauces are bright and bold. The music is mixed including punk, reggae, blues and college rock. From the second floor outdoor porch you can soak up the ever-changing scene on Ponce. Beer is sold; credit cards are not accepted. Tortillas is open daily from 11 AM to 11 PM.

U.S. BAR Y GRILL
2202 Howell Mill Rd. N.W.   352-0033
$$

The folks here quickly point out that their fare is coastal Mexican, not "Tex-Mex." Their specialties are cabrito (baby goat), seafood and steaks, and they mix a mighty margarita. A mariachi band plays on Thursday, Friday and Saturday nights. On Monday through Friday, there's a happy hour appetizer buffet. It's open daily for lunch and dinner but closed for lunch on Sunday.

Seafood

ATLANTA FISH MARKET
265 Pharr Rd.   262-3165
$$$

A pleasing combination of casual atmosphere and superior food, this restaurant is part of the kingdom of Panos Karatassos and the Buckhead Life restaurant outfit. The Savannah-style fish house is designed to look weathered and as if it grew in a hodge-podge fashion. Fresh seafood favorites are rarely done at other places as well as at the Atlanta Fish Market. The menu changes daily, and the catch of the day can be prepared to your order, charbroiled, blackened, sauteed, fried or steamed. Everything meets the legendary Panos standards. Reservations are suggested for dinner seven nights a week. Lunch is served every day except Sunday.

Pano's Food Shop on the premises offers prepared fancy foods, fresh seafood and baked goods to take home.

JIM WHITE'S HALF SHELL
2394 Peachtree Rd.   *237-9924*
$$$

Another Buckhead staple, this restaurant has long delighted diners with house specialties of stone crab claws and Maryland crab cakes. Other favorites include fresh fillet of trout Pontchartrain, sauteed and topped with fresh tomatoes and crab meat. Among the extensive seafood standards is Shoreman's Delight, a winning combo of rock lobster tail, crab and shrimp. In the Peachtree Battle Shopping Center, this casual-dress restaurant with a full-service bar serves dinner every night but Sunday. It is wheelchair accessible and offers a children's menu. Reservations are recommended for parties of five or more.

INDIGO COASTAL GRILL
1397 N. Highland Ave. N.E.   *876-0676*
$$$

An open kitchen will allow you to watch the magic happening here. Prepare for a wait to be seated in this highly popular place that draws crowds with its varieties of coastal cuisine including tastes from Cape Cod to the Caribbean. The rustic decor's relaxed ambiance has overtones of Key West. Brown butcher paper covers the tables, and paraphernalia abounds. Check out the conch fritters. The fresh catch of the day, wrapped in parchment, is a favorite. Indigo is open for dinner seven nights a week.

MARRA'S SEAFOOD GRILL
1782 Cheshire Bridge Rd. N.E.   *874-7347*
$$

The chic setting here befits the elegant cuisine, which has won the *Wine Spectator* magazine award of excellence. Grilled swordfish, tuna, black pepper oysters and salmon from the Pacific are popular features. Unique dishes include the Thai steamed mussels and shrimp Portofino. Beef entrees, appetizers and light fare are offered as well. Marra's serves lunch on weekdays and takes reservations for dinner seven days a week.

McKINNON'S LOUISIANE RESTAURANT AND SEAFOOD GRILL
3209 Maple Dr. N.E.   *237-1313*
$$$

For more than 20 years, McKinnon's has provided superior Cajun seafood to appreciative diners in two settings: the upscale dining room and the casual Grill Room. The fare is traditional Creole and Cajun cuisine in addition to fresh seafood. There's nothing ordinary about the

---

The old Southern names for meals — "dinner" for the midday and "supper" for the evening — are seldom used anymore, but you may encounter them. If you're in doubt about which meals a restaurant serves, you can clear up the question by asking the hours of service.

Insiders' Tips

offerings, such as a crab cake appetizer with corn butter and jalapeno sauce. Blackened amberjack, cooked to a moist and tender state, is a favorite. Crawfish Etouffe, served over rice, is another. A sing-along piano bar entertains guests on Fridays and Saturdays. Located at the intersection of Maple and Peachtree Road, the restaurant accepts reservations for dinner every night except Sunday.

RAY'S ON THE RIVER
6700 Powers Ferry Rd.   955-1187
$$$

Voted best Sunday brunch by *Atlanta* magazine, Ray's has drawn a lively crowd to its riverside setting since 1984. Seafood flown in daily and fresh pasta are favorites here. Grilled, blackened, broiled, sauteed, baked or fried — have your choice of how your entree is prepared. Among the popular choices are oysters on the half shell and blackened fish Alex, which is topped with Mornay sauce, shrimp and scallops. Other entrees include prime rib, chicken, large salads, homemade soups and desserts. A full-service bar, extensive wine list and live jazz music creates an enjoyable atmosphere. A call for priority seating will move you to the head of the line if you arrive at your appointed time. Ray's serves lunch and dinner seven days a week, plus Sunday brunch. On Tuesday through Saturday evenings, Ray's features jazz by an Atlanta favorite, Elgin Wells and his combo.

Southern Food and Barbecue

BARBECUE KITCHEN
1437 Virginia Ave., College Park   766-9906
$

If you love Southern food and lots of it, you'll flip at the Barbecue Kitchen. The main dishes include country ham, fried chicken and the restaurant's own pork barbecue, which is smoked right out back. Your dinner comes with three vegetables, such as mashed potatoes, collards and fried okra, and you can get a free reorder of each — but since you can order the same vegetables or three different ones, you're really getting a meat and six. All this place lacks is someone to help happy diners waddle back to their cars. It's open daily from 7:30 AM to 10:30 PM; no alcohol; no credit cards.

THE BEAUTIFUL RESTAURANT
2260 Cascade Rd. S.W.   752-5931
$

Fresh vegetables, baked chicken, beef ribs and banana pudding are all popular with diners at the Beautiful soul food restaurants. The Cascade Road location is open 24-hours, seven days; the Auburn Avenue restaurant, which is across from Ebenezer Baptist Church, is open from 7 AM to 7 PM daily. No alcohol; no credit cards.

Additional location: 397 Auburn Avenue N.E., 233-0080.

BUCKHEAD FEED MILL
35-A W. Paces Ferry Rd. N.W.   233-0134
$

For more than 20 years, the Feed Mill has been cooking inexpensive Southern food in the heart of Buckhead. Perennial favorites are country-fried steak with mashed potatoes, grilled Cajun catfish and salmon croquettes. It's open Monday through Friday from 6 AM to 8 PM and Saturday from 6 AM to 3 PM; closed Sunday. No alcohol; no credit cards.

BURTON'S GRILL
1029 Edgewood Ave.   658-9452
$

Serving breakfast and lunch on weekdays only, Burton's is a legend in soul food. Founded by the late Deacon Burton, this modest restaurant's tender skillet-fried chicken is the best bird in all Atlanta. The vegetables, such as collard greens, cream corn and mashed potatoes, are thoroughly cooked and deliciously flavored. Burton's is a favorite with everyone, from TV and print media people to civil rights leaders. It's right beside the Inman Park/Reynoldstown MARTA station. No alcohol; no credit cards.

THE COLONNADE
1879 Cheshire Bridge Rd. N.E.   874-5642
$

This large Southern restaurant has been an Atlanta tradition since 1927 and is a favorite with the older set as well as young people and families. Turkey and dressing tops the list of entrees, and there are generally some 30 vegetables on the menu. After church on Sundays, things really get crowded here. The Colonnade is open daily for lunch and dinner; it has a full bar but does not accept credit cards.

DAMON'S CLUBHOUSE
76 Wall St. at Underground Atlanta   659-7427
$$

Damon's is at the top of the main steps leading to Underground Atlanta. Ribs are it's pride, but you might go for the prime rib or chicken. The atmosphere is sporty casual, and there are five big-screen TVs. During the 1994 Superbowl in Atlanta, Damon's cooked outdoors and had a big bash. It's open daily for lunch and dinner.

DUSTY'S BARBECUE
1815 Briarcliff Rd. at Clifton   320-6264
$

There's always country music playing at Dusty's, which is decorated entirely in a "pig" motif. The barbecue (pork, beef or chicken) is the main attraction at Dusty's, but the potato salad, fried okra and hushpuppies are good too, and the sweet

tea is excellent. Beer and wine are available. Dusty's is open daily for lunch and dinner.

EVANS FINE FOODS
2125 N. Decatur Rd. at Clairmont   634-6294
$

Evans has been fixing Southern food since 1958. Specialties include smothered breast of chicken, country-fried steak, ribeyes and blueberry and blackberry cobbler. About 15 vegetables are offered daily. Evans is closed on Sunday and open other days from 5:30 AM to 9 PM; no alcohol; no credit cards.

FAT MATT'S RIB SHACK
1811 Piedmont Ave.   607-1622
$

Fat Matt's has a cool exterior by Atlanta airbrush legend "J.J. of L.A.," whose mouthwatering paintings of food embellish numerous stores and restaurants in the city. Matt's fixes ribs, chopped pork barbecue and barbecued chicken, plus side dishes. It's open every day for lunch and dinner, and there's live blues every night. Beer is sold; no credit cards.

THE FLYING PIG
856 Virginia Ave., Hapeville   559-1000
$

The new management of this spot, which originally opened in the 1950s, has quickly won the respect of barbecue-lovers. Beef, pork and ribs are pit-cooked on-site. All the food is prepared in the kitchen right in front of the customers. A new outside deck is scheduled to open this spring. It's closed on Sunday and Monday; no alcohol; no credit cards.

MARY MAC'S TEA ROOM
224 Ponce de Leon Ave. N.E.   876-1800
$

Mary Mac's has been in business for 50 years at this location, and, although the founding Lupo family is no longer involved in its management, the restaurant remains an institution in Southern food. Governor Zell Miller eats here often; Georgia's Secretary of State Max Cleland comes in frequently with his mother. Favorites at the Tea Room include baked chicken and dressing, fried chicken, sweet potato souffle, fresh baked yeast rolls and the rich "pot liquor" broth. There's a full bar, but smoking is not allowed; no credit cards.

OUR WAY CAFE
303 E. College Ave., Decatur   373-6665
$

This friendly Decatur cafeteria offers a delightfully updated Southern menu. Yes, you can get meatloaf, but other entrees typically include dishes such as spicy chicken enchiladas, salmon loaf and lemon pepper chicken. More than 10 vegetable choices are available, plus several desserts. Our Way is open weekdays for lunch only; no alcohol; no credit cards.

PASCHAL'S RESTAURANT
830 Martin Luther King Dr. S.W. 577-3150
$

Much history in the civil rights movement is said to have taken place over Paschal's soul food, and the restaurant remains a landmark in the African-American community. Brothers James and Robert Paschal founded the restaurant in a smaller building across the street in 1947; it was so successful that they eventually built the current restaurant,

150-room motor hotel and lounge. There's a full bar; Paschal's is open daily for breakfast, lunch and dinner. There's free parking in the lot behind the motor hotel.

SILVER GRILL
900 Monroe Dr. at Eighth St.   876-8145
$

Now being run by the third generation of its founding family, the Silver Grill has been cooking Southern food at this location since 1945. Fried chicken, country-fried steak and grilled chicken breast are longtime menu standouts; about 10 vegetables are generally offered each day. The Grill is open weekdays for lunch and dinner; no alcohol; no credit cards.

SOUTHERN STAR RESTAURANT
231 W. Ponce de Leon Ave.
Decatur   377-0799
$

Open for breakfast and lunch Monday through Saturday, Southern Star began fixing its regional fare in 1980. It's in downtown Decatur and attracts many local office workers and people with business at the courthouse. Popular dishes include turkey and dressing, meatloaf, beef tips and Greek-style baked chicken. Fourteen to 18 vegetables are generally available; no alcohol; no credit cards.

Cajun

DUX'S
248 Pharr Rd. N.E.   814-0558
$$

Dux's is a New Orleans-style eatery

with a full bar in Buckhead. Lunch is served Tuesday through Sunday; dinner is served nightly. Crawfish etouffee, blackened red fish and barbecued shrimp are just a few of the delicacies you can try. The music ranges from blues to alternative rock. Large parties may call ahead for reservations.

FRENCH QUARTER FOOD SHOP
923 Peachtree St. N.E.   875-2489
$

Here's a little of the bayou right on Peachtree. This small restaurant swings to Louisiana music and serves up spicy dishes such as etouffee and jambalaya at bargain prices. The fried shrimp and fried oyster po' boys are also popular. The owner, who is from Lafayette, Louisiana, proudly says that some of the same conventioneers come in to eat year after year whenever their business brings them back to Atlanta. Both locations have beer and wine and are closed on Sunday.

Additional location: 2144 Johnson Ferry Road, 458-2148.

TASTE OF NEW ORLEANS
889 W. Peachtree St. N.E.   874-5535
$$

Cajun and Creole food is served in a fun environment at this restaurant. Popular lunch dishes include the oyster po' boy and jambalaya; etouffee, seafood pasta and fish moutarde are dinner recommendations. Taste of New Orleans is open Monday through Saturday for dinner and on weekdays for lunch. Beer and wine are served; reservations are accepted for dinner.

Thai

ANNIE'S THAI CASTLE
3195 Roswell Rd.   264-9546
$$

The word has spread about this hospitable place. Lunch and dinner are served Tuesday through Saturday. On Sundays, Annie's stays open from 1 PM to 10:30 PM. Pud Thai, a tasty noodle dish accompanied by egg, bean spouts and ground peanuts, is a favorite. Or try the spicy spaghetti with hot chili peppers. A shrimp-filled noodle dish pleases the regulars.

PHUKET THAI RESTAURANT
2839 Buford Hwy.   325-4199
$$

Locals find their way to this crisply appointed setting, where the food is the standout. Family owned and operated, Phuket Thai offers many specials, such as Pud Thai noodles and Phuket Scallops. Beer and wine are served; parking is plentiful. The restaurant is open for dinner seven nights a week and for lunch Monday through Friday.

SURIN OF THAILAND
810 N. Highland Ave.   892-7789
$$

Since opening in 1991, Surin continues to draw faithful followers with delicacies served in a candlelit setting. Gleaming wooden floors, dark blue tablecloths and Thai banners create a charming backdrop. Among the traditional dishes are chicken in curry paste, Thai noodles and chicken coconut soup. This soup features

---

Vegetarians find like-minded souls by calling the Vegetarian Society of Georgia's 24-hour recording, 662-4019, for updates on cooking classes, educational programs and a complimentary copy of the society's newsletter.

chunks of chicken, tiger shrimp and fresh mushrooms. The array of appetizers tempts you to make a meal of them. Try the tender poached rice paper rolls filled with shrimp, shredded pork and bean sprouts. Surin offers a full bar and validated parking. Reservations are not accepted. Surin serves lunch and dinner seven days a week. Be sure to check the specials.

BANGKOK THAI RESTAURANT
1492 Piedmont Rd. N.E.   874-2514
$$

Bangkok, which opened in 1977, claims to be the oldest Thai restaurant in Atlanta. In the Ansley Square Shopping Center, just south of the intersection of Piedmont and Monroe in Midtown, Bangkok serves an adventurous and delicious version of Thai cuisine: If you like it hot, start with the spicy, aromatic tom yum (lemon grass) soup, then go for the stir-fry vegetables with chili peppers. Afterward, cool off with the exquisite homemade coconut ice cream. Your bill will likely be in the low end of this price range. Bangkok has beer and wine; it's open weekdays for lunch and nightly for dinner.

KING & I
1510-F Piedmont Ave. N.E.   892-7743
$$

Delicious Thai food served by a friendly staff is the attraction at King & I, which joined the Atlanta restaurant scene in the early '80s. Recommended dishes include the spring roll appetizer, Pud Thai noodles and shrimp with hot garlic sauce. The prices are reasonable, and the portions are large. Beer and wine are available; the restaurant serves lunch on weekdays and dinner nightly.

Additional location: 4058 Peachtree Road N.E., 262-7985.

Vegetarian

EAT YOUR VEGETABLES CAFE
428 Moreland Ave. N.E.   523-2671
$

Set in Atlanta's eclectic Little Five Points district, this vegetarian stronghold has presented tasty, healthful dishes in a laid-back atmosphere for 15 years. Select a glass of beer or wine to go with your tofu manicotti or veggie burger. Or go for one of the chicken or seafood entrees. A favorite with many is the Chicken Pesto. Be sure to ask about the organic and pasta specials, which change daily. Reservations for six or more are accepted. Lunch and dinner are served seven days a week.

THE FLYING BISCUIT
1655 McLendon Ave. N.E.   687-8888
$$

Known to many as an all-day breakfast cafe, The Biscuit displays its unique personality for lunch and dinner as well. This cozy 30-seater-plus counter has a welcoming ambiance that's as pleasing as the food. For breakfast, try Eggceptional Eggs, served yolk up on black bean cakes with a fresh tomatillo salsa. For a side order, how about fresh turkey sausage with sage and creamy rosemary potatoes? Or dig into fluffy stacks of organic oatmeal pancakes topped with warm maple syrup. Among lunch and dinner choices are hearty burgers (grain, vegetable or turkey) and moist turkey meat loaf dressed with horseradish sauce. Service is friendly in this homey place, where you can graze for little or spend more to feast on food prepared as if it were for friends and family. Closed on

Monday, the cafe eschews credit cards and reservations to keep prices low.

LETTUCE SOUPRISE YOU
245 Pharr Rd. N.E.   841-9583.
$

With seven locations in Atlanta, it's easy to see why this group of restaurants continues to grow — for families or singles, there are fresh, satisfying choices for everyone. Selection and reasonable prices are why we include it even though it is part of a chain. The salad bar's extensive ingredients are pleasingly displayed to whet the appetite. Soups, chili, baked potatoes and pasta salads precede the fruit bar and extraordinary muffins. Some sites have added rotisserie chicken. All are open seven days a week for lunch and dinner. Other locations inside the Perimeter: 2470 Briarcliff Road, 636-8549; 1109 Cumberland Mall, 438-2288; 595 Piedmont Avenue, 874-4998. Outside the Perimeter: 1474 Holcomb Bridge Road, Roswell, 642-1601; 3525 Mall Boulevard N.W., Duluth, 418-9969; 5975 Roswell Road, 250-0304.

Vietnamese

VIETNAMESE CUISINE
3375 Buford Hwy. N.E.   321-1840
$$

Bring your appetite to this storefront eating place, owned and operated by one family. They promise gourmet Vietnamese food and lots of choices for the low end of this price range. A favorite is stir-fried chicken with lemon grass. Beef and pork entrees, pepper rolls and good vegetable soup are popular. Serving lunch and dinner seven days a week, the restaurant also offers beer and wine. It is in the Northeast Plaza, which means convenient parking.

CHA GIO
966 Peachtree St.   885-9387
$

This restaurant has been voted best Vietnamese cuisine every year since 1991 by the readers of *Creative Loafing*, a local weekly newspaper. The $5 lunch buffet gives you a chance to familiarize yourself with the classic and provincial dishes popular here. Sample a variety of vegetarian entrees, noodle and rice specialties, five-spice fish or Cha Gio's famous summer rolls seasoned with basil and cilantro with a pepper-peanut sauce. The restaurant is open seven days a week for lunch and dinner.

DONG KHANK
VIETNAMESE RESTAURANT
4646 Buford Hwy.   *457-4840*
$$

Open seven days a week for lunch and dinner, Dong Khank offers many specials at reasonable prices. Among them are a spicy version of chicken with lemon grass, barbecue dishes and summer rolls with the fillings of your choice. Beer and wine are available.

SONG HUONG BELLA
4795 Buford Hwy.   *451-2944*
$$

Serving a combination of Vietnamese and Chinese dishes, Song Huong's food reflects many nationalities. The barbecue beef roll is popular, as are the vermicelli with egg roll and several creative seafood entrees. Vietnamese and American beers and wine are offered. On Saturday evenings, a live band plays music that ranges from Vietnamese favorites to American rock (there's a small cover).

Beyond Atlanta

American

AMERICAN PIE
5840 Roswell Rd. N.W.   *255-7571*
$$

American Pie is the restaurant that thinks it's on Ocean Boulevard in Myrtle Beach instead of on Roswell Road in Sandy Springs. The swinging atmosphere is that of a beach club bar and grill, and the gaudy decor carries the theme through. You want TV? The Pie has about 30 TVs. You want booze? The Pie has four full bars. You want food? Try the grilled chicken supreme sandwich with barbecue sauce. You want big events? The Pie frequently stages big radio station promotions and other happenings to amuse its guests, who tend to be sports-loving singles out for fun. It's open daily from 11 AM to 4 AM, but closes at 3 AM Saturday night.

BABY DOE'S
2239 Powers Ferry Rd. S.E.
Marietta   *612-8588*
$$

Built to look like a Colorado silver mine from the frontier days, Baby Doe's is a multilevel restaurant with views of the Chattahoochee River and the Perimeter highway. It's decorated in period furnishings and has numerous seating areas. Lobster tail, prime rib and fillets are top entrees, and the restaurant presents a huge buffet on Sunday. It's open daily for lunch and dinner; reservations are accepted.

JOEY D'S OAK ROOM
1015 Crown Pointe Pkwy.
Dunwoody   *512-7063*
$$

American cuisine takes center stage at this upscale casual restaurant. Recommended items include New Orleans spicy shrimp, chicken salad and steaks. Joey D's opened in 1990 and has a full bar. Reservations are accepted.

VAN GOGH'S RESTAURANT & BAR
70 W. Crossville Rd.
Roswell   *993-1156*
$$$

Van Gogh's likes to think of itself as a bit of Buckhead out in Roswell. The five dining rooms are adorned with original art, which is for sale; there's a fireplace and a lovely antique bar. The ethnic-influenced American fare includes fresh lump meat crab cakes, grilled portobello mushrooms, fresh pastas and veal chops. There's a full bar; reservations are accepted for all meals except Friday and Saturday night dinner. Lunch and dinner are served seven days a week, except there's no lunch on Sunday.

RUTH'S CHRIS STEAKHOUSE
5788 Roswell Rd.   255-0035
$$$

Ruth's offers fine dining in a clubby, casual atmosphere. The split-level building has four fireplaces and an overall attitude of luxury. Popular menu items include the stuffed mushroom appetizer, fillet, fresh lobster, bread pudding with whiskey sauce and chocolate mousse cheesecake. Ruth's is said to be a frequent stop for Atlanta Braves players. Both locations serve dinner nightly; the Buckhead restaurant (below) also serves lunch on weekdays. Reservations are recommended. Additional location: 960 E. Paces Ferry Road N.E., 365-0660.

LICKSKILLET FARM RESTAURANT
1380 Old Roswell Rd., Roswell 475-6484
$$$

Lickskillet Farm is set in an 1846 farmhouse with fireplaces and several dining rooms. Fine dining in a casual setting is the offering here: The American continental menu features Cornish hen, rack of lamb and snapper Alicia. It's closed on Monday; lunch and dinner are served the rest of the week; there's a Sunday brunch. Reservations are accepted.

MAGNOLIA TEA ROOM AND RESTAURANT
5459 E. Mountain St.
Stone Mountain   498-6304
$$

On 2.5 acres in an 1854 Victorian home, the Magnolia Tea Room presents new American and French cuisine in a Southern setting. Specialties include the salmon-in-puff pastry with asparagus and the banana cheesecake with pralines. The Magnolia is open Tuesday through Saturday for lunch, Friday and Saturday for dinner, and Sunday for brunch. Reservations are encouraged; beer and wine are served; credit cards are not accepted.

1848 HOUSE
780 S. Cobb Dr., Marietta   428-1848
$$$

The setting for this restaurant is an authentic 1848 Greek Revival plantation home on 13 acres of land. Six of the 10 dining rooms feature fireplaces. The fare is contemporary Southern and American; the owner recommends the Charleston she-crab soup, the Vidalia onion tart appetizer, the sauteed slow-cooked pepper duck and the grilled quail on crawfish rice. During the Civil War, the house was used as a Union hospital, which may explain why it wasn't reduced to rubble. The house is listed on the National Register of Historic Places. Dinner is served Tuesday through Sunday; a jazz brunch is presented Sunday; reservations are accepted.

PUBLIC HOUSE ON ROSWELL SQUARE
605 Atlanta St., Roswell   992-4646
$$

This restaurant is in an 1854 brick warehouse building on the historic Roswell Square; the structure was used as a Confederate hospital during the Civil War. Public House opened in 1976 and was the third restaurant in the Peasant Restaurants group. Standout dishes include peach pecan rack of lamb, grilled swordfish with rosemary buerre blanc and steak au poivre. Lunch and dinner are served daily; reservations are not accepted.

LONGHORN STEAKS

6390 Roswell Rd.   843-1215
$$

Established in Buckhead in 1981, Longhorn now has 45 restaurants in Georgia and five other states. The steaks, such as the seven- or nine-ounce fillet and the 20-ounce Porterhouse, are cut fresh daily by hand; the salmon (an addition in recent years) is farm-raised in Canada. The atmosphere is steakhouse-Western, and the service is friendly. All locations are open daily for dinner; some are open weekdays only for lunch. Call as you're heading out to get your name on the waiting list.

Additional metro-Atlanta locations: 2151 Peachtree Road, 351-6086; 5403 Old National Highway, College Park, 761-8018; 900 Mansell Road, Roswell, 642-8588; 2700 Town Center Drive, Kennesaw, 421-1101; 7882 Tara Boulevard, Jonesboro, 477-5365; 2120 Killian Road, Snellville, 972-4188; 1355 East-West Connector, Austell, 941-4816; 4721 Lower Roswell Road, Marietta, 977-3045; 4315 Hugh Howell Road, Tucker, 939-9842; 8471 Hospital Drive, Douglasville, 942-7795; 3525 Mall Boulevard, Duluth, 476-9026.

Continental and Fine Dining

ACACIA

Atlanta Doubletree Hotel
7 Concourse Pkwy.   395-3900
$$$

The Doubletree is off Peachtree Dunwoody Road just outside I-285. Acacia,

its fine dining restaurant, seats 52 in an intimate, dark-colored ambiance. Selections from the creative American and continental menu include lamb, salmon and wild game. Dinner is served Monday through Saturday; reservations are recommended.

CAFE RENAISSANCE

7050 Jimmy Carter Blvd.
Norcross   441-0291
$$

Cafe Renaissance is a touch of the city in the suburbs: a New York-style bistro featuring Country French and continental specialties. The fresh fish of the day is always the bestselling menu item; other recommendations include the escargot appetizer, pheasant and country grilled vegetables. The emphasis is on service. Beer and wine are sold; reservations are accepted.

LE CLOS

Chateau Élan Resort & Winery
100 Tour de France Dr.
Braselton   932-0900
$$$$

Le Clos is the fine dining restaurant at the Chateau Élan Resort & Winery complex about 45 minutes northeast of Atlanta (Exit 48 off I-85). The six-course prix fixe meal includes specially selected wines from the resort's own winery. Elegant Le Clos attracts diners from Atlanta, Athens, Gainesville and elsewhere. Dinner is served Wednesday through Saturday evenings; the first seating is at 6 PM. Jackets are requested for the gentlemen; call for reservations.

Greek/Mediterranean

DIMITRI'S

4651 Woodstock Rd.
Roswell   587-2700
$$

In the Sandy Plains Village Shopping

Center, Dimitri's has been delighting diners since 1992 with many Greek specialties served in a fine dining atmosphere. Among them are braised leg of lamb and salmon marinated in maple. A full-service bar is provided for your enjoyment. Dimitri's is open seven days a week for dinner and for lunch on weekdays. The restaurant accepts reservations every night except Friday and Saturday for parties of any size.

GYRO AND FALAFEL SHOP

2250 Cobb Pkwy.
Marietta   *984-1010*
$

Walk in and make your choice for takeout, or eat in the tiny dining area. Tasty and satisfying falafels are among the traditional fare. Try the grilled eggplant or the platters of gyro and tabouli with vegetables, dressed with tahini sauce, lemon juice, garlic and parsley. Then check out the array of exotic staples offered in the grocery next door. The restaurant is open six days a week for lunch and dinner (till 7 PM) and closed on Sundays.

Indian

DAWAT INDIAN CUISINE

4025-K Satellite Blvd.
Duluth   *623-6133*
$

Tiny but tidy, Dawat offers a sumptuous vegetarian lunch buffet with curries, soup, rice pilau and more. You'll find some standards and some surprises on the menu: Lentil-stuffed potato patties and dosa pancakes are favorites. Ample parking is provided. Lunch and dinner are served every day but Monday.

INDIAN DELIGHTS

3675 Satellite Blvd. Ste.1000   813-8212
Duluth
$

Low on atmosphere but high on food

quality, this vegetarian restaurant features dishes from the southern part of India. The spotlight here is on creatively seasoned grains and vegetables at inexpensive prices. Masala dosa, a large crepe filled with curried potatoes, is a favorite. Spicy soups, homemade noodles and hot sauces will bring you back for more. Additional location: 1707 Charles Street, Decatur, 296-2965.

HAVELI INDIAN CUISINE

2650 Cobb Pkwy. S.E.   955-4525
$$

Popular choices here are the lentil-based entrees and fresh vegetable dishes. The restaurant also offers kebabs, chicken and seafood dishes for non-vegetarians. Open for dinner seven nights a week, Haveli serves lunch every day except on Sunday.

Italian

ALTOBELI'S FINE ITALIAN CUISINE

3000 Old Alabama Rd.
Alpharetta
$$ *664-8055*

Specializing in veal dishes, Altobeli's nonetheless offers an impressive array of pasta, chicken, beef and fish entrees. For instance, the dish called Fusilli à la Pescatore combines shrimp, scallops, mussels, calamari and clams simmered in marinara sauce and wine. Casual dress is suitable for both locations, which are open for dinner seven nights a week with a full-service bar. Reservations are recommended.

BROOKLYN CAFE

220 Sandy Springs Cr. N.W.   843-8377
$$

Crowds flock to this New York art deco setting for the imaginative, high-quality food. After opening in 1993, the cafe was voted one of the top-10 best new restaurants by *Atlanta* magazine. Happily, its standard has persisted. The Italian continental cuisine includes delectables such as Veal Sorrentino, a sauteed scallopine dish topped with red and yellow peppers, and Pasta Bucatini, a tubular pasta with tomatoes, red peppers, garlic and Parmesan cheese. An extensive wine and beer list is offered. Open seven days a week for dinner and on weekdays for lunch, the Brooklyn Cafe recently added brunch on the weekends. In lieu of reservations, call ahead to put your name on the priority seating list, which puts you first in line when you arrive at your appointed time.

CAPRI RISTORANTE ITALIANO
5785 Roswell Rd.   255-7222
$$

Called chic and intimate, Capri is simple but stylish, making it an ideal spot for either a social or business occasion. The owners bring solid experience, based on their European training, to their second restaurant endeavor. Delectable entrees include shrimp gamberoni piccata over angel hair pasta and fresh mussels with marinara sauce. Among the veal dishes, scaloppine di vitello veronese, with roasted peppers, mushrooms, garlic and white wine cream sauce, is a real favorite. Open for lunch and dinner, Capri is just north of I-285 at Carpenter Drive.

MI SPIA RISTORANTE-BAR
4505 Ashford Dunwody Rd.   393-1333
$$

The sophisticated Mi Spia offers Italian food with a contemporary flair. This neighborhood bar and grill features a garden patio and a lively cocktail hour. Wood-trimmed French doors overlook a courtyard and enliven the airy dining room. Fresh seafood, pasta and veal combos, homemade breads and desserts keep the customers coming back. The in-house pastry chef creates unusual treats, such as the olive and walnut loaf. Among Mi Spia's specialties are the saffron fettuccine and marinated grilled jumbo shrimp. Dinner is served every night, and lunches are served on weekdays. Smoking is allowed in the bar area only. Reservations are accepted.

Japanese

UMEZONO
2086-B Cobb Pkwy.
Smyrna   933-8808
$$

Reasonable costs and high-quality food make the drive to Umezono worth it. You'll find delicious versions of tempura, noodle dishes and teriyaki made with salmon. A favorite here is the beef teriyaki and sushi combination, perhaps accompanied by a Japanese beer. An ice cream with red bean dessert comes with entrees. Dinner is served seven days a week; lunch is served every day but Sunday.

SHIKI JAPANESE RESTAURANT
1492 Pleasant Hill Rd.
Duluth   279-0097
$$

Shiki was voted best Japanese restaurant two years in row by *Atlanta* magazine. It's a place with two faces: a traditional style dining room where, among many other entrees, impeccably fresh fish in an artful design will delight your eye as well as your palate. Dinners here run a bit more, from the $18-or-more range. And there's a sushi bar at the rear of the main room, where a chef prepares a wide variety of tempting treats.

On the hibachi side of the restaurant, you'll find quality steaks and seafood cooked on tableside grills. How does a chicken combo dinner with appetizer, soup and dessert for $12 sound? Or a steak and scallop combo for $18? Beer and wine are offered. No matter which section you choose, exquisite presentation added to thoughtful and gracious service makes a return visit likely. It's open seven days a week, with two-day advance reservations highly recommended.

Korean

GARAM KOREAN RESTAURANT
5881 Buford Hwy.
Doraville   454-9198
$$

Offering an extensive menu, Garam will cook fresh vegetables at your table or serve heaping portions of their Korean barbecue. The restaurant is open for both lunch and dinner seven days a week.

SHI GOL HOUSE
570 Cobb Pkwy.
Marietta   425-1462
$$

If there's anyone who knows spicy barbecue (besides Texans), it's Koreans. Shi Gol has a way with hot pepper, garlic and barbecued meats. And to go with it, help yourself to a serving of bool go gi, which is finely shaved marinated steak accompanied by side dishes such as spicy hot pickled cabbage. Servers are glad to advise you on delectable choices from the extensive menu. Shi Gol serves dinner every night and lunch on weekdays.

Latin

AZTECA GRILL
1140 Morrow Industrial Blvd.
Morrow   968-0908
$$

Spicy specialties at this Mexican and Southwestern restaurant include poblano corn chowder and a Mexican version of tur-nip greens that has people talking. Your total could easily be less than $20 for two, or you could try everything and live it up at the full bar. There's outside dining in the warm weather; parties of 10 or more may call for reservations.

CHIPICUARA
711-D Industrial Blvd.
Gainesville   531-0290
$$

This delightful Mexican restaurant attracts diners from as far away as Atlanta and Athens who come to feast on authentic poblano chile relleno and quesadillas. Beer and wine are sold; prices are at the low end of this range. Reservations are not necessary, although certain exotic specialties (such as paella) are not on the menu and can be prepared for groups with a day's advance notice. Lunch is served Monday through Saturday; dinner is served Wednesday through Saturday.

COZUMEL MEXICAN RESTAURANT
2697 Spring Rd., Smyrna   801-1487
$

This Mexican eatery northwest of Atlanta offers popular items such as steak ranchero, mixed fajitas and carne asada. Beer and wine are available. Cozumel is open every day for lunch and dinner.

Seafood

EMBERS SEAFOOD GRILL
234 Hildebrand Dr. N.W.   256 0977
$$

Excellent preparation, good service, sizable portions — what more could you ask for? The Embers' decor could be called a dressed-up seafood shack scheme. Good service and well-trained staff will gladly explain the details of entrees, which will likely run to the high end of this price category.

The catch of the day may be mahi mahi, grilled and served in a spicy Cuban sauce with banana peppers, accompanied by red rice and beans. Grilled salmon and trout are other favorites. The Combo Kebab presents two pieces of swordfish, two of tuna, one sea scallop, red onion and green peppers, served with teriyaki sauce. Blackened amberjack is another favorite. Other menu selections include grilled swordfish, tuna, grouper, scallops, shrimp, lobster, steaks and chicken. A few pasta and entree-size salads, made with fish, are on the menu. For an appetizer, you might try the smoked barbecued shrimp or the delicious crab cakes. Casual dress and a children's menu make the Embers a comfortable setting. A full-service bar is on the premises. It's open for dinner seven days a week and for lunch on weekdays.

SLOCUM'S
6025 Peachtree Park Way
Norcross   446-7725
$$

Believed by many to be the best yellowfin tuna in Atlanta, Slocums' house specialty is marinated in teriyaki sauce, then grilled. The casual setting may surprise you. It's been called a suburban Bubba bar and grill, complete with neon beer signs. The bar has country music and TV tuned to sports; you can be seated away from all this if you wish. Slocum's draws families, singles and just about anyone else who loves juicy, fresh fish. The steak and burger crowd has their say on the menu too. Slocum's serves lunch Monday through Saturday and dinner seven nights a week.

The restaurant takes reservations for six or more. The other locations are 8849 Roswell Road, Dunwoody, 587-3022;

1433 Terrell Mill Road, Marietta, 951-2090; 4977 Memorial Drive, Stone Mountain, 299-9872.

Southern Food and Barbecue

BLUE WILLOW INN RESTAURANT
294 N. Cherokee Rd.
Social Circle   464-2131
$

On five acres of land, the Blue Willow is housed in a 1907 Greek Revival mansion. The fare, served buffet style, is authentic Southern cooking, including fried chicken and fried green tomatoes. Four to five meats and 10 to 12 vegetables are generally offered. In warm weather, you may choose to dine outside by the pool. Credit cards are not accepted, but reservations are. Due to local regulations, no alcohol is sold; however, patrons are welcome to bring their own wine or champagne. Social Circle is 45 minutes east of Atlanta; take I-20 to Exit 47.

L&K CAFE
839 Broad St., Gainesville   531-0600
$

L&K serves breakfast, lunch and dinner every day of the year except Christmas. Menu favorites include fried chicken and cobbler; eight vegetables are generally offered. No alcohol; no credit cards.

PUCKETT'S RESTAURANT
119 S. Lee St., Buford   945-6031
$

Puckett's fixes breakfast, lunch and dinner on weekdays only. A typical day begins at 4:30 AM, when the homemade pies are baked. Other specialties include fried chicken and country fried steak; seven or so vegetables are available. Friendly, down-home Puckett's has been in business since 1953; no alcohol; no credit cards.

SONNY'S REAL PIT BAR-B-Q

625 Morrow Industrial Blvd.
Jonesboro   968-0052
$

Sonny's big draw is the $8.95 all-you-can-eat Chuck Wagon special, which includes barbecued pork, beef, chicken and ribs and all the fixings. There are also daily all-you-can-eat specials, plus regular orders for smaller appetites; beer is sold.

Additional locations: 6869 Peachtree Industrial Boulevard, Doraville, 447-6616; 160 Cobb Parkway S.E., Marietta, 428-1534; 2717 New Spring Road S.E., Smyrna, 955-1597; 11170 Alpharetta Highway, Roswell, 664-8930; 1235 Indian Trail-Lilburn Road, Norcross, 381-7357; 1870 Highway 20 S.E., Conyers, 860-0099.

DOWN EAST BAR-B-QUE

2289 S. Cobb Dr., Smyrna   434-8887
$

Down East opened in 1994 and quickly built a reputation for powerful 'cue. The owners proudly point out that their barbecue is pit-cooked North Carolina-style and is served with a vinegar-type sauce. Also on hand are all the home-made fixings, such as potato salad and cole slaw. Down East is closed on Sunday; no alcohol; no credit cards.

Thai

ROYAL THAI CUISINE

6365-A Spalding Dr.
Norcross   449-7796
$$

Take your seat in the cozy upholstered booths surrounded by wood paneling and deep green fabric panels. Or dine on the outdoor deck of this small place known for good food. Sauteed pork, seasoned with black pepper and garlic, is popular as is the lamb with fresh basil. Tea rose dumplings deserve their spot on the menu. Thai beer is served. You'll find efficient friendly service at Royal Thai, which offers lunch on weekdays and dinner every night.

Vegetarian

CAFE SUNFLOWER

5975 Roswell Rd.   256-1675
$$

Just a half-mile outside the Perimeter in Hammond Square Shopping Center, Cafe Sunflower is on the flip side of the building from the Lettuce Souprise You Roswell Road location listed above. This comfortable restaurant specializes in imaginative and well-prepared whole-some food. The cuisine is a combo of Asian, Mediterranean and Southwestern influences. An overall soothing atmosphere is launched at the front door, where an art piece spouting rippling water greets you. Try the fresh vegetables over fluffy brown rice or the wild mushroom pizza. While you could eat for less than the price range shown, you may find the menu's temptations impossible to resist. No alcohol is served, nor is smoking allowed. Reservations are welcome.

VEGGIELAND

220 Sandy Springs Cr. N.W.   252-1165
$$

Fresh and healthy food is the treat here, with lots of vegetables and salads to satisfy your hunger. Try the pesto pasta, made just to your liking. Lunch and dinner are served every day but Sunday. Additional location: 211 Pharr Road, in the Buckhead area, 231-3111.

Photo: Theatre In The Square

Marietta's Theatre In The Square is housed in a former cotton warehouse.

Inside
Nightlife

"I love the nightlife!
I've got to boogie!"
— Atlanta's own Alicia Bridges

When the sun goes down, Atlanta gets a new attitude. Night brings an end to the day's problems, replacing them with more pleasant concerns. For a few hours, "Where are we going?" "Who's meeting us there?" and "What's everyone doing later?" become the most important issues.

Actually, the nightlife scene has always been a part of Atlanta. The first tavern, after all, opened 10 years before the first church. And Moses Formwalt, a tinsmith and still-maker backed by the Free and Rowdy Party, defeated the Morals Party's temperance candidate in the first mayoral election in 1848. Prohibition, needless to say, did not go over well in Atlanta (see sidebar).

The ever-changing nature of life in Atlanta is nowhere more evident than in the city's nightlife. Clubs, bars and coffeehouses open, close, remodel and disappear with amazing speed. We could tell you about the pricey seafood restaurant that's now a live music club showcasing the latest bands or the leather bar that became an upscale steakhouse, but take our word for it: Everything about Atlanta nightlife is subject to change.

Theme nights are very big in Atlanta clubs. A club may have live rock bands one night, a gay dance party the next and attract a largely African-American singles crowd yet another evening. Even though a club's name might remain the same, the nightly themes and entertainment offerings can change with the wind.

Don't assume, just because you've been to a club before, that its entertainment and door policies will be the same when you return. It's always a good idea to call first if you're not sure. Many of the larger clubs now have sophisticated answering systems you can access with a touch-tone phone; these give directions to the club and information about entertainment, nightly specials and cover charges.

Several local periodicals offer up-to-the-minute coverage for Atlanta's night-crawlers: These are the best ways to find out what's happening on any given night or weekend in Atlanta. The following publications are all free and are distributed in various locations around town; if you don't run across the periodical you're looking for, call the numbers shown during business hours and ask about nearby distribution points.

Creative Loafing, 688-5623, is published weekly and carries features and an entertainment calendar with extensive information on the nightly action at dozens of clubs.

The University Reporter, 315-7650, is a monthly paper that spotlights places and shows of interest to college students and 20-somethings. Its "SCENE" chart gives a quick rundown on the recreational opportunities and cover charges of some 50 bars.

The Hudspeth Report, 255-3220, another monthly, targets an affluent professional crowd; its coverage focuses on Buckhead and Northside clubs and restaurants.

Atlanta has some 30 bars that cater to gays and lesbians. For the latest on these clubs, pick up the free weekly publications *Etcetera Magazine,* 525-3821, and *Southern Voice,* 876-1819.

Please note this general information: Bars in Atlanta may stay open as late as 4 AM, though not all do. On Saturday nights, all bars are required to close an hour earlier, at 3 AM. A handful of clubs have special licenses that allow them to stay open and serve liquor around the clock: Two of these are Club Anytime, 1055 Peachtree Street N.E., 607-8050, and Backstreet (see item under dance clubs).

Acceptance of credit cards varies. Some places that don't accept plastic at the door will let you pay your tab with a card. Others don't accept credit cards but have an ATM on the premises. If your plan is "party now, pay later," it's best to call the club and make sure your card will be accepted.

All persons entering a bar are required to have a picture ID. This is not about how old you look, and it's not about doormen who want to hassle you. Most clubs will refuse admittance to anyone — regardless of age — who does not have a picture ID. Avoid aggravation by making sure each person in your group has one.

Information on cover charges is given as a guide only and may not reflect the actual cost to enter a club on a given night; for example, many clubs dramatically raise the door charge on special evenings such as New Year's Eve and Halloween. In the listings that follow, a small cover charge means less than $5; a moderate cover charge means $5 to $10.

The drinking age for liquor, beer and wine in Georgia is 21. "Eighteen to party, 21 to drink" is the rule at some clubs, which usually issue a special bracelet required to order alcohol.

Finally, Georgia's drunk driving laws are very strict and getting stricter all the time. A driver who registers a blood-alcohol level of 0.08 gm or higher is considered drunk. The police use random roadblocks to apprehend drunk drivers; these are often on two-lane (as opposed to wider) streets in areas with a heavy concentration of nightclubs. Rather than taking a chance on getting busted or endangering yourself or others, take a cab, use a sober designated driver or ride MARTA. It's hard to hail a cab on the street, but they are generally available in areas with lots of clubs. If you don't see cabs outside, ask the doorman to call one for you a few minutes before you're ready to leave.

Any discussion of Atlanta nightlife has to begin with Buckhead. Buckhead is not only the shopping center of the Southeast — with 1,400-plus retail units ringing up more than $1 billion in sales annually — it's also the nexus of Atlanta nightlife and dining. Certainly, other sections, such as Virginia-Highlands, Midtown and Little Five Points, have their own unique bars and nightlife scene, but for sheer critical mass of clubs, nowhere else even comes close to Buckhead.

In this chapter, we'll begin our bar-hopping tour of Atlanta in Buckhead. After we've touched on some of the after-dark diversions there, we'll move on to several categories of clubs around town that offer live music, dancing and more.

Swinging Buckhead

Within the Buckhead district are more than 210 eating and drinking establishments. Dozens of these businesses are within walking distance of each other, primarily in the area where Peachtree Road intersects with Pharr Road and E. Paces Ferry Road. If you want to spend an evening in one district with lots of entertainment options, come on up to Buckhead.

When **Tongue & Groove**, 3055 Peachtree Road N.E., 261-2325, opened in Buckhead in 1994, it promised to "turn down the music and turn up the taste, letting people and their personalities take center stage in a stunningly designed space filled with subtle beauty." The club's interior is contemporary yet romantic and features custom furnishings and flattering lighting. Sushi and paté are available; there's a moderate cover charge after 10 PM.

Otto's, 265 E. Paces Ferry Road N.E., 233-1133, is a sleek, very upscale nightclub featuring nightly live music downstairs and a Top-40 dance floor upstairs. On Friday and Saturday after 9:30 PM, there's a moderate cover charge for gentlemen; there's never a cover for ladies. Otto's casually elegant dress code is strictly enforced; the club is closed on Sunday.

Rupert's, 3330 Piedmont Road N.E., 266-9834, occupies the huge space that was originally home to the famous disco temple Limelight back in the '70s and early '80s. (It was during the Limelight era that the supermarket beside the club picked up the nickname it's still known by: "Disco Kroger.") Rupert's has a moderate cover charge and a strict dress code; call for details. On Tuesday, Thursday, Friday and Saturday nights, there's live dance music as Rupert's orchestra performs the hits of yesterday and today.

Abri, 3029 Peachtree Street, 237-6848, has a piano bar on the first floor. The upstairs room has a dance floor and a nice view. There's a moderate cover charge on Friday and Saturday.

The Odyssey, 210 Pharr Road, 261-8476, is three bars in one. There's live acoustic music on the covered deck; the rock 'n' roll sports bar has more than 30 TVs; the disco features hits from the '70s through today. The crowd is diverse, but most guests are in their 20s. The Odyssey is open every night, and there's never a cover.

No mere piano bar, **Jellyroll's**, 295 E. Paces Ferry Road N.E., 261-6864, is a dueling piano bar! Four piano players, in teams of two, take turns banging out the hits of yesterday and today. The audience participates, and the singing, dancing waitstaff has been known to leap onto the bar to demonstrate "The Time Warp" from *The Rocky Horror Picture Show*. Jellyroll's rocks Wednesday through Saturday nights; there's a small cover nightly.

Aunt Charley's, 3107 Peachtree Road N.E., 231-8503, has been Buckhead's neighborhood pub for about 20 years. The menu includes hamburgers, rib-eyes and salads, and the full bar includes the suds of some 60 microbreweries. It's closed on Monday.

"No theme, no attitude, just Bar" is the slogan at this bar without a story. At **Bar**, 250 E. Paces Ferry Road, 841-0033, patrons enjoy such pastimes as free pool and chugging "bobsled shooters," which are poured through an ice sculpture. Bar is open Wednesday through Saturday nights, and there's never a cover.

The World Bar, 3071 Peachtree Road. N.E., 266-0627, has a dance floor and pool tables, and it's open Tuesday through Saturday nights. There's a small cover on Friday and Saturday nights only.

If your taste runs more to Big Band than to loud band, head up to **Johnny's Hideaway**, 3771 Roswell Road, 233-8026. This self-described "nightclub for big kids" showcases the music of the '40s, '50s and '60s. Dress is business casual, and the crowd tends to be 35 and older. Johnny's is open every night, and there's never a cover.

Dance

Within six months of its 1991 opening, **Velvet**, 89 Park Place, 681-9936, was named one of the nation's four hottest dance clubs by *Newsweek*. In a turn-of-the-century downtown building that was a saloon and pool hall, it has old brick walls, an imposing mahogany bar and patterned tin ceilings. The building may look nostalgic, but the crowd and the music are totally today. Madonna and other celebrities have popped in to party and dance the night away. Various theme nights attract college kids, African-Americans and gays; call for the latest party information. There is a moderate cover charge.

Backstreet Atlanta, 845 Peachtree Street, 873-1986, is Atlanta's biggest gay bar and it's open 24 hours every day. This huge cha-cha palace is an entertainment complex with a high-energy disco and a separate room for live shows. Backstreet is a membership club but also welcomes nonmembers. The cover charge for nonmembers is small during the week and moderate on the weekends. Some of Atlanta's best-known female impersonators perform upstairs Wednesday through Sunday evenings; the weekend shows go until dawn. Although Backstreet is way-gay, many fun-loving straights love this place — particularly if they're into dancing. Backstreet has a Peachtree address, but the entrance is through the parking lot on the Juniper Street side.

Club Echelon, 585 Franklin Road S.E., Marietta, 419-3393, attracts an upscale, predominantly African-American clientele. It's open Thursday through Saturday nights; the moderate cover charge varies with the entertainment, which spotlights hot stars such as Ce Ce Peniston. The club welcomes persons 23 and older and has a strict dress code; call for details.

Live Music

Rock

Masquerade, 695 North Avenue, 577-8178, is the kind of place your mama must have warned you about: The average Masquerade patron probably has more body piercings and tattoos than the average business person has credit cards. But those into the gothic, punk and alternative rock scenes will have a blast here. In an antique factory that once turned out excelsior (wood shavings used for packing straw, much as foam "peanuts" are used today), Masquerade's cavernous space is divided into three theme areas: Hell, the throbbing downstairs dance room; Heaven, the big upstairs concert hall; and Purgatory, a more low-key performance art space that's — you guessed it — between the two. Masquerade showcases lots of local talent and books national acts for major concerts almost every week. It's open Wednesday through Sunday; the cover charge is moderate to higher, depending upon the evening's entertainment.

Hidden behind the Winn-Dixie shopping center at Monroe Drive and Virginia Avenue and next to the Midtown 8 cinema is **Midtown Music Hall**, 872-8570, a popular venue for alternative and college rock bands. There's a full bar, and there's a moderate cover charge in the showroom.

In Virginia-Highlands, the **Dark Horse Tavern**, 816 N. Highland Avenue N.E., 873-3607, has a conversation bar upstairs and a showroom in the basement where exciting local and national alternative bands play every night. A full menu is available; the small cover charge varies with the entertainment.

Like its sister bar in New York, **Scrap Bar**, 1080 Peachtree Street, 724-0009, is decorated with 30 tons of scrap metal. While the look is definitely "heavy metal," this club books all sorts of rock bands for shows on Thursday, Friday and Saturday nights. There's a full bar; a small cover charge applies, but only on nights with live music.

Smith's Olde Bar, 1578 Piedmont Avenue N.E., 875-1522, occupies the building that many will remember as Gene & Gabe's restaurant. Smith's features live entertainment seven nights a week. It opens daily for lunch, prepared in the full kitchen, and stays open until 4 AM weekdays and 3 AM on Saturday. There are four pool tables; cover charge in the showroom varies from small to moderate, depending on who's playing. Recent shows have headlined national acts such as Jonathan Richman and local favorites such as Atlanta recording artist Richard Bicknell.

Dottie's, 307 Memorial Drive S.E., 523-3444, is a fun little honky-tonk near Grant Park. Dottie's has a full bar and is open every night. There's usually a live band of the alternative music genre on Wednesday, Friday, Saturday and Sunday. There might be a small cover on entertainment nights.

The Point, 420 Moreland Avenue N.E., 659-3522, is open every night in the heart of Little Five Points. Up-and-coming college rock bands play Tuesday through Saturday nights, when there's also a small to moderate cover charge. You can trip out at the Sunday psychedelic disco party for just a buck. The Point has a full bar and serves food.

Also in Little Five Points, the **Star Community Bar**, 437 Moreland Avenue N.E., 681-9018, is open nightly and has a full bar. College, garage and rockabilly bands play here five or six nights a week; occasionally there's a show by a national

The sale of alcohol in retail stores (including liquor stores) ends before midnight on Saturday night and does not resume until Monday morning.

Underground Atlanta is a unique place to shop and dine.

act on the college circuit. The Star has an all-Elvis juke box and an Elvis shrine housed in a former bank vault.

Out in Marietta, **The Edge** has live rock bands seven nights a week. There are 15 pool tables; the restaurant serves until 1 AM. There's a small cover charge nightly, which increases when national acts perform.

Jazz and Blues

A neon alligator in the window welcomes you to **Blind Willie's**, 828 N. Highland Avenue N.E., 873-2583. Big names, such as Mose Allison and Jr. Wells, have played this small blues joint that features live entertainment every night. Sundays are usually acoustic. There's a full bar with bar food; a moderate cover is charged nightly.

Both the Underground Atlanta, 577-1800, and Buckhead, 266-1600, locations of **Dante's Down the Hatch** swing to live jazz nightly and charge a small to moderate cover. For details, please see the listing in the Continental section of the Restaurants chapter.

Yin Yang Cafe, 64 Third Street, 607-0682, serves beer and wine and food. There's a small cover on nights with live jazz, usually Thursday through Sunday.

Teddy's Live, Underground Atlanta, 653-9999, features live R&B and contemporary jazz nightly. Teddy's serves lunch on weekdays and dinner nightly. There's a small to moderate cover on most nights, depending upon the entertainment.

In Sandy Springs just north of I-285, **Cafe 290**, 256-3942, is open nightly with live jazz or blues. A separate section houses a sports bar. A full menu is available; there's never a cover.

Folk and Acoustic

In Decatur, **Eddie's Attic**, 515 McDonough Street, 377-4976, includes a restaurant, a tavern and a 225-person-capacity music hall. There's live original acoustic entertainment seven nights a week. The restaurant serves sandwiches and nachos; there's a year-round patio. The cover charge ranges from low to high for big-name acts.

Also in Decatur, the **Freight Room**,

301 E. Howard Avenue, 378-5365, spotlights a variety of music, including acoustic, bluegrass, jazz and zydeco. There's a small cover on Thursday, Friday and Saturday; cover may be moderate to higher when national acts perform. There's a full-service restaurant, and the club is open nightly with live music. The Freight Room occupies a 110-year-old building that was once Decatur's railway station.

Country

Country music never went out of style in Atlanta, and in recent years it's become more popular than ever. The biggest honky-tonk inside I-285 is **Mama's Country Showcase**, 3952 Covington Highway, Decatur, 288-6262. Mama's has a 3,000-square-foot dance floor and holds about 2,000 boot-scooters. Ladies are admitted free on Wednesday and Thursday, and there are free dance lessons and a free buffet; there's a moderate cover for the cowboys. The moderate cover on weekend nights is higher for those 18 to 20. There's a restaurant on premises; a live country band plays nightly. If you're brave, you can hop on Tornado the mechanical bull. Mama's is closed Sunday through Tuesday.

Out in Marietta, **Miss Kitty's Saloon & Dancehall**, 1038 Franklin Road S.E., 424-6556, is a country club with pool tables and live music Tuesday through Saturday nights. Different nights feature dance lessons, country karaoke and more. There's a small cover charge.

Also northwest of town, the **Crystal Chandelier**, 1750 N. Roberts Road in Kennesaw, 426-5006, welcomes you and all your rowdy friends. This 4,800-square-foot country club has a 4,000-square-foot dance floor and holds about 3,700 cowboys and cowgirls. Wednesday is ladies

night. The cover is small to moderate but goes higher when national acts are featured.

Amphitheaters

CHASTAIN PARK AMPHITHEATER
Powers Ferry Rd. at Stella Dr.   *733-4800*

One of Atlanta's least-kept secrets, Chastain Park offers world-class entertainment in an outdoor dining environment that makes for a truly enjoyable evening. The gently sloping amphitheater with 7,000 seats means good sight lines to the stage, where internationally known performers such as Tony Bennett, Natalie Cole, James Taylor and Nancy Wilson have weaved their magic in the soft summer air.

Classical, country, jazz, rock 'n' roll — you name it, Chastain presents it. The Atlanta Symphony Orchestra calls Chastain home during the summer while backing the big showbiz names.

Peer around you at the repasts created by those attending. You'll see a few brown-baggers. But more often you'll see full-blown dinner parties, complete with linen cloths, candles, silver and champagne-filled crystal goblets.

For a complete schedule of park-managed concert dates and performances, call 733-4800; for Southern Concerts Promotion events, call 231-5888.

COCA-COLA LAKEWOOD AMPHITHEATER
2002 Lakewood Way   *627-9704*

Beginning in 1916, Lakewood Fair Grounds was the site of the Southeastern Fair, which drew exhibitors and visitors from across the South. Today the Lakewood Amphitheater is the site of a concert series that runs from May to October. In 1994, headliners included Jimmy Buffett, Crosby, Stills & Nash, Steely Dan,

Atlanta Home Brews Hop to Big Time

Atlanta jumped into the microbrewery craze in 1994 when two local companies premiered ales that are brewed right here in town.

Red Brick Ale is a traditional top-fermented ale. It's brewed with spring water from the North Georgia mountains using five American malts and a special blend of domestic and European hops. It's a deep copper-red color. In Red Brick's debut in the annual beer tasting at R.J.'s Uptown Kitchen & Wine Bar, 870 N. Highland Avenue N.E., 875-7775, the brew beat out suds from 60 other microbreweries to be crowned "Best Beer in Atlanta." The ale is brewed by Atlanta Brewing Co. at 1219 Williams Street in Midtown and is available bottled and on draft in close to 1,000 metro stores, restaurants and bars. The introduction of the new Red Brick Golden Lager is scheduled for this spring.

Marthasville Brewing Company — whose name honors one of Atlanta's several early names — produces unpasteurized Martha's Pale Ale and Sweet Georgia Brown Ale. Just after its introduction, Martha's Pale Ale beat out 47 other microbrews in a tasting at Aunt Charley's.

Marthasville Ales are now on tap at more than 75 metro bars and restaurants, and bottling is scheduled to begin in spring 1995.

Complimentary ale tastings and tours of Marthasville's southwest Atlanta brewery, 3960 Shirley Drive. S.W., are offered every Tuesday night at 7. For information call Barbara, 713-0333.

Harry Connick Jr. and the Allman Brothers Band. The two-day Lollapalooza festival drew thousands of tattooed and pierced devotees of punk and alternative rock.

Lakewood seats more than 18,000: Reserved seats are under the covered pavilion, while the broad lawn is general admission. Big-screen TVs suspended from the pavilion roof bring the action up-close for those on the lawn. Shows at Lakewood go on rain or shine. To charge tickets by phone, call 249-6400.

To reach Lakewood, take I-75/85 south from downtown to the Lakewood Freeway East Exit and follow the signs, or take the Lakewood Freeway West Exit to Stewart Avenue and follow the signs. Several parking lots are available; the closest lots are the most expensive.

Note: For an outdoor facility, Lakewood has a lot of rules. You may bring in a blanket to sit on, but you may not bring in the following: coolers, containers, drinks or food prepared off-premises, lawn chairs, cameras and recording equipment. Avoid hassles by leaving prohibited items in your car. Alcohol and a full menu are available at all shows, but the prices are steep.

Comedy

A list of comedians who have played the **Punch Line**, 280 Hilderbrand Drive N.E., reads like *TV Guide*: Jerry Seinfeld, Ellen Degeneres, Tim Allen and Brett Butler have all cracked up audiences there. Pam Stone of the TV series *Coach* got her start here as a waitress. The club is open Tuesday through Sunday; the cover charge is moderate to high, depending upon who's performing.

The **Uptown Comedy Corner**, 2140 Peachtree Road N.W., showcases popular black comedians and draws a primarily African-American, upscale crowd. The club holds about 300, and there are three shows nightly on Friday and Saturday; Tuesday is open mic night. The cover charge is moderate during the week and higher on Friday and Saturday.

Concert Theaters

Atlanta has several venues that offer the experience of seeing nationally known performers in fairly intimate surroundings. Ticket prices at these theaters vary with the acts appearing there.

Center Stage, 1374 W. Peachtree Street N.W., 874-1511, proudly proclaims that "every seat is the best seat in the house." The Midtown theater holds only 1,000 people in a steeply raked, amphitheater-style setting, which gives great sightlines to the stage. There's a full bar and a restaurant on-premises. Recent shows here have starred Jackson Browne, B.B. King, Greg Allman and Jerry Seinfeld. Tickets are available at the box office, or you can charge tickets by calling TicketMaster, 249-6400.

In Buckhead, **The Coca-Cola Roxy Theater**, 3110 Roswell Road, 233-ROXY, holds 1,100 to 1,500 people in a space that was once a cinema and drafthouse.

Recent shows have starred Joe Cocker and Bryan Ferry of Roxy Music. The Roxy has a full bar. Tickets are sold through TicketMaster, 249-6400; the box office sells tickets for events only on the day of the show.

Variety Playhouse in Little Five Points, 1099 Euclid Avenue N.E., 521-1786, seats 800 to 1,000 patrons in a former movie theater with a balcony and space for dancing in front of the stage. Doc Watson, the Seldom Scene, Grover Washington Jr., MagnaPop and Everything But The Girl have played the Variety recently. The theater features beer, wine and snacks. Tickets are available at the box office (there's a $1 service charge for credit card sales). To charge by phone, call TicketMaster, 249-6400.

Pubs

Manuel's Tavern, 602 N. Highland Avenue N.E., 525-3447, has been a favorite in-town watering hole since 1956. Many customers are regulars who pass the time table-hopping and visiting other regulars. For more information, please refer to the separate item in the American section of the Restaurants chapter.

Limerick Junction, 822 N. Highland Avenue, 874-7147, in Virginia-Highlands celebrates Celtic culture. There's an Irish sing-along nightly Wednesday through Saturday; on Sunday and Monday nights, there's live contemporary Irish or folk music. There's a small cover only on Friday and Saturday nights.

County Cork Pub, 5600 Roswell Road, 303-1976, is an Irish pub with darts, food and live Irish music Tuesday through Saturday nights. There's a small cover on Friday and Saturday nights; the pub is closed on Sunday.

Dave and Buster's

This incredible amusement park for adults defies easy classification. Dave and Buster's, 2215 D&B Drive, Marietta, 951-5554, is a 53,000-square-foot world of fun with some 300 employees. Here are 19 world-class mahogany and slate billiard tables, seven shuffleboard courts, the Million-Dollar Midway with more than 100 video games and virtual reality simulators, a "for-fun" casino, a restaurant, full-service bars and a mystery dinner theater where the audience helps solve the crime. Dave & Buster's is open every day from before noon until midnight or later. Accompanied children are welcome but must remain with their parents at all times. After 10 PM, minors are allowed only in the dining room.

Adult Entertainment Clubs

Because they offer totally nude dancers, Atlanta's adult entertainment clubs are controversial — but they're also legendary. These establishments advertise heavily in print, on billboards and on the radio; even the city's own official tourist magazine *Atlanta Now* incudes a listing of some of them. You can find many adult clubs listed under "Nightclubs" in the Yellow Pages. Also check the "Adult Scene" pull-out section in the free weekly *Creative Loafing*.

The following clubs are among those with nude female dancers: **The Gold Club**, 2416 Piedmont Avenue N.E., 233-1210; **The Goldrush Showbar**, 2608 Stewart Avenue S.W., 766-2532; and **The**

Cheetah, 887 Spring Street N.W., 892-3037. Two clubs showcase nude female and male dancers: **Guys and Dolls**, 2788 E. Ponce de Leon, Decatur, 377-2956; and **The Coronet Club**, 5275 Roswell Road N.E., 250-1534.

Coffee Culture

Atlanta, like other cities, is getting a case of the java jitters. Coffeehouses can pop up anywhere in any sort of space: At the intersection of Piedmont and Monroe, a coffeehouse in a former Texaco percolates across from a coffeehouse in a former dry cleaners. More java joints seem to open every month; here are a few hot ones to visit.

Café Diem, 640 N. Highland Avenue N.E., 607-7008, is open seven days a week serving coffee, cordials, wine, beer and food. There's a classical guitarist on Sunday; the cafe hosts a big poetry reading on the first Tuesday of each month. Artists, students and international visitors dig Café Diem.

By day, **Kalo's Coffeehouse**, 1248 Clairmont Road, Decatur, 325-3733, is a big, sunny study hall for students from Emory University, which is about a mile away. Kalo's offers a light fare menu and 25 to 30 desserts. On Sunday, Monday and Tuesday evenings, there's live acoustic entertainment; there's no cover charge.

Caffeinds, 3095 Peachtree Road, 262-7774, is right in the heart of Buckhead and features live entertainment (from jazz to poetry readings) every night except Sunday and Wednesday. On Friday and

---

Insiders' Tips

Before you head out on your bar-hopping adventure, make sure everyone in your party has a government-issued picture ID card — even those of you obviously older than 21.

Prohibition in Atlanta: Not a Good Idea

Prohibition in Atlanta was imposed once by a county referendum, then later by the state and the federal governments. These laws, in general, were not popular and were widely disregarded.

The second volume of Franklin Garrett's exhaustive *Atlanta and Environs* reports that Atlanta first went dry on July 1, 1886, after a Fulton County referendum. But on November 26, 1887, the law was repealed — again, by referendum — and 40 liquor stores were operating in 1888.

A state prohibition law took effect in 1908, shutting down more than 100 Atlanta saloons and liquor stores and one brewery. A loophole allowing alcohol sales in private clubs led to the proliferation of "locker clubs," typically upstairs in office buildings, which called themselves private clubs but were basically bars. Legally, at least, Atlanta had been dry for a dozen years when prohibition became law nationally.

Following the 1933 repeal of prohibition, Governor E.D. Rivers signed legislation in 1938 allowing local option alcohol sales. Fulton County went wet by a margin of better than three to one. A dozen liquor stores opened on April 25, 1938, and the *Constitution* reported: "With their tongues 'hanging out', hundreds of Atlantans flocked to the legal liquor stores to make purchases of state-stamped legal whiskey, many of them buying legal liquor for the first time in their lives."

Saturday it's open until 2 AM; there's no cover charge.

Also in Buckhead, **Cafe Intermezzo**, 1845 Peachtree Road N.E., 355-0411, is a European-style coffeehouse with bistro food and some 50 desserts. It's open every day and draws a cross section of locals and visitors.

Java Jive, 790 Ponce de Leon Avenue, 876-6161, is a brightly colored shrine to the styles of the 1930s, '40s and '50s set to a Big Band soundtrack. The desserts are homemade — most popular is the chocolate truffle tort with raspberry sauce. Java Jive is open until 2 AM on Friday and Saturday nights.

Less a hangout and more a "Joe to go" joint, there are four locations of **Aurora Coffee**, including Little Five Points,

523-6856, and Virginia-Highlands, 892-7158.

Way downtown at 255 Trinity Street S.W., **Homage**, 681-2662, was a coffeehouse before coffeehouses caught on. It features live alternative music several nights a week for a small cover. Call for show information and directions.

Caribou Coffee, 733-5539, is at the intersection of Monroe and Piedmont in a former Texaco whose big windows are great for viewing the passing parade in this busy Midtown shopping area. Sweets are sold; Caribou has three other locations.

The Cinematic Theater

Even though most theaters begin screening early in the afternoon, we'll cover movies in our Nightlife chapter since that's when most people have time to attend the cinema.

A recent check of the Sunday Atlanta *Journal and Constitution* turned up 68 theaters showing movies on more than 475 screens throughout metro Atlanta. Some first-run theaters accept credit cards and sell advance tickets by phone; their recorded messages let you know if this is the case. Most theaters have special matinee prices until 4 PM; some go as late as 6 PM.

Considering the speed with which new movies now move from first-run houses to bargain theaters, many people prefer to wait a few weeks and catch new flicks at lower prices. The typical price at bargain theaters is $1.50 to $1.75 for all seats. Here are some discount theaters within Atlanta's Perimeter highway.

GREENBRIAR CINEMA
I-285 and Lakewood Fwy.   629-9999

LEFONT PLAZA THEATER
1049 Ponce de Leon Ave. N.E.   873-1939

NORTHEAST PLAZA CINEMA 12
3365 Buford Hwy.   248-0624

TOCO HILLS THEATER
3003 N. Druid Hills Rd.   636-1858

TOWER PLACE 6
Peachtree at Piedmont   594-4595

If you crave the experience of watching a movie from the comfort of your car, head for one of Atlanta's drive-in. (Can

you believe it, we still have these!) On the northeast side, there's the **North 85 Drive-In**, 3265 Northeast Expressway Access Road, Chamblee, 451-4570. On the south side, visit the **Starlight Drive-In**, 2000 Moreland Avenue S.E., 627-5786.

One unhappy side effect of development in Atlanta has been the loss of several movie theaters that specialized in limited-run, revival and art films. Many theaters are doomed by the valuable real estate they occupy, and owners choose to develop the property for other, more lucrative purposes. You can, however, still catch art and foreign-language films at the **Screening Room**, 2581 Piedmont Road, 231-1924, and at the **Lefont Garden Hills Cinema**, 2835 Peachtree Road, 266-2202.

Cinéfest is in the University Center building at Georgia State University, 66 Courtland Street, Suite, 211, 651-2463. The movie theater is sponsored in part by GSU's students. Many programs are double-features, including new popular movies, art films and cult classics. The program usually changes on Friday and again on Monday. The monthly schedule of coming attractions is available free in some in-town restaurants and bars. At the theater, you may sign the mailing list and receive the calendar free by mail.

IMAGE Film/Video Center, Suite M-1 in the TULA arts complex, 75 Bennett Street N.W., 352-4225, has hundreds of public screenings annually of hard-to-find films and videos. In addition, the group offers more than 40 workshops each year and sponsors the annual Atlanta Film and Video Festival. Call for schedule information.

Screenings of alternative and art movies also take place from time to time at the **Rich Auditorium of the High Museum of Art**, 1280 Peachtree Street N.E., 733-4570; at the **Goethe-Institut Atlanta**, Colony Square, 892-2388; and at other libraries, colleges and universities around Atlanta. To see what's playing where, check the "Alternative" listing in Rob. Walton's "Short Subjectives" capsule reviews in the free weekly *Creative Loafing*.

And on about a dozen nights between June and September, the **Fox Theatre's** summer film series lets you revel in the experience of seeing a movie in the lush, exotic environment of an authentic movie palace. The series shows a mix of current and classic films. Doors open at 6:45 PM; the sing-along with the Mighty Moeller organ begins at 7:20 PM; and a cartoon precedes the main feature, which begins at 8 PM. Leaving the humidity and heat outside and luxuriating in the Fox's cool darkness is the perfect way to enjoy a sultry Atlanta night.

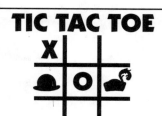

Inside
Shopping

A transportation hub from its beginning, Atlanta naturally became a retail center as well. Just two years after the Civil War, more than 250 stores were wheeling and dealing in Atlanta. (Remember all the money Scarlett O'Hara and her second husband Frank Kennedy made with their store and lumberyard during Reconstruction?)

Today Atlanta is a booming retail market with amazing extremes. Here you can shop Saks, Tiffany & Co., Gucci, Cartier and Neiman Marcus in megamalls that have become tourist attractions in themselves. Just a few rail stops away, you may find vendors selling obviously fake designer goods for a tiny fraction of the original's cost. And on every weekend with halfway decent weather, you'll find streets full of yard sales around town — there's always lots of moving going on around the first of the month.

Here's a quick trip through some of Atlanta's best-known retail centers and some lesser-known ones too. We'll start our trip at the city's three most famous malls: Lenox Square, Phipps Plaza and Underground Atlanta.

Malls

Atlanta

LENOX SQUARE
3393 Peachtree Rd. N.E.
at Lenox Rd.   233-6767
Atlanta's first large suburban shopping center opened in 1959 with 52 stores and 665,000 square feet. Buckhead was still on the fringes of Atlanta, and Atlantans were stunned at the $32 million cost of the new shopping center. The shopping center was enclosed and expanded in 1972 and expanded again in 1987; its food court was expanded in 1993.

Today, at 1.4 million square feet, Lenox is the largest mall in Atlanta. It has 200 stores, attracts 14 million visitors annually, and its rate of sales per square foot is among the highest of all U.S. shopping centers. And, naturally, it's under renovation again: A $60 million expansion, to be completed before the 1995 holiday season, will increase its size to 1.5 million square feet.

Macy's, Neiman Marcus and Rich's anchor the 61-acre mall; other shops include Louis Vuitton, Cartier, Warner Bros., Disney, Metropolitan Museum of Art and Snooty Hooty, where celebrities shop for exotic outfits. There are acres of free parking, or you can take the train to the Lenox MARTA station. Opposite the station is the J.W. Marriott Hotel; adjacent to it, the Lenox Building has an enclosed passageway leading directly to the mall.

PHIPPS PLAZA
3500 Peachtree Rd.
at Lenox Rd.   262-0992
Diagonally across Peachtree from Lenox Square, Phipps Plaza is devoted strictly to upscale stores. When it opened in 1969, Phipps was the first two-story mall in the Southeast. A $140 million renovation in 1992 added a new three-level wing

and Parisian (an Alabama-based department store), which joined existing anchors Lord & Taylor and Saks Fifth Avenue. Other shops of note include the amazingly designed, 24,000-square-foot Nike Town and the only Atlanta locations of Tiffany & Co. and Gucci. The mall also has a 12-screen movie theater.

Like its older neighbor across the street, Phipps just can't stop growing. A massive expansion scheduled for completion before the '96 Olympics will bring its total size to almost 1.4 million square feet, adding prestigious Bloomingdale's and 130 new specialty shops.

UNDERGROUND ATLANTA
Peachtree at Alabama   *523-2311*

Underground Atlanta evolved as a curious byproduct of the city's growth. By 1890, more than 100 trains a day were passing through the downtown depot. Temporary iron bridges were built across the tracks to alleviate traffic congestion; then, in the 1920s, a permanent concrete viaduct was added, and the street was elevated. Businesses on old Alabama Street relocated upward to new Alabama Street, and the old storefronts sat abandoned below the street until they were developed as a retail and entertainment center in 1969.

Throughout most of the 1970s, Underground boomed as a rowdy party spot that was a favorite of locals and tourists. But after it lost about half its space to MARTA construction and the perception of crime became a problem, the old Underground closed in 1981.

Redeveloped as a public/private venture, the new Underground opened in 1989 and is almost three times the size of its predecessor. Shops and vendor carts line both subterranean Lower Alabama Street and the above-ground pedestrian-only Upper Alabama Street. Shops of note include Everything's a Dollar, Eddie Bauer, Doubleday Books, The Gap, Limited Express, Victoria's Secret and Warner Bros. The food court has a good mix of ethnic and fast food. The open-air Kenny's Alley is a courtyard of bars and restaurants. Heritage Row is a chronological documentary of Atlanta's history from past to present, and the Olympic Experience honors the '96 Olympics.

The entrance to the Underground parking decks is on M.L. King Jr. Drive (one-way, westbound); there are other decks in the area, as well. Or take MARTA to the Five Points station and enter through the pedestrian tunnel under Peachtree; it's on your right just before you exit the station.

CNN CENTER
Marietta St. at Techwood Dr.   *827-2491*

CNN Center includes the Omni Hotel and the studios and world headquarters of the Cable News Network. It offers fine dining (the hotel's Bugatti), fast food and a variety of Atlanta-themed gifts (The Atlanta Store, Braves Clubhouse Store and The Turner Store).

You can take a 45-minute tour of the CNN headquarters between 9 AM and 5 PM, seven days a week. Space is limited, and tours sometimes sell out in advance. Admission is $6 for adults, $4 for seniors and $3.50 for kids; call 827-2300 for information and reservations. You can also reserve a seat in the audience of CNN's interactive show *TalkBack Live*: call (800) 410-4CNN.

CUMBERLAND MALL
Intersection of I-285, I-75 and Cobb Pkwy.
Cobb County   *435-2206*

The 1.2 million-square-foot Cumberland Mall was renovated in 1989;

its anchors are Rich's, Macy's, Sears and JCPenney. The food court offers an array of choices, including the popular Atlanta-based restaurant Mick's.

GALLERIA SPECIALTY MALL
One Galleria Pkwy., I-75 at I-285
Cobb County   955-9100
The Cobb Galleria Centre complex includes a 108,000-square-foot exhibition hall, the Stouffer Waverly Hotel and the Galleria Specialty Mall, which has 32 unique, owner-operated stores and an eight-screen theater.

GREENBRIAR MALL
2841 Greenbriar Pkwy. S.W.
I-285 at Lakewood Fwy.   344-6611
Another one of Atlanta's first malls, Greenbriar opened in August 1965. Its 678,000 square feet include Rich's, Circuit City, 50 Off, Woolworth and Cub Foods, plus a big selection of stores carrying Afrocentric fashions and accessories for the home.

THE MALL AT PEACHTREE CENTER
Peachtree St. at International Blvd.   614-5000
This is the retail component of the huge Peachtree Center complex designed by famed Atlanta architect John Portman. The Mall is connected by pedestrian bridges to many downtown buildings, including the Marriott Marquis, Hyatt Regency, Westin Peachtree Plaza and Apparel and Merchandise Marts. Its 75 businesses include elegant restaurants and fast food places, plus apparel (including Brooks Brothers and Muse's) and services (Continental Styles hair salon). Peachtree Center is served by the Peachtree Center MARTA station.

MARKETSQUARE AT NORTH DEKALB
Lawrenceville Hwy. at N. Druid Hills Rd.
I-285 at Decatur Exit   320-7960
One of Atlanta's first malls (it opened in 1965), Market Square was renovated in 1986. Its 650,657 square feet include Mervyn's, Rich's and Stein Mart.

NORTHLAKE MALL
4800 Briarcliff Rd.
I-285 at LaVista Rd., Exit 28   938-3564
Northlake has 125 specialty stores, along with Sears, Macy's, JCPenney and Parisian.

At nearby Northlake Tower Festival (3983 LaVista) are numerous "superstores," such as PetSmart and Toys 'R' Us.

Come Play With Us!

Gainesville Hall- The *heart* of Northeast Georgia

GAINESVILLE HALL COUNTY, GA
Convention & Visitors' Bureau

Gainesville Hall County Convention and Visitors Bureau
830 Green Street
Gainesville, GA 30501
(404) 536-5209
Ext. 1230

• 45 minutes NE of Atlanta • Relaxed Southern charm • Appalachian Mountain folklore • Sailing, fishing, boating, swimming and more on Lake Sydney Lanier and Lake Lanier Islands • Nature galore: Waterfalls, hiking paths, camping • Elachee Nature Center • Motor Sports at Road Atlanta and Lanier Raceway • History: General Longstreet, Beulah Rucker, Chief Whitepath Cabin, antiques, and the Nations 1st Gold Rush

RIO SHOPPING CENTER

Corner of Piedmont and North Ave. 874-6688

This is easily the most unusual shopping center in Atlanta. Miami-inspired Rio's centerpiece — a huge geodesic dome made of tubular metal — sits in the middle of a pool surrounded by giant gold-painted frogs. Rio has a variety of specialty tenants: These include **Tic-Tac-Toe**, which sells men's and women's hats and unique T-shirts, 888-0118; **Blue Moon at Rio**, which offers original black art and fine home accessories, 874-1855; the popular Crab House Restaurant, 872-0011; and **The 3rd Act** musical revue dinner theater, 897-3404.

Beyond Atlanta

Cobb

TOWN CENTER AT COBB

I-75 at Exit 116, Kennesaw   424-9486

Opened in 1986 and expanded in 1992, this 1.2 million-square-foot mall has 200 stores including Macy's, Mervyn's, Parisian, Rich's and Sears.

DeKalb

PERIMETER MALL

4400 Ashford Dunwoody Rd., I-285 at Exit 21 Ga. 400 at Exit 5   394-4270

Perimeter Mall opened in 1971, expanded in 1982 and was renovated in 1993. Sitting just outside I-285, the 1.2 million-square-foot mall is the nerve-center of the hyper-developed, always busy northeast Perimeter sector. Its anchors are JCPenney, Macy's, Rich's and Rich's main furniture showroom.

Just across Ashford Dunwoody is Perimeter Expo, which includes Home Depot's upscale Expo Design Center and Best Buy, a large discounter of electronics, appliances and CDs.

Fulton

NORTH POINT MALL

1000 North Point Cr., east of Ga. 400 between Mansell and Haynes Bridge Rds.   740-9273

Opened in 1993, the 1.1 million-square-foot North Point features JCPenney, Lord & Taylor, Mervyn's, Rich's and Sears. Average household income in its affluent trading area is $72,000. The food court has 15 restaurants and an outdoor patio. In a huge glass atrium beside the food court is a 30-foot-high carousel that accommodates 38 riders; rides are $1 per person.

SHANNON SOUTHPARK MALL

I-85 at Exit 13, Union City   964-2200

Shannon opened in 1980 and expanded in 1986. Its 770,651 square feet comprise 110 stores including anchors Macy's, Mervyn's, Rich's and Sears.

Gwinnett

GWINNETTPLACE

I-85 at Exit 40
Gwinnett County   476-5160

This 1.2 million-square-foot mall opened in 1984 and expanded in 1993. It has 220 shops and the department stores Macy's, Mervyn's, Parisian, Rich's and Sears.

The surrounding streets are a favorite stop for car buyers: Most of the major car-makers have dealerships in this area, which is known as "Motor Mile."

Clayton

SOUTHLAKE MALL

I-75 at Hwy. 54, Morrow   961-1050

On 88 acres south of town, one million-square-foot Southlake Mall includes JCPenney, Macy's, Rich's, Sears and some 120 shops. Southlake, which opened in

1976, annually welcomes more than 11 million shoppers.

Outlet Shopping

Atlanta

MCO (MACY'S CLOSE-OUT)

Avondale Mall, Memorial at Columbia Drs.
Decatur   286-0829

This is where much unsold Macy's merchandise ends up. Goods come in marked at 40 percent off the retail price, and additional markdowns are taken later. You can get some terrific bargains here, but all sales are absolutely final, so examine everything carefully before you buy. This store is packed on the weekend; the best times to shop are days and evenings during the week.

OUTLET SQUARE MALL

4166 Buford Hwy. at Clairmont Rd.   633-2566

This 303,000-square-foot mall is anchored by Marshall's and Burlington Coat Factory and has 40 additional shops. Despite of its name, it's more of an off-price retail clearance mall than a traditional manufacturer's outlet center.

Beyond Atlanta

CALHOUN OUTLET CENTER

455 Bellwood Rd., I-75 to Exit 129
Calhoun   (706)602-1300

This center is closer to Chattanooga than Atlanta, but its 33 shops include outlets for Anne Klein, Nike, Adolfo II and Cape Isle Knitters.

TANGER FACTORY OUTLET CENTER

I-85 to Exit 53, Hwy. 441
Commerce   (706)335-4537

About an hour north of Atlanta, this

LITTLE FIVE POINTS

center has 44 shops and promises savings of up to 70 percent off retail. Among others, you'll find Geoffrey Beene, Bass, Liz Claiborne, Reebok and London Fog factory stores. It's open seven days, year round.

Shopping Districts

Atlanta

Five Points/Downtown

In downtown Atlanta, as in many other cities, much of the high-end retail long ago made for the malls. The days when polite Southern ladies met for lunch at the Magnolia Room are no more; Rich's famous flagship store closed in 1991, and much of it has since been demolished.

But downtown still has its charms. The big Macy's store, 180 Peachtree, 221-7221, opened in 1927; its tall, chandelier-lit main floor recalls the glory days of elegant department store shopping. Underground Atlanta (see listing under malls) offers gifts at nearly every price level, beginning with the always-lively Everything's A Dollar store. At the east end of Underground, the World of Coca-Cola has a shop filled with Coke-theme gifts, 676-5151; there's no admission charge to visit the store.

Downtown's most unusual and fun stores are south of Five Points. The Five Points Flea Market, 82 Peachtree S.W., 681-9439, is a bazaar of designer-lookalike T-shirts, gold-tone jewelry and cheap sunglasses. Scope out the bargains at Kesslers Department Store, 87 Peachtree S.W., 525-8594; pick up that new costume or disguise at Sun Wigs, 69-B Peachtree Street S.W., 522-0510;

buy some flashy trinkets at Atlanta Gift and Novelty, 80 Peachtree Street S.W., 524-7200; and, for good luck, swing by Rondo, 171 Mitchell Street S.W., 522-4379, and get a "Money-Drawing" or "Law Stay Away" prayer candle. For a few cents extra, the clerk will "dress" it, sprinkling your candle with glitter and a fragrant, dark green oil. And, for a perfectly charming old-fashion downtown lunch, stop into Tasty Town Grill, 67 Forsyth Street N.W., 522-8565.

Especially during the day, downtown is relatively safe; but use the same precautions you would in any large city. Watch your belongings, and don't talk to strangers.

Little Five Points

The area around the intersection of Moreland, Euclid and McLendon avenues is Little Five Points. It's rather like Atlanta's answer to New York's East Village: hip, funky and artistic. The district's many old storefronts make it a favorite location site for movies and TV: Most memorably, this was where Morgan Freeman drove Jessica Tandy to the store in Driving Miss Daisy. The part of the Piggly-Wiggly was portrayed by Sevananda Natural Foods Community-Owned Grocery, 1111 Euclid, 681-2831. Other fun stores include: Wish, high-style hip-hop wear, 447 Moreland, 880-0402; Throb, shiny clubwear and accessories, 1140 Euclid, 522-0355; Boomerang, terrific '50s- and '60s-style furniture, 1145 Euclid, 577-8158, and Junkman's Daughter, new and used clubwear and novelties, 464 Moreland, 577-3188. Little Five is served by the Inman Park/Reynoldstown MARTA station. From the station walk

north on Hurt, then right on Euclid (about six blocks); or take the 48 Lenox bus.

Buckhead

Buckhead retailing is dominated by the huge malls Lenox Square and Phipps Plaza, but there are also plenty of small shops with unusual merchandise. The heart of Buckhead is the intersection of Peachtree and Roswell roads, but the district covers a big area. A few of the shops in Buckhead include: **Axis Twenty**, 200 Peachtree Hills Avenue, 261-4022, selling 20th-century classic furniture; **Play It Again**, 273 Buckhead Avenue, 261-2135, better secondhand women's apparel; **Laura Ashley Home Store**, 1 West Paces Ferry Road, 842-0102, home furnishings and fabrics; **Beverly Bremer Silver Shop**, 3164 Peachtree Road, 261-4009; **Pepperidge Farm Thrift Store**, 318 Pharr Road, 262-7580; and **Beverly Hall Furniture Galleries**, 2789 Piedmont Road, 261-7580.

Virginia-Highland

You'll see plenty of interesting retail and street life in the Virginia-Highland section. There's a cluster of shops and restaurants on N. Highland Avenue near the intersection of St. Charles Avenue and another half-mile north near the intersection of Virginia Avenue. The last shopping section is at the intersection of N. Highland and Lanier Boulevard, after which the neighborhood is all residential. (By the way, that pleasant street scene on the cover of our book was shot in Virginia-Highland.) Some interesting shops: **20th Century Antiques**, home furnishings, gifts and accessories from around the world, 1044 N. Highland Avenue, 892-2065; **Earth**

Baby, organic cotton clothing for babies and children, wooden toys and rattles and organic baby food, 776-B N. Highland Avenue, 607-1656; **Back to Square One**, antiques, handmade crafts by regional artists for the home and garden, 1054 N. Highland Avenue, 815-9970; **Bang! and Rapture** featuring modern men's and women's apparel, 1039 N. Highland, 873-0444; **Maddix Deluxe** with flowers and gifts, 1034 N. Highland, 892-9337; **Bill Hallman Designs** offering hip clothes for men and women, 876-6055; **The Common Pond**, 1402 N. Highland Avenue, 876-6368, specializing in environmentally friendly gifts for people and their pets (Emily Saliers of Atlanta's own Indigo Girls is an investor in the store).

Amsterdam Avenue

Monroe Drive intersects with Amsterdam Avenue about a half-mile north of the corner of Monroe and Virginia. Turn left; at the end of this dead-end street you'll find an eclectic mix of off-price and specialty shops, including **Shoemaker's Warehouse**, 881-9301; **Malepak**, 892-8004, with bodybuilder wear; and **Let The Music Play**, 892-6700, a mecca for nightclub DJs.

Buford Highway

Thanks to a large concentration of apartment complexes, Buford Highway is home to many international Atlantans, especially people from Central and South America and Asia. The stretch of Buford Highway between Shallowford Road and the Perimeter has dozens of Asian stores, restaurants and service companies. **Koreatown Shopping Center**, 5302

Buford Highway, is home to **Yen Jing**, 454-6688, a good Chinese restaurant. In **Asian Square Shopping Center**, 5150 Buford Highway, the major tenant is **99 Ranch Market**, 458-8899, a full-size supermarket packed with amazing Asian products.

Chattahoochee Avenue Warehouse Shopping District

On the west side of town off Howell Mill Road, bargains abound in the Chattahoochee Avenue warehouse shopping district. **Freedman Shoes**, 1240 Chattahoochee Avenue, 355-9009, offers discounts on name-brand men's shoes. **LoLo**, 935-D Chatahoochee Avenue, 352-9355, discounts women's apparel. **AJS Shoe Warehouse**, 1788 Ellsworth Industrial Boulevard, 355-1760, offers deals on women's shoes, handbags and accessories. **K&G Men's Center**, 1750-A Ellsworth Industrial Boulevard, 352-3527, discounts men's wear.

Beyond Atlanta

Stone Mountain

EAGLE'S NEST GIFTS
994 Main St.   *498-9078*

In a house built in 1847, this shop offers a variety of unusual gifts and collectibles. You'll find Baldwin brass candle holders, designer baskets of willow and pine and handmade treasure boxes from Vintage Lumber made by Georgia artisans. Eagle's Nest has plenty of hand-carved miniatures, leaded glass crystal, antique furnishings, Georgia honey and peach spreads. It's closed on Mondays January through March.

GRANDMA'S STUFF
994 Main St.   *498-9078*

This charming shop, situated in the Eagle's Nest (described previously), is chock-full of affordable country and primitive antiques. The owner chooses each piece personally and in most cases can provide buyers with detailed background information on the store's wide array of accessories and small furniture pieces. Unusual quilts, one-drawer stands and wooden boxes are among the finds here. This shop is closed on Mondays from January through March.

STONES
955 Main St.   *469-5536*

With an array of semiprecious stones, this store offers several ways to adorn yourself. You can make your own jewelry from loose beads. Choose from the pieces on display, or let the owners do the work on a custom-designed pin or pair of earrings. Repair services and jewelry classes are offered.

KELLY KAYE'S OF STONE MOUNTAIN
913-C Main St.   *469-0779*

Choose from around 400 handbags and travel cases made of 100-percent leather. The items originate in Mexico and sell in the $20 range. Souvenir T-shirts, other apparel, costume jewelry, sunglasses, umbrellas and more complete the wares.

COUNTRY MANOR
933 Main St.   *498-0628*

Very traditional Southern antiques and decorative pieces abound here. Among them are local folk art pieces, such as bird houses and wood carvings. Gift items include Rowe pottery, hand-carved wooden decoys and Bob Timberlake furniture and accessories.

One of the first antique malls in the city. A cluster of unique shops located on an oak covered hill offering a skyline view of Atlanta.

Hawthorne Village Gallery & Design Center
Hawthorne Village Book Shop
Make It Lovely • Make It Lovely Blue Bird Tea Room
As Time Goes By • The Old Village Custom Frame Shop
Hawthorne's House of the Arts

3032 N. Decatur Road   Scottdale, GA 30079 • 404-294-4585

MAXWELL'S
5367-A E. Mountain St.   879-4797

Collectibles, gourmet specialties, gift items and greeting cards comprise the unique merchandise in Maxwell's two locations. One popular feature is the very large selection of seasonally oriented decorations. You'll find many items for the garden, such as wind chimes, bird feeders and statuary. For collectors, the store carries a significant selection of Precious Moments, Harbor Light and Department 56. Angel-motif gifts include everything from lapel pins to figurines. A second store is at 1715 Howell Mill Road, 351-3931.

Antiques, Decorator Items and Flea Markets

In addition to dozens of yard and estate sales nearly every weekend, Atlanta has several antique shopping districts and large flea markets. Prices at these establishments range from rock-bottom to sky-high. In many antique shops the price tag is just a starting point for negotiations; if you like to bargain hard, you may save big bucks. Use your common sense at the flea markets: We hope you're not too shocked to learn that those red vinyl bags on sale for $10 are not real Chanel — even though they are crudely stitched with the famous double-C logo.

Atlanta

ATLANTA ANTIQUE CENTER & FLEA MARKET
5360 Peachtree Industrial Blvd.
1.5 miles inside the Perimeter, Exit 23458-0456

Open every weekend with free parking and admission, this 80,000-square-foot market features more than 150 dealers.

ATLANTA SWAP MEET AND FLEA MARKET
3265 N.E. Expressway Access Rd.
Chamblee   451-4570, 233-3889

Every Saturday and Sunday of the year, the North 85 Twin Drive-In hosts this popular market where bargains abound. The drive-in is 2 miles inside the Perimeter on the one-way access road between Shallowford and Chamblee-Tucker roads; from Atlanta, exit at Shallowford. Park alongside the access road; admission is free. The market opens at 8:30 AM on Saturday and 6 AM on Sunday.

BARGAINATA

791 Miami Cr.   *262-7199*

This big sale comes only once a year (around the second week in November) and lasts just five days, but it always causes quite a stir. Bargainata, which marked its 25th year in 1994, is a secondhand clothing sale held by the National Council of Jewish Women. The sale starts with designer and other fine apparel priced low; by the last day, the remaining merchandise is sold off at an additional 50-percent discount.

BENNETT STREET

Three blocks north of Piedmont Hospital on the west side of Peachtree, little Bennett Street is home to a large selection of antique and decorative art dealers. These are not junk shops; most of the merchandise here is of the "better" category, and the prices reflect this. If you're looking for fine antiques, you'll find them here. Near the end of Bennett Street is the TULA complex of showrooms and galleries (see TULA's listing under Galleries in The Arts chapter).

BUFORD HIGHWAY FLEA MARKET

5000 Buford Hwy.   *452-7140*

This market features lots of designer-look goods, Atlanta souvenirs and flashy home accessories. It's open Friday, Saturday and Sunday.

CHESHIRE BRIDGE ROAD

On Cheshire Bridge Road between Piedmont and LaVista, numerous antique dealers are scattered among the restaurants, bars and "lingerie modeling" businesses. The larger antique shops rent out spaces to dealers, who always seem to be moving in or out. Competition for customers (and dealers) is keen. Expect to save at least 10 percent off the asking price unless an item is already marked down. Worth noting: **A Cherub's Attic**, 2179 Cheshire Bridge Road, 634-9577; **Milou's Market**, 1927 Cheshire Bridge Road, 892-8296; and **Cache Antiques**, 1845-47 Cheshire Bridge Road, 872-0095.

GOLD'S ANTIQUES AND AUCTION GALLERY

1149 Lee St.   *753-1493*

Gold's presents a variety of antiques Monday through Saturday. It holds an auction at 6 PM every Tuesday night.

GREAT GATSBY'S

2 miles inside I-285
5070 Peachtree Industrial Blvd.   *457-1905*

This 100,000-square-foot "wholesale to the public" market is one of Atlanta's most fun stores. You can spend hours ogling everything from exquisite antiques to kitschy advertising memorabilia to huge architectural fragments. Gatsby's supplies hotels worldwide with unusual furnishings; a guitar that had belonged to John Lennon was once sold here at auction.

HISTORIC HAWTHORNE VILLAGE ANTIQUES AND GIFTS

3032 N. Decatur Rd.
Scottdale   *294-4585*

Just east of Decatur and inside I-285, this is a sort of mini-mall of antiques and collectibles. In addition to the main cottage store, seven shops offer their own unusual and interesting goods. The merchandise includes antique prints, framed artwork, furniture, glassware, silver, gifts, jewelry and Civil War memorabilia and books. From time to time, the village delights children by staging a Victorian tea party with teddy bears.

Rich's

Founded just two years after the Civil War, Rich's Department Stores' history is inextricably tied to the history of Atlanta. The company began in 1867, when Morris Rich borrowed $500 from his brother William to open a dry goods store on Whitehall Street. By 1948, the store, which had relocated in 1924 to 45 Broad Street, occupied two downtown

Photo: Chuck Morgan

Rich's Department Store was founded two years after the Civil War.

blocks, with the buildings connected by a four-story glass bridge.

From 1948 until 1990, thousands of Atlantans concluded their Thanksgiving Day festivities by gathering in the chill to sing Christmas carols while awaiting the lighting of Rich's Great Tree, which stood majestically atop the bridge. Nearby on the store's rooftop, a miniature monorail with pig-shaped cars delighted children throughout the holidays. Those "I Rode The Pink Pig At Rich's" stickers were cherished souvenirs.

In 1959, Rich's began its suburban store expansion by opening a store at Lenox Square, Atlanta's first suburban shopping center. The first Rich's stores in malls opened at Greenbriar and North DeKalb malls in 1965. More stores followed in Atlanta and Augusta and in Alabama and South Carolina. Rich's was sold to Federated Department stores in 1976. After being acquired by Campeau Corp. in 1988, Federated declared bankruptcy in 1990. Rich's historic downtown store, which had been completely renovated in 1987, was closed in 1991, and much of it was imploded in 1994.

But the lighting of Rich's Great Tree still takes place before thousands of people downtown on Thanksgiving night; now it stands atop Underground Atlanta. The Pink Pig was donated to Egleston Children's Hospital's annual Festival of Trees fund-raiser, where it continues to enchant children.

Since 1957, Rich's Fashionata fall fashion preview has raised hundreds of thousands of dollars for nonprofit organizations. Rich's parent company Federated emerged from bankruptcy in 1992. And, with 12 department stores and more than 7,000 employees in the Atlanta area, Rich's remains very much a part of Atlanta's life.

LAKEWOOD ANTIQUES MARKET
2000 Lakewood Ave. S.W.   622-4488

This popular market is held on the second weekend of each month and features thousands of unusual antiques and collectibles. Parking is free; admission is $3 for adults and free for children. The market is held Friday, Saturday and Sunday, but there's a special early buyers' day on Thursday, when admission is $5. Take I-75/85 south from downtown; exit at Lakewood Freeway East and follow the signs.

MIAMI CIRCLE

This short street is full of antique and decorator merchandise. As you drive north on Piedmont, Miami Circle is on your right; it's north of the Lindbergh MARTA station and just past the Cub Foods shopping center. Shops of note include: **Bobby Dobb Antiques & Kilims,** 231-0580 and **Hilderbrand & Star Antiques,** 814-0692.

THE WRECKING BAR

292 Moreland Ave. N.E.   525-0468

On Moreland, just south of the Little Five Points intersection, The Wrecking Bar sells architectural art and antiques, from hardware and chandeliers to large mantles and statuary. The store occupies an 1895 mansion listed on the National Register for Historic Places.

Beyond Atlanta

GWINNETT FLEA MARKET

5675 Jimmy Carter Blvd.
Norcross   449-8189

This big flea market is open daily, except Monday and Tuesday, from 11 AM to 8 PM. From Atlanta, take I-85 N. to Jimmy Carter Boulevard; exit and turn left; the market will be on your right.

LAMPS N THINGS

1205 Johnson Ferry Rd. N.E.
Marietta   971-0874

In the Woodlawn Square Shopping Center, this 3,800-square-foot store offers thousands of lamp shades, plus lamps, mirrors, art, antiques and other home accessories. The store's personnel will also custom-make shades and lamps for indi-

viduals and decorators. Lamp repair services are offered.

PRIDE OF DIXIE ANTIQUE MARKET

1700 Jeurgens Ct., Norcross   279-9853

Held monthly on the fourth weekend, this market hosts some 800 vendors. It's held in the North Atlanta Trade Center in Norcross. Take I-85 to Exit 38; east on Indian Trail; right on Oakbrook Parkway; right on Jeurgens Court. The $3 admission is good for Friday, Saturday and Sunday; parking is free.

Thrift Stores

Confirmed thrift store shoppers know that little islands of great value can sometimes be found amid the oceans of junk in Atlanta's thrift stores. If you're of an adventurous mind, you might discover an elegant outfit — or at least maybe your next Halloween get-up. Large thrift stores typically don't have dressing rooms, but you can still try before you buy if you dress appropriately. If you wear close-fitting shorts, a T-shirt and loafers you can easily kick off, you can try on your new outfit right in the store. Believe us, in these no-frills stores, no one will even notice. We've described some of the major thrifts; see the Yellow Pages for the location nearest you.

Atlanta

AMVETS

3651 Memorial Dr.
Decatur   286-1083

The early bird gets the best junk: Experienced bargain hunters hit the yard sales and flea markets early, before everything gets picked over.

Insiders' Tips

GOODWILL INDUSTRIES
2201 Glenwood Ave., plus nine other locations
373-5815

JUNIOR LEAGUE OF ATLANTA
2581 Piedmont at Sidney Marcus Blvd.
233-6639

SALVATION ARMY
740 Marietta St. N.W., plus five other locations
523-6214

ST. VINCENT DE PAUL
3660 Clairmont Rd., plus five other locations
457-9648

THRIFT HOUSE OF THE
CATHEDRAL OF ST. PHILIP
2581 Piedmont at Sidney Marcus Blvd.
233-8652

UNIQUE THRIFT STORE
3655 Memorial Dr., Decatur   286-9526

VALUE VILLAGE
1320 Moreland Ave., plus five other locations
416-1110

Vintage

Vintage wear is a step-up from thrift store goods in quality and price. Some clothing that starts out in thrift stores winds up cleaned, pressed and marked-up in the vintage shops. Still, because the thrifts can be downright grungy, many people who can afford to prefer to shop the vintage stores, which are generally cleaner, take credit cards and have dressing rooms.

Atlanta

FROCK OF AGES
1653 McLendon Ave. N.E.   370-1006

CLOTHING WAREHOUSE
Toco Hills Shopping Center   248-1224
1146 Euclid Ave.   524-5070

DAYS GONE BY
1150 Euclid Ave. N.E.   523-8478

JUNKMAN'S DAUGHTER
464 Moreland Ave.   577-3188

STEFAN'S
1160 Euclid Ave. N.E.   688-4929

Costumes

Whether you're impersonating a pope or a pirate, a belle or a baboon, you'll find just the right disguise at an Atlanta costume shop. These stores are busiest in October; don't wait until the day before Halloween to make your selection.

Atlanta

ABBEY PARTY RENTALS
670 14th St. N.W.   873-0833

ATLANTA COSTUME
2089 Monroe Dr. N.E.   874-7511

COSTUMES ETC.
3224 Peachtree Rd. N.E.   239-9422

EDDIE'S TRICK & NOVELTY
3665 Roswell Rd. N.E., plus two more locations
264-0527

Farmers Markets

Atlanta

DeKalb Farmers Market, 3000 E. Ponce de Leon Avenue, Decatur, 377-6400, is a big, bustling, truly international food market. Employees come from every corner of the globe and wear badges listing the languages they speak. This market is sometimes affectionately described as a less-yuppified version of Harry's (see later entry). This is real mar-

ket shopping; don't take it personally if someone bumps into your cart.

International Farmers Market, 5193 Peachtree Industrial Boulevard at Chamblee-Tucker Road, 455-1777, offers fresh fruits and vegetables and meats and cheeses; spices are sold in bulk. **Harry's in a Hurry** is a gourmet takeout shop that's the answer to an overworked cook's prayers, 1875 Peachtree Road, 352-7800.

Beyond Atlanta

Atlanta State Farmers Market, Exit 78 off I-75, 16 Forest Parkway, Forest Park, 366-6910, a 146-acre open-air retail and wholesale market claims the distinction of being the largest in the Southeast and one of the largest in the world. It's open to the public round-the-clock every day except Christmas. More than 7,000 people visit the market each day. Inside the fenced compound, you drive your car around to visit vendors of everything from fresh produce to homemade preserves to Christmas trees during the holidays.

Harry's Farmers Markets are a gourmand's dream-come-true, filled with delicacies from around the world. From the commonplace to the exotic, including fish, cheese, wine, flowers, coffee and gourmet meals to-go, at Harry's you can eat well and grow large. You'll find three locations: 2025 Satellite Parkway, Duluth, 416-6900; 1180 Upper Hembree Road, Alpharetta, 664-6300; and 70 Powers Ferry Road, Marietta, 578-4400.

Books and Periodicals

Atlanta

Oxford Book Store, 360 Pharr Road, 262-3333, is Atlanta's premier book retailer, with more than 140,000 titles in computerized inventory. An array of out-of-town newspapers, international magazines, sheet music, CDs, videos and more are all available, along with coffee and a knowledgeable, book-loving staff. Big-name authors on autograph tours are a regular feature at Oxford; fans show up for hours in advance of signings to get a good place in line. The 30,000-square-foot main store is busy just about any time you come here; there are three additional stores; all are open 365 days a year. Oxford stores discount *The New York Times* bestselling hardbacks 30 percent every day. Outside Atlanta, call Oxford's nationwide customer service line, (800)476-3311.

Barnes & Noble, 2900 Peachtree Road N.W., 261-7747, is still new on the Atlanta book scene. Here you'll find books, magazines, CDs and hot coffee in a roomy store that's easy to shop. There are two additional Atlanta locations.

Borders Book Shop at the corner of Roswell and Piedmont in Buckhead, 633-1328, is a large store with more than 83,000 titles and lots of newspapers and magazines.

At the Ansley Mall, Monroe at Piedmont, **Chapter 11 Discount Books**, 872-7896, knocks 30 percent off *The New York*

Times bestsellers every day. There are six more Atlanta locations.

Tall Tales, 2999 N. Druid Hills Road in Toco Hills Shopping Center, 636-2498, is a full-service independent book store. Customer service is the specialty here: Special-order books can often be delivered the very next day. The store will also search for out-of-print books. The highly literate staff will gladly help you make your selections.

Book Nook, 3342 Clairmont Road N.E., 633-1328, sells new and used books, records, comics and CDs.

Here are some special-interest book shops:

Inside the Cyclorama in Grant Park, the **Eastern National Park & Monument Association Book Store,** 622-6264, is a small shop with a fine collection of Civil War books and maps.

Old New York Book Shop, 1069 Juniper Street N.E., 881-1285, sells used books and also carries some rare volumes.

Religious books and gifts are for sale at the bookstore in the **Episcopal Cathedral of St. Philip,** 2744 Peachtree Road N.W., 237-7582.

St. Mary's Bookstore & Church Supply, 2140 Peachtree Road N.W., 351-2865, sells religious books and materials of special interest to Catholics.

Presbyterian Book Store of Atlanta, 1455 Tullie Road N.E., 728-9985, carries Bibles, devotionals and other religious items.

Cokesbury Books and Church Supplies, 2495 Lawrenceville Highway, Decatur, 320-1034, sells religious books and other materials. It's affiliated with the United Methodist Church.

Iwase in the Around Lenox Shopping Center, 814-0462, has thousands of Japanese-language books and periodicals.

The Civilized Traveller, Phipps Plaza, 264-1252, offers a big selection of travel books and tour guides, plus luggage, binoculars and other travel accessories.

In Little Five Points, **Charis Books,** 1189 Euclid Avenue, 524-0304, is a pleasant store selling feminist books and music and children's books.

Outwrite, 607-0082, is in the Winn-Dixie shopping center at the corner of Virginia and Monroe in Midtown. Outwrite sells gay and lesbian books, magazines and cards and coffee.

Brushstrokes, 876-6567, in the Ansley Square Shopping Center just south of the intersection of Piedmont and Monroe, is a popular stop for gay and lesbian magazines and gifts.

In the same shopping center, **The Sphinx,** 875-2665, is a lovely shop with metaphysical books, statues, incense and music.

On the campus of Atlanta University Center, **Soul Source,** 118 James P. Brawley Drive S.W., 577-1346, offers Afrocentric books and gifts.

In West End, you'll find an excellent source of African-American books for both adults and children at the **Shrine of the Black Madonna,** 946 Ralph David Abernathy Boulevard, 752-2165.

And if you just have to find out whodunit — or you think you already know — sleuth on over to the **Science Fiction & Mystery Book Shop,** 2000-F Cheshire Bridge Road in the Cheshire Pointe Shopping Center, 634-3226.

For a truly enjoyable treat, get a copy of *The Booklover's Guide to Atlanta,* by Cal Gough and Celeste Tibbets. These two professional librarians present detailed profiles of bookstores large and small plus specialized information on the library system. The guide is a treasure of little-known facts about Atlanta's literary events and significant literary landmarks. We wonder how many locals know that Atlanta has a reproduction of poet Robert Burns' birthplace in Alloway Scotland. There's even a section on favorite outdoor spots for reading. The softcover book sells for $5 at Oxford Books and Border Books Shop. If you don't find it, ask the store to order it or call the authors directly, 377-0476.

Beyond Atlanta

Greater Atlanta Christian Bookstore, 1575 Indian Trail-Lilburn Road N.W., Norcross, 923-9285, has a big selection of Christian books, music, gifts and cards. It's on the campus of the Greater Atlanta Christian School.

Music

Atlanta

Blockbuster Music, formerly Turtles, is the dominant music chain in Atlanta, with 65 metro locations. The largest store is at 2099 Peachtree Road, 605-7131, just opposite the entrance to Bennett Street. Following are some other Atlanta record retailers.

In Lenox Shopping Center next door to Lenox Square, **Tower Records**, 264-1217, is a music superstore with a large separate classical room, thousands of books and magazines and sing-along tapes for karaoke. Pick up the slick, informative free magazines *Pulse!* and *Classical Pulse!* There's a second location in the GwinnettPlace Mall area at 2330 Pleasant Hill Road, 623-6688.

Following are some other record stores of note:

Wax 'n' Facts, 432 Moreland Avenue N.E., 525-2275, sells new and used records, CDs and tapes and band T-shirts. The new music in this Little Five Points shop tends toward underground; the used stuff is all over the charts. A bit of trivia: Back in the '70s, the owner's independent record label released the first single by the B-52's.

One mile east of Little Five Points, **Full Moon Records**, 1653 McLendon Avenue N.E., 377-1919, buys, sells and trades records, tape and CDs. Full Moon has a big selection of $1 records.

Near Emory University, **Wuxtry**, at the corner of Clairmont and N. Decatur, 329-0020, also sells new and used records, tapes and CDs.

E D's Gourmet Records, 867-1557, in the Ansley Square Shopping Center near Piedmont and Monroe, has the dance hits and is a favorite stop for club DJs.

Earwax Records, 1052 Peachtree Street, N.E., 875-5600, specializes in hip-hop, house and R&B.

Also in Midtown, **Sounds from the Lion's Den**, 699 Ponce de Leon Avenue N.E., in the Kroger shopping center, 607-0608, concentrates on reggae, hip-hop and jazz.

Third World Enterprises, 824 McDonough Boulevard S.E., 627-6176, specializes in African-American music. There are six other Atlanta locations.

Beyond Atlanta

Best Buy, 1450 E. Park Place Boulevard S.W., Stone Mountain, 469-9848, sells home electronics and appliances. The large music department discounts the latest releases and has a selection of discontinued CDs at bargain prices. All six Atlanta area Best Buy stores are outside the Perimeter.

Inside
Attractions

Let the adventures begin! It's safe to say your dilemma will be finding time for the boundless attractions the metro area has waiting for you. Our dilemma was fitting a representative sample into one chapter. The solution was highlighting some favorites that draw visitors year after year.

Some attractions are covered more thoroughly in other chapters and are listed here as a reminder. In these cases, references are given. Don't miss the Fun Freebies section toward the end of the chapter. You'll find lots of inviting destinations in Kidstuff, Daytrips, Recreational Sports, History, The Arts and other chapters. Whatever your activity of choice, it's almost certain Atlanta has what you're seeking. Whether you want high-voltage activity or more laid-back entertainment, jump in and enjoy yourself. An important note: Always call first to verify hours, dates of operation and admission prices. Several attractions plan changes sometime in 1995, with information unavailable prior to publication of this book.

Less than 150 years have passed since Atlanta was first chartered as a city, but those years have been action-packed. Though still young compared to many other U.S. cities, Atlanta has seen a lot of history.

And though we Atlantans are always excited about the new and improved, we also very curious about those places that speak to us about where our city and its people came from. All around the modern metropolis are vivid reminders of other eras with their own triumphs, trag-

edies, heroes and villains. Let's begin our tour of Atlanta's attractions by looking at some of the places where bright glimpses of yesterday can still be seen today.

Historic Sites and Attractions

Atlanta

THE APEX MUSEUM
135 Auburn Ave. N.E.   521-APEX

The APEX, African American Panoramic Experience, Museum is housed in a small building beside the Auburn Avenue Research Library on African-American Culture and History and across the street from the headquarters of Atlanta Life Insurance Co. Eventually, plans call for the museum to have its own specially designed 97,000-square-foot facility on this site; its different sections will spotlight African-American achievement in various areas of endeavor, such as politics, entertainment and sports.

The present facility includes a replica of an Atlanta streetcar where visitors sit to watch a film, with narration by Julian Bond and a dramatic reading by Cicely Tyson, that tells of Auburn Avenue's rich history as a center of black commerce and culture. Exhibits of African and slavery-era artifacts occupy the museum's main room, along with a replica of Yates & Milton, a black-owned drug store that originated on Auburn and eventually had four Atlanta locations. Among other

The Atlanta Cyclorama depicts the 1864 Battle of Atlanta.

items, the gift shop offers a reasonably priced and fascinating pictorial history book, *Sweet Auburn — Street of Pride*, published by the museum. Admission is $3 for adults and $2 for students and seniors.

THE ATLANTA CYCLORAMA
800 Cherokee Ave. S.E. (in Grant Park) 624-1071

At the Atlanta Cyclorama, the scene never changes: It is forever 3:30 on the blistering afternoon of July 22, 1864, and out by the Georgia Railroad line 2 miles east of Five Points, thousands of men are locked in a desperate battle whose outcome will lead to the fall of Atlanta and the Confederacy's defeat.

Housed in a massive, custom-built structure in Grant Park, the Cyclorama is an amazingly vivid re-creation of the Battle of Atlanta. Taller than a five-story building and 358 feet in circumference, the 9,334-pound oil painting on canvas is considered the world's largest and has quite an interesting history.

Huge, round panorama paintings, most often depicting battle scenes, were once a popular form of entertainment.

In 1885, the Milwaukee-based American Panorama Studio brought a team of expert European panorama artists to Atlanta. From a 40-foot observation tower constructed near the present-day intersection of DeKalb and Moreland avenues, the artists surveyed the battlefield, which had changed little in the two decades since the war. During their months of research in Atlanta, the artists sought the war recollections of numerous veterans and citizens.

The artists worked for 22 months in the studio to complete the painting, which was first exhibited in Minneapolis in 1887 and then brought to Atlanta in 1892. Patronage waned by the following year, and the painting was sold at a sheriff's auction for $1,000. It was eventually donated to the City of Atlanta in 1898 and displayed in a wooden building in Grant Park. Fear of fire lead to the construction of the current artificial stone structure, which was dedicated in 1921. A huge central column was both the viewing platform and the roof's support. During the Depression, Works Progress Administration artists crafted the many foreground figures of soldiers, horses and wagons that make the Cyclorama a three-dimensional experience.

By 1979, the deteriorating Cyclorama was attracting more rats than tourists and badly needed extensive repairs. Noted conservator Gustav A. Berger's restoration team undertook the task. But the artists needed access to the fragile painting's back as well as its front, and it could not be removed from its specially designed building. Ingeniously, they removed a section of the structure's wall and hung the painting from an overhead track; this allowed them to rotate various sections into the work area as needed.

The project was not only tedious but downright dangerous, since the canvas had been coated with lead, arsenic and other toxins to repel insects. The diorama figures were restored under the direction of Joseph Hurt, a descendent of Troup Hurt, whose large brick house dominates the painting. The rather odd-looking modern space-frame system that spans the building's roof was necessitated when the load-bearing central column was replaced with a better viewing area. The $11 million restoration was completed in 1982.

Your visit to the Cyclorama begins with a 14-minute film, narrated by James Earl Jones, that features hundreds of costumed Civil War re-enactors. The film recounts Confederate generals Johnston and Hood's increasingly desperate efforts to protect Atlanta from Sherman's advancing troops. The guide then directs everyone upstairs to the Cyclorama. There, surrounded by the battle scene, the audience sits on a tiered viewing platform that slowly revolves as various parts of the painting come alive with computerized narration, light and sound effects.

For the most dramatic experience, skip the Cyclorama's front rows and head up to the back section. These high seats afford a wider view of the entire battle scene and better capture the original panoramic effect. It's fun to bring a pair of binoculars to spot small details in the painting and see where the artists attached the figures to the canvas.

In the Cyclorama's museum are numerous informative displays about the Civil War and the painting itself. A half-hour video explains the tremendous restoration project. The museum also houses the locomotive *Texas*, which was used in the Great Locomotive Chase (see separate listing). It's worth mentioning that the Cyclorama does not espouse the Confederate point of view: It was restored during the tenure of Atlanta's first African-American mayor, Maynard Jackson, and its prevailing mood is anti-war, not pro-South.

The Atlanta Cyclorama is open daily 9:30 AM to 4:30 PM from Labor Day through May 31 and until 5:30 PM during the summer. Presentations begin every 30 minutes throughout the day. Admission is $5 for adults, $4 for senior citizens, $3 for children 6 to 12 and free for children younger than 6. Very small children are likely to find the realistic attraction too frightening.

ATLANTA HERITAGE ROW
THE MUSEUM AT UNDERGROUND
55 Upper Alabama St.   584-7876

This interactive walk-through history museum is on pedestrians-only Upper Alabama Street in Underground Atlanta. The exhibit is presented as a time-line, beginning with Atlanta's earliest days and progressing through the jet age. Operations of the museum have recently been taken over by the Atlanta History Center. The museum was under renovation at this writing, with completion scheduled for late winter 1995. Admission is $2 per person; admission is free for children younger than 6.

ATLANTA HISTORY CENTER
130 W. Paces Ferry Rd. N.W.   814-4000

Why was Atlanta of such strategic value in the Civil War? What was it like to live on a rural farm in the antebellum South or in an opulent Atlanta mansion in the 1930s? And what was a shotgun house, anyway?

You'll find the answers to these and many more questions at the Atlanta Historical Society's Atlanta History Center. The society was formed in 1926; in 1966 it acquired the Edward Inman family's grand Swan House mansion on a 22-acre Buckhead estate. Many improvements were made over the years, culminating with the 1993 opening of the new 83,000-square-foot Atlanta History Museum. The history center is fun as well as educational. Here are a few of its highlights.

Start off at the permanent museum exhibit "Metropolitan Frontiers," a walk-through installation where you can learn about the Native Americans who once called this region home, the arrival of the railroads, Atlanta's destruction and renaissance, and the modern city's achievement of international esteem. In the museum's galleries are large, themed exhibits. Recent major installations have included "The Herndons: Style and Substance of the Black Upper Class in Atlanta 1880-1930" (through August 31, 1995) and "Gone for a Soldier: Transformed by War, 1861-1865" (through December 31, 1995).

Behind the museum is the Tullie Smith Farm, an 1845 house that was moved to the center from its original site on an 800-acre tract near the present-day N. Druid Hills Road and I-85. A cos-tumed guide takes guests through the house and describes the farm family's daily routine. Outside are a separate kitchen, a blacksmith shop and other outbuildings.

Farther south is the Swan House, the elegant 1928 mansion built by cotton magnate Edward Inman and designed by Philip Trammell Shutze. A guide shows visitors through the classically influenced yet personal home, whose futuristic residents insisted on having the recently invented shower instead of an old-fashioned tub in three of their four bathrooms. The Atlanta History Center's distinctive "star" emblem duplicates the pattern on the floor of the Swan House's foyer.

The center also includes the Swan Coach House Restaurant (open for lunch, Monday through Saturday), the Victorian Playhouse for children and 32 acres of botanically labeled gardens. The 3.5-million-item McElreath Hall research facility and archives is free and open to the public (closed Sundays).

The center's regular hours are Monday through Saturday, 10 AM to 5:30 PM and Sunday, noon to 5:30 PM. Admission is $7 for adults, $5 for students older than 18 and seniors, $4 for youths 6 to 17 and free for kids 5 and younger. Add $1 per visit to each of the historic homes.

ATLANTA MUSEUM
537 Peachtree St. N.E.   872-8233

Diversity reigns in this upstairs museum in a Historic Register Victorian home (downstairs is a antique shop). How diverse? You'll find a lock of Napoleon's hair, personal articles that belonged to Adolf Hitler, a rare Japanese "zero" warplane and paw signatures of dog movie stars. The museum is usually open Monday through Friday, 10 AM to 5 PM; call to verify hours. Admission is:

adults, $3; children younger than 12 and senior citizens, $2.

THE ATLANTA PRESERVATION CENTER WALKING TOURS

156 Seventh St. N.E., Ste. 3   876-2041

This nonprofit organization offers 10 guided walking tours in Atlanta. Tour fees go toward the preservation of the city's architecturally, historically and culturally significant buildings and neighborhoods.

Most tours are from 1½ to 2 hours long. Some tours are offered March through November in good weather; the Fox Theatre District Tour is available year round. Call 876-2040 for a recorded message with tour days and times. The fee is $5 for adults, $4 for seniors 65 and older, $3 for students and free to members of the Atlanta Preservation Center. Reservations are required for groups of 10 or more. No tours are offered on legal holidays. Trained guides for tour buses are available.

The Fox Theatre District Tour reveals the mysteries of the 1920's Moorish movie palace on Peachtree Street. You'll marvel at the architecture and interiors, reminiscent of King Tut's tomb, and the castle-like auditorium. The Historic Downtown Tour brings history alive with accounts of past movers and shakers responsible for the businesses, the buildings and the parks in center city.

Atlanta's first suburb, Inman Park, has its own tour of Victorian mansions (some restored, some in the process), including the home of Asa Candler, Coca-Cola king. The Historic Underground/Birth of Atlanta Tour will give you an understanding of Atlanta's beginnings and Georgia's present-day legislative setting. The Reverend Dr. Martin Luther King Jr.'s boyhood home and church are part of the Sweet Auburn Tour, which includes the foundations of this historically significant African-American community.

A combined West End and Wren's Nest Tour will show you Victorian homes and churches in the West End district, including the home of Joel Chandler Harris, *Tales of Uncle Remus* author. Movie fans will recognize scenes from *Driving Miss Daisy* in the Druid Hills Tour. This elegant neighborhood was designed by the great landscape architect Frederick Law Olmsted and remains the site of particularly gracious architecture.

The three newest stars in APC's tour lineup are Atlanta University Center, Ansley Park and Piedmont Park. The AUC tour covers Vine City, mother lode of Atlanta's African-American heritage, and includes prominent colleges and churches. Ansley Park was one of Atlanta's first garden suburbs and remains the setting for lovely homes. An exploration of Piedmont Park's rich history includes its former lives as a farm, a Civil War encampment and a driving club.

THE CARTER PRESIDENTIAL CENTER

I Copenhill Ave. N.E.   331-0296

President Carter's accomplishments and administration are thoroughly documented in this 30-acre setting graced by Japanese gardens. Even the location has historical significance. From the hilltop site, Gen. Sherman watched the Battle of Atlanta. But Carter planned the facility for the future, not the past, with designated space for organizations addressing such issues as child welfare and human rights.

Important moments in history are put into perspective in the well-organized exhibits drawn from 1.5 million photographs, plus hundreds of hours of tapes. Visit a replica of the Oval Office during Carter's presidency and a display devoted to Rosalynn Carter's activities. See the impressive array of mementoes presented to the Carters from world leaders, such as a bisque doll in a silk kimono given to Amy Carter by the Emperor of Japan.

The Library is open Monday through Saturday, 9 AM to 4:45 PM; Sunday, noon to 4:45 PM. The adjoining cafe with a view of downtown Atlanta's skyline is open 11 AM to 4 PM daily. Admission is $4 for adults, $3 for seniors; children 16 and younger get in free.

A COCA-COLA EXCURSION
Various sites around Atlanta

Make no mistake: When you're in Atlanta, you're in Coca-Cola country. The world's most popular soft drink was invented here, and it was all the rage in Atlanta before it was available anywhere else. Over the years, the company's leaders, especially founder Asa G. Candler and longtime president Robert W. Woodruff, poured money into worthy Atlanta institutions (most notably Emory University), often through generous but anonymous gifts.

Cola-Cola was invented by Dr. John S. Pemberton in his home, which stood at 107 Marietta Street. It was first served to a thirsty world in May 1886 at Jacobs' Pharmacy, 2 Marietta Street, and first bottled at 125 Edgewood Avenue, now home to Georgia State University's Baptist Student Center. The recipe for Coke's top-secret essence, code-named "Merchandise 7X" is kept under lock and key in a vault in the Trust Co. of Georgia building, Park Place at Auburn Avenue. The nearby 17-story Candler Building, Peachtree at Dobbs, was once home to Coke's executive offices. An architectural marvel when new, the Candler Building has recently been grandly restored.

In Midtown, Coca-Cola's world headquarters building towers at 310 North Avenue. Just down the street is The Varsity, North Avenue at Spring Street, the world's largest drive-in and predictably the world's largest retail user of Coca-Cola syrup. May Heaven protect you should you ask for that "other" cola drink here.

Inman Park, Atlanta's first suburb, was home to Coke's founder Asa Candler from 1903 to 1916. His red brick mansion, now a private residence, stands on the corner of Euclid Avenue and Elizabeth Street and was named Callan Castle after the family's ancestral home in Ireland. Candler's eldest son Howard built the magnificent Gothic-Tudor mansion Callanwolde at 980 Briarcliff Road; today it's a fine arts center maintained by DeKalb County (see item in "The Arts" chapter). Lullwater House, the Clifton Road home of another Candler heir, is now the residence of Emory University's president. St. John's Melkite Catholic Church, 1428 Ponce de Leon Avenue N.E., is another former home of Asa Chandler.

Atlanta's loyalty to the Coca-Cola tradition is steadfast — remember the backlash against that all-but-forgotten marketing disaster "New Coke"? When company executives rolled out the "new, improved taste" in a flashy downtown celebration at Woodruff Park on April 23, 1985, the crowd included lifelong Atlanta Coke consumers who — in front of the world's media — poured bottles of the new, sweeter drink onto the street. Less than three months later, with Coke drinkers around the country still clamoring for their old favorite, the corporation acquiesced and returned the original formula to the market as "Coca-Cola Classic."

If you'll settle for nothing less than being fully awash in a river of Coca-Cola

The story of Coke — past, present, and future — will entertain you at the World of Coca-Cola.

Photo: Georgia Tourist Division

history, images and lore, go directly to the World of Coca-Cola (see separate item in the general Attractions section of this chapter). And while you're in Atlanta, don't forget: Things go better with the pause that refreshes! It's the real thing! Refreshing! Delicious!

DECATUR DOWNTOWN DEVELOPMENT AUTHORITY

100 E. Trinity Pl., Decatur   371-8386

The lovely city of Decatur is 6 miles east of downtown Atlanta. Founded in 1823, it's more than a decade older than its big, noisy neighbor.

It's said that Decatur was considered as the terminus point for the Western & Atlantic railroad in the 1830s, but local residents objected, fearing the smoke and general confusion. Instead, the railroad line ended at what became Five Points, and the rest, as they say, is history. On July 22, 1864, a skirmish at Decatur's cemetery resulted in one of the few Confederate victories in the fighting around Atlanta.

Decaturites are proud that their city, so near the center of the Atlanta metropolitan region, has been able to preserve its village-like atmosphere. Surrounding the square are numerous interesting structures from the early 20th century and even some from before the Civil War. Available at the above address and from the DeKalb Historical Society, in the old courthouse on the square, 373-1088, are two helpful free booklets: *Tour and Discover Historic Decatur — A Driving Tour* and *Historic Downtown Decatur — A Walking Tour*.

THE FOX THEATRE

660 Peachtree St. N.E.   881-2100

To visit the Fox Theatre is to be swept into another world. In an age of minimalist architecture and 12-plex movies in festival mini-malls, the Fox is the real deal: No mere theater but a complete environment, lush and ornate and almost beyond belief. This dazzling movie palace is so closely associated with Atlanta today that it's inconceivable it was almost torn down just 20 years ago — but that's exactly what happened.

Planning for the structure began in 1916: It was to be the headquarters for the Yaarab Temple of the Ancient Arabic Order of the Nobles of the Mystic Shrine (the Shriners). In 1929, as it neared completion, financial difficulties forced the Shriners into a deal with movie magnate William Fox, and the temple's plans were altered to include a spectacular movie theater and exterior street-level retail space.

Oozing with Middle Eastern opulence, the Fox opened on Christmas Day, 1929; just 125 weeks later, squeezed by the Great Depression, it closed. In 1935 it reopened; then, in 1947, gained prestige as the site of the Metropolitan Opera's annual week of Atlanta performances. The Met's stars often got lost inside the Fox's cavernous backstage areas until someone came up with an ingenious solution: The names of the New York streets around the Metropolitan Opera House were chalked on the Fox's walls to help the singers find their way.

By 1975, unable to fill its nearly 5,000 seats as a first-run movie house, the Fox closed again; this time things looked grim indeed. Plans were to raze the theater to make way for a skyscraper. But thanks to the contributions of thousands of people and the work of Atlanta Landmarks Inc., the Fox was saved and reopened in time to celebrate its 50th birthday. Today it's a favorite venue for concerts and touring Broadway shows; a summer film series still affords the lavish experience of seeing a movie in a "real" movie theater.

The Fox is too amazing to describe briefly, but here are a few highlights and tips:

• With six motorized elevator lifts, the 140-foot-wide stage remains one of the largest ever built. Another elevator raises and lowers the 3,610-pipe Mighty Moller organ, which is played for a sing-along before each movie during the summer film series, just as it was in the 1930s.

• The ceiling of the 64,000-square-foot auditorium suggests night under a bedouin chieftain's tent beneath a clear desert sky. The tent is not canvas as might be expected but a reinforced plaster canopy that helps draw sound up to the rear of the balcony. The stars twinkling in the blue sky are 11-watt bulbs fixed above four-inch crystals. Clouds, rain and other special effects are produced by projector. The pre-movie sing-along usually includes "Sunrise, Sunset," during which the theater's sky brightens from darkness to day before slipping back to dusk.

The entire second level of the Fox (the loge, first and second dress circles and gallery) and the front of the orchestra section enjoy views of the sky. To the rear of row M in the orchestra section, the balcony overhang hides the sky. Especially for movies, the front rows of the loge are the best in the house.

• Don't miss the rest rooms and their lounges! Even these areas are fabulous in the Fox.

• The several full bars serve cocktails and other beverages during all events, including movies, and you're welcome to enjoy drinks and snacks inside the auditorium. Smoking is permitted only in the exterior entrance arcade and on the smoking porch facing Ponce de Leon.

For information on touring the Fox, see our item on the Atlanta Preservation Center's walking tours.

GEORGIA DEPARTMENT OF ARCHIVES AND HISTORY
330 Capitol Ave. S.E.   *656-2393*

Although not set up as a tourist attraction, the Georgia Department of Archives and History is an invaluable resource for serious scholars and those researching genealogy. The department was created in 1918; from 1931 to 1965, the state's archives were maintained in Rhodes Hall (see separate listing).

The Ben W. Fortson, Jr., State Archives and Records Building between the Capitol and Atlanta Fulton County Stadium is often mistaken for a prison, but the tall, windowless structure provides a secure, controlled environment for some 85,000 cubic feet of official records and more than 65,000 reels of records on microfilm. Among these governmental and nongovernmental documents are family letters and papers, business account books, organizational and church records and photographs.

To gain access to the Search Room, visitors must show identification and complete an application for a research card. To protect the fragile records, the building has strict rules about what materials may be brought inside.

GEORGIA'S FILM AND TELEVISION INDUSTRY

Here's a bit of trivia: Since the Georgia Film and Videotape Office, 656-3545, was formed in 1973, more than 350 motion pictures and TV movies have been filmed in the state, with an economic benefit of nearly $2 billion.

Of these, 165 were filmed entirely or in part on location around Atlanta. These include *Smokey and the Bandit I & II, Wise Blood, The Bear, The Slugger's Wife, Sharky's Machine, Tanner '88, Consenting Adults, Free Jack, Basket Case III* and *The Oldest Living Confederate Widow Tells All.*

Two of the best-known Atlanta movies are Spike Lee's *School Daze,* filmed on the campus of Atlanta University Center, and the 1989 Oscar-winner for best picture *Driving Miss Daisy,* filmed in the elegant Druid Hills district and in Little Five Points.

THE GEORGIA GOVERNOR'S MANSION
391 W. Paces Ferry Rd. N.E.   *261-1776*

The Georgia Governor's Mansion was dedicated in 1968. Like the state's first Governor's mansion, built in Milledgeville in 1838, the modern mansion is in the Greek Revival style; it was designed by Georgia architect A. Thomas Bradbury. The 24,000-square-foot house is the property of Georgia's citizens and, by law, remains the same even when its primary resident changes.

Neoclassical paintings and furnishings from the 19th century complement the mansion's design. On the main floor are a library with many books by Georgia authors and the state drawing and dining rooms. The second floor is the first family's private home and includes the large Presidential Suite for visiting dignitaries. The lower floor of the mansion boasts a ballroom that seats 150 for dinner.

The Governor's Mansion is open to the public each week on Tuesday, Wednesday and Thursday from 10 AM to 11:30 AM. The tour is self-guided, but hostesses in each room explain items of significance. The tour is free, but reservations are required for groups of 20 or more. Drive up to the main gate; there's parking on the 18-acre grounds. While you're out at the mansion, you may wish to visit the Atlanta History Center; it's right across the road.

GEORGIA'S HISTORICAL MARKERS
Various locations around Atlanta and Georgia

As you explore Atlanta and Georgia, you can gain a wealth of background from the state's historical markers. You can't miss them: The olive-green cast-aluminum signs are 42 by 38 inches and are emblazoned with the state seal. Statewide, there are some 2,000 markers, about 700 of which concern the Civil War. The metro Atlanta area has about 600 historical markers.

The program was launched in 1951 and strongly emphasized Civil War history in the buildup to the 100th anniversary of the conflict. Artist and historian Wilbur Kurtz, who was a consultant on the movies *Gone With the Wind* and *Song of the South*, wrote the text for the markers between Tennessee and Atlanta. Another prominent historian, Col. Allen P. Julian, described Sherman's March to the Sea on the markers south of Atlanta to Savannah.

Historical markers are scattered across metro Atlanta. You can see some along DeKalb Avenue about 2 miles east of Five Points, the area at the center of the Battle of Atlanta. There are several markers around the Inman Park/Reynoldstown MARTA station; the fighting at this location is depicted in the Atlanta Cyclorama.

GEORGIA'S STATE CAPITOL
Intersection of Capitol Ave., M.L. King Jr. Dr., Washington Ave. and Mitchell St. 656-2844

The Georgia Legislature first met in Atlanta in 1868, but the $1 million needed for construction of the Capitol was not provided until 1883. Work got under way in October of 1884; when it was completed, the state treasury had spent all but $118.43. The building was dedicated on July 4, 1889.

The Chicago architectural firm Edbrooke and Burnham designed the Capitol, which was built of Indiana oolitic limestone by Miles and Horne of Toledo, Ohio. Georgia marble, judged impractically expensive for the exterior, was used for the floors, walls and steps. The open rotunda peaks at a height of more than 237 feet.

Outside, atop the dome, stands a 15-foot-tall, 2,000-pound Greek-inspired statue of a female figure holding a torch in one hand and a sword in the other: It commemorates Georgia's war dead.

During a 1956 renovation program, 43 ounces of native gold, donated by the people of Dahlonega and Lumpkin County, site of America's first gold rush in 1828, were applied to the dome's exterior. Another application of gold in 1981 restored the dome to its original brilliance. The Capitol was named a National Historic Landmark in 1977.

Inside and out, the Capitol's memorials and mementos tell Georgia's diverse history. Statues of famous segregationists

Insiders' Tips

When driving in metro Atlanta, always have your driver's license, proof of liability insurance and vehicle registration card with you to avoid inconvenience at police roadblocks.

share the grounds with the touching modern sculpture "Expelled Because of Their Color," commissioned in 1976 by the General Assembly's black legislative caucus. It is "dedicated to the memory of the 33 black state legislators who were elected, yet expelled from the Georgia House because of their color in 1868" and is on the northeast side of the grounds.

The **Georgia State Museum of Science and Industry** on the first and fourth floors showcases Georgia's wildlife and minerals; other features include Native American artifacts and battle flags flown by Georgia regiments in various wars.

Free guided tours of the Capitol are offered year round, Monday through Friday, at 10 AM, 11 AM, 1 PM and 2 PM. The tour desk is on the main floor in the West Wing just outside the Governor's office. The Capitol is open on weekends, but no tours are given. Call for more information or to arrange a group tour or tour for hearing- or sight-impaired persons.

THE GREAT LOCOMOTIVE CHASE
Various sites of interest in the metro area

This bizarre railroad adventure has been the subject of two famous motion pictures: Buster Keaton's *The General* and Walt Disney's *The Great Locomotive Chase*. On April 12, 1862, in the town of Big Shanty, now called Kennesaw, a party of Union spies led by James J. Andrews stole the locomotive *General* while its conductor and crew were breakfasting nearby. They absconded northward on the Western & Atlantic line with the intention of burning bridges and cutting the rail line to Chattanooga.

Their plan might have succeeded but for the *General's* conductor, Capt. William Fuller, and his crew, who gave furious chase on foot, on a push car and on three different locomotives. Finally, running the locomotive *Texas* in reverse, Fuller and his men caught up to the *General* above Ringgold, Georgia, before the raiding party could burn the targeted bridges. Of the captured raiders, some escaped to Union lines; others were held as prisoners of war until the following year; seven were executed by hanging at the present intersection of Memorial Drive and Park Avenue in Atlanta; Andrews was hanged at the present intersection of Juniper and Third Street in Midtown.

In 1972, following a legal battle over its ownership that went all the way to the U.S. Supreme Court, the *General* steamed into an old cotton gin that had been newly renovated as its permanent home, Big Shanty Museum, 2829 Cherokee Street, 427-2117, in the center of Kennesaw, Exit 118 off I-75 N. The museum tour includes numerous descriptive exhibits and a narrated slide presentation. Admission is $3 for adults, $2.50 for seniors, AAA members and military personnel and $1.50 for kids 7 to 15.

The reverse-racing *Texas* is on permanent display in the lobby of the Atlanta Cyclorama.

THE HERNDON HOME
587 University Pl. N.W.   581-9813

This 1910 Beaux-Arts Classical mansion near Atlanta University is as amazing as the African-American family that built it. Alonzo Herndon began life as a slave in Social Circle, Georgia. As a young man possessing only one year of formal education, he learned the barbering trade and moved to Atlanta. Here Herndon's hard work was richly rewarded: His barber shop eventually employed some 40 men, and he founded the Atlanta Life Insurance Co. and became the city's wealthiest African American.

On a tall hill overlooking the city,

Herndon and his wife, the former Adrienne McNeil, built their dream home, designing it themselves without an architect. Constructed entirely by black craftsmen at a cost of $10,000, the mansion was completed in 1910 after 2½ years of work and included such ultramodern conveniences as electricity, central plumbing and steam heat. Tragically, the ailing Mrs. Herndon died just one week after moving into the home. The Herndons' only son, Norris, lived in the house until his death in 1977; since then, the Herndon Foundation has owned and operated the home.

The Herndon Home is opulent and magnificent, with nine fireplaces, a lavish mahogany dining room and a recurring lion's-head motif. Other aspects, though, are charmingly personal. In the living room is a mural that tells the story of the elder Herndon's rise from slavery to riches. The flat roof was Adrienne's idea: A drama teacher and Shakespearean actress, she envisioned it as the ideal place for outdoor dramatic performances.

The Herndon Home is open to the public Tuesday through Saturday from 10 AM to 4 PM. Guided tours begin on the hour. Donations are accepted, but there is no admission charge.

THE MARTIN LUTHER KING, JR. CENTER FOR NONVIOLENT SOCIAL CHANGE
449 Auburn Ave. N.E. 524-1956

The King Center is Atlanta's preeminent tourist attraction, each year receiving more than 3.5 million visitors. All day, every day, visitors make their way past the eternal flame in the center's plaza and toward the tiered reflecting pool, in the center of which stands Dr. King's elevated marble tomb. West of the tomb is Ebenezer Baptist Church, where Dr. King

was co-pastor. East of the tomb is the King Center's main facility. Across Boulevard on the east side of the 23-acre National Historic Site and Preservation District is King's restored birth home, 501 Auburn Avenue.

King was assassinated on April 4, 1968, while in Memphis, Tennessee, lending his support to striking sanitation workers. Upon learning of the sudden tragedy, Atlanta Mayor Ivan Allen Jr. immediately began to prepare the city for the funeral, which would become one of the largest events in its history. When Dr. King won the Nobel Peace Prize in 1964, Robert Woodruff led the movement to honor him with a gala banquet. In the hours after the tragedy, the Coca-Cola president called the mayor and insisted that no expense be spared in preparing the city to accommodate thousands of mourners and the international media; Woodruff himself guaranteed payment of any cost overruns.

During the grief-stricken days that followed the assassination, rioting in 126 U.S. cities claimed some 46 lives — but Atlanta remained calm. Mayor Allen and Police Chief Herbert Jenkins walked the streets of the city's black neighborhoods, expressing their sympathy and support. Hundreds of volunteers at the Southern Christian Leadership Conference offices worked around the clock to assist the thousands of mourners streaming into the city. Central Presbyterian Church downtown announced it was opening its doors to black visitors; hundreds of other white churches followed suit.

On April 9, more than 100,000 people crowded around Ebenezer Baptist Church for the funeral. Hundreds of dignitaries and celebrities attended, including Jacqueline and Bobby Kennedy, Wilt Chamberlain, James Brown, Nelson Rockefeller, Richard Nixon, Harry

Belafonte and Vice President Hubert Humphrey. Georgia's Governor Lester Maddox, a pick-handle-waving segregationist who had complained about plans to fly flags at half-mast in the city, remained in his office under the protection of state troopers.

Some 200,000 mourners followed the humble mule-drawn wagon that carried Dr. King's body along Auburn Avenue and back to his alma mater Morehouse College, where he had lain in state. There he was eulogized by Dr. Benjamin E. Mays, president emeritus of Morehouse.

Incredibly, Mrs. Coretta Scott King and 7-year-old son Dexter went to Memphis only four days after the murder to march with the striking sanitation workers. Within just three months, the King Memorial Center had opened. Mrs. King and her children have continued working to keep Dr. King's dream alive. Following extensive lobbying and much controversy, Dr. King's birthday became a national holiday in 1986.

The King Center's exhibition hall contains a permanent display of photographs and memorabilia of Dr. King's public and private life. Freedom Hall is a space for meetings and other gatherings. The center's library and archives house the world's largest collection of primary information on the civil rights movement.

In 1994, a dispute arose between the center's directors and the U.S. National Parks Service, which operates the National Historic Site, over plans for future development in the district. Tours of the King birth home, which were suspended for several months, had resumed at press time.

There is no charge to visit the King Center, which is open daily from 9 AM to 5:30 PM, with extended hours during the summer and other peak periods. There is limited parking in the area; the Parks Service operates a free parking lot one block south of the center on Edgewood Avenue.

MARGARET MITCHELL HOUSE
Peachtree St. at 10th St.   870-2360

To Margaret Mitchell, it was affectionately known as "The Dump." Some look at the ramshackle, abandoned apartment house and see nothing but a prominent eyesore on Peachtree Street; others,

Margaret Mitchell and her husband John Marsh are buried in historic Oakland Cemetery.

however, see a place where a dream was formed and the city's future was forever altered.

From 1925 to 1932, Mitchell and her husband John Marsh lived in this modest building; theirs was the first-floor, left corner apartment on the building's rear, Crescent Avenue, side. Here, typing at the sewing table she used as a desk, she wrote *Gone With the Wind*, whose worldwide popularity remains second only to the Bible.

Mitchell was intensely private. She specified that nearly all her papers, including the carbon copies of her correspondence, be burned after her death; those who possessed letters from her were requested to destroy them as well, and she is said to have opposed the building of any memorial to herself.

However, tourism officials report they annually receive more than 1 million inquiries about Mitchell and the book, and many tourists are aghast that the city has no official memorial to the author who told its story to the whole world. The dilapidated building was spared the wrecker's ball in 1988, and a board of distinguished Atlantans came together and began raising money to perpetuate "The Dump" as a museum.

The project is expected to cost $3.6 to $4.5 million. A fire in September 1994 further damaged the property, but not the enthusiasm of its supporters, who still plan to have it restored and open to the public before the 1996 Olympics. (The fire broke out after the roof had been covered with thousands of inflated rubber gloves in a conceptual art piece symbolizing world peace as part of the Arts Festival of Atlanta.) The group's marketing studies project that the house would attract 160,000 visitors in its first year alone.

This section of Peachtree Street figured prominently in the final chapter of Mitchell's own life. Three blocks north of her old apartment on August 11, 1949, Mitchell and Marsh were on their way to see the British art film *A Canterbury Tale*. The pair was halfway across Peachtree in the unmarked crossing at 13th Street when a speeding car appeared. Mitchell panicked, screamed and bolted back across Peachtree toward her parked car. As he swerved left to miss the couple, the driver struck the retreating Mitchell directly; Marsh was unharmed.

Mitchell died on August 16 at Grady Memorial Hospital. Her funeral cortege followed the same route as the December 15, 1939, parade when 300,000 people had packed Atlanta's streets to celebrate the world premiere of *Gone With the Wind* and get a glimpse of its stars. Mitchell and Marsh, who died in 1952, are buried at Oakland Cemetery.

OAKLAND CEMETERY
248 Oakland Ave.   688-2107

Almost in the shadows of downtown's skyscrapers lies one of Atlanta's most serene places: shaded, hilly Oakland Cemetery. In 1850, city leaders purchased six acres of land east of the city limits for a municipal burial ground. Private or church graveyards were thus unnecessary, and so very nearly every person who died in Atlanta between 1850 and 1884, when Westview Cemetery opened, was buried at Oakland. The result is a vivid and often touching picture of Atlanta a century ago.

Oakland's brick walls now enclose 88 acres. Here are the unmarked graves of black and white paupers; here also are the stunning monuments and private mausoleums of the city's wealthiest families. In the Jewish section are closely spaced monuments with Hebrew inscrip-

Photo: Chuck Morgan

A replica of Georgia's first black-owned drugstore is one of the
exhibits at the APEX.

tions. Beneath the 65-foot memorial obelisk lie thousands of Confederate dead; the nearby statue of a lion, with a sword through its back and its head lying across the fallen Rebel flag, honors the unknown Confederate soldiers buried around it.

The most famous person buried in Oakland is not easy to find. The author of *Gone With the Wind* lies beneath a simple headstone reading "Margaret Mitchell Marsh;" it's said she requested a plain marker on her grave. Other well-known people buried at Oakland are golfer Bobby Jones, Moses Formwalt (Atlanta's first mayor), Rich's founder Morris Rich and several of the Southerners who participated in the Great Locomotive Chase.

A helpful brochure for sale ($1.25) at the white tower building will assist you in locating graves and sections of interest. From March through October, a guide leads a tour of Oakland at 10 AM and 2 PM on Saturdays and at 2 PM on Sundays. The tour is $3 for adults and $2 for seniors and students. From Midtown, take Boulevard south to Memorial; turn right, drive past the long brick wall and turn right on Oakland Avenue. You are permitted to drive around Oakland, but proceed slowly and only on the asphalt-paved roads. Stone rubbings are prohibited. From the King Memorial MARTA station, walk south on Grant Street; the cemetery gate is on your left just before you reach Memorial.

RHODES HALL

Georgia Trust for Historic Preservation
1516 Peachtree St. N.W.   881-9980

Lavish Victorian-era mansions once lined parts of Peachtree Street, but very few remain today. One that does is Rhodes Hall, built in 1902-1904 by furniture tycoon Amos G. Rhodes. He asked architect Willis Denny to design the home in the style of the Rhineland castles Rhodes had seen in Europe. The result is a most unusual, eclectic, Romanesque Revival mansion.

The house's most imposing feature, however, is not European at all, but distinctly Southern. As a boy growing up in Kentucky during the Civil War, Rhodes often saw both Yankee and Rebel troops. For his mansion, he commissioned a series of elaborate painted and stained-glass windows as a memorial to the Confederacy. In nine panels, the windows show Jefferson Davis' inauguration, the firing on Ft. Sumter, Stonewall Jackson at Manassas and Robert E. Lee at Appomattox. The windows curve around the massive carved mahogany staircase between the first and second floors.

Mr. Rhodes died in 1928; the following year, his family deeded the home to the state of Georgia. It was listed on the National Register of Historic Places in 1974. Georgia's official archives were maintained in the mansion from 1931 to 1965. The original 150-acre estate has been reduced to a single acre. Since 1983 the mansion has been the headquarters for the Georgia Trust for Historic Preservation; it's also available as a rental reception facility. Rhodes Hall is open to the public Monday through Friday from 11 AM to 4 PM; admission is $2 for adults, $1 for children and $1 per person for groups of 10 or more.

ROAD TO TARA MUSEUM

The Georgian Terrace
659 Peachtree St.   897-1939

This 6,000-square-foot museum takes its name from the title Margaret Mitchell originally gave her best-seller. Now a condominium, the Georgian Terrace was once a hotel. It was here that Mitchell gave her typewritten manuscript to MacMillan agent Harold Latham and here that the stars of *Gone With the Wind* stayed during the gala 1939 premiere.

The collection includes autographed and foreign editions of the book, movie posters, artists' renderings of key scenes, costume prints and reproductions and 100 different GWTW dolls. The 35-seat theater shows film clips of the making of the movie.

The museum is open 10 AM to 6 PM Monday through Saturday, and 1 to 6 PM on Sunday. Admission is $5 for adults, $4.25 for seniors, $3.50 for students and free for kids 11 and younger.

SOUTHERN CHRISTIAN LEADERSHIP CONFERENCE NATIONAL OFFICE
334 Auburn Ave. N.E.   *522-1420*

Founded in 1965 by Dr. Martin Luther King Jr., its current president Dr. Joseph E. Lowery and others, the SCLC continues to fight for civil rights. The group's Auburn Avenue national headquarters is a working office (not a tourist attraction), but visitors are welcome to stop in, examine the historic photos from the civil rights movement and take photos of their own.

UNITED STATES PENITENTIARY
601 McDonough Blvd. S.E.   *622-6241*

Be very glad you're seeing this historic building from the outside. Standing solemnly at the south end of Boulevard, the Atlanta Penitentiary was one of the first three Federal prisons. Congress voted to build the prisons in 1891 but did not appropriate the funds until later. The Atlanta Penitentiary was built by prison labor between 1899 and 1902, when it received its first prisoners.

The tract of land was several miles from Atlanta when the government acquired it; since that time, of course, the city has grown to surround the prison. The high-security facility is the largest Federal penal institution located inside a major city. Famous inmates at the penitentiary have include mobster Al Capone and mafiosi-turned-state's evidence Joseph Valachi.

In 1923, two men living in an outdoor tent for tubercular inmates dug a tunnel eight feet beneath the ground, eventually reaching the outside world. Four men used it to escape on a Sunday afternoon; all were recaptured. Between 1980 and 1987, the Atlanta Pen primarily held Cuban detainees from the Mariel boatlift. On November 23, 1987, Cuban inmates rioted and set a huge fire whose smoke was visible beyond the Perimeter; authorities regained control of the facility when the prisoners surrendered on December 4.

In 1920, an inmate at the Atlanta Penitentiary received almost 1 million votes in the U.S. Presidential election. Eugene V. Debs was a socialist who had run for President four times previously. Because of his outspoken opposition to World War I, Debs was convicted under the Espionage Act in 1918 and sentenced to 10 years in prison. He ran his fifth campaign from behind the prison's walls and got more than 900,000 votes. In 1921, Debs' sentence was commuted by President Warren G. Harding. (Interestingly, Georgia politician Tom Watson, who also criticized WWI and even urged young Georgians to dodge the draft, is immortalized in bronze on the Capitol grounds.)

WESTVIEW CEMETERY
1680 Westview Dr. S.W.   *755-6611*

In 1884, a private corporation purchased the land for Westview Cemetery. This enormous graveyard comprises some

600 acres, of which 300 are yet to be developed. Within Westview's walls are 22 miles of paved roads. During the Civil War, the city's western siege line passed through Westview's rolling hills; a fragment of Confederate breastwork remains.

Although other mausoleums have grown larger through additions, Westview Abbey is the largest mausoleum ever built from a single set of plans: It has spaces for 11,444 entombments. Its exotic design is a bit reminiscent of the Fox Theatre. Twenty-seven stained-glass panels depict the life of Christ. The hushed and shadowy chapel, with its marble floors and stained-glass windows, is especially opulent.

Well-known persons buried at Westview include journalists Joel Chandler Harris, Henry Grady and Ralph McGill; Coca-Cola's leaders Asa G. Candler and Robert W. Woodruff; and Atlanta mayors I.N. Ragsdale and William B. Hartsfield. A free map of the cemetery is available in the office near the main gate.

To reach Westview from downtown, take I-20 W. to Ashby Street, turn left, then turn right at the second light onto Ralph David Abernathy Boulevard. Stay on Abernathy when it bears right (about three-fourths of a mile past the Wren's Nest, near a Kentucky Fried Chicken restaurant) and follow Abernathy a little more than three-fourths of a mile; you'll see Westview's entrance on your left. An alternate route is to take Westview Drive from the Atlanta University Center area directly to the cemetery's front gate.

WINECOFF HOTEL FIRE SITE
Peachtree at Ellis Sts.

Beside the downtown Macy's department store, a vacant building and a his-torical marker commemorate a most dreadful day in Atlanta's history.

In the early morning hours of December 7, 1946, a fire broke out in the Winecoff Hotel. It was not the first blaze at the supposedly fireproof hotel: A spectacular fire had raged there on February 18, 1942, though miraculously no one perished. This time the outcome was horribly different.

The Winecoff had neither fire escapes nor sprinklers, and its open central stairway to the penthouse acted as a huge chimney. The fire department's ladders were too short to reach the upper floors of the 15-story building, and dozens of terrified guests jumped to their deaths; many more perished in the smoke and flames. Among the dead were 28 of 51 boys and girls in town for a youth conference. The Winecoff's original owner, W. F. Winecoff, died with his wife in their 14th-floor rooms.

In all, 119 people perished in the 3-hour conflagration, which is still America's worst hotel fire. Many grim lessons learned from the disaster have improved fire safety in modern hotels.

On the anniversary of the fire in 1994, some of its survivors gathered to unveil the historical marker outside the still standing, vacant, building.

THE WREN'S NEST
1050 Ralph David Abernathy Blvd. S.W.
753-8535

Joel Chandler Harris was a teenager during the Civil War; there is some evidence to suggest that his mother, a seamstress, may have cleverly altered his age to save him from sacrifice on the altar of the doomed Confederacy. At the Turnwold plantation near Harris' hometown of Eatonton, Georgia, about 70 miles east of Atlanta off I-20, the young Harris learned the printing trade and spent many hours listening wide-eyed to an elderly slave, George Terrell, who amused the boy with folk tales and fables of African origin.

Harris' printing background led him into journalism. After a stint at *The Macon Telegraph*, he went to work at the Atlanta *Constitution* where, in 1877, he was asked to write a story in dialect; such pieces were popular features and continued to appear in some Southern newspapers as late as the 1960s. He called upon memories of his happy boyhood hours with Terrell and penned a story in which kindly Uncle Remus fascinates a young boy with a fable about plucky Br'er Rabbit. Harris' work instantly resonated with both black and white readers, many of whom recalled similar tales from their Southern childhoods.

Not content to rely on his memory alone, Harris meticulously researched the folk tales, eventually collecting more than 200 of them. Although the dialect in the stories understandably makes some modern-day readers uncomfortable, many scholars credit Harris, a charter member of the American Folklore Society, with preserving a fragile literary heritage that otherwise might have been lost.

In 1881 Harris and family rented a five-room West End farmhouse that had been built shortly after the Civil War. He bought the house in 1883 and added several rooms. One day, when Harris discovered that tiny wrens had built a nest in his mailbox, the house got its nickname. The shy and gentle Harris wrote many of his stories in his "summer living room" (the broad front porch), and folks enjoyed riding by to glimpse the famous author at work. Harris died in 1908; the Uncle Remus Memorial Association operated the house from 1913 to 1984.

In 1984, the Joel Chandler Harris Association took over and began painstak-ingly restoring the house, which had undergone many historically inaccurate makeovers, to its original condition. Today, the Wren's Nest is again as it was when Harris lived there. On display are original and foreign editions of his works and some of the many gifts he was sent by admiring readers, including a stuffed great horned owl from President Theodore Roosevelt, whose mother was from Roswell, Georgia, and who entertained Harris at a White House dinner.

The Wren's Nest is open Tuesday through Saturday from 10 AM to 5 PM and Sunday from 1 to 5 PM. The last tour begins at 4 PM. Admission is $4 for adults, $3 for seniors and teens and $2 for children 4 to 12. Storytelling is often an added attraction, and there's a small shop with lots of Uncle Remus books and gifts.

Beyond Atlanta

Clayton County

CLAYTON COUNTY CONVENTION & VISITORS BUREAU
8712 Tara Blvd., Jonesboro   *478-4800*

Clayton County is Atlanta's southern neighbor and was the site of an important Union victory in the siege of Atlanta, but every day visitors go there looking for a house that never existed: the O'Hara family's Tara from *Gone With the Wind*. As a girl, Margaret Mitchell often visited elderly relatives in Clayton County. Though later she used the county as the location of Scarlett's plantation, Tara and the other homes described were entirely products of her imagination.

Nevertheless, there are numerous reasons to visit Clayton, including the 1839 Stately Oaks plantation, the 1880 Ashley Oaks mansion and the Spivey Hall performing arts center (see The Arts chapter). Stop by the bureau and pick up the "self-driving tour" and other free brochures about the area's attractions.

Cobb County

KENNESAW MOUNTAIN NATIONAL BATTLEFIELD PARK
900 Kennesaw Mountain Dr.
Kennesaw 427-4686

In the spring and summer of 1864, the armies of U.S. Gen. William Sherman and Confederate Gen. Joseph Johnston played a deadly game of cat and mouse across north Georgia. Each time Sherman encountered strong Rebel lines, his troops would swing wide around them in a flanking maneuver, forcing the Confederates to drop back and retrench — a pattern that brought the fighting ever-closer to Atlanta.

When the Union troops reached Kennesaw Mountain, they found the Confederates strongly entrenched in superbly prepared fortifications. On June 27, in a rare blunder, Sherman ordered an assault on these Confederate positions. It was bloodily rebuffed, and the North lost 3,000 men to the South's 800. Sherman resumed his flanking strategy, and the Rebels, on July 2, were forced to abandon their fortifications and fall back yet again.

Today the Kennesaw battlefield is preserved as part of a 2,884-acre National Park with 16 miles of hiking trails featuring troop movement maps, historical markers, monuments, cannon emplacements and preserved trenchworks. In the visitors center you'll find a good selection of Civil War books for sale and a slide presentation that explains the Atlanta Campaign and the importance of the area's several battles.

Atlanta's Got It!

• The tallest building in the Southeast: the 1,023-foot NationsBank Plaza (the ninth tallest building in the world).

• The tallest hotel in the western hemisphere: the 73-story Westin Peachtree Plaza.

• The largest hotel in the southeast: the 1,674-room Marriott Marquis.

• The largest painting in the world: the Cyclorama.

• The largest bas-relief sculpture in the world: the Confederate Memorial at Stone Mountain.

• The largest toll-free dialing area in the world: 3,300 square miles.

• The second-largest U.S. convention center: the 2.5-million-square-foot Georgia World Congress Center.

• The largest cable-supported domed stadium in the world: the Georgia Dome.

• The national or world headquarters facilities for:

American Cancer Society
Arthritis Foundation
Atlanta Life Insurance
Cable News Network (CNN)
CARE
Chick-fil-A
Coca-Cola
Days Inns of America
Delta Air Lines
Equifax
Georgia-Pacific
Holiday Inn Worldwide
Home Depot
Maxell Corp. of America
Rich's Department Stores
Ritz-Carlton Hotels

Scientific Atlanta
Turner Broadcasting
Sportstown
United Parcel Service
The U.S. Centers for Disease
    Control and Prevention
The Weather Channel

On weekdays you can drive your own car to the top of the mountain. Due to the high volume of visitors, the mountain road is closed to private vehicles on weekends for much of the year, but there's a free shuttle bus to the top every 30 minutes. From the summit on a clear day, you can easily see downtown Atlanta, Decatur and Stone Mountain. To preserve the fragile mountain ecology, hikers must stay on trails or roadways. The possession or use of metal detectors on park grounds is illegal. The park is free and open daily to the public.

MARIETTA WELCOME CENTER AND VISITORS BUREAU
No. 4 Depot Square, Marietta   429-1115
Marietta was founded in 1834, making it older than Atlanta. The town was captured by Union troops during the Civil War; but, as Sherman seemed to be saving his matches for Atlanta, it escaped the ordeal with its antebellum town square and many homes and churches remaining intact. For a free brochure with a map to historic homes and sites, stop by the Welcome Center; it's open daily.

CONFEDERATE CEMETERY
Corner of N. 120 Loop and Cemetery St. Marietta   No phone
Established in 1863, this cemetery holds the remains of more than 3,000 Confederate soldiers, buried in graves arranged by home state. Most of the sol-diers fell in the fighting around Kennesaw and Marietta.

MARIETTA NATIONAL CEMETERY
500 Washington Ave. Marietta   428-5631
More than 18,000 veterans — from the Civil War through Desert Storm — are buried in this 25.3-acre cemetery. Some 10,000 known and 3,000 unknown Civil War soldiers are interred here.

Fulton County

BULLOCH HALL
189 Bulloch Ave., Roswell   992-1731
One block west of the Roswell town square, Bulloch Hall is a Greek Revival mansion constructed of aged heart pine and completed in 1840. At the home in 1853, Maj. Bulloch's daughter Mittie married Theodore Roosevelt Sr.; from their marriage came the future President Teddy Roosevelt, who visited his mother's childhood home in 1905. The senior Roosevelt's other son was the father of Eleanor Roosevelt, the wife of FDR. During her husband's therapeutic visits to Warm Springs, Georgia, Mrs. Roosevelt would sometimes drive to Roswell for a visit at the hall.

Bulloch Hall is open to the public for tours; it's also home to guilds that keep alive such crafts as quilting and basketry. Periodic activities include the re-enactment of Mittie's 1853 wedding, Civil War encampments and cannon-firing demonstrations. Admission is $3 for adults and $2 for children 6 to 16.

HISTORIC ROSWELL CONVENTION & VISITORS BUREAU
617 Atlanta St., Roswell   640-3252
Wisely convinced that the rushing waters of Vickery Creek would power in-

dustry, Mr. Roswell King founded Roswell as a textile mill town in the 1830s. King and his associates built lavish mansions for themselves and cottages and apartments for their workers. Today the town prides itself on its 1839 town square and its many old homes and churches. The historic district trail is a 4.5 mile route that takes guests to some of the town's attractions. A tour guide pamphlet is available for $1 at the visitors bureau.

Gwinnett County

Gwinnett Historic Courthouse
185 Crogan St., Lawrenceville   822-5450

Designed by E.G. Lind in 1885, the Gwinnett County Courthouse evolved in an eclectic combination of Romanesque, Second Empire and Works Progress Administration styles. It was last an active courthouse in 1988; an extensive renovation and restoration program was completed in 1992.

The courthouse stands on a full block at the center of Lawrenceville town square, and around it are monuments, picnic tables and a gazebo. In their upstairs headquarters, members of the Gwinnett County Historical Society, 822-5174, will gladly give you information on other county attractions and historic sites.

Visitors are welcome to explore the courthouse on a self-guided tour weekdays from 9 AM to 4 PM, and there is no admission charge. The courthouse is available as a rental facility for public and private gatherings both large and small.

Hall County

Green Street Historic District
Gainesville Hall County Chamber of Commerce
230 E.E. Butler Pkwy., Gainesville 532-6206

In downtown Gainesville, northeast of Atlanta off I-985, a half-mile corridor of Green Street has been included on the National Register of Historic Places. The street features 19th and 20th century Victorian and Neoclassical homes and businesses. Stop by the Chamber of Commerce for free information on walking and driving tours to area sites of interest.

General Attractions

Atlanta

Welcome South Visitors Center
200 Spring St.
In the Atlanta Gift Mart   224-2000

Seven Southeastern states joined Georgia to develop the $6.5 million Welcome South Visitors Center. The 23,000-square-foot downtown facility is a walk-through attraction that features various displays, a feature film, two retail stores and extensive visitor information services.

The center's multilingual staff and volunteers greet visitors and help them learn about the region's recreational opportunities. Visitors can make travel arrangements, purchase tickets, exchange currency and conduct ATM transactions all within the center. Olympic tickets will go on sale at ACOG's (Atlanta Committee for the Olympic Games) kiosk in 1995.

The center includes a working press facility, complete with computers, telephones and fax machines, which visiting journalists can access when working in the region.

Atlanta Botanical Garden
1345 Piedmont Ave. N.E.   876-5859

In Piedmont Park, just 3 miles from downtown, discover and enjoy more than 60 acres of the Atlanta Botanical Gardens. Three main components make up ABG:

Storza Woods, which is spread over Piedmont Park; the outdoor gardens, which showcase plants that thrive in the north Georgia climate; and the Fuqua Conservatory. For a complete description of ABG, see our Green Atlanta chapter.

CNN Center

I CNN Center
Marietta St. at Techwood Dr. 827-2491

Spend the day touring three studios, CNN, Headline News and CNN International. Visit such shops as the Braves Clubhouse and the Turner Store, snack in the food court, dine in full-service restaurants or take in a movie in the Cinema Six. Take your seat and play broadcaster on a mock-up set, or step in front of the camera for a turn as weathercaster. Tours are 9 AM to 5 PM daily. Admission is: adults, $6; seniors, $4; children 12 and younger, $3.50. CNN is also listed in our Media chapter.

Fernbank Museum of Natural History

767 Clifton Rd. N.E. 378-0127

Don't miss this environmental and educational complex that includes a major museum of natural history, a science center, a planetarium and observatory, gardens and the Fernbank Forest. See our Kidstuff chapter for a complete description.

Fernbank Science Center

156 Heaton Park Dr. N.E. 378-4311

Marvel in one of the nation's largest planetariums, and enjoy an array of scientific exhibits. See our Kidstuff chapter for a complete description.

SciTrek

The Science and Technology Museum of Atlanta
395 Piedmont Ave. 522-5500

Enjoy a variety of interactive exhibits, live science demonstrations, workshops, programs, parties and more. See our Kidstuff chapter for a full description.

Underground Atlanta

Peachtree at Alabama Sts. 523-2311

In the heart of Atlanta, six city blocks have been transformed into an intriguing marketplace of more than 100 speciality shops and a dozen restaurants and entertainment spots. Pushcart vendors hawk everything from fudge to sunglasses. Special events, some on the wacky side, draw crowds year round. See our Shopping chapter for more details. Underground Atlanta is open Monday through Saturday, 10 AM to 9:30 PM; Sunday, noon to 6 PM. The bar and restaurant section swings until well after midnight. See our Nightlife chapter for more information.

The World of Coca-Cola

55 Martin Luther King Jr. Dr. 676-5151

Ever thought you'd visit the life history of a soft drink? The story of Coke — past, present and future — is so well told, you'll need at least an hour to take it all in. Amuse yourself at a futuristic soda fountain that defies description. See the mammoth collection of memorabilia. Check out how many of the classic radio and TV ads you remember. Enjoy the entertaining facsimile of the bottling process.

The World of Coca-Cola receives an average of 1 million visitors each year. There is also a shop with Coca-Cola merchandise — everything from hats to T-shirts to dancing coke cans, (you don't need to buy a ticket just to enter the store). Next to Underground Atlanta, this attraction features self-guided tours. It's open Monday through Saturday, 10 AM to 9:30 PM; Sunday, noon to 6 PM; closed holidays. The last admission is 1 hour before closing time. Admission is: adults, $2.50; seniors older than 55, $2; children 6 to 12, $1.50.

Zoo Atlanta

Grant Park
800 Cherokee Ave. S.E. 624-5600

This is one of those Cinderella stories Atlantans are proud to repeat. Rising from poor circumstances, Zoo Atlanta has become a top-ranked facility with an international reputation for excellence in conservation, education and science. In June 1994, *Good Housekeeping* magazine named it one of the 10 best zoos in the United States.

In their natural habit, you'll see orangutans, tigers, elephants, birds and more of the 250-species collection. The five-acre Ford African Rain Forest is home to three families of gorillas. Make the acquaintance of Willie B., Atlanta's favorite gorilla, who became the father of baby Kudzu in '94 at a ripe old (gorilla) age of 35 years. You may notice "Way to go, Willie B.!" bumper stickers as you cruise around town. By the way, the big ape's name is a playful tribute to William B. Hartsfield, the forward-looking mayor who helped ready Atlanta for the jet age.

A must-see is the Masai Mara exhibit of an East African habitat, with giraffes, lions and zebras. The kids are sure to love the World of Reptiles, the OK-To-Touch Corral and the Sheba Sumaran Tiger Forest.

The zoo is open 10 AM to 5:30 PM daily; it closes at 6:30 PM on summer weekends. Admission is: adults, $7.50; seniors, $6.50; children, $5; children younger than 2, free. Prices drop $1 each during winter months.

Beyond Atlanta

Cobb County

SIX FLAGS OVER GEORGIA
7561 Six Flags Rd. S.W. at I-20 W.   948-9290

A monster 331-acre theme park for everyone in the family, Six Flags is 12 miles west of downtown. Since opening in 1967, the park has entertained visitors with more than 100 rides, shows and attractions. Rides include the Z-Force roller coaster, the Mind Bender and the Free Fall.

Younger children will love Looney Tunes Land's play fort, scaled-down rides and merry-go-round. For everyone in the family, there's the entertaining Bugs Bunny Show, the Crystal Pistol and many others. Six Flags is open weekends during the spring and fall, daily during summer months. Admission is: adults, $28; children ages 3 through 9, $20; children younger than 3, free; senior citizens older than 55, $15. A two-day pass for adults and children is

Photo: Chuck Morgan

Zoo Atlanta was named one of the best 10 zoos in the United States.

offered for $32. Season tickets and group rates are available. Parking, food and souvenirs are extra.

DeKalb County

GEORGIA'S STONE MOUNTAIN PARK
Exit off U.S. Hwy. 78
Stone Mountain   498-5600

This major 3,200-acre attraction in a scenic park setting has something for everyone and then some. With its easily reached location (about 30 minutes from downtown), Stone Mountain is a prime vacation site for many visitors.

The park's name comes from the enormous exposed mass of granite, the world's largest, on which is carved a 90-foot-high by 190-foot-wide memorial to Robert E. Lee, Stonewall Jackson and Jefferson Davis. The carving of the Confederate war heroes on horseback, more than 50 years in the making, has a fascinating history all its own.

Mrs. C. Helen Plane, charter member of United Daughters of the Confederacy (UDC) launched the idea of a carving in 1912. Subsequently, the Venable family deeded the north face of the mountain to the UDC. A man named Gutzon Borglum conceived a plan and began work on the mountain sculpture in 1923. Ten years later, serious technical problems and internal disputes caused him to abandon the work. An artist named Augustus Lukeman worked on the edifice for three years till the owners lost patience and reclaimed the property. Borglum eventually gained fame as the creator of Mount Rushmore in South Dakota.

Finally in 1958, the state bought the land and mountain for a park. Work resumed in 1964 under the direction of Walter Kirkland Hancock and Roy Faulkner and was completed in 1970. Today, you can view the mountain from a walking trail that crosses its moss-covered slopes, where you may spot rare wildflowers. Or ride in comfort to the top aboard a tram equipped with an informative narration; the trams run about every 20 minutes.

A skylift, a riverboat and a steam engine locomotive are just a few of the things you'll find in Stone Mountain. Then there's the antique auto and music museum, plus a game ranch with petting area. For active pastimes, try the hiking trails and the outstanding facilities for fishing, tennis and golf (see our Recreational Sports chapter). Waterworks is a special beach area with waterslides and miniature golf.

A big favorite with Atlantans is Lasershow, a spectacular event complete with fireworks. Summer evenings after dark, cartoons, stories and graphics, complete with choreographed music, light up the mountain. Lasershow begins in April on Friday through Sunday evenings; from early May to Labor Day every night; Friday through Sunday in September; then Friday and Saturday only in October before adjourning for the winter. As always, call to verify show dates.

Another of the park's don't-miss attractions is the Stone Mountain Scenic Railroad. Take the 25-minute ride around the 5-mile base of Stone Mountain in one of three Civil War steam trains. Your trip will begin at Memorial Depot, an old-fashioned train station with a restaurant on premises that serves chicken dinners with all the fixings. Or maybe you'd prefer a tasty morsel from the barbecue snack bar.

Not a train aficionado? You can cruise the 363-acre Stone Mountain Lake in the *Scarlett O'Hara*, a paddlewheel riverboat.

Six Flags over Georgia is located just 12 miles west of downtown Atlanta.

And for animal lovers, more than 20 acres of natural woodlands are home to cougar, elk, bison and other species once native to Georgia. The Traders Camp Petting Farm provides a chance for up-close contact with domesticated creatures.

The Antebellum Plantation will expose your children to bygone ways, with authentic furnishings and detailed descriptions of how they were used. Self-guided tours are offered in 19 buildings. Hosts in period dress will assist you. An 1830's country store, the 1850 neoclassic Dickey House (with its Tara-like overtones), clapboard slave cabins and a coach house are among the sights.

On the plantation's grounds are formal gardens and a kitchen garden. This sight-within-a-sight takes at least an hour to tour. Sometimes, especially in summer, you'll find storytellers, balladeers and medicine shows. A 20-minute carriage ride around the area is available.

Special events scheduled throughout the year, ranging from a Taste of the South food festival to the Scottish Festival Highland Games, make Stone Mountain worth many repeat visits.

Attractions are open 10 AM to 9 PM daily June through August; 10 AM to 5 PM September through May. General admission is $5 per car; an annual pass for $20 is offered. Most adult attraction tickets are around $2.50; children's are $1.50. A non-refundable ticket package called the Big Ticket admits you to the six major attractions with no expiration dates; adults, $13.50; children 3 to 11, $9. The Big Ticket is available at any attraction or ticket information center. Group rates for 25 or more are offered.

Fulton County

CHATTAHOOCHEE NATURE CENTER
9135 Willeo Rd., Roswell   992-2055

Enjoy nature trails, ponds, exhibits, activities for children of all ages and more. See our Kidstuff chapter for a complete description.

Rockdale County

CONYERS APPARITION SITE
2324 White Rd., Conyers   922-8885

We mean no disrespect by including

this unusual site in our Attractions chapter — but it is, by any definition, an attraction of the first order. At noon on the 13th of every month, thousands of people from throughout the United States and parts beyond flock to a farmhouse in Conyers, 30 minutes east of Atlanta off I-20, where a woman says she receives divine messages.

In February 1987, housewife Nancy Fowler says she began receiving visions of Jesus and the Virgin Mary. A series of mystical experiences followed, and on October 13, 1990, Fowler says the Virgin began visiting her in Conyers to deliver special messages for the United States.

On the 13th of every month since that time, devotees have journeyed to the farm to await the divine message. Some pilgrims claim to experience an overpowering scent of roses; others say they see the sun spinning in the sky. Crowds have sometimes numbered more than 50,000. In March 1993, a howling March blizzard dubbed the "storm of the century" did not keep some people from making their pilgrimage.

Fowler says that in May 1994, the Virgin Mary announced that her monthly messages would cease. However, since then, Fowler says she has continued to see visions of Mary and to see and receive messages from Jesus. Prayer services are held daily at the farm.

The monthly gatherings are entirely outdoors, so bring a blanket or lawn chairs and dress according to the weather. The prayer services and messages are broadcast live over local radio 1540 AM. Drinking water and sanitary facilities are available on site. A group called Our Loving Mother's Children directs activities at the site and publishes Fowler's recitation of the messages. To hear the most recent message, call (404) 922-8885; to receive the message by fax, call (404) 413-1656 from a touch-tone fax machine.

From Atlanta, take I-20 E. to Exit 42, Conyers. Turn left (north) onto Ga. 138 N.; travel 4.9 miles, then turn left on White Road; the farm is a third of a mile ahead on the left. Law officers and volunteers will direct you to the parking area. There is no charge to park or visit the farm, although donations are accepted.

Fun Freebies

Many of these attractions are covered in other parts of this chapter and elsewhere. We're listing them all together here to remind you of one important fact: They're free!

ATLANTA INTERNATIONAL MUSEUM OF ART AND DESIGN
Peachtree Center, Marquis Two
285 Peachtree Center Ave.   688-2467

This museum celebrates the craftsmanship of the world's cultures through ethnographic, folk art and design exhibits. See The Arts chapter for a complete description.

CALLANWOLDE FINE ARTS CENTER
980 Briarcliff Rd.   872-5338

Originally the home of Howard Candler, the eldest son of Coca Cola's founder, Callanwolde now is a fine arts center. A nonprofit foundation directs a variety of arts programs, including dance, drama, painting, photography, pottery, textiles, writing and more. See The Arts chapter for a complete description.

COBB COUNTY PETTING ZOO
1060 County Farm Dr.   499-4136

Go see Miss Wiggy, the 900-pound pig, and her friends, the goats, chickens, deer, ferrets and sheep. Behind the Cobb County Animal Shelter, the zoo includes a pond with ducks and geese. It's open Monday through Friday, 9:30 AM to 5:30 PM; Saturday, 9:30 AM to 4 PM. Reservations are required.

CRAWFORD W. LONG MUSEUM
550 Peachtree St. N.E.   686-2631

This medical museum honors Dr. Crawford Long, who died in 1878. He is said to be the first physician to use anesthesia during surgery. Tour the fine array of medical tools and accessories from the days of horse-and-buggy doctoring. The museum is open Monday through Wednesday, 10 AM to 2 PM.

FEDERAL RESERVE BANK MONETARY MUSEUM
104 Marietta St.   521-8747

Here you'll see all the various forms our currency has taken over the decades — everything from beads to bars of gold — as well as the history of the banking system. Samples of gold coins minted just north of Atlanta in Dahlonega are exhibited. Appointments are required for groups. It's open Monday through Friday, 9 AM to 4 PM.

THE GEORGIA GOVERNOR'S MANSION
391 W. Paces Ferry Rd. N.E.   261-1776

See Historic Attractions in this chapter for a complete description.

GEORGIA STATE CAPITOL
Martin Luther King Jr. Dr. and
Washington St.   656-2844

See Historic Attractions in this chapter for a complete description.

THE HERNDON HOME
587 University Pl. N.W.   581-9813

See Historic Attractions in this chapter for a complete description.

THE HIGH MUSEUM OF ART
Folk Art and Photography Galleries
30 John Wesley Dobbs Ave. N.E.   577-6940

See the Arts chapter for a complete description.

KENNESAW MOUNTAIN NATIONAL BATTLEFIELD PARK
900 Kennesaw Mountain Dr.
Kennesaw   427-4686

See Historic Attractions in this chapter for a complete description.

THE MARTIN LUTHER KING, JR. CENTER FOR NONVIOLENT SOCIAL CHANGE
449 Auburn Ave. N.E.   524-1956

See Historic Attractions in this chapter for a complete description.

JOHNNY MERCER EXHIBIT
100 Decatur St. S.E.   651-2476

Music lovers will enjoy seeing displays of awards, manuscripts, photos and letters from the life of this composer of enduring music. The exhibit is open Monday through Friday, 8:30 AM to 5 PM.

MARGARET MITCHELL EXHIBIT
Central Library
One Margaret Mitchell Sq.   730-1700

This permanent display on the main floor of the library features the author's typewriter, pages from the *Gone With the Wind* manuscript and movie script and other rare memorabilia.

OLYMPIC EXPERIENCE
Underground Atlanta
At Peachtree and Alabama Sts.   658-1996

Get a preview of the 1996 Centennial Olympic Games in this walk-through audiovisual exhibit. A complete history of the Olympics, lodging and employment information, background on the Cultural

Olympiad and wall maps showing sites for the games in Atlanta are all part of this attraction. Izzy, the Games' mascot, is your guide for the interactive system presented in original music, still photos and full-motion video.

It's open Monday through Saturday, 10 AM to 9:30 PM; Sunday, noon to 6 PM. Another Information Center is in Lenox Square on Peachtree Road.

SOUTHEASTERN RAILWAY MUSEUM
3966 U.S. Hwy. 23, Duluth   476-2013

Train buffs will revel in the displays of rail travel from days gone by. This outdoor museum contains more than 40 diesel locomotives, freight cars and passenger cars. It's open Saturdays only, 9 AM to 5 PM.

TELEPHONE MUSEUM
675 W. Peachtree St. N.E.   223-3661

This unusual attraction presents the social and political history of the communications systems we depend on so heavily. In the plaza level of the Southern Bell Center, it's open Monday through Friday, 11 AM to 1 PM.

WORLD CHAMPIONSHIP WRESTLING
Center Stage
1374 W. Peachtree St.   874-1511

For a wild and wooly time, howl along with the audience at stars such as Hulk Hogan, as well as newer performers on their way up. These matches, another Ted Turner enterprise, are taped for national broadcast. Free tickets are available at current sponsors' places of business. For information, call 827-2066. See our Spectator Sports chapter for more information.

Photo: Chuck Morgan

The Science and Technology Museum of Atlanta (SciTrek) has been named
one of the top-10 science centers in the United States.

Inside
Kidstuff

Grownups, don't let the title of this chapter keep you from joining in the pleasures to be found in these varied attractions. Why let children have all the fun? Be sure to read our Attractions chapter for complete descriptions of the Six Flags Over Georgia amusement park, Zoo Atlanta, the plethora of activities available at Georgia's Stone Mountain Park and other attractions your whole family will enjoy.

AMERICAN ADVENTURES
250 N. Cobb Pkwy., Marietta   424-9283

This is Atlanta's amusement park for kids of all ages. You'll find rides, indoor and outdoor miniature golf, a race track, a train ride, a carousel, a balloon ride, go-carts, a skill arcade and many other attractions. American Adventures opens at 11 AM daily; closing times vary. There is no admission charge, and amusements generally range less than $2. Economy packages are available.

CENTER FOR PUPPETRY ARTS
1404 Spring St. N.W.   873-3089, 873-3391

Enjoy this unique museum's collection of puppets, the largest such collection in the country. There you'll find everything from Chinese hand puppets to ritualistic African figures and the Muppets. In fact, when the center opened in 1978, Kermit the Frog performed the ribbon-cutting ceremony with the assistance of the late Jim Henson. See The Arts chapter for a complete description.

CHATTAHOOCHEE NATURE CENTER
9135 Willeo Rd., Roswell   992-2055

On the border of the Chattahoochee River, you'll find a delightful change of pace in 100 acres of nature trails, ponds, activities for all ages and a boardwalk over marshlands. A wildlife rehabilitation program makes small animals available for children to see. A center with exhibits and classes on nature entertain as they teach. The center is open daily from 9 AM to 5 PM. Admission is $2 for adults, $1 for children.

FERNBANK MUSEUM
OF NATURAL HISTORY
767 Clifton Rd. N.E.   378-0127

The very popular Fernbank is many things rolled into one: a 150-acre environmental and educational complex that includes a major museum of natural history (the largest in the Southeast), a science center, a planetarium and observatory, gardens and the Fernbank Forest.

Since opening in 1993, the museum, owned and funded by the DeKalb County School System, has attracted more than 900,000 visitors.

The permanent exhibits at Fernbank include A Walk Through Time in Georgia, which shows the chronological development of life on earth. Six galleries recreate landform regions such as the pine-forested Piedmont Plateau and the Okefenokee Swamp.

Fernbank teems with other delights too. The *Origin of the Universe*, a high-definition video, projects the drama of the Big Bang theory on the 30-foot by 10-foot screen in the Cosmos Theater. Another is the spectacular Dinosaur Hall, with seven life-size dinosaurs and three massive murals of the Cretaceous, Jurassic and Triassic eras. The Okefenokee Swamp gallery surrounds you with the sights and sounds of this stunning swampland.

Georgia's first IMAX Theater is here at Fernbank. The 52-foot by 70-foot screen is the largest film format in the world. If you've never seen an IMAX film, prepare yourself: You'll feel like you're inside the action. The larger film also makes the image a lot clearer than regular theater screen formats. IMAX movies employ a special, curved screen and powerful sound that is digitally-recorded on CDs. Fernbank's IMAX system cost about $2 million. It's one of only five in the Southeast and one of only 100 in the world.

Spectrum of the Senses presents interactive exhibits on light and sound. This gallery brims over with computers, colored lights, video projectors and lasers. This very popular gallery's exhibits can be experienced at several intellectual levels; some are simple, while others involve high technology.

There's much more to see here, including a museum shop and restaurant. All facilities are accessible to disabled visitors. The museum is open Monday through Thursday and Saturday, 10 AM to 5 PM; Friday, 10 AM to 9 PM; Sunday, noon to 5 PM. Hours may vary with the season; call to confirm. Museum admission is: adults, $5.50; students, seniors and children, $4.50; museum members and children younger than 2, free. Combination IMAX and museum tickets cost $9.50 for adults, $7.50 for students and seniors.

FERNBANK SCIENCE CENTER
156 Heaton Park Dr. N.E.   378-4311

Home to one of the nation's largest planetariums (70 feet in diameter), the Science Center is also the location of an exhibit hall featuring moon rocks, the original *Apollo* space capsule and much more. In the greenhouses, open on Sundays only, your child can pot a plant and take it home.

The observatory is open Thursday and Friday evenings when the sky is clear. For nature lovers and explorers, the 65-acre Fernbank Forest has 2 miles of trails through some 65 acres; some trails are adapted for heart patients and the visually impaired. Active research programs are conducted by staff members and visiting scientists. Currently a 132-foot-high meteorological tower is in the forest and is used to study low-level ozone and the effects of vegetation on mediating weather.

The center is open Monday, 8:30 AM to 5 PM; Tuesday through Friday, 8:30 AM to 10 PM; Saturday, 10 AM to 5 PM; and Sunday, 1 PM to 5 PM. Hours may vary with the season; call to confirm. There is no general admission charge. Admission to planetarium shows is $2 for adults and $1 for students.

LAKE LANIER ISLANDS
6950 Holiday Rd.
Lake Lanier Islands   932-7200

A premier full-service resort on one of the country's most popular lakes, recreational facilities here spread over the 1,200 acres surrounded by water. A beach, golf course, water park with eight water slides, stable, bike rentals, cottages, camp sites and boat rentals of all kinds (including houseboats) are just part of the picture.

The islands are open all day, every day. General admission is $3 per car or

WhiteWater offers nearly 40 acres of wet fun with a separate activity area for small children.

Photo: Georgia Tourist Division

$15 for an annual pass. Children less than 42 inches tall pay $4.50; seniors and children 2 and younger are free. See our Daytrips and Recreational Sports chapters for more information.

MALIBU GRAND PRIX

5400 Brook Hollow Pkwy.
Norcross   416-7630
3005 George Busbee Pkwy.
Kennesaw   514-8081

Here you'll find Formula One racing for the whole family. Sprint car racing, miniature golf, sports arcade, batting cages, bumper boats — this is the place to let off some steam. The Norcross location is open Sunday through Thursday, 11 AM to 11 PM; Friday and Saturday, 11 AM to midnight. The Kennesaw location summer hours are seven days a week, 11 AM to midnight. Prices vary according to the feature chosen; call for specifics.

ARKENSTONE PAINT BALL GAMES

7257 Cedarcrest Rd. N.W.
Acworth   974-2535

This is where the big kids come to play! A 1,750-foot clubhouse and paint ball supply store, Arkenstone is open weekends for beginner and intermediate sportsters. (In paint ball, by the way, you use air guns and pellets of water-soluble paint to shoot your opponents.) The location features 10 fields with forts, bunkers foxholes, ravines and streams. Owner Mike Lanier says mostly business groups come in, playing corporate team-building games. Arkenstone is open Saturdays and Sundays year round from 10 AM to 5 PM. An all-day rental charge is assessed, averaging about $45 for a full day.

SCITREK

The Science and Technology Museum of Atlanta
395 Piedmont Ave.   522-5500

More than 100 interactive exhibits await you at SciTrek, named one of the top 10 science centers in the United States. Since its opening in 1988, SciTrek's doors have admitted more than 360,000 school children from 28 countries.

Sure to pique the curiosity of both kids and adults, the hands-on exhibits will bring the mysterious and the everyday to life like never before. Marvel at the scaled-down exhibits for children from ages 2 to

7, specially designed to develop their cognitive, social, emotional and fine motor skills.

You'll enjoy live science demonstrations, workshops, films, traveling exhibits, overnight programs, parties and a unique museum shop with special gifts for kids. For grownups, SciTrek offers an adult lecture series given by scientists, professors and other business people. The series is held at 7:30 PM on the third Thursday of each month in the Sponsor's Room.

Want an example of SciTrek fare? During summer '94, the big show was Masters of the Night: The True Story of Bats. The interactive exhibit contained a realistic rain forest, a cave, fossils and models of bats, plus detailed presentations of the creatures' roosting habits, migration patterns and hibernation periods.

SciTrek is open Tuesday through Saturday, 10 AM to 5 PM; Sunday, noon to 5 PM. Call for extended summer hours. Admission is $6.50 for adults and $4.25 for children 3 to 17. Reduced rates are offered Tuesday though Friday, 2 to 5 PM.

SUN VALLEY BEACH
5350 Holloman Rd., Powder Springs 943-5900

Fourteen miles west of Atlanta and billed as the Southeast's largest swimming pool, this recreation area has a full roster of fun for all. The pool covers 1.5 acres, has seven water slides and a Tarzan swing. Play volleyball on a half-mile sand beach, or try your hand at miniature golf, tennis and horseshoes. The kids will take to a romp in the four kiddie play areas. Picnic spots with concession stands dot the 34-acre site, which is open weekends in May, daily from Memorial Day to Labor Day. Call for prices.

WHITE WATER PARK
250 N. Cobb Pkwy., Marietta 424-WAVE

Nearly 40 scenic acres of water attractions, adjacent to American Adventures, make for a wild day of fun. You'll find raft rides, body flumes, a wave pool and lots of attractions from the relaxing to the shriek provoking. The Bahama Bobslide, the Atlanta Ocean and Dragon's Tail Falls are just a few. At Little Squirt's Island, a separate activity area is scaled to kids under 48 inches tall.

With five restaurants on premises, guests aren't allowed to bring their own food. No thong or G-string bathing suits are allowed either. The park opens at 10 AM from Memorial Day through the first weekend in September; closing times vary. Group rates and season passes are available. Call for admission prices.

WREN'S NEST
1050 R. D. Abernathy Rd. S.W. 753-8535

A gentler attraction is found here in the Victorian home of Joel Chandler Harris, author of the Uncle Remus tales. Storytelling times, a museum shop with Br'er Rabbit memorabilia and guided tours are offered. See our Attractions chapter for a complete description.

YELLOW RIVER WILDLIFE GAME RANCH
4525 Hwy. 78, Lilburn 972-6643

This wildlife reserve shelters rarely seen animals native to Georgia. They roam freely on 24 wooded acres where you may pet, feed and photograph them. The ranch is open daily from 9:30 AM till dark. Admission for adults is $4.50; children 3 to 11, $3.50; it's free for wildlife enthusiasts younger than 3. Rates for groups of 15 or more are available.

Inside
Annual Events and Festivals

Atlantans love any excuse to throw a party. Most weekends throughout the year, you can find several festivals or special events going on somewhere in the metro area. Whether cozy block parties, neighborhood tours of homes, large church-sponsored festivals or huge celebrations that draw more than 100,000, Atlanta offers pleasant diversions throughout the year.

Here's a look at some of the annual events that make life in Atlanta special. Approximate dates are given for most festivals; call the sponsoring groups to confirm specifics before you make plans to attend.

Outdoor festivals are generally free; we'll let you know if there is an admission charge. A typical neighborhood festival has many free attractions and a few that charge admission, such as a tour of homes or a street dance; we've designated these, "Free admission to most events."

Tours of homes have become especially popular festival attractions. These tours feature different homes each year and are a great way to get the Insiders' view of a neighborhood. In most cases, tours are self-guided: Visitors pay an admission fee and receive a descriptive brochure with a map. Call the sponsoring organizations to learn where this year's tours begin and what admissions are charged.

Many festivals are held in parks. For specific information on Atlanta's parks, see our Green Atlanta chapter. Here's a quick guide to the location of major parks.

Piedmont Park is in Midtown; most concerts are given on the main stage facing the rolling hillside along 10th Street between Monroe Drive and Piedmont; food, drink and merchandise vendors sell their wares along the paved car-free road that circles the lake.

Grant Park is in southeast Atlanta; its main entrances are on Cherokee Avenue and on Boulevard. Zoo Atlanta and the Cyclorama occupy the southern portion; festivals take place in the park's northern area.

Chastain Park is in northwest Atlanta; take Roswell Road north through Buckhead; turn left on W. Wieuca Road and follow the signs.

To reach **Georgia's Stone Mountain Park**, take U.S. 78 (Ponce de Leon Avenue - Scott Boulevard - Lawrenceville Highway - Stone Mountain Parkway) east of Atlanta to the Stone Mountain Park Exit. A per-vehicle admission is always charged here: It's $5 per car. An annual pass is $20. There is an additional charge for some special events at Stone Mountain; these are noted "Fee in addition to park admission."

January

KING WEEK AND THE MARTIN LUTHER KING JR. NATIONAL HOLIDAY

Martin Luther King, Jr. Center for
Nonviolent Social Change   524-1956
449 Auburn Ave. N.E. (and other locations)
The week preceding the Martin Luther King, Jr.
National Holiday

Dr. Martin Luther King Jr. was born in Atlanta on January 15, 1929. A national holiday was declared in his honor in 1986. Long before that, we Atlantans had been staging an annual celebration to laud our Nobel laureate. King Week includes performances, concerts, special religious services, educational events and the National March of Celebration — a parade on Peachtree Street and Auburn Avenue with bands, floats and visiting celebrities.

February

BLACK HISTORY MONTH

Numerous educational and entertainment events commemorate Black History Month all over Atlanta throughout February.

RINGLING BROS. AND BARNUM & BAILEY CIRCUS

The Omni
100 Techwood Dr. N.W.   681-2100
Mid-February
Admission fee

By February, most people have had enough of winter and need cheering up. And just like magic, the circus comes to town! The big show rolls in this month for a 10-day run at The Omni; call TicketMaster for tickets, 249-6400; a convenience charge applies.

March

ST. PATRICK'S DAY

March 17

Atlanta goes green with St. Patrick's Day celebrations. There are parades both downtown (sponsored by the Hibernian Benevolent Society — contact Mac McKenna, 449-6601 extension 103) and in Buckhead (sponsored by the Buckhead

The Callanwolde Fine Arts Center hosts "Christmas At Callonwolde" and was once the home to the eldest son of Coca-Cola's founder.

Village Merchants Association, 266-9209).

CONYERS CHERRY BLOSSOM FESTIVAL
Conyers   *918-2169*
Various events during March
Free admission to most events

In 1980, Hitachi Maxell's president donated 500 cherry trees to the city of Conyers, 30 minutes east of Atlanta on I-20, home to Maxell Corp. of America. The Conyers Cherry Blossom Festival has greeted spring here since 1981. The month-long calendar of events includes art exhibits, a road race, other sporting tournaments, a beauty pageant, music and more.

THE ANTEBELLUM JUBILEE
Georgia's Stone Mountain Park   *498-5702*
A weekend in late March
Fee in addition to park admission

Y'all had better practice up on your Rebel yell for this trip back in time to the prewar South. You'll find folk music, crafts, open-hearth cooking, storytelling, an authentic Civil War encampment and more.

ATLANTA PASSION PLAY
Atlanta Civic Center
395 Piedmont Ave. N.E.   *347-8400*
Final three weekends of Lent and Easter Sunday
Admission fee

Since 1976, the First Baptist Church of Atlanta has annually presented this pageant portraying Christ's life, death and resurrection. The elaborately staged and costumed play is the work of more than 300 people, including a chorus and full orchestra. Due to the 3-hour length, the sacred nature of the performance and the graphic portrayal of Christ's death, children younger than 5 are not admitted. The church sets ticket prices well below the cost of other shows with comparably high production values.

EASTER SUNRISE SERVICES
Georgia's Stone Mountain Park   *498-5702*
Easter Sunday
Free with park admission

In the predawn darkness on Easter Sunday morning, the faithful gather atop Stone Mountain to await the sunrise on the holiest day of the Christian year. As morning breaks, local ministers lead an ecumenical worship service. This inspiring celebration is a long-standing Atlanta tradition. The weather is often windy and cold, so you might need to bring a blanket.

April

EASTER SUNRISE SERVICES
See March entry.

THE GREAT ATLANTA POT FESTIVAL
Piedmont Park   *522-CAMP*
A Saturday in early April

It's no coincidence that this one-day event is held on the weekend following the annual Atlanta Omni concerts of the perpetually touring Grateful Dead. The festival of bands and leftist politics attract a multicultural and generally well-behaved crowd in the tens of thousands for a good time and a good smoke. Note: Atlanta Mayor Bill Campbell opposes the event; its future is hazy.

ATLANTA DOGWOOD FESTIVAL
Piedmont Park   *952-9151*
A weekend in late April

Atlanta's legendary springtime floral trademark is paid homage at this popular festival, whose highlights include a colorful hot-air balloon race, concerts, children's parades and the dog Frisbee championships. Note: Atlanta's beautiful dogwoods and azaleas bloom on a schedule all their own, and their peak does not always coincide with this festival!

Earth Jam

Georgia's Stone Mountain Park 498-5702
A Saturday in late April
Fee in addition to park admission

Earth Jam is a musical event dedicated to raising awareness about Earth's ecology and limited resources. Big-name stars headline; Jackson Browne played in 1994. Concert tickets are available through TicketMaster, 249-6400; a convenience charge applies.

Freaknik

Piedmont Park and various locations
A weekend in late April

In the past, this massive event has drawn more than 200,000 African-American college students from across the country for a weekend of partying and driving very slowly around town. Unfortunately, round-the-clock traffic jams, noise and disorderly conduct have made Freaknik unpopular with many Atlantans. Mayor Bill Campbell has said the party is no longer welcome here; organizers say they plan to hold it anyway. Stay tuned for more details, or call the Mayor's office, 330-6100. Traffic-wise, this is unquestionably the worst weekend of the year.

Inman Park Festival

Various Inman Park neighborhood streets
A weekend in late April 242-4895
Free admission to most events

About 2 miles east of Five Points, Inman Park was developed as Atlanta's first suburb, and along its broad, tree-lined streets are imposing Victorian mansions and charming bungalows. Coca-Cola founder Asa Candler lived here in the early 1900s; Mayor Bill Campbell lives here today. A parade, a tour of homes, antiques, food, crafts, music and more can all be found at this two-day street party. This is the oldest of Atlanta's many neighborhood festivals.

Georgia Renaissance Festival

I-85 at Exit 12
Fairburn 964-8575
Late April to mid-June
Admission fee

Forsooth, this rollicking recreation of the English Renaissance features more than 100 performances daily on 10 stages scattered across the 30-acre festival grounds. Strolling musicians, minstrels, magicians and other costumed characters are all part of the fun, along with knights in armor jousting on horseback. The festival is open Saturdays and Sundays only, plus Memorial Day; it's such a popular event that it's presented again (with some different attractions) in October.

May

Lasershow

Georgia's Stone Mountain Park 498-5702
Early May through late October
Free with park admission

Seven nights a week all summer long, the sky over Stone Mountain explodes with a rainbow of laser light. To stirring musical accompaniment, lasers are projected on the mountain's north face, which becomes a natural million-square-

Insiders' Tips

Admission to Georgia's Stone Mountain Park is charged per vehicle: $5 per car. An annual pass costs $20.

foot screen. Bring a blanket and relax under the stars. After Labor Day, the show is presented on Friday and Saturday nights only.

SPRINGFEST '95 AND THE SOUTH'S LARGEST GARAGE SALE

Georgia's Stone Mountain Park   498-5702
A weekend in early May
Free with park admission

Cooks from around the South compete in a barbecue cookoff for thousands of dollars in cash and prizes. In addition to live music, the weekend includes a huge garage sale that's a junk lover's dream come true. A registration fee is required for sellers.

WEST END TOUR OF HOMES

Various West End neighborhood homes
A weekend in mid-May   755-2000
Admission fee

This event spotlights the proud and historic southwest Atlanta neighborhood, West End, the location of the Wren's Nest, the lovely restored Victorian home of Uncle Remus' creator Joel Chandler Harris. Ten area homes are included on the tour.

LAKE CLAIRE TOUR OF FUNKY HOMES

Various Lake Claire neighborhood homes 373-4744
A weekend in mid-May
Admission fee

There's no lake in this pleasant neighborhood just east of Little Five Points and Candler Park, but there are many affectionately restored large and small homes. Lake Claire overflows with writers, artists and other freethinkers: The emphasis here is on creativity. Look for imaginative and eccentric touches in the homes and gardens of this easygoing neighborhood.

OLD MIDTOWN TOUR OF HOMES

Various Midtown neighborhood homes   876-3201
A weekend in mid-May
Admission fee

Midtown, the heavily wooded neighborhood that has Piedmont Park for its front yard, hit the skids in the 1960s before again becoming a preferred address in the late '70s and the '80s. Some of Midtown's large homes were built before the turn of the century and survived the great fire of 1917, which makes them positively ancient compared to most Atlanta houses. About a dozen outstanding homes are featured on the tour each year.

KINGFEST INTERNATIONALE

Martin Luther King, Jr., Center for Nonviolent
Social Change   524-1956
449 Auburn Ave. N.E.
A weekend in late May

The King Center welcomes everyone for a celebration with international music and dance, art exhibits and more.

MIDTOWN MUSIC FESTIVAL

Peachtree at 10th in Midtown   872-1115
A weekend in late May
Admission fee

First held in 1994, this outdoor festival scored an immediate hit. 1994 acts included James Brown, Bobby "Blue" Bland, Joan Baez and Al Green.

The biannual National Black Arts Festival will next be held June 28 through July 7, 1996.

Insiders' Tips

GEORGIA SPECIAL OLYMPICS

Emory University
Corner of N. Decatur and Oxford rds. 414-9390
A weekend in late May

The athletic accomplishments of mentally handicapped Georgians are showcased in this three-day event of competition and recognition.

ATLANTA JAZZ FESTIVAL

Grant Park and Underground Atlanta
A weekend in late May   817-6815

The City of Atlanta sponsors this festival, which brings in big-name jazz and pop acts for a series of free concerts.

TASTE OF THE SOUTH

Georgia's Stone Mountain Park   498-5702
Memorial Day weekend
Fee in addition to park admission

If you've always been curious about okra (boiled or fried), grits (cheese or regular) and greens (collard or turnip), here's your chance to taste what you've been missing. Each Southern state shows off its best offerings in food, entertainment, travel and more.

ATLANTA PEACH CARIBBEAN FESTIVAL

Various locations   220-0158
Memorial Day weekend
Free admission to most events

Atlanta is home to many people who trace their roots to the Caribbean islands. This festival celebrates Caribbean culture with a parade, a soccer tournament, parties, art shows and performances.

DECATUR ARTS FESTIVAL

Decatur town square and other locations
Memorial Day weekend   371-9583
Free admission to most events

The lovely city of Decatur, 6 miles east of downtown, hosts this popular festival, which has grown substantially in recent years. Among the many activities to enjoy are art exhibits, a children's festival, international music and dance and literary events.

June

LASERSHOW

See May entry.

KINGFEST INTERNATIONALE

Martin Luther King, Jr., Center for Nonviolent Social Change, 449 Auburn Ave. N.E. 524-1956
A weekend in mid-June

The King Center presents another weekend of international music and dance, art exhibits and more.

NATIONAL BLACK FAMILY REUNION

Georgia World Congress Center and Piedmont Park   524-6269
A weekend in mid-June
Free admission to most events

This three-day event begins with a leadership forum on Friday; on Saturday there's a free expo in the Georgia World Congress Center with seminars, health screenings and merchandise vendors. An R&B show caps Saturday's activities. On Sunday the festival moves to Piedmont

Construction continues on the Olympic Stadium as Atlanta looks forward to the summer of 1996.

Park for a gospel concert, where food and more merchandise are available.

JUNEENTEENTH
Washington Park, Lena St. at Ollie 876-6346
A weekend in mid-June

The Juneteenth festival commemorates the day, June 19, 1865, when slaves in Texas finally found out they had been freed by the Emancipation Proclamation more than two years earlier. Washington Park is just northwest of the Ashby Street MARTA station; in segregated times, it was the only city park open to Atlanta's black citizens.

ATLANTA LESBIAN AND GAY PRIDE FESTIVAL
Piedmont Park and various locations
A weekend in late June 662-4533

Like similar celebrations across the United States, the Atlanta Lesbian and Gay Pride Festival commemorates the day, June 27, 1969, when patrons at New York's Stonewall Inn fought back against police oppression and ignited the modern gay liberation movement. Founded in 1970, Atlanta's Pride Festival is now among the largest in the nation: It features an artists' market, merchandise vendors and two days of continuous entertainment. The weekend's highlight, a Sunday afternoon march from the Civic Center to Piedmont Park with a rally and show afterward, attracts more than 150,000 people.

July

LASERSHOW
See May entry.

FANTASTIC FOURTH CELEBRATION
Georgia's Stone Mountain Park 498-5702
July 4
Free with park admission

The park throws a four-day birthday party for America, with major concerts and other entertainment, plus nightly fireworks in addition to the Lasershow.

INDEPENDENCE DAY
Various locations
July 4

There's almost too much fun to be had around Atlanta on the 4th. The action gets under way at the crack of dawn as thousands of spectators line Peachtree to watch 50,000 runners compete in the annual Peachtree Road Race, 231-9065. Midday there's WSB-TV's Salute 2 America parade, 897-7385, the largest Independence Day parade in the nation. After dark there are fireworks all over town, with magnificent displays at Lenox Square, the Southeast's largest, and at Atlanta Fulton County Stadium following the Braves game. With so many people heading to the same destinations and some major streets closed for the road race and the parade, traffic can be difficult; plan accordingly, or take MARTA.

August

LASERSHOW
See May entry.

WING FLING AND COLLECTIBLES SHOW
Georgia's Stone Mountain Park   498-5702
A Saturday in early August
Free with park admission

Cooks from around the South sling wings and fry for prizes in the wacky "Wing-lympics" at this food-fest, which also includes entertainment and a big collectibles show.

HOTLANTA RIVER EXPO
Chattahoochee River and various venues
A weekend in mid-August   874-3976
Admission fee

Thousands of gay men from around the nation arrive for this weekend of intense partying and a raft trip down the Chattahoochee.

This is an especially festive weekend in the gay clubs in Midtown and elsewhere.

September

LASERSHOW
See May entry.

A TASTE OF ATLANTA
Peachtree at 10th   248-1315
Admission fee

You can sample the cuisine of more than 40 of Atlanta's tastiest restaurants in this eat-a-thon benefiting the National Kidney Foundation of Georgia. (The cost of the foods you select is in addition to the admission charge.)

WEST END FESTIVAL
Howell Park   752-9329
The second weekend in September

Founded in 1975, this two-day affair is the second oldest of Atlanta's many neighborhood festivals. Saturday's activities spotlight the district's cultural landmarks, including The Wren's Nest, home of Joel Chandler Harris, the Hammonds House Galleries and the Shrine of the Black Madonna Culture Center. On Sunday, the festival moves to Howell Park, Peeples Street at Ralph David Abernathy Boulevard, for an outdoor celebration with entertainment.

GRANT PARK TOUR OF HOMES
Various Grant Park neighborhood homes
A weekend in mid-September   522-7131
Admission fee

Grant Park is named for Col. Lemuel

P. Grant, the transplanted Yankee civil engineer who designed the elaborate fortifications around Atlanta during the Civil War and who later donated much of his wooded, hilly land to the city. The neighborhood around the park has many historic Victorian homes, both massive and modest. Ten homes are open to visitors during this event, which also includes carriage rides through the neighborhood.

YELLOW DAISY FESTIVAL

Georgia's Stone Mountain Park   *498-5702*
A weekend in mid-September
Free with park admission

For more than 25 years, Stone Mountain Park has staged this celebration of the Confederate Yellow Daisy, fields of which adorn the mountainside and bloom about this time. The festival features a big arts and crafts sale with more than 400 vendors, live entertainment, a flower show, lots of food and more.

ARTS FESTIVAL OF ATLANTA

Piedmont Park   *885-1125*
Mid-September

The largest annual event of its kind in the city, the Arts Festival draws an amazing 2 million visitors during its nine-day run at Piedmont Park. Hundreds of vendors sell arts, jewelry and crafts. Leading restaurants offer their specialities. Every day there are concerts, dance performances, movie screenings, art exhibits and more. *Creative Loafing*, the free entertainment weekly, includes extensive schedule information the week of the festival to help you plan your visits. Opening and closing weekends are the most crowded; weekday afternoons are the least crowded.

Parking for this massive event has always been a problem, as the available street spaces fill up fast. There's paid parking at nearby Grady High School on the corner of 10th and Charles Allen Drive; the money collected benefits the school's PTSA. Or you can take MARTA to the Arts Center station, where a special festival shuttle bus operates every 6 to 10 minutes. For handicapped parking only, enter at the Park Drive entrance off Monroe Drive. Especially on weekends, MARTA is your best bet.

SWEET AUBURN FESTIVAL

Auburn Ave.   *524-1956*
A weekend in late September

For nearly a century Auburn Avenue has been the backbone of black Atlanta. It picked up the "sweet" label at a time when it was functioning as the city's "other" main street, offering a full array of commercial, religious and entertainment institutions. Dr. Martin Luther King Jr.'s birth home, church and tomb are part of a National Historic Site on Auburn. The famous Royal Peacock Lounge once showcased soul music stars such as James Brown and Stevie Wonder; it continues to operate today. This festival celebrates the street's rich heritage with three days of music, food, fun and shopping.

ATLANTA GREEK FESTIVAL

Greek Orthodox Cathedral of the Annunciation
2500 Clairmont Rd.   *633-5870*
A weekend in late September
Admission fee

This annual fall tribute to Greek culture attracts more than 50,000 people in four days. There's Greek music, dancing, wine, and oh, the food: souvlaki, moussaka, gyros and honey-dripping baklava. There is no parking on-site, but the festival operates free shuttles to nearby parking; call for details.

ALPENFEST

Georgia's Stone Mountain Park   *498-5702*
A late September weekend
Fee in addition to park admission

Get ready to "oom-pah-pah" around the rock. Attractions at this two-day party include a German beer and wine garden serving wursts, kraut and strudel and a Festhalle with polka music and other entertainment.

OLDE ENGLISH FESTIVAL

St. Bartholmew's Episcopal Church
1790 LaVista Rd.   *634-3336*
A weekend in late September
Admission fee

Knights and knaves alike will enjoy this pleasant festival on the wooded grounds of St. Bart's church. The admission fee is good for all three days; attractions include a flea market, a raffle, entertainment, wine, tea and more. There's no parking on-site; instead, park for free at Georgia Mental Health Institute, 1256 Briarcliff Road, and take the complimentary double-decker bus to the festival.

October

LASERSHOW

See May entry.

GEORGIA RENAISSANCE FALL FESTIVAL

Fairburn, I-85 at Exit 12   *964-8575*
Weekends in October
Admission fee

The Spring Renaissance Festival was so much fun they decided to have another one in the fall. Lords and ladies, wenches, vassals and the occasional fool roam the 30-acre festival grounds, where more than 100 daily performances take place on 10 stages. Special attractions at the fall celebration include the Haunted Castle and the Octoberfest WurstHaus. The festival is open Saturdays and Sundays only.

TOUR OF SOUTHERN GHOSTS

Georgia's Stone Mountain Park   *498-5702*
Mid-October through Halloween
Fee in addition to park admission

Be very afraid: Something terrifying is happening out at the old plantation house. Seven nights a week, spooks, monsters and "haints" galore take over the mansion at Stone Mountain where storytellers spins webs of horror. Tours begin at 7 PM; the last tickets are sold at 9 PM.

AIDS WALK

Piedmont Park and various streets   *876-WALK*
A Sunday in mid-October

One part of Atlanta's response to the ongoing AIDS tragedy, this annual walk-a-thon raises thousands of dollars for AID Atlanta, which offers a variety of services to persons with AIDS; Project Open Hand, which delivers free meals to people with HIV; and other worthy organizations. Look for big stars (sometimes Atlanta's own Elton John) to perform at the after-walk concert.

SCOTTISH FESTIVAL AND HIGHLAND GAMES

Georgia's Stone Mountain Park   *498-5702*
A weekend in late October
Fee in addition to park admission

Aye, 'tis the sons and daughters of Burns a-gathering for this annual celebration of Scottish heritage, also known as "Scots on the Rock." Kilted clans engage in athletic events, plus there are parades and pageantry galore with bagpiping, drumming and folk dancing.

ATLANTA MINI GRAND PRIX AT BUCKHEAD

Buckhead neighborhood streets   *872-7100*
A Sunday in late October

Atlanta is home to the headquarters of the Arthritis Foundation, which stages this benefit event. Several Buckhead streets are closed to traffic and taken over by tiny cars, which zip around in a grand prix-style race.

LITTLE FIVE POINTS HALLOWEEN FESTIVAL
Little Five Points neighborhood
The weekend before Halloween

The cynic may sneer that every day looks like Halloween in Little Five, but Atlanta's most eclectic shopping district really goes over the edge this weekend. The shops are filled with costume ideas, and sidewalk vendors hawk accessories. Now is the perfect time to pick up that rainbow wig or beatnik cigarette holder.

November

VETERANS DAY PARADE
Downtown Atlanta   416-0377
November 11

On the day World War I ended in 1918, Georgia honors all its veterans with a downtown parade.

LIGHTING OF RICH'S GREAT TREE
Underground Atlanta   523-2311
Thanksgiving evening

Even though Rich's once-proud downtown flagship store is gone, this holiday tradition begun in 1948 still continues. At 7 PM, thousands of Atlantans gather to sing carols with mass choirs and await the lighting of Rich's Great Tree, an enormous tree decorated with basketball-sized ornaments atop Underground Atlanta's parking garage. Even the scroogiest Scrooge is hard pressed to produce a "bah, humbug!" when (during the highest note of "Oh, Holy Night") the switch is thrown, and the huge tree explodes with light. To share the fun but not the frostbite, tune into the live broadcast on WSB-TV channel 2.

HOLIDAY CELEBRATION
Georgia's Stone Mountain Park   498-5702
Thanksgiving Friday through New Year's Eve
Fee in addition to park admission

The park's holiday party goes on seven nights a week, with horse-drawn carriage rides, a decorated plantation home, Christmas music and a holiday laser show. The guest of honor, of course, is jolly old St. Nick, accompanied by his merry elves.

CANDLELIGHT TOURS
Atlanta History Center
130 W. Paces Ferry Rd.   814-4000
Late November or early December
Admission fee

Hundreds of candles illuminate acres of gardens and nature trails at the History Center. Traditional music and a bonfire enliven the Tullie Smith farm house; the grand 1928 Swan House mansion shimmers in holiday finery to the accompaniment of jazz music. For an additional charge, guests can enjoy a traditional three-course holiday dinner at the Swan Coach House restaurant. Many of the center's paths are unpaved and not suitable for wheelchairs, but center personnel will gladly make arrangements for physically challenged persons: Phone ahead for assistance.

December

CHRISTMAS AT CALLANWOLDE
980 Briarcliff Rd. N.E.   872-5338
First two weeks of December
Admission fee

This elaborate, 27,000-square-foot mansion was once home to the eldest son of Coca-Cola's founder; now it's operated as a fine arts center. Some 20,000 people tour the lavishly decorated home during this two-week event each December. A special attraction is holiday music played on the gigantic 3,752-pipe, 20,000-pound Aeolian organ, the largest of its kind still in playable condition, around which the house was built.

EGLESTON CHRISTMAS PARADE

Downtown Atlanta streets   264-9348
The first Saturday morning in December

Egleston Children's Hospital sponsors this annual Christmas parade through downtown Atlanta. It features giant balloons, celebrities, bands, floats and Santa Claus. WSB-TV 2 broadcasts the parade live.

COUNTRY CHRISTMAS

Atlanta Botanical Garden
1345 Piedmont Ave., at The Prado   876-5859
The first Sunday in December

For more than 15 years, the Atlanta Botanical Garden has presented this one-day event, which attracts more than 2,000 visitors, as its gift to the city. The garden and conservatory are bedecked in high holiday style with decorated trees and thousands of poinsettias, including some unusual varieties. There's fun for the whole family, with face painting, dance, other entertainment and storytelling. Vendors sell a variety of foods, plus fresh greenery. There's very little parking in the area, but you can park free at the IBM building garage, 14th Street at W. Peachtree, and take the free shuttle to the garden.

FESTIVAL OF TREES

Georgia World Congress Center
285 International Blvd.   325-NOEL
A week in early December
Admission fee

The GWCC sparkles with more than 200 trees and holiday vignettes created by noted interior designers especially for this event, a fund-raiser for Egleston Children's Hospital. Two kiddie rides are magical attractions: an antique carousel

and the original Pink Pig, the little monorail with pig-shaped cars that delighted generations of children on the rooftop of Rich's now-demolished downtown store.

ATLANTA SYMPHONY ORCHESTRA HOLIDAY CONCERTS

Symphony Hall, Woodruff Arts Center
1280 Peachtree St. N.E.   733-5000
Various performances throughout December
Admission fee

From joyful gospel music to the grandest Baroque oratorio, there's something in the ASO's December lineup to get everyone into the holiday spirit. There are concerts for kids, programs spotlighting both traditional songs and rousing gospel Christmas music (The Pointer Sisters headlined at these shows in 1994) and performances of the Christmas portions of Handel's *Messiah*.

THE ATLANTA BALLET PRESENTS THE NUTCRACKER

The Fox Theatre
660 Peachtree St. N.E.   873-5811
Early December through Christmas
Admission fee

The Atlanta Ballet's annual production of *The Nutcracker* has long been a holiday tradition. In 1994, for the first time in 10 years, the production returned to The Fox, which was the Atlanta Ballet's home for many years. (The ballet company and the movie palace share a common birth-year: 1929.) The production includes an orchestra, a full company of dancers and more than 200 children.

THE ATLANTA OPERA PRESENTS AMAHL AND THE NIGHT VISITORS

Georgia Tech Center for the Arts
349 Ferst Dr. N.W.   355-3311
Mid-December
Admission fee

Written by Gian Carlo Menotti, the one-act opera *Amahl and the Night Visi-*

tors is the touching story of a crippled boy whose humble gift for the newborn Christ child earns him a great reward. The Atlanta Opera's three public performances of the English-language work are preceded by a week of performances for metro-area school children at Spivey Hall on the campus of Clayton State College in Morrow.

PEACH BOWL PARADE

Downtown Atlanta streets   586-8500
Around New Year's Eve

The Peach Bowl is played in the Georgia Dome each year on or near New Year's Eve. A big downtown parade preceding the game honors the collegiate contenders. For more information about the football game, see our Spectator Sports chapter.

FIRSTNIGHT ATLANTA

Midtown streets   892-4782
New Year's Eve
Admission fee

Following a trend made popular in other cities, Midtown businesses sponsor this alcohol-free, family-oriented street party featuring music, art, theater and dance. Peachtree Street is closed for several blocks in Midtown, and patrons buy a badge that entitles them to attend the performances being offered continuously throughout the evening.

ATLANTA RINGS IN THE NEW YEAR

Underground Atlanta   523-2311
New Year's Eve

A huge throng gathers every New Year's Eve to ring out the old and ring in the new on the plaza at Underground. Never to be outdone by the Big Apple, Atlanta drops its own enormous piece of electrified fruit (a peach, of course!) down a tower to mark the beginning of the New Year. Fun, but not for the claustrophobic.

Photo: Kevin C. Rose

The Fox Theatre hosts a wide array of live performances and is on
the National Register of Historic Places.

Inside
The Arts

Gone With the Wind's Gerald O'Hara notwithstanding— "Look at the way they go tearing up to New York and Boston to hear operas and see oil paintings," he said disparagingly of his neighbors, the Wilkeses — the arts have always been a vital part of life in the American South.

From the town's early days, Atlanta's people developed a taste for the flashy entertainments common to larger American cities. Atlanta's ever-increasing population and its position as a rail hub made it a natural stop for touring theater and opera companies, orchestras and lecturers. Even during the tough years of Reconstruction, the arts were becoming big business: Two new opera houses opened in 1866, less than two years after Atlanta was put to the torch.

In 1882 Oscar Wilde, the then 27-year-old Irish poet and apostle of Aestheticism, stopped in Atlanta near the end of his very successful U.S. lecture tour. (The long-haired "sunflower psalmist" was so well-known here that a local man, Smith Clayton, had made a name for himself impersonating Wilde in a comedy act called *Wild Oscar*.) The Atlanta *Constitution* reported that on July 4 Wilde lectured on "Decorative Art" before "quite a large crowd" at DeGive's Opera House. He urged the audience to support the arts and encourage young artists: "The world underestimates the value of its own praise. Bring to their faces the flush that praise will bring. They will put in marble and in painting the flowers that adorn your hillsides and your valleys, and there they will live forever."

As years passed and the city grew, Atlantans weary of importing their art from elsewhere formed and supported the city's own performance companies. The Atlanta Ballet danced its inaugural season in 1929; the Atlanta Symphony Orchestra first tuned up in 1945. In the 1970s and '80s, entrepreneurial directors and their supporters boldly launched theater groups in storefronts and attics. Some of these modest efforts survived to become leading Atlanta companies with widespread reputations for innovative theater.

Atlanta's position as the cultural capital of the South affords patrons an array of arts options. The presence of both traditional and experimental arts organizations means that neither the classics nor avant-garde works are neglected in a typical year's offerings: Traditional Shakespeare, symphony and grand opera can all be found — but so can adult-oriented puppet theater, post-modern psychological drama and alternative productions of well-known works.

Offerings are various in the visual arts too. There's the architecturally renowned High Museum of Art, and the city has dozens of private and public galleries, including traditional, primitive and modern.

We've organized this chapter into the following categories: Music and Dance, Theater, Performance Beyond Atlanta, Visual Arts and Visual Arts Beyond Atlanta. Recently produced or upcoming shows or events are cited to give you an idea of an organization's areas of specialization. Call for performance dates and ticket information. We'll let you know when a group's performance venue is different than the address given after its name.

Music and Dance

ATLANTA BALLET
477 Peachtree St. N.E.   *873-5811*

The Atlanta Ballet has been a part of the city's life since the Fox Theatre opened in 1929. In 1994, for the first time in 10 years, the Ballet returned to the Fox, its old home, for the annual nonsubscription holiday production of *The Nutcracker*, which included a cast of more than 200 children. Regular-season ballet performances are given at the Atlanta Civic Center, Piedmont Avenue at Ralph McGill Boulevard. Call the Atlanta Ballet for season ticket and schedule information. For individual performance tickets, call TicketMaster, 817-8700; a convenience charge applies.

THE ATLANTA OPERA
1800 Peachtree St. N.W., Ste. 620   *355-3311*

Opera has long held an important place in Atlanta's cultural life. For seven decades between 1910 and 1987, the city was a regular stop on the Metropolitan Opera's tour, and Atlantans were treated to such legendary vocal talents as Enrico Caruso, Geraldine Farrar, Olive Fremstad and Birgit Nilsson. When the Met gave up touring for financial reasons in 1987, Atlanta was said to be the only city on the tour still meeting its obligation to the company.

Atlanta was the birthplace of the great diva Mattiwilda Dobbs. When she made her operatic debut at age 25 at LaScala in Milan, Italy, the soprano was the first black person to perform in that famous opera house. Dobbs, who graduated from Spelman College, went on to sing with the Metropolitan Opera. When her nephew, Maynard Jackson, was elected Atlanta's first black mayor, Dobbs returned to Atlanta to sing at his inauguration.

Several local companies produced a variety of operas through the years; then, in 1985, The Atlanta Opera was formed. The company produces fully staged operas with an excellent chorus of local singers and principal singers from around the nation and the world. Numerous veterans of the Metropolitan Opera have appeared in recent years, including Martile Rowland, Jan Grissom, Tatiana Troyanos, Hao Jiang Tian and Timothy Noble.

All performances are given in the original language with English supertitles projected above the stage. While renovations are under way at its home stage (Symphony Hall), The Atlanta Opera moves to the Fox Theatre (site of many Met performances) for its two 1995 productions: Gounod's *Faust* on June 1 and 3 and Verdi's *Aida* on August 31 and September 2.

In addition, the company stages an annual nonsubscription holiday production of Menotti's *Amahl and the Night Visitors* at the Georgia Tech Center for the Arts. The company's Atlanta Opera Studio is an educational outreach program that brings fully staged and costumed operas into schools across Georgia.

To charge season or individual tickets, call The Atlanta Opera.

ATLANTA SYMPHONY ORCHESTRA
Symphony Hall, Woodruff Arts Center
1280 Peachtree St. N.E.   *733-5000*

In only 50 years, the ASO grew from an inspired group of high school music students into a major orchestra with an international reputation. Since the 1976 release of its first commercial recording, the ASO's work has earned 14 Grammy Awards. The orchestra's renown grew steadily under the leadership of Robert Shaw, who passed the baton to Yoel Levi in 1988 after 21 years as music director. The ASO has commissioned and premiered works by Aaron Copland, Leonard Bernstein, Philip Glass and Gian Carlo Menotti. In 1994, the Pointer Sisters headlined the ASO's "Gospel Christmas" concerts, which were taped and broadcast nationally on PBS.

The regular ASO season runs from September to May. The festive summer series, inaugurated in 1972, takes place under the stars in the 6,000-seat amphitheater at Chastain Park, northwest of Buckhead. This very popular series, attracting more than 140,000 patrons, has grown to include 30 concerts headlined by famous pop or country stars. All shows feature reserved tables for picnicking in style.

Also during the summer, watch for the orchestra's free concerts in Piedmont and other city parks. Here you'll find tens of thousands of Atlantans lounging on blankets amid flickering candles, transported by the magic of music as the heat of the day breaks and the evening cool sweeps through the park.

A variety of full- and partial-season subscription packages is offered; call 733-4800. Ticket prices are reduced for family concerts and youth orchestra concerts. Public sneak preview rehearsals are held before the opening of six regular season concerts. These previews are given in Symphony Hall on the Thursday morning before the program's Thursday night premiere; general admission tickets are only $8.50.

CAPITOL CITY OPERA COMPANY
3235 Ridgewood Rd. N.W.   *355-8685*

This local company produces traditional and modern operas at various performance venues during the year. Its 1994 offerings included Britten's *The Turn of the Screw* and a program of madrigals at the Episcopal Cathedral of St. Philip.

GEORGIA TECH CENTER FOR THE ARTS
349 Ferst Dr. N.W.   *894-9600*

On the campus of Georgia Tech, this center houses galleries, a student-run theater and the 1,200-seat Robert Ferst Theatre. Between September and April, the Ferst Theatre hosts an eclectic arts series, which typically includes leading artists in

On most Sunday afternoons from September through May, there's an Evensong recital in the soaring, inspiring Episcopal Cathedral of St. Philip, 2744 Peachtree Road N.W., in Buckhead. Various organists, vocalists and other musicians are featured. Recitals are at 3:30 PM. Admission is free, and the public is invited. Recitals are not given every Sunday, and no recitals are presented in December. Call the Cathedral music office for more information, 365-1050.

Insiders' Tips

international and classical music, dance and opera. Series tickets are available. In the Dean James E. Dull Theatre, the student group DramaTech presents three major productions annually, plus several one-acts.

SAVOYARDS LIGHT OPERA

34 Old Ivy Rd. N.E., Ste. 202   233-0750

Established in 1980, the Savoyards present the works of Gilbert and Sullivan as well as other light opera favorites. Performances are given at the Georgia Tech Center for the Arts, 349 Ferst Drive N.W. The 1994-95 season included Gilbert and Sullivan's *Ruddigore*, *Camelot* and Romberg's *The Student Prince*.

Theater

THE ACADEMY THEATRE

501 Means St. N.W.   525-4111

Active in the Atlanta theater scene since 1956, Academy produces all-original works. Performances are given before school and community groups, as well as at the playhouse.

Coming in 1995 are the Fifth Annual Three Plays in May staged readings and the Third Annual Summer Drama Camp at the Georgia Tech Center for the Arts.

ACTOR'S EXPRESS

887 W. Marietta St. N.W., Ste. J-107
(In King Plow Arts Center)   607-7469

Founded in 1988 in a church basement, Actor's Express has grown into one of Atlanta's most respected theater companies. The group got its big break in 1991 when it produced the world premiere of *The Harvey Milk Show*, a musical based on the life of the assassinated San Francisco gay rights leader. It played to sold-out audiences and was later produced in other cities.

"In the midst of one of the most chaotic and spiritually hungry cultures in history, Actor's Express is in the business of helping myths sing for our time," says the company's mission statement. A typical season includes classics, comedies and tough psychological dramas. Included in the 1995 season are *Hamlet*, *The Night of the Iguana* and Paul Rudnick's *Jeffrey*.

ALLIANCE THEATRE COMPANY

Woodruff Arts Center
1280 Peachtree St. N.E.   733-5000

If there were any lingering doubts about the Alliance's status as a company of national importance, all were dispatched in 1994 when it was one of only four U.S. theaters chosen by playwright Tony Kushner to mount productions of his Tony Award- and Pulitzer Prize-winning play *Angels in America: Millennium Approaches*. (The Alliance production was sponsored in part by our celebrity-in-residence Elton John.)

Established in 1968, the Alliance is a nonprofit, professional company producing mainstage, studio and children's productions at its facility in the Atlanta Memorial Arts Building. The Broadway-style mainstage space is an especially comfortable place to see theater. The Alliance presented the world premiere productions of Tennessee Williams' *Tiger Tale* and Ed Gracyk's *Come Back to the Five and Dime, Jimmy Dean, Jimmy Dean*, among other premieres. Seasons typically include new and classic dramas and musicals. Season ticket-holders save 45 percent off the single-ticket price; call 733-4600 for details.

AGATHA'S — A TASTE OF MYSTERY

693 Peachtree St. N.E.   875-1610

Here's where you go when you can't decide whether to have dinner or solve a murder. Agatha's is a "mystery dinner theatre" where the audience is part of the show. When guests arrive, each is given a small assignment, such as making up goofy song lyrics or delivering a short line upon request. The plays are all originals, with absurd names such as *An Affair to Dismember* and *Cat on a Hot Tin Streetcar*.

But while you're being entertained, you're also being wined and dined in high style: The evening includes a five-course meal, wine and beverages. (Cocktails, tax and gratuity are extra.) Admission is $39 per person Sunday through Thursday, $42 per person on Friday and $45 per person on Saturday. Monday through Saturday, seatings are at 7:30 nightly; on Sundays the fun starts at 7 PM. Agatha's is across from the Fox Theatre; call for reservations.

AMERICAN EXPRESS
ATLANTA BROADWAY SERIES
659 Peachtree St., Ste. 900   873-4300

The Fox Theatre is the setting for the American Express Atlanta Broadway Series, which presents national touring companies in top-notch productions of Broadway hits. Shows in the 1994-95 season included *The Phantom of the Opera, Jesus Christ Superstar, Joseph and the Amazing Technicolor Dreamcoat*, Maurice Hines in *Jelly's Last Jam* and Petula Clark in *Blood Brothers*. In October 1995, the blockbuster *Miss Saigon* comes to the stage of the Atlanta Civic Center (the Fox just wasn't big enough to hold this one).

Tickets go on sale at the Fox box office six to eight weeks before a show opens. To charge by phone, call TicketMaster, 817-8700; a convenience charge applies.

CENTER FOR PUPPETRY ARTS
1404 Spring St. at 18th   873-3391

Founded in 1978, this unusual theater and museum annually attract more than half-million visitors. Regular programs include 13 shows and 12 puppet-making workshops weekly, plus six adult-oriented shows per year. Housing three separate theaters and a museum featuring authentic Muppet characters plus puppets from around the world, the center is the largest facility of its kind in North America. The center is closed Sundays and holidays; museum admission is $3 for adults (14 and older) and $2 for children; performances are extra. Call for schedules and admission prices.

GEORGIA SHAKESPEARE FESTIVAL
501 Means St. N.W.   688-8008

This festival has seen its annual attendance more than double since its inaugural season in 1985. Performances are held on the campus of Oglethorpe University, 4484 Peachtree Road N.E., whose Gothic architecture affords a fine setting for productions of Shakespeare.

An evening at the festival begins at 6:30 when the grounds open for picnicking (pack your own or call ahead for catering). At 7, there's cabaret-style entertainment. Then, at 8, it's into the great festival tent for an evening of the Bard's best.

The Atlanta Symphony Orchestra presents a public sneak preview dress rehearsal prior to six of its regular season concerts. These previews are held in Symphony Hall on the Thursday morning before the program's Thursday evening opening. Tickets are $8.50, general admission. Call 733-5000.

Insiders' Tips

Yoel Levi is Music Director of the Atlanta Symphony Orchestra.

The 1995 10th anniversary season includes performances of *King Lear, Much Ado About Nothing* and the restoration comedy *The Country Wife*.

HORIZON THEATRE COMPANY
1083 Austin Ave. N.E.   **584-7450**

Horizon operates an intimate, 170-seat theater in a rehabilitated school building at the intersection of Euclid and Austin avenues in Little Five Points. In business since 1983, the professional, non-profit company's productions range from satire to drama, with a special emphasis on new plays and playwrights. In addition to four mainstage productions annually, Horizon develops new writers through its New Horizons readings and cultivates new theater-lovers through its Teen Ensemble program.

JOMANDI PRODUCTIONS
1444 Mayson St.   **876-6346**

Founded in 1978, Jomandi is Georgia's oldest and largest African-American professional theater company. Jomandi has received numerous grants from prominent national arts organizations and tours more extensively than any other professional company in the Southeast. More than half its mainstage productions have been premieres; the remainder have been stage adaptations of works by established black writers. Performances are given at 14th Street Playhouse, 14th at Juniper. The 1994-95 season included *Sophisticated Ladies* and *Servant of the People: The Rise and Fall of Huey P. Newton and the Black Panther Party*. Jomandi also produces the annual Juneteenth emancipation celebration; see June in our Annual Events and Festivals chapter.

ONSTAGE ATLANTA
420 Courtland St.   **897-1802**

Onstage Atlanta is a big stage in a small theater: Its 124 seats are arranged on three sides of the stage, creating an experience that's instantly intimate. A typical season runs from September to June and includes drama, comedy and musicals; two additional shows play during the summer. Many shows were first mounted off-Broadway. The Abracadabra! Children's Theatre presents five shows on Saturday mornings and afternoons during its season, also September to June. The theater is one block off Peachtree behind St. Luke's Episcopal Church; there's free secured parking for patrons.

OutProud Theater
191 Howard St. N.E.   *373-8750*

OutProud is the theatrical arm of SAME, the Southeastern Arts, Media and Education project. The group was founded in 1985 by members of the gay and lesbian community "to use the arts for social change." OutProud presents several productions annually; these include works by both locally and nationally known playwrights.

Other SAME activities include an arts and crafts festival, the literary magazine *Amethyst* and cosponsorship (with *Southern Voice* magazine and Maddix Deluxe gift shop) of the annual Atlanta Lesbian & Gay Film Festival, which celebrated its seventh anniversary in 1994.

7 Stages
1105 Euclid Ave.   *523-7647*

From its humble beginnings in a storefront in 1979, 7 Stages has grown into a major company operating two theaters in a former Little Five Points moviehouse. Risk-taking is a hallmark: An anti-Klan musical staged here in 1986 provoked the first Klu Klux Klan rally in the city in 30 years. Typical productions include experimental plays, dramas by local writers, international works and alternative stagings of classics. The com-

plex has a 200-seat mainstage and a 90-seat black box space (entrance in the rear).

The Shakespeare Tavern
499 Peachtree St.   *874-5299*

Four blocks south of the Fox Theatre, this company produces the plays of Shakespeare and other Elizabethan authors. Although the setting is casual (chairs and tables for 175 are arranged tavern-style), the productions are traditional — no need to worry that you'll find *King Lear* pushing a shopping cart through a post-nuclear slum. The company produces the tragedies as well as the comedies and tries hard to incorporate some of the lesser-known works. A British pub-style menu and beer and wine are sold before performances and at intermission.

Theatre Gael
P.O. Box 77156, Atlanta   *876-1138*

Theatre Gael explores Celtic culture through the plays, poetry and music of Ireland, Scotland and Wales. Most performances are given at the 14th Street Playhouse, 14th at Juniper. The 1995-96 season includes Wilde's *The Importance of Being Earnest*, Shaw's *Arms and the Man* and Thomas' *Under Milk Wood*.

Theater of the Stars
P.O. Box 11748, Atlanta 30355   252-8960

Since 1952, Theater of the Stars has brought national touring companies' shows to Atlanta. Theater of the Stars' regular season runs from June to August, and performances are given at the Fox

For a listing of various classical concerts and recitals — many of them free — check "Music Performances" in the "Happenings" section of the free weekly *Creative Loafing*.

Insiders' Tips

From Great Tragedy, Great Hope

Atlanta's vibrant and thriving arts scene is a living and fitting memorial to the victims of one of the saddest events in the city's history. As part of a European tour organized by the Atlanta Art Association, 106 Atlantans boarded a chartered Air France 707 on June 3, 1962, at Orly airport in Paris. But, as it taxied down the runway, the jet was unable to reach takeoff speed. The pilot tried unsuccessfully to abort, and the plane ran off the runway and exploded into flames. All 130 people on board, except three flight attendants in the tail section, were killed.

In that awful moment, Atlanta lost many of its most ardent patrons of the arts. The arts movement in the city might have died with them but for the determination of Atlantans to continue the mission for which the 106 had lost their lives. In their memory, $13 million was raised through private donations to build the Atlanta Memorial Arts Center, 1280 Peachtree Street N.E., which opened in 1968. The Richard Meier-designed High Museum of Art opened next-door in 1983.

The 10-acre arts complex was renamed the Robert W. Woodruff Arts Center in 1985, but the structure that houses Symphony Hall, the Alliance Theatre and the Atlanta College of Art retains the name Memorial Arts Building. On the landing in the building's south staircase is a casting of Rodin's "L'Ombre," donated by the French government as a tribute to the crash victims.

After a quarter-century as the physical and symbolic center of the Atlanta arts scene, the much-used Memorial Arts Building needed refurbishing. A $15 million renovation program, to be completed in time for the '96 Olympics, was undertaken in mid-1994. Long criticized for its boxy appearance, the remodeled Memorial will include more glass and more curves, making it architecturally more harmonious with the award-winning High Museum next-door.

Theatre. Recent presentations have included *Cats*, Shirley Jones in *The King and I*, Georgia native Marla Maples Trump in *The Will Rogers Follies* and Jennifer Holiday in *Dream Girls*.

THEATRICAL OUTFIT

P.O. Box 7098
Atlanta 30357   872-0665

Theatrical Outfit was founded in 1976 in a space above an old laundromat in Virginia-Highland. In 1985, the company scored a big hit with a lavish production of *The Rocky Horror Show*, which featured soon-to-be famous Atlantan RuPaul. Now the company stages four productions a year between October and May at the 14th Street Playhouse, 14th at Juniper. The Outfit's annually updated *Appalachian Christmas* show has become an Atlanta holiday tradition. The 1994-95 season included *The Scarlet Letter* and *The Beggar's Opera*.

Performance Beyond Atlanta

SPIVEY HALL

Clayton State College, Morrow   961-3683

Fifteen miles south of Atlanta (Exit 76 off I-75), Clayton State College is home to what many view as the finest performance venue in the entire metro area. Since it opened in 1991, the $4 million Spivey Hall has won raves from critics and performers alike. Overlooking a 12-acre lake, the 398-seat hall's centerpiece is its 79-rank, 4,413-pipe Ruffatti organ.

Some 60 concerts covering a broad range of musical traditions are presented between September and June; subscription packages let patrons choose to attend all the concerts of a certain type, such as piano, organ or jazz, or custom-design their series with six or more concerts for a 20-percent discount off the single-ticket rate. The 1994-95 season includes performances by violin sensation Midori, organist Diane Bish, the Vienna Boys Choir, Preservation Hall Jazz Band and Metropolitan Opera stars Camellia Johnson and Annie Sofie von Otter.

THEATRE IN THE SQUARE

11 Whitlock Ave., Marietta   422-8369

This professional company, whose 225-seat facility is housed in a former cotton warehouse, attracts the second-largest audience of any Atlanta area theater. The company found itself at the center of an international controversy when local politicians, outraged at a risqué comedy staged here, passed Cobb County's divisive resolution condemning "the gay lifestyle." The ensuing uproar caused the Atlanta Committee for the Olympic Games to move the preliminary Olympic volleyball events Cobb County had been scheduled to host.

The theater's 1995 offerings include Ibsen's *An Enemy of the People*, the 25th anniversary production of *Company* and the annual production of *The 1940's Radio Hour*, an Atlanta holiday tradition since 1981.

THE VILLAGE PLAYHOUSES OF ROSWELL

617 Holcomb Bridge Rd.
Roswell   998-3526

This lucky company has two stages and so runs two productions simultaneously for much of the year. In the Village Center Playhouse (theater in-the-round), the 1995 season includes *Heaven Can Wait, Life with Father, Oliver* and *I Remember Mama*. In the Roswell Village Theater (traditional proscenium stage), the 1995 season includes *To Kill a Mockingbird, Brighton Beach Memoirs* and *The Unsinkable Molly Brown*.

Visual Arts

Art Museums

THE HIGH MUSEUM OF ART

Woodruff Arts Center
1280 Peachtree St. N.E.   733-HIGH

When The High Museum of Art opened in its new building in October 1983, *The New York Times* called it "among the best museum structures any city has built in at least a generation." Richard Meier designed the gleaming white museum with its curved glass wall overlooking Peachtree Street. Its effect is at once both classical and ultramodern, rather like a wedding cake for The Jetsons. The $20 million High has won numerous design awards; in 1991, the American Institute of Architects named it one of the top 10 works of American architecture of the 1980s.

Inside the huge, skylit central atrium, sloping, half-circular ramps conform to the front wall's curve and climb to the top floor. You may wish to start at the top: It's fun to take the elevator all the way up, then walk through the galleries and down the ramps at your own pace. The museum's 10,000-piece permanent collection includes contemporary and classical paintings and sculpture by European and American artists, plus African art, photography and folk art. Throughout the year, selections from the permanent collection share the space with major traveling exhibitions. The museum gift shop offers many exhibition catalogs, posters and gifts.

The High Museum is open daily, except for Mondays and holidays, Tuesday through Saturday, 10 AM to 5 PM; Sunday noon to 5 PM; Friday nights until 9. Admission is $6 for adults, $4 for students with ID and persons older than 64, and $2 for youth 6 to 17. Admission is free for museum members and children younger than 6. Occasionally, a special exhibition may have a surcharge. Admission is free to all on Thursday afternoons from 1 to 5 PM.

The 135,000-square-foot High Museum of Art is part of the Robert W. Woodruff Arts Center and is served by the Arts Center MARTA station. Paid parking is available in the Arts Center garage; there is limited on-street parking behind the Arts Center. You may also park on some streets in the Ansley Park neighborhood across Peachtree, but be sure to obey all posted regulations and cross busy Peachtree only at the pedestrian crosswalks.

THE HIGH MUSEUM OF ART
FOLK ART AND PHOTOGRAPHY GALLERIES
30 John Wesley Dobbs Ave. N.E. 577-6940

On the ground floor of the Georgia-Pacific Center, corner of Peachtree and Dobbs, just north of Woodruff Park, the multilevel downtown branch of the High showcases photography and folk art. The museum is open Monday through Friday, 11 AM to 5 PM, and admission is always free. Take MARTA to the Peachtree Center station; follow the signs to the station's south exit at Ellis Street; the 51-story Georgia-Pacific Center is across Peachtree; the museum's main entrance is on the Dobbs Avenue side; you may also enter through the building's lobby.

ATLANTA INTERNATIONAL
MUSEUM OF ART AND DESIGN
Peachtree Center, Marquis Two
285 Peachtree Center Ave.   688-2467

Established in 1989, this museum celebrates the craftsmanship of the world's cultures through ethnographic, folk art and design exhibits. It is a nonprofit educational organization supported by public and private funds. Admission is free; the museum is open Tuesday through Saturday, 11 AM to 5 PM.

The Cultural Olympiad and The 1996 Olympic Arts Festival

The Atlanta Committee for the Olympic Games Cultural Olympiad, the cultural component of the 1996 Centennial Olympic Games, will culminate in the Olympic Arts Festival in the summer of '96.

The Cultural Olympiad got under way in February 1993 with a month-long celebration of the culture of Norway, host of the '94 Winter Olympic Games. Other events have honored the art of Mexico and the art of Africa. More than half the living Nobel laureates in literature are expected to attend an unprecedented convocation at the Carter Center in April 1995. Marking the 100th Anniversary of World Cinema, the Cultural Olympiad and the High Museum of Art are presenting a two-year long series showcasing 100 classic feature films.

The Olympic Arts Festival will be held from June to October 1996, with most performances taking place during the Olympic Games, July 19 through August 4. The festival will present entertainment ranging from storytelling and puppetry to major play premieres and concerts by world-famous artists. To receive information about upcoming Cultural Olympiad events, call 224-1835.

THE HAMMONDS HOUSE GALLERIES AND RESOURCE CENTER OF AFRICAN-AMERICAN ART

503 Peeples St. S.W.   *752-8730*

Housed in one of the oldest homes in historic West End, Hammonds House is the only Georgia museum dedicated to African-American fine art.

What is believed to have been the first kindergarten in Atlanta once operated in one wing of this pre-Civil War Victorian-style home. Today, the building houses a collection of more than 250 works of art, mainly by African Americans. National and local artists are represented in the collection, which also includes African and Haitian works. In addition to exhibitions, Hammonds House offers lectures, classes and a resource center for scholars (by appointment).

Admission is a $2 donation for adults and a $1 donation for children and se-niors; the facility is closed to the public on Mondays.

MICHAEL C. CARLOS MUSEUM

Emory University, 571 S. Kilgo St. 727-4282

Internationally acclaimed architect Michael Graves designed this 45,000-square-foot building on the quadrangle at the heart of Emory University. Finished in rose and white marble, the museum's striking design suggests a temple. Dramatic twin staircases on the building's front rise to the third level, which is adorned by three levels of columns.

The design's interpretation of ancient and classical elements is strikingly appropriate to the museum's 12,000-piece collection, which, although varied, is strongest in its selection of objects from antiquity. Art and objects of daily life from ancient Egypt, Greece, Rome, Africa and the Americas are displayed inside galleries whose proportions and features honor timeless design ideals.

Free parking is allowed on campus except where restricted or reserved; there's a small lot right behind the museum; paid parking is available in the Boisfeuillet Jones Building lot nearby. If you visit the Carlos on a weekend, you should have no trouble parking. On MARTA, take the 6 Emory bus (from Lindbergh or Edgewood/Candler Park stations) or the 36 North Decatur (from Arts Center or Avondale stations) and get off at the university's white front gate; follow the signs to the museum.

The museum is open seven days a week: Monday to Saturday, 10 AM to 5 PM (except Friday until 9 PM); Sunday noon to 5 PM; it's closed on major holidays. Admission is by donation; $3 is suggested.

Arts Centers

800 EAST

800 East Ave.   522-8265

This alternative performance space and gallery is just a stone's throw from the Freedom Parkway, but you can't reach it from the four-lane. Its attitude, like its location, is definitely on the edge: 800 East is a privately owned art center that accepts no government funding. Consequently, its programs tend to risk-taking and experimental: adult-oriented art exhibits and performance events share the space with audience-involvement plays and walk-through installations. Events are held sporadically; call for dates and admission prices. Take N. Highland south from Ponce de Leon past Elizabeth Street; after you cross the bridge, turn right on Alaska and follow it until it dead-ends at 800 East.

CALLANWOLDE FINE ARTS CENTER

980 Briarcliff Rd.   872-5338

Today operated as a fine arts center in a combined public/private effort, Callanwolde was originally the home of Howard Candler, the eldest son of Coca-Cola's founder. The dramatic Gothic-Tudor style mansion was designed by Henry Hornbostel, designer of Emory University, and completed in 1920. The 27,000-square-foot mansion's plan stresses openness: Almost all rooms adjoin great halls on each floor, and the entire building is centered around a large enclosed courtyard.

In addition to details, such as walnut paneling, stained glass and delicate ceiling and fireplace reliefs, the house has an amazing feature: a 3,752-pipe, 20,000-pound Aeolian organ, the largest of its kind still in playable condition, that is audible in every room. New, the organ cost $48,200.

Callanwolde is in the elegant Druid Hills section (of *Driving Miss Daisy* fame) laid out by famed landscape architect Frederick Law Olmstead, who also designed Central Park in New York. The original 27-acre estate has been reduced to 12 acres. With assistance from the federal Housing and Urban Development department and DeKalb County, a neighborhood association purchased the property in 1972 for $360,000, then turned it over to the county to maintain as an arts center.

Today a nonprofit foundation directs the arts programs, which include classes, performances and exhibitions. Dance, drama, painting, photography, pottery, textiles, writing and more are all part of Callanwolde's art offerings.

"Christmas at Callonwolde" is the center's most popular event: Each year during the first two weeks of December,

Photo: Woodruff Arts Center

Concrete comes down off Woodruff Arts Center — literally tearing down walls to let people in.

more than 20,000 visitors tour the lavishly decorated mansion and enjoy holiday music on the grand organ: See December in our Annual Events and Festivals chapter.

Except for special events, admission to Callonwolde and its formal garden is free. The gallery is open Monday to Saturday 10 AM to 3 PM. The art shop is open Tuesday through Saturday, 10:30 AM to 2:30 PM. The conservatory is open Monday through Friday, 10 AM to 4 PM.

KING PLOW ARTS CENTER

887 W. Marietta St. N.W.   *885-9933*

In an amazing transformation, an antiquated, 165,000-square-foot plow factory near the waterworks in northwest Atlanta became an exciting arts center. King Plow Arts Center, whose first phase opened in 1991, now houses more than 50 tenants. These include galleries representing both fine and commercial art, artists' residential and working space, architectural and graphic design firms and the Actor's Express theater.

Take 10th Street west until it dead-ends at Brady Avenue; turn left; when Brady dead-ends at West Marietta, turn right; King Plow is on your right just past the bridge.

NEXUS CONTEMPORARY ART CENTER
535 Means St. N.W.   688-1970

Nexus has been a vibrant force on the Atlanta art scene since it was founded as a co-op storefront gallery in 1973. Later it occupied a former elementary school; then, in 1989, it purchased a historic warehouse complex west of Five Points. The 40,000-square-foot center houses an art book press, studios and a large gallery that presents six major exhibitions annually. A 100-seat theater (under development) will complete the multipurpose project.

The gallery is open Tuesday through Saturday, 11 AM to 5 PM. From Five Points, go west on Marietta Street, then left on Ponders Avenue and right on Means Street.

TULA ARTS COMPLEX
75 Bennett St. N.W.   351-3551

TULA is at the end of the Bennett Street antique shopping district (left off Peachtree just north of Piedmont Hospital). A privately developed, multi-use arts center, it houses more than 45 galleries, artists' studios and arts-related businesses. TULA is home to IMAGE Film/Video Center, 352-4225, which promotes the cinematic arts and exhibits lots of offbeat and experimental movies.

Galleries

ART & FRAME CLASSICS
4135 LaVista Rd., Ste. 220
Tucker   270-0542

This shop specializes in military and aviation prints with a large selection of Civil War art. Prices range from less than $100 to $10,000. Custom framing is also offered.

BLUEMOON AT RIO
Rio Shopping Center
Piedmont at North Ave.   874-1855

BlueMoon specializes in African-American art. The collection includes oil and acrylic paintings on canvas and paper, wood carvings, sculptures and masks, soft-sculpture figures and more. Fine home accessories are also offered, including blown glass, Italian leather furniture, pottery, pillows and dining sets.

CITY GALLERY EAST
675 Ponce de Leon Ave.   817-7956

Operated by the city's Bureau of Cultural Affairs, the 6,000-square-foot City Gallery East is on the first floor of the City Hall East government building. (Built by Sears, Roebuck & Co., the massive red brick structure opened in 1926 and for decades was the retailer's Southeast catalog order center. Directly across the street stood the stadium where the Atlanta Crackers baseball team played in the days before Major League ball came to town.) The gallery presents five major exhibitions each year spotlighting contemporary visual art. Atlanta artists are a special focus, but the gallery does not exclude the works of other U.S. and international artists.

FAY GOLD GALLERY
247 Buckhead Ave.   233-3843

This contemporary gallery has enjoyed phenomenal success since its 1980 opening and now occupies a 7,000-square-foot space in the heart of Buckhead. A list of artists brought to the gallery for major solo exhibitions reads like a who's who of the modern art world: Andres Serrano, Keith Haring, Bruce

Weber, Herb Ritts and Annie Leibowitz, to name just a few.

JACKSON FINE ART

3115 E. Shadowlawn Ave.   233-3739

Specializing in 20th century and contemporary photography, Jackson's client list includes the Metropolitan Museum of Art, the High Museum of Art, the Los Angeles County Museum of Art, Coca-Cola, Delta Airlines and the Woodruff Foundation. The gallery's inventory includes works by Ansel Adams, Walker Evans, Edward Steichen and Eudora Welty.

KOOLHIPFUNKYSTUFF

1030 Monroe Dr. N.E.   607-1095

The Good Samaritan Project, a non-profit organization that provides an array of services to people with HIV/AIDS, operates this unusual gallery. Following a very successful fund-raising art auction, the gallery opened in November 1993. Artwork in various media is displayed on a consignment basis; the money raised by the sale of art is split 50/50 between the artist and the project. Established as well as new artists are featured. The project provides emotional, practical and spiritual support for those living with HIV disease and also furnishes speakers who help raise community awareness about AIDS.

THE MCINTOSH GALLERY

One Virginia Hill, 587 Virginia Ave. 892-4023

Established in 1981, the McIntosh features works of emerging and established

U.S. and European artists but focuses primarily on Southeastern talents.

THE MODERN PRIMITIVE GALLERY

1402 N. Highland Ave.   892-0556

Both serious collectors and curious browsers feel right at home at Modern Primitive, which offers folk, self-taught and local art. Famous folk artists represented here include the Rev. Howard Finster, Archie Byron and Minnie Evans.

SANDLER HUDSON GALLERY

1831-A Peachtree Rd. N.E.   350-8480

The gallery's intent is "to exhibit provocative, psychologically motivated imagery." Painting, drawing, photography, sculpture and jewelry are among featured media. Its primary focus is established contemporary artists from the Southeast.

NANCY SOLOMON GALLERY

1037 Monroe Dr.   875-7100

International contemporary art is the focus of Nancy Solomon Gallery. Solomon, who is a graduate of Barnard College in art history, grew up in France and Switzerland and has worked in galleries in London, Paris and New York. The gallery emphasizes conceptual painting and sculpture.

URBAN NIRVANA

15 Waddell St.
Corner of DeKalb Ave.   688-3329

Housed in a former meat-packing plant, Urban Nirvana is easily Atlanta's most unusual art gallery. The complex is home to goats, sheep, rabbits, turkeys,

Admission to The High Museum of Art is free on Thursday afternoons from 1 to 5 PM.

Insiders' Tips

Atlanta Arts Hotline

Looking for an art or performance event? You can get free information on the Atlanta arts scene 24 hours a day by calling the Arts Hotline, 853-3ART. A recording will give you instructions on how to use the service. Press one of the following numbers to hear detailed listings of events. To move from one listing to another, press the # button.

1. Theatrical performances
2. Musical performances
3. Dance events
4. Films, lectures and book signings
5. Museums and galleries
6. Festivals and workshops
7. Opportunities for artists
8. Special messages

peacocks, ducks — and lots of art. The proprietor, Christine Sibley, is known for her garden sculptures and ornaments; the gallery also exhibits other art in a variety of media. If you're riding the MARTA east rail line toward downtown, you can get a quick but amazing glimpse of Urban Nirvana's fantastical facade shortly after you leave the Inman Park/Reynoldstown station; sit on the right side of the train and keep a lookout for metal dinosaurs, fountains and other objects bizarre.

MARCIA WOOD GALLERY
1198 N. Highland Ave. 885-1808

Marcia Wood Gallery showcases contemporary art, especially painting, although other media using narrative imagery are also shown. Important artists featured in recent exhibitions include Cornel Rubino, Phyllis Stapler and Marcia Cohen.

Visual Arts Beyond Atlanta

Cobb County

MARIETTA/COBB MUSEUM OF ART
30 Atlanta St., Marietta 424-8142

This museum is housed in a 1909 Greek Revival-style Post Office building just off the square in Marietta. Typical offerings include mainstream exhibitions of American and European art from the 19th and 20th centuries and highlights from the museum's own collection of American art.

Admission is $2 for adults and $1 for seniors and students; the museum is open Tuesday through Saturday, 11 AM to 5 PM.

Inside
Recreational Sports

Atlanta's temperate climate and great natural beauty make it a natural for year-round outdoor recreation. Often called the city in a forest, it lures residents and visitors to active pastimes.

If you're a newcomer and fear you've left behind certain sports, chances are you'll be pleasantly surprised. Sports enthusiasts among the constant influx of new residents have formed a league, a club or a network of some kind to support an amazing array of sports addictions. From martial arts to snow skiing, boardsailing to bocci ball, this chapter presents a glimpse at what keeps Atlantans busy and fit. No matter what your age, the metro area offers pleasurable pastimes to shake loose the cobwebs of workday worries.

Parks and Recreation Departments

Surely some of the metro area's greatest assets are the services offered by our fine parks and recreation departments. All four counties present programs at various skill levels for youth, adults, seniors and the physically challenged. Complete written information, well designed for easy reading, is yours with a call to the county of your residence.

What is available through these departments would encompass a book in itself. Safe to say, virtually no athletic interest is left out. Fitness, music

instruction, after-school tutorials, arts and crafts and so much more are offered free or for small fees.

The City of Atlanta alone maintains 319 park sites, 2,600 acres of park land, 114 playgrounds, 34 recreation centers, 50 tennis courts, a Lake Alatoona camp, 95 ballfields, 18 outdoor pools, three indoor pools, four 18-hole golf courses, one nine-hole course and a five-hole youth course. Be assured that whatever your interest, the opportunity for instruction and league play is not far away.

CITY OF ATLANTA PARKS & RECREATION
675 Ponce de Leon Ave. N.E.
                                817-6744

COBB COUNTY PARKS & RECREATION
1792 County Farm Rd.
Marietta   *528-8808*

DEKALB COUNTY PARKS & RECREATION
1300 Commerce Dr.
Decatur   *371-3621*

FULTON COUNTY PARKS & RECREATION
1575 Northside Dr. N.W.   *730-6200*

GWINNETT COUNTY PARKS & RECREATION
75 Langley Dr.
Lawrenceville   *822-8840*

Participants in some of the lesser-known sports that are gaining popularity in Atlanta in many cases have formed informal groups with no official meeting places. We've provided addresses when possible. Loosely organized around a shared activity, these groups may be short-lived or may thrive for years. We've arranged this chapter alphabetically.

Ballooning

More than a half-dozen companies will take you up, up and away to commemorate marriage proposals, anniversaries, birthdays or just plain fun. You may be able to schedule your flight at your favorite time of day.

In business 20 years, **Aeronautical Enterprises**, 972-1741, offers group rates seven days a week, FAA-certified pilots and gift certificates. In addition, **Peach Blossom Balloons**, 565-9023, provides champagne picnics with flights and first-class comfort in its "chase" vehicle; you can see videos of your flight in the specially equipped motor home while being transported back to your launch spot.

Bocci Ball

VENI, VEDI, VICI RESTAURANT
41 N. 14th St. N.E.   875-8424

Betcha never thought you'd find bocci ball in the South, did you? The timeless sport of Italian lawn bowling is played on the grounds of this elegant Midtown restaurant. The games are played Mondays through Thursdays from 11:30 AM to 11 PM; Fridays from 11 AM to midnight; Saturdays from 5 PM to midnight; Sundays from 5 PM to 10 PM. Call for additional details on how you can get in the game and set the standard.

Bowling

BRUNSWICK LANES
3835 Lawrenceville Hwy.
Lawrenceville   925-2000

The Atlanta area Brunswick Lanes are most crowded in the evenings (when leagues bowl) and on rainy days (when everyone wants to get out of the house). To check on lane availability and make a reservation, call the alley of your choice before you head out. Additional metro Brunswick lanes are: 2750 Austell Road S.W., Marietta, 435-2120; 2749 Delk Road S.E., Marietta, 988-8813; 6345 Spalding Drive N.W., Norcross, 840-8200; 785 Old Roswell Road, Roswell, 998-9437.

EXPRESS BOWLING LANES
1936 Piedmont Cr. N.E.   874-5703

This bowling alley closes at 2 AM on Monday and Wednesday nights; otherwise, it's open 24 hours. Groups of 15 or more may call to make a reservation. You don't bowl but you crave the spotlight anyway? No problem! Head for Sugar Daddy's lounge, where the laser karaoke machine may make you a star.

Cricket

The Cricket Champions of Atlanta invite you to join them in this traditionally British sport. The club meets on the last Saturday of every month in different members' homes. For details, call 455-8482.

Camping

Some of the country's most unspoiled land is in Georgia, where state protection has preserved great areas of natural beauty. We recommend you begin with the state park system, which will furnish you with well-designed information to help plan your trips.

Georgia State Parks and Historic Sites, part of the Georgia Department of Natural Resources, is your best source of guidance.

GEORGIA STATE PARKS & HISTORIC SITES
1352 Floyd Tower East
205 Butler St. S.E.   656-3530

Georgia's 40 state park campgrounds are well worth exploring as an introduction to the state's abundant natural resources. They include tent or trailer camping, RV sites and group camp facilities. A concept called pioneer camping, more primitive and rustic in nature, offers water and basic sanitary facilities only, with no RVs allowed.

Campgrounds are open from 7 AM to 10 PM. Registration is required at the park office before 8 PM prior to setting up camp. Credit cards are honored. Check out time is 1 PM.

Most campsites are available on a first-come, first-served basis. However, reservations for a minimum of two nights are accepted for a limited number of campsites at some parks, with a nonrefundable deposit required within one week of making the reservation. Special winter prices are offered. The parks accept reservations in person or by phone up to three months in advance. Campers younger than 18 must be accompanied by an adult.

Tent/RV campsites offer electrical and water hookups, cooking grills and picnic tables. Many sites have laundry facilities and camping supplies. Fully equipped cottages and lodges are available at many state parks.

A 28-page booklet, *Special Events,* will alert you to fun happenings from April to December each year. Here's just one example: the Sheep to Shawl event, held at Jarrell Plantation Historic Site in Juliette. You can see the production of a wool garment including the shearing of the sheep and spinning, dyeing and weaving of the cloth, just as it was done in the 1800s.

Two of the parks closest to Atlanta are Red Top Mountain Park and Lodge and Victoria Bryant Park.

RED TOP MOUNTAIN PARK
653 Red Top Mountain Rd. S.E.
Cartersville   975-0055

One-and-a-half miles east of I-75 at Exit 123, Red Top offers 90 tent and trailer sites, a 33-room lodge and 18 cottages. Adding to the pleasures are 50 picnic sites, a lake for fishing, tennis facilities, nature trails and a boat ramp.

VICTORIA BRYANT PARK
1105 Bryant Park Rd.
Royston   (706)245-6270

This park is 4 miles west of Royston off U.S. Highway 29. It offers 125 tent and trailer sites, with 107 picnic sites. You can fish in the lake and swim in the pool. Golf facilities are offered as well.

Canoeing

For canoeing adventures close to the city, go to the Providence Outdoor Recreation Center. Qualified instructors will guide you through day-long classes teaching the basics of canoeing in both moving and flat water. For more information on class dates, write or call the center at 13440 Providence Park Drive, Alpharetta, 30201; 740-2419.

Climbing

ATLANTA CLIMBING CLUB
DeKalb Northlake Library
3772 La Vista Rd., Tucker   621-5070

If climbing up tall structures turns you

Photo: Georgia Tourist Division

The Chattahoochee River offers a fun way to beat the heat.

on, the folks in the Atlanta Climbing Club are your kind of people. They meet at 7:30 PM on the second Tuesday of each month.

Cycling

When you're tired of walking, what better way to survey the scene than from the seat of a bike? You'll have lots of company. Cycling grows in popularity each year as Atlantans discover the pleasures and environmental benefits of the sport. Bike to Work Day in May 1994 drew an estimated 1,000 cyclists during Atlanta's Clean Commute Week. Convoys left from designated areas, and special passes were sold for the city's rapid transit system, which allowed bikes on trains that day.

Lots of informal groups schedule regular bike rides and welcome newcomers. For a good source of these sometimes temporary groups, check the recreation and sports listings in *Creative Loafing*, a free weekly newspaper available at many bookstores and retail establishments. One such group meets each Sunday at 2 PM

at the Trust Company Bank, 4030 Peachtree Road N.E., across from the Brookhaven MARTA station. Riders have distance options of 5, 10, 15 or 25 miles. For details, call 417-1821.

Piedmont Park, Piedmont Avenue and 14th Street, 892-0117, a 185-acre getaway in the Midtown area, is popular with residents for cycling and other recreational sports. You can ride MARTA to Midtown and walk to the park. On the Piedmont Avenue border of the park, where the main entrance is, you can rent bicycles, helmets and accessories by the day or hour, usually $5 an hour or $20 a day. See the skating section of this chapter for rental information.

SOUTHERN BICYCLE LEAGUE
1285 Wileo Creek Dr., Roswell   594-8350

Pick up a copy of the organization's monthly magazine *Freewheelin'* in local bike shops. It's full of safety tips, ride calendars and directions to the best trails. The league sponsors bike rides of about 11 miles at 2 PM on the second and fourth Saturdays of the month. Starting location is The Freight Room, a restaurant/ tavern at 301 E. Howard Avenue in the DeKalb County town of Decatur.

NORTH ATLANTA ROAD CLUB
2800 Canton Rd. N.E.
Marietta 422-5237

Call this club for friendly cycling guidance. With a $25 annual membership, you get a host of goodies: a discount in the Free Flite shop in the northwest metro area of Marietta, a point system for ride participation earning further discounts, newsletters and info about practice rides and more.

Field Hockey

GEORGIA FIELD HOCKEY ASSOCIATION
2840 Peachtree Rd., No. 103 346-3982

Some 25 teams are currently playing through the association. There are teams for male, female and children players. The above hotline number will give you current information on leagues and how to join. To reach the president, call 262-1633.

Fishing

Now for some watery sports, from the chills of white water adventures to the more placid art of angling. You gotta have a ticket to get in this game. A license, that is.

For nonresidents, an annual license costs $24; a seven-day license is $7; a one-day license is $3.50 Each of these except the one-day license also requires a $13 trout stamp when fishing in designated trout waters. Georgia fishing licenses are available in many convenient locations. Call first to be sure the outlet hasn't temporarily run out of the type of license you need.

Locations include these area stores: Kmart, Wal-Mart, Sports Authority, Sports Town and many bait and tackle shops.

THE FISH HAWK
283 Buckhead Ave. N.E. 237-3473

At the venerable Fish Hawk, you can get a full line of tackle, gear and outdoor clothing. What's more, you'll find advice and another source for fishing licenses. As fishing fanatics know, haunts like this will likely turn up information on where the fish are biting.

THE GEORGIA WILDLIFE RESOURCE DIVISION
2123 U.S. Hwy 278 S.E.
Social Circle 918-6418

These are the people who operate public fishing areas around the state. Largemouth bass, bream, blue gill, sunfish and channel catfish are species commonly managed in these areas. Generally, the hours of designated trout stream areas are from 30 minutes before sunrise to 30 minutes after sunset from the last Saturday in March to the last day in October. Different hours exist for specific managed areas; the Wild Life Resource Division will provide detailed information about this and the special rules on bait and tackle.

Anglers from 16 to 65 years of age must have a Wildlife Managed Area Stamp to fish, as well as a trout stamp attached to the Georgia fishing license when fishing in designated trout waters. Landowners fishing on their own property do not need a trout stamp.

Golf

Public Courses

Several municipal golf courses offer convenient locations and excellent playing conditions. Most of these courses feature greens of Bermuda grass on a rolling landscape, with rental clubs available. Unless otherwise noted, these are 18-hole courses. The following is a representative sampling; for complete lists, call the specific locality's parks and recreation departments listed at the beginning of this chapter.

In the past six years, more than 15 public courses have opened in the metro Atlanta area in addition to the already existing facilities. Fees listed here are subject to change; please call before heading out. For municipally owned courses, resident and nonresident fees are quoted; otherwise, one fee applies to all. Weekdays on the golf course means Mondays through Thursdays.

Cobb County

BOULDERS AT LAKE ACWORTH
4200 Nance Rd., Acworth   917-5151
Whenever prominent attorney Houston Lennard can break away from a full schedule, he heads for his favorite links at Boulders. "The course is so well maintained and the greens are pristine all seasons of the year," he says. "It's not an easy course, it offers challenges with choices to be made."

Designed by course architect Ken Dye, the facility offers a golf shop and clubhouse. Dye says, even though the course isn't a monster lengthwise, it's interesting and allows golfers to use everything in their bags. Many golfers enjoy the therapeutic benefit from the combination of natural beauty and athletic challenge.

Weekday fees for residents are $27 to walk; $37 with a cart. Nonresidents pay $44 to walk. Cobb County residents can get an annual discount card that shaves $10 off the fees.

CENTENNIAL
5225 Woodstock Rd., Acworth   975-1000
The Georgia Association of Golf headquarters is at this fine par 72 course. It's the signature course of Larry Nelson, PGA pro, who designed Centennial. Considered one of the very best daily-fee facilities, its winding creeks gives golfers a challenge for their fees. These begin at $35 weekdays, $45 on weekends.

LEGACY GOLF LINKS
1825 Windy Hill Rd., Smyrna   434-6331
A combination of beauty and challenge await you at this 18-hole course designed by Larry Nelson. Called a challenging executive course, it features sloping doglegs and rolling fairways that conceal fairway bunkers and traps. It has well-maintained Penn Links Bentgrass greens. A driving and practice range, a clubhouse and a putting course are on the premises.

Weekday fees for women and seniors are $10; all others pay $15. Carts are $9.45 per person.

DeKalb County

CLIFTON SPRINGS COURSE
2340 Clifton Springs Rd., Decatur 241-3636

This par 3, 18-hole course offers instruction and rental equipment. Carts are available, as are custom clubs. Fees for weekday play are $8 for 18 holes; $6 for nine holes.

MYSTERY VALLEY
6094 Shadowrock Dr.
Lithonia   *469-6913*

Pro Dave Ayers describes this course as a championship caliber layout that makes for a challenging round of play. Designed by Dick Wilson, the 18-hole, par 72 course has Bermuda fairways and greens. Fees begin at $13 for weekdays and go up to $15 on weekends. For non-DeKalb County residents, the fees are $17 weekdays and $20 weekends. Carts cost $9.50 per person.

Fulton County

ALFRED TUP
2300 Wilson Dr. S.W.   *753-6158*

This 18-hole course has a par score of 72, with PGA-approved pro Carl Seldon overseeing the operation. Bermuda greens cover the only slightly hilly terrain with wooded areas nearby. Intermediate golfers find the course a pleasure. Eighteen-hole fees for weekday play for residents begin at $14.84 and rise to $16.96 on the weekends. For nonresidents, the weekday fee is $19. Carts cost $10 for one person

and twice that for two. Nine holes of play will set you back $7.

BOBBY JONES
384 Woodward Way N.E.   *355-1009*

This is an 18-hole course with a par score of 71. The course has 16 different types of fees that begin with weekday rates of about $15 for residents and a $9.50 cart charge. For nonresidents, the weekday rate is $19. The Bermuda greens and fairways are popular with intermediate golfers.

CANDLER PARK
585 Candler Park Dr. N.E.   *373-9265*

With nine holes and a par of 36, fees at Candler Park start at the low end with $4.50, $3.75 for students and seniors. No carts are available.

CHASTAIN GOLF COURSE
216 W. Wieuca Rd.   *255-0723*

The Chastain course was built in the 1940s. Its low, rolling terrain is called a championship course. The stone clubhouse, perhaps in tribute to the country synonymous with golf, is modeled after venerable structures in Scotland. Here you will find a pro shop and snack bar. Resident weekday fees to walk are $14.84; with a cart, $29.38. For nonresidents, the basic weekday fee is $19; with a cart, $29.

CHAMPIONS CLUBS OF ATLANTA
15135 Hopewell Rd.
Alpharetta   *343-9700*

These attractive public courses play

well for golfers of most any experience level, making it a perfect spot for the visiting boss or favored client. You can find a relaxing day on the links at any one of the Champions Clubs' locations. For the Apalachee Farms course in Dacula (northeast metro Atlanta), call 822-9220; in Alpharetta (north metro), call the above number; the Club in Gwinnett County, (Snellville, northeast metro), call 978-7755. At the Alpharetta club, fees are $42 weekdays, $49 on Fridays, $55 on Saturdays and Sundays.

Gwinnett County

SPRINGBROOK GOLF COURSE
585 Camp Perrin Rd.
Lawrenceville   822-5400

Beautiful Bermuda fairways with Bent grass greens makes this course a pleasure to view as well as to play. The Gwinnett County links feature a clubhouse, restaurant, driving range and putting green. Club and cart rentals are available. Other amenities in this county-operated complex include tennis courts and a pool. Weekday resident fees are $17 to walk; with cart, $25.13. Nonresidents add $2.

Privately Owned Courses Open to the Public

CHATEAU ÉLAN GOLF CLUB
6060 Golf Club Dr.
Braselton   271-6050

At the Chateau Élan resort and winery (30 minutes northeast of Atlanta, Exit 48 off I-85) is a par 71 — 18-hole course designed by Dennis Griffiths. Spread across 170 acres, the course includes three lakes and two creeks; water comes into play on 10 of the 18

holes. A practice facility simulates the course's challenges and prepares golfers to meet them. Rates — $55 per person Monday through Thursday, $60 per person Friday through Sunday — include cart rental.

LAKE LANIER ISLANDS HILTON RESORT
7000 Holiday Rd.
Lake Lanier Islands   945-8787

Designed by Joe Lee, this 18-hole, par 72 course features 13 holes on the shores of Lake Lanier. In 1989, *Golf Digest* named the course one of the top five in its listing of the best new U.S. resort golf courses. Fees include the mandatory cart rental. In-season rates are in effect March 1 through October 31: $42.50 per person Monday through Thursday, $47.50 per person Friday through Sunday and on holidays. From November 1 through February 28, the rate is $39 per person, seven days a week.

STOUFFER RENAISSANCE PINEISLE RESORT
9000 Holiday Rd.
Lake Lanier Islands   945-8921

This resort's 18-hole championship course was designed by Gary Player and Ron Kirby & Associates. From 1985-89, it was the site of the LPGA Nestle World Championship; eight holes skirt Lake Lanier. *Golfweek* magazine named the course to its list of America's best in 1992 and 1994. Greens fees and cart rental are $54 per person Monday through Thursday, $59 per person Friday through Sunday.

STONE MOUNTAIN GOLF COURSE
U.S. Hwy. 78
Stone Mountain   498-5717

Stone Mountain Park's beautiful 36-hole course, designed by expert Robert

Trent Jones, is open to the public. The course has been rated among the top 25 public courses in the country by *Golf Digest*. Nine of the holes lie beside the park's lake.

There's a pro shop on the premises, with lessons and rental clubs available. Weekends and holidays require about a week's advance reservation. Otherwise, it's first come, first served. You'll pay a $5 fee for each car entering the park. Stone Mountain course is open Mondays through Fridays, from 8 AM to dark and from 7 AM to dark on weekends and holidays. For more information, call the course number above or the general information number, 498-5690.

METROPOLITAN CLUB OF ATLANTA
3000 Fairington Pkwy.
Decatur   *981-5325*
This 18-hole course was designed by Robert Trent Jones. Monday through Thursday you'll pay $30 for greens fee and cart; Friday through Sunday, $38. Rental clubs are available.

Horseback Riding
Riding enthusiasts of all ages have lots of company here. Close to 20 riding academies and stables in the metro area offer lessons, rental riding time, boarding and an assortment of equestrian services. For a list of horseback riding organizations, call the Georgia Department of Agriculture, 656-3685. Here are a couple of well-recommended facilities.

CHASTAIN STABLES
Chastain Memorial Park
4371 Powers Ferry Rd. N.W.   257-1470
Basically a school and boarding facility, Chastain is open seven days a week, and the public is invited. Bring the children, some carrots and apples and feed the horses.

This 10-acre park offers English riding lessons for children and adults Monday through Friday. Times and costs vary with experience level, which ranges from beginner to advanced. Three barns house some 35 school and boarding horses; no rental rides are offered. Pony birthday parties are a specialty.

WILLS PARK
11925 Wills Rd., Alpharetta   740-2400
Although there is no riding or boarding service at this 46-acre equestrian park, the draw is the events put on by major saddle clubs year round in the three-ring facility. One biggie is the Southeastern Charity Horse Show held each September, a four-day event that benefits Scottish Rite Childrens' Medical Center in Atlanta. The schedule is filled, with an event for just about every weekend. Many of the shows are free, while others levy a minimum charge. The Annual Rodeo, to be held in mid-August, draws thousands of enthusiastic spectators. The charge is approximately $10, children younger than 10 get in free.

Ice Skating

ATLANTA ICE FORUM
2300 Satellite Blvd., Duluth   813-1010
This ice rink is off Exit 42 from I-85 northeast of the city. It's open seven days a week with varying hours; it's closed on Monday and Wednesday evenings. Admission is $6 on Friday and Saturday. Skate rental is $2.

PARKAIRE OLYMPIC ICE ARENA
4880 Lower Roswell Rd.
Marietta   *973-0753*
For ice skating, Parkaire has been a favorite with northwest area dwellers for the past 20 years. The arena is

MARTA makes it easy to get around.

the practice site for the Atlanta Knights, the city's professional hockey team. Youth hockey league play is a feature; for information call 816-3033. Lessons, offered in seven-week series, are available; $75 children and $80 adults. Admission in 2-hour increments is $5.75 for adults, $5.25 for kids 12 and younger, plus $1.25 skate rental. Public hours vary, so call for more information.

Juggling

ATLANTA JUGGLERS ASSOCIATION
Little Five Points Community Club
1083 Austin Ave. N.E.   522-2926

The Atlanta Jugglers Association unites amateurs and professionals for a few hours of fun every Tuesday and Thursday from 7:30 PM to 10 PM at the Little Five Points Community Club. Call for information.

Lacrosse

The Atlanta Lacrosse Club seeks new players to join in the excitement. The club's hotline is 332-0014. The Women's Lacrosse Club invites newcomers to call 303-1160 or 888-6738 to learn about this group's activities.

Martial Arts

Among the martial arts represented in Atlanta are aikido, kung fu and shotokan.

AIKIDO CENTER OF ATLANTA
639 Valley Brook Rd.
Decatur   449-6333, 297-7804

Here you can study the defensive martial art in classes seven days a week. Aikido stresses channeling energy rather than brute strength for the purpose of self-defense. Increased strength and spiritual awareness are among the aims of devotees of aikido.

ATLANTA SHOTOKAN
801 Tree Lodge Pkwy.
Dunwoody   391-9418

To promote strength, confidence and flexibility for self-defense, study this traditional Japanese form of karate with Randall Hackworth. He offers classes in two locations: the Concourse Athletic Club, 8 Concourse Parkway, just north of Atlanta; and at Georgia Tech University in the Athletic Complex. Training is offered six days a week.

IMPERATORI FAMILY KARATE CENTER
5290 Roswell Rd.   252-8200

This large 8,000-square-foot center houses training for men, women and children, plus a martial arts supplies store. Nationally ranked husband and wife team Joey and Sheldon Imperatori teach clients discipline and self-defense techniques while increasing confidence and fitness levels.

DAVE YOUNG'S WORLD CLASS KARATE & MARTIAL ARTS ACADEMY
5400 Chamblee Dunwoody Rd.
Dunwoody   394-5425

Men, women and children can learn tai chi, kickboxing, jujitsu and other arts here. Competition training is offered, as are summer camps, body guard service and even karate birthday parties. Women's self-defense classes are popular. This organization has operations in at least five states.

A HOUSE OF KARATE
1104 Ridge Ave.   413-9139

In the Stone Mountain area, this center is designed for the serious martial artist. Instructors Phil and Donna Robinson boast 25 years of experience. A family atmosphere is provided for ages 7 and older.

Racquetball

TUCKER RACQUET & FITNESS CENTER
3281 Tucker Norcross Rd.   *491-3100*

This facility has an open court for guests, who can play all day after paying a $10 guest fee and signing a liability waiver. Eight racquetball courts are joined by tennis courts and aerobics and weight exercise equipment.

SOUTHERN ATHLETIC CLUB
754 Beaver Ruin Rd. N.W.
Lilburn   *923-5400*

For an $8 guest fee, you can play all day on one of seven courts, two of which are challenge courts. Call ahead to reserve a spot. Other facilities include an outdoor pool, a volleyball court, tennis courts, basketball courts and a sun deck. Among the full club amenities are a steam room, a sauna, a whirlpool, lockers and showers. Full workout equipment includes Nautilus, free weights, Stairmasters and more.

SOUTHLAKE ATHLETIC CLUB
1792 Mt. Zion Rd., Morrow   *968-1798*

Eight indoor courts await you for a guest fee of $10. Manager David Hansen describes Southlake as a family-oriented facility with child care available. A pro instructor is on staff. Members and guests can engage in tournaments and league play. Fitness is assisted in several ways such as aerobics and free weights. Memberships are available on a month-to-month basis or up to three years.

Rowing

At the Chattahoochee River Park, 203 Azalea Drive, Roswell, a group devoted to rowing on the river meets regularly. Contact The Atlanta Rowing Club, 8351 Rosewell Road, Suite 103, 30350; 993-1879.

Rugby

The **Atlanta Rugby Football Club** practices its moves each Tuesday and Thursday. To find out more, call 240-0280 during the day or 449-6274 in the evenings. Another group called the **Atlanta Renegades Rugby Club** has a hotline to tell you about activities; call 365-2442.

Running/Walking

A strong case can be made that Atlanta's most popular recreation is human locomotion. When a city's track club has 10,000 members and when 50,000 participants show up on July Fourth for the world's largest 10K race, you know the place is carrying on a love affair with running and walking.

The city's environment encourages exploration amidst the ivy-covered lawns, the towering tree canopy and the flower-bedecked walkways. From mall strollers to competitive athletes, Atlanta offers a trail for everyone. And besides, it's a great way to meet people while you become acquainted with the city.

Neighborhood-based running and walking clubs encourage participation.

Among these are the **Chattahoochee Road Runners**, 425-8184; **The Virginia Highlands Running Club** (call the Atlanta Track Club for information); and the **South Fulton Running Partners**, 762-0667.

The **Roswell Striders**, a walking/jogging club meets the third Wednesday of each month at 7:30 PM in the community activity building of Roswell Area Park. Call 641-3760 for more details. **Walking Club of Georgia** sponsors walks in various locations in Atlanta. For times and locations of events, plus membership information, call 593-5817.

Indoor walking programs, jogging with your dog, runners who prefer track running, walk/runs for kids, speed runners — a program for just about everyone is listed in Atlanta Track Club's *The Wingfoot*. Many groups welcome newcomers and sometimes finish off their workout with a meal.

For guidance in walking the city neighborhoods, read a delightfully detailed book called *Atlanta Walks*, by Ren and Helen Davis. Published by Peachtree Publishers, the book sells for $9.95 in local bookstores. It will greatly enhance your walking experience, giving you a thorough grounding in the history and architecture of your favorite routes.

Atlanta runners march to their own tune via an upbeat audio tape by Greg Blum created to inspire runners. The tape is available at Wax 'N' Facts, Wuxtry, Rainy Day Records and Eat More Records for $8, with $2 going to charity. Specially designed to give runners a lift at key points during a 10K run, the rock tape called *2nd Wind* features musical talent such as the Ellen James Society and the Viceroys.

ATLANTA TRACK CLUB
3097 E. Shadowlawn Ave.   *231-9065*

Have questions about running and walking in the metro area? Call the Atlanta Track Club, a top-notch source. To quote directly from the club's monthly magazine, *The Wingfoot,* the club "is a nonprofit, membership organization dedicated to the promotion of health and fitness for youth and adults through programs of amateur road racing, cross country, and track and field in the spirit of fun and competition."

Organized in 1964, ATC has grown to become one of the most active clubs of its type in the country. Under the expert guidance of Executive Director Julia Emmons and the ATC board of directors, the club promotes some 25 events each year, such as the Thanksgiving morning **Atlanta Marathon and Half Marathon**.

King of them all is the gigantic **Peachtree Road Race**, a USA Track and Field-sanctioned event limited to 50,000 runners. Thousands of spectators, armed with water guns and shouts of encouragement, create an exhilarating scene along the entire route. Hundreds of volunteers support the race by handling pre-race registration, staffing water stations, assisting runners in trouble and performing dozens of other unseen but necessary tasks behind this major event.

Besides the major races, ATC sponsors low-key biweekly road races and a summer series of informal track and field meets. To get information about each week's events, call the ATC-sponsored phone line, 262-RACE. ATC also maintains a list of sports medicine specialists.

Hundreds of members volunteer at events, helping with coaching or with administrative matters. ATC's Volunteer Coaching Program, in its 13th year of service to members, has approximately 50 big-hearted people who will work with you at your level as part of your membership benefits. Whether you're just getting started and want to form good habits to avoid injury or graduating to marathon level, you can be paired with an experienced runner near your residence.

ATC takes part in many community support efforts, among them the Adopt-A-Highway Program and the State of Georgia Games, which are patterned after the Summer Olympic Games. The ATC Shoe Project coordinates members' donation of running shoes (unfit for running but still wearable) to such agencies as the Salvation Army and the Battered Women's Shelter.

Annual memberships in the ATC take three forms: $20 for individuals; $30 for couples; $45 for families. Benefits include free entry to most ATC races (14 in this category in 1994), the monthly magazine, a membership card, which will get you a 10 percent discount in certain bike and running equipment stores, and voting rights in the annual board of directors election.

One of the most coveted advantages of membership has been the members' advance sign-up date for the Peachtree Road Race, now limited to those who joined be-

fore July 1994. Applications from around the world flood ATC headquarters to fill all available slots within hours of the opening application date.

Racewalking

Racewalking gains advocates among those who seek the benefits of running without the injury rate. Classes held in several metro locations over an eight-week period help beginners get into the swing of things; the fee is $75. For more information, call 847-WALK.

Sailing

LANIER SAILING ACADEMY
8000 Holiday Rd.
Lake Lanier Islands   945-8810

Private and group instruction is available here for beginners and more seasoned sailors. Racing clinics and junior programs are also offered. Boat rental, charter cruises and more are part of this large academy. The setting is unbeatable and draws Atlantans by the thousands. The marina provides complete sailboat facilities for rent, as well as those for motorboats. Take that dream vacation aboard a houseboat here at Lake Lanier, the body of water so large it spans three counties.

WINDSONG SAILING ACADEMY
Holiday Marina, Lake Lanier   256-6700

With two locations on the largest lakes in the Atlanta area, Lake Lanier and Lake Alatoona, this outfit offers numerous sailing opportunities. While basically a school, many people continue to sail through the academy after taking courses for the $30-per-session fee.

The academy's programs are approved by Cobb, DeKalb and Gwinnett counties and are offered year round. You may take courses in chartering, boat purchase and navigation, safety, weather, celestial navigation, on-board gourmet cooking and many other topics.

Barefoot Sailing

The Barefoot Sailing Club meets at 7:30 PM on the fourth Monday of each month at the Sheraton Century Center Hotel, 2000 Century Boulevard N.E., 256-6839.

Boardsailing

ATLANTA BOARDSAILING CLUB
Norcross   908-0348

The Atlanta Boardsailing Club promotes and supports this thrilling sport on various Southeastern lakes. The group meets in different members' homes in the Norcross area (northeast of the city) on the second Tuesday of each month. Membership fee is $20. Call 908-0348 for more details.

Scuba Diving

The Atlanta Reef Dweller Scuba Club meets monthly to plan trips, listen to guest speakers and view films on the sport. For more details, call 457-6008.

Skating

For fast movers who still want to take in the scene, skating provides the solution for many Atlantans and visitors. Catch MARTA to the Midtown area and walk to prime skating territory in Piedmont Park.

SKATE ESCAPE
1086 Piedmont Ave. N.E.   892-1292

Skate Escape is open Monday through Saturday, 10 AM to 7 PM; on Sunday,

noon to 7 PM. Rental requires identification, such as a driver's license or major credit card, or a hefty $100 deposit.

You can rent skates, both conventional and in-line, for $4 per hour or $12 per day. Skate Escape also rents helmets, accessories and skate boards — in short, everything you need to glide through the park to your heart's content.

For indoor skating, you have your choice of a good dozen or more skating rinks. Following are a couple of suggestions to give you an idea of what's available.

THE GOLDEN GLIDE ROLLER SKATING RINK
2750 Wesley Chapel Rd.
Decatur   288-7773

This rink designates specific nights for special age groups, with a basic rate of $1 skate rental plus admission price. Mondays through Wednesdays are reserved for private parties. On Thursdays, 8 PM to midnight the rink is reserved for skaters older than 21, with an admission price of $4.

Family Night is Friday from 7:30 PM to 11 PM, $3.50 admission fee. Open skating is Saturday afternoons from 1 to 5 PM and Sundays from 3 to 6 PM, $3 admission fee. Teen Night is Saturday from 7:30 to 11:30 PM, $4 admission fee. On Adults Only Ladies Night, the minimum age is 21; ladies pay $2, and men pay $4.

INLINE HOCKEY CLUB
1250 Franklin Dr.
Marietta   528-9809

In Cobb County just across from Dobbins Air Force Base, this club offers league play for kids and adults of all ages and all levels of experience. Players range from beginners to those who play on traveling teams. Participation in an eight- or nineweekseason costs $120 for children during the first season, which includes a one-time registration fee, and $95 per season thereafter. For adults, a first season's play costs $130, $105 for subsequent seasons.

Skiing

For skiing, get in touch with Atlanta Ski Club, one of the largest of its type in the world with approximately 4,000 members. Among features are extensive snow skiing programs, year-round adventure trips and social events. Membership dues are $60 to join; $50 annual thereafter. The club's information line is 255-4800. The College Park Recreation Department offers two annual trips to Beech Mountain Ski Resort at Banner Elk, North Carolina, in January and February. Call 669-3773 for information.

Soccer

Soccer fans bow to no one in their enthusiasm, and Atlanta offers both kids and adults ample opportunity to indulge in the sport. Here are some examples of where to find information on league teams and other forms of play.

GEORGIA STATE SOCCER ASSOCIATION
3684 Stewart Rd., Doraville   452-0505

In metro Atlanta, there are approximately 27 kids' leagues and 11 adult leagues. All registration, insurance and other administrative matters for organized league play are handled through this office.

The association certifies coaches and referees. It also offers a coaching school and a referee program. The Soccer Booster Club gives members priority access to seating for Olympic soccer events. Call for information on league locations in your area.

STONE MOUNTAIN YOUTH SOCCER ASSOCIATION
5585 Rockbridge Rd.
Stone Mountain   879-1123

Boys and girls from ages 4 to 19 enjoy the sport in this league in spring and fall. Two types of programs are offered, recreational and select, the select being the more competitive. Costs may vary with seasons, but average between $50 and $70.

TOPHAT SOCCER CLUB
1900 Emery St. N.W.   351-4466

This is an all-girls soccer club of about 700 players in the Buckhead area of Atlanta. It is one of the highest-ranked clubs in the Southeast and is very competitive on state and national levels.

TUCKER YOUTH SOCCER
2803 Henderson Rd., Tucker   414-0538

Approximately 1,000 players make up this club of boys and girls. Both recreational and select programs are available for fall and spring seasons. Costs average $65.

Softball

SOFTBALL COUNTRY CLUB
3500 N. Decatur Rd.   299-3588

From about the second week of February through the first of December, the Softball Country Club swings with all-adult, slow-pitch play. The club has nine fields and an air-conditioned clubhouse for savoring those moments of glory after the big game. Most people come here as part of existing teams, but individuals are welcome to sign up for available slots; sometimes even spectators are pressed into service. Team members typically split the cost of play, which works out to between $40 and $60 per person for the season.

Leagues play Sunday through Friday; tournaments are held on Saturday.

Swimming

We may be a distance from the ocean, but there's no lack of pools to frolic in. For visitors, most hotels and motels have swimming facilities. Residents journey down to their local municipal pool where, for a small fee, they can splash away a summer day. Some pools have seasonal membership cards available.

Atlanta

The City of Atlanta Bureau of Parks maintains 18 outdoor swimming pools and three indoor pools. For a complete listing or the pool nearest you, call the **Department of Parks & Recreation**, 817-6744. Following are a few of the city's major municipal facilities.

CHASTAIN MEMORIAL PARK
235 W. Wieuca Rd. N.W.   255-0863

GRANT PARK
625 Park Ave. S.E.   622-3041

PIEDMONT PARK
Piedmont Ave. and 14th St.   892-0117

Cobb County

The **Cobb County Aquatics Center**, near the Cobb County Civic Center, houses two heated pools, a diving well, a fitness room and locker facilities. The center offers instruction, a year-round competitive swim program, public swim times and a diving program. Two more pools in Cobb County are Sewell Park in East Cobb and Powder Springs in West Cobb. Get all the details by calling 528-8467.

DeKalb County

The county operates 12 pools open daily during the summer months, closing each year around Labor Day. The pools are staffed by certified lifeguards. Annual passes and family discounts are offered. For information on DeKalb's pools, call 371-2631.

Fulton County

The county's Clarence Duncan Park Natatorium has open swim hours every day of the week and is open year round. Swim passes in three-month increments are available. More than a half-dozen different classes, from water safety to arthritis exercise, are offered. Hours and classes are subject to change, so call ahead to inquire. The natatorium is at 6000 Rivertown Road, Fairburn; call 306-3137.

Gwinnett County

Gwinnett operates five aquatics centers, four of which are open from Memorial Day weekend to Labor Day weekend. The fifth facility at Mountain Park in Lilburn is open year round. Each facility offers a variety of swim lessons and classes. Season passes are available. For year-round information on schedules, costs and hours of operation, call Mountain Park Pool, 564-4650.

Tennis

Tennis is big in the metro area, as you'll see by the many city and county parks with courts. The City of Atlanta alone maintains 50 tennis court locations.

With our temperate weather, the heartiest of aficionados can play pretty much year round. We'll begin with information on the organization credited with changing the tennis scene in the metro area.

ATLANTA LAWN TENNIS ASSOCIATION (ALTA)
1140 Hammond Dr. N.E.   399-5788

A solid boost to popularity of the sport came in 1971 when ALTA began league play with 1,000 members. Today 73,000 individuals and more than 3,500 doubles teams take part.

League play is scheduled for women, men, juniors and wheelchair competitors. Leagues are divided according to expertise. Call ALTA's office for more information.

PIEDMONT PARK TENNIS CENTER
Piedmont Park
Piedmont Ave. and 14th St.   872-1507

In yet another attraction of this sizeable park in Midtown Atlanta, one of the largest in the Southeast, 12 outdoor hard courts are lighted for night play. Showers, lockers and a pro shop are on the premises. The facility is operated by the City of Atlanta Parks and Recreation Department. Hours are Monday through Friday, 10 AM to 9 PM. On Saturday and Sunday, hours are from 9 AM to 6 PM. The fee is $1.50 per person per hour; $1.75 for lighted courts. Reservations are made for team practices only.

BITSY GRANT TENNIS CENTER
2125 Northside Dr. N.W.   351-2774

Among the courts operated by the city's Parks and Recreation Department is the popular Bitsy Grant, named for the local player who became a champion. Thirteen outdoor clay courts (six lit at night) and 10 outdoor hard courts (four lit) are available. Showers, lockers and a pro shop are on site. Call for hours of operation, which vary with the season.

LENOX PARK TENNIS CENTER
3375 Standard Dr.   237-7339

A management group called Tennis Tech runs nearly a dozen courts at this facility a mile north of Lenox Square on Peachtree Road. Lessons, a pro shop, showers and lockers are offered. You can reserve a court 24 hours in advance. Call for prices and hours of operation.

CHASTAIN PARK TENNIS CENTER
Chastain Memorial Park   255-9798
W. Wieuca, Powers Ferry and Lake Forrest Dr.

The It's A Match Club offers an opportunity to play mixed doubles and round robins each week from 7 to 9 PM on Fridays at Chastain Tennis Center. Tennis trips, partner matching and team play are all offered. For more details, call 255-1993 or 662-6162.

GEORGIA'S STONE MOUNTAIN PARK
Stone Mountain Sports Complex Tennis Center
Ga.   78   498-5728

At the fabulous Stone Mountain Park's Sports Complex, enjoy the game on eight lighted courts. The facility also provides a multilevel range of batting cages so you can practice your swing. Fees are $2.50 per person per hour. Call 498-5600 for more information.

COBB COUNTY PARKS & RECREATION
Tennis Hotline   421-1109

Cobb County offers several designated tennis centers with league play, partner matching, classes and tournaments. For the location of the center closest to you and for the latest programming information, call the number above. Phone numbers for the centers are: the Harrison Center, 591-3151; Kennworth, 917-5160;

Sweetwater, 819-3221; Fair Oaks, 528-8480; and Terrell Mill, 644-2771.

DeKalb County Recreation Parks
General Information Line   371-3621

Residents of DeKalb County, just east of downtown, enjoy playing on more than 50 recreational tennis courts in parks throughout the county, including eight new courts at Wade-Walker Park.

Three of the centers offering tennis facilities in DeKalb are the Sugar Creek Center, 243-7149; the Blackburn Center, 451-1061; and the DeKalb Center, 325-2520. Call these centers for more information on programs. ·

Fulton County
Parks & Recreation
Office of the Director   730-6200

Fulton County operates eight tennis facilities. To highlight just one, we'll look at the North Fulton Tennis Center, 500 Abernathy Road, 303-6182. Here you'll find 24 lighted courts, 20 hard surface and four soft courts. The Tennis Center is complete with a pro shop, showers and lockers, a full-time teaching staff, lounges and viewing areas. North Fulton was named as one of the top-50 public tennis facilities in the United States by *Tennis* magazine.

Gwinnett County
Parks and Recreation
Information Line   822-8840

To the northeast of the city, Gwinnett County residents flock to a beautiful tennis/golf/aquatics complex called Springbrook, 585 Camp Perrin Road, Lawrenceville. Just north of the city of Lawrenceville, the park offers three hard courts. Six other tennis centers also offer league play, lessons and tournaments on lighted courts.

Ultimate Frisbee

The **Atlanta Flying Disc Club** focuses on perfecting the sport of ultimate Frisbee. Co-ed play is staged weekly. Co-ed winter and summer leagues are available. For more information, call the AFDC hotline, 351-0914.

Whitewater Rafting and Tubing

For thrills that last long after you've soaked your clothing, try your hand at whitewater river rafting. Within easy distance of Atlanta, you'll find adventures galore via raft, canoe and kayak.

The scenic Chattooga River, scene of the movie *Deliverance*, is one of the last undammed whitewater streams in the Southeast. You can choose your level of difficulty on a variety of rapids, but if you dare, you can tackle one of the five rapids that drops more than 70 feet. The challenge varies with the season of the year as water levels change.

Thousands throng to these waters, so make your reservations early. Most companies require children to be 10 years old for lesser rapids and 12 or 13 for the wilder ones. The season runs generally from March into November, with wet suits and paddle jackets provided as needed.

Weekdays are cheaper than weekends. Prices vary with the length and difficulty of the trip. Half-day trips start around $30, full-day trips start around $50 and usually include a guide, lunch, necessary equipment and transportation from the outpost down to the river.

Southeastern Expeditions
2936 N. Druid Hills N.E.   329-0433
(800)868-7238

This is a company that has organized outings since 1973. Ropes challenges, overnight trips, personalized instruction and group outings are among Southeastern's services.

From Atlanta, it takes about 60 to 90 minutes to reach the company's Chattooga Outpost. Take I-85 N. to I-985 N.; you'll see a left-hand fork. I-985 eventually turns into Ga. Highway 441. Continue on to the town of Clayton. At the first light in town, turn right on Ga. Highway 76. Go 8 miles, and you'll see the outpost on the right-hand side of the road.

NANTAHALA OUTDOOR CENTER'S CHATTOOGA OUTPOST
13 miles east of Clayton   (800)232-7238

Farther north, the Nantahala Outdoor Center's Chattooga Outpost is in Georgia's northeast corner. Twenty-two years' experience underlies this employee-owned company based in Bryson City, North Carolina.

NOC offers outings on five rivers: the Nantahala, Ocoee, Chattooga, Nolichucky and French Broad. Call (800)232-7238 for information. A division of NOC, the Great Smokies Rafting Company, specializes in the dam-controlled, icy Nantahala; call (800)238-6302 for details.

THE APPALACHIAN OUTFITTERS
P.O. Box 793, Dahlonega 30533 (706)864-7117

How about some kinder, gentler fun on the water? Two outfitters have set up operations near Dahlonega, about an hour north of Atlanta, to offer a couple of hours' lazy drifting on the Chestatee River.

The Appalachian Outfitters has an outing called Miner's Run after the gold rush days of Dahlonega. It runs 3.5 miles for 2½ hours of lovely scenery. You'll get a look at historic landmarks where present-day miners pan the gold veins that empty into the Chestatee, making prospecting seem awfully easy. Appalachian Outfitters is open May through September, 10 AM to 3 PM on weekends; 10 AM to 2 PM on weekdays. Rates are: adults, $7.50; children 6 to 12, $5. The price includes a double-walled tube, a life jacket, floating buckets, river information, safety instructions and a shuttle back to your car.

GENTLEWATERS TUBING
Hwy. 60 at Chestatee River Bridge

GentleWaters Tubing offers long trips of 3.5 miles and short ones of 1 mile with very similar services. Rates are: adults, $7 long trip, $6 short trip; children, $5 long trip, $4 short trip.

GEORGIA BLIND ADVENTURES
3680 Lindley Cr.   943-3296

Georgia's many scenic settings are accessible to the visually impaired through this organization. Canoeing trips, whitewater rafting and rappelling are among the group's outings, which participants take with the assistance of sighted volunteers.

The group needs volunteers' eyes, elbows and cars to help serve people who won't let a disability stop them from exploring the world.

Volleyball

Volleyball games tend to be informal and impromptu neighborhood-based activities. One likely spot to find a game is at Mercer University. Call 986-3369 for information on times and locations.

A co-ed volleyball tournament is held each October at Boatrock Recreation Center, 5800 Boatrock Road S.W. Call 346-8395 for more information.

Volleyball is played regularly at

Hammond Park, 705 Hammond Drive. Beginners', women's and men's teams are formed here. Call 303-6176 for information.

ATLANTA BEACH SPORTS & ENTERTAINMENT PARK

2474 Walt Stephens Rd.
Jonesboro   *478-1932*

Twenty minutes south of Atlanta off I-75, Atlanta Beach will be the beach volleyball venue for the 1996 Olympics. The 32-acre park is part of a Clayton County park of more than 200 acres. It has an eight-acre filtered and treated spring-fed lake with a white sand beach and a stocked 15-acre fishing lake. Beach volleyball, softball and horseshoes are all popular pastimes here. The park features an 18-hole mini-golf course, go-carts and a kiddie play area with 14 slides. It's open from 10 AM to 8 PM weekends in May and daily from Memorial Day to September. Admission is $8.75 for adults and $5.75 for kids; group packages are available.

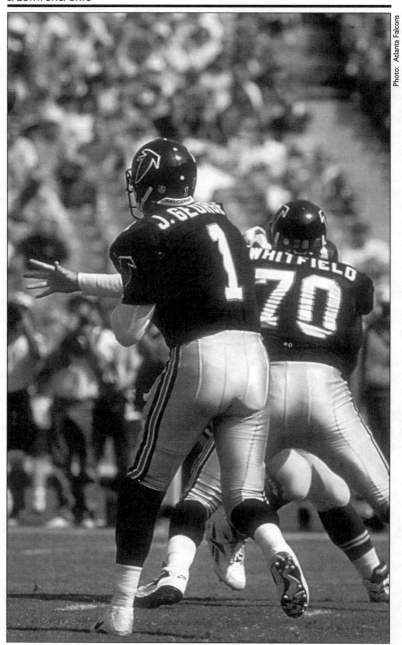

Photo: Atlanta Falcons

The Atlanta Falcons provide NFL action at the Georgia Dome.

Inside
Spectator Sports

For many years, Atlanta was the only city in the South with big league baseball, football and basketball teams. Our teams, therefore, were "adopted" as the home team by millions of Southerners, many of whom seldom travel to Atlanta and have never been to a game in person. These long-distance fans are fiercely loyal and follow the action as closely as folks in Atlanta.

In the 1960s, Atlanta's acquisition of major league teams was an important milestone in its growth. Win or lose, the media attention the teams generated gave people across the country a reason to think — and talk — about the perpetually building city.

At times, Atlantans may seem to take their teams for granted. Hardly anybody paid attention to the Braves during their many losing seasons. Sometimes even winning isn't enough. When the Hawks won the NBA central division in 1994, tickets to their playoff games at the Omni were available right up to the last minute.

But at other times, sports are a city-wide mania. The Braves have generated so much interest in baseball there's a scramble every spring for little league team slots in the rapidly growing suburbs. Now it's something of a late-winter tradition: TV news reports show shivering parents camping in line all night to get their kids signed up for a league close to home.

And no event in Atlanta's modern history, of course, has consumed the public like the 1991 and 1992 World Series. After the Braves lost in '91, the city honored them with a downtown parade that drew 750,000 people — far more fans than turned out in Minneapolis to cheer the victorious Twins.

In 1994 Atlanta hosted Super Bowl XXVIII in the Georgia Dome. More than 800 million people worldwide, including 133 million in the United States, tuned in, making the game the most-watched event in TV history. And, looking ahead, in 2002, the Dome will host the NCAA Final Four.

Our biggest sporting event, of course, is yet to come. In 1996, the attention of the whole world will be on Atlanta, where elite athletes will compete in the 17-day XXVI Olympiad, the 100th anniversary of the modern Olympic movement.

So, sports fans, no matter what time of year you're coming to Atlanta, you're sure to find lots of action and excitement. What follows is a rundown of major spectator sporting events in Atlanta, together with a brief look at how the city is preparing for the 1996 Olympics and how you can get tickets!

(Note: Though correct at press time, ticket prices and policies for all sporting events are subject to change. Not all seats are available in all venues; many sections sell out to season ticket holders.)

Baseball

Atlanta Braves

Play Ball! Major league baseball came to Atlanta on April 12, 1966, when the newly relocated Milwaukee Braves played the Pittsburgh Pirates, losing 3-2 in 13 innings. Chief among the Braves' assets were future Hall of Famers Phil Niekro and Hank Aaron. In 1969, the Braves took the National League West title but lost the pennant in three games to the "Miracle" Mets.

In 1973, Hank Aaron, Dave Johnson and Darrell Evans made the record books by each hitting more than 40 homers. Then came the big moment: On April 8, 1974, millions watched as Hank Aaron smashed his 715th home run, besting Babe Ruth's long-standing record (a moment now immortalized in a large statue outside the stadium).

Back in the early 1980s, Braves games sometimes felt more like minor league contests. Attendance at games was often below 10,000; fans roamed the stadium freely and sat where they liked. But all that changed in 1982 when the Braves set a new record for the most games won (13) at the beginning of a season. Suddenly the Braves weren't a joke anymore, and Atlantans by the thousands spent their lunch hour standing in line for tickets.

In 1982 and 1983, Dale Murphy won back-to-back National League Most Valuable Player awards, helping the Braves capture the Western Division title in '82 and finish second in '83.

Then came the biggest shock. In 1990, the basement Braves chafed under the worst record in baseball. One year later, the

amazing Braves brought the World Series to Atlanta, becoming the first team in baseball history to go from worst to first in a single season. New records were set for Atlanta wins (94) and for attendance (more than 2.1 million). After beating out the L.A. Dodgers for the Western title, the Braves fell behind the Pittsburgh Pirates three games to two in the playoffs then came back to win the pennant in the seventh game. In the first World Series ever played in Atlanta, the Braves held on to the end, losing to the Minnesota Twins 1-0 in the 10th inning of game seven.

In 1992 the Braves were back: They set a modern-day franchise record with 98 wins and topped 3 million in attendance. They took their second-straight division title, then beat the Pirates in a seven-game series to win the league championship, becoming the first National League team since the 1977-'78 Dodgers to win back-to-back pennants. Again, Atlanta hosted the World Series, but again the Braves came up just short, losing to the Toronto Blue Jays in six games.

1993 saw more records set, as the team won 104 games (53 on the road) and drew almost 3.9 million fans to the ballpark. Ten games behind at the All-Star break, the Braves battled back to grab the division title from the San Francisco Giants in the final game of the regular season. Atlantans were again talking World Series, but this time the honor went to the Philadelphia Phillies, who took the pennant in six games but lost the Series to the Toronto Blue Jays.

When the players' strike ended the 1994 season, the Braves were in second-place in the National League East with a record of 68 wins and 46 losses.

Tickets

The days when you could show up at any Braves game and buy great tickets at

Photo: Georgia Tourist Division

Everybody loves the Braves!

the last minute are gone with the wins; most of the best seats are now snatched up by season-ticket buyers (often for corporate entertaining). However, if you're not too picky about where you sit, you'll usually find tickets available.

At the stadium, tickets are sold at the ticket stand near gate G. In-park patrons may buy tickets to future games at the in-park ticket window on aisle 119. Tickets are also available by mail: Atlanta Braves Mail Order, P.O. Box 4064, Atlanta 30302. Tickets are $18, $15, $12, $10 and $5.

You may order by phone and charge your tickets to your VISA, MasterCard, Discover or American Express card through the TicketMaster service. Call 249-6400 in Atlanta; long distance, dial (800)326-4000. Tickets are also sold at TicketMaster's 91 retail locations in Georgia, including Blockbuster Music and Tower Records. All TicketMaster retail centers require cash payment. TicketMaster adds a service charge for both phone and in-person orders.

Season and group tickets are available directly from the Braves: Call 577-9100.

If you don't have tickets, you can watch the Braves on SuperStation WTBS and the SportSouth cable network and can hear every game on the 150-station Braves Radio Network, whose Atlanta flagship station is WSB-AM 750.

BRAVE NEW STADIUM

Braves home games are played at the Atlanta-Fulton County Stadium downtown where I-20 and I-75/85 intersect. The circular stadium was completed in 1965 after a quick 51 weeks of work. It's a convertible stadium and was originally home to both the Braves and the Atlanta Falcons, but the football team flew the coop in 1992 to roost in the new Georgia Dome.

The Braves play their final season at the stadium in 1996. Beginning in 1997, they'll be swinging at their new home currently under construction right next door.

Beside the Atlanta-Fulton County Stadium, the 85,000-seat Olympic stadium is rising from the ground. Following the Olympic Games, the new stadium will be converted to a permanent baseball venue, seating 48,000 fans.

"Like the older, more intimate ballparks, this one will put the fans really close to the action," says Janet Marie Smith, director of planning and development for the Braves and vice president of sports for TBS Properties. Smith is working with the Atlanta Stadium design team; her previous experience includes planning Baltimore's extremely popular and well-received Camden Yards ballpark. Smith stresses that Atlanta's new stadium is being designed as a baseball stadium that will be temporarily expandable for the Olympics, not as an Olympic stadium where baseball is an afterthought.

Smith describes the plan for the new stadium's look as "very traditional," with dark green accents and liberal use of the Braves' team colors of red, white and blue. It will feature three levels of seating and 60 private suites.

Following the 1996 baseball season, Atlanta-Fulton County Stadium, once the pride of Atlanta and the South and the site of two World Series, will be demolished to create more parking spaces. Once again, nostalgia counts for little in Atlanta when something newer and better looms on the horizon.

STADIUM AMENITIES

The stadium opens 2 hours before game time, and fans who arrive early can watch batting and fielding practice. Those lucky enough to snag a foul ball may take it to the guest relations window at aisle 119 to receive an official "grandstand fielder" certificate.

Homer the Brave and Rally, the official team mascots, pose with kids (who are accompanied by an adult) near aisle 124 between the fourth and seventh innings.

Lots of food, drink and souvenir retailers operate during games. Food courts with a variety of snack options are located between aisles 105 and 106 on the field level concourse and between aisles 308 and 314 on the upper level concourse. Concessionaires with food, beer and sodas make regular rounds.

The Stadium Club restaurant overlooking the third-base line is open year-round for lunch Monday through Friday. Call 577-4476 for reservations. The club is open only to members and guests during games.

Private luxury suites are available for rental. Call 577-9100 for information.

Photo: Georgia Dome

The Georgia Dome, home to the Atlanta Falcons, is as tall as a 27-story building.

Wheelchair-accessible locations (and adjoining companion seats) are available at the top of each field level aisle on row 27. Tell your ticket agent if you need a wheelchair location.

STADIUM RULES

Some Atlanta sports and concert venues have more rules than a religious order. In comparison, the Braves gate policies are positively liberal. Ticket-takers typically perform a cursory inspection of carry-in items looking for obvious violations of these rules.

• Fans may bring in their own food and beverages in small coolers and plastic containers, providing these are small enough to fit easily under the seat or in one's lap.

• No alcoholic beverages may be brought into the ballpark.

• Glass bottles and cans of any kind (except medicinal aerosol cans) are not allowed.

• Foam tomahawks are allowed; wooden or metal tomahawks are not.

• Smoking is not allowed in the stadium except in designated areas on each concourse.

• Fans may photograph or videotape the ball game, provided their equipment does not obstruct the view of other fans. However, no film or videotape may be reproduced or broadcast without the Braves' permission.

• Reselling tickets for more than their face value is a violation of Georgia law; both sellers and buyers are subject to prosecution.

PARKING AND MARTA

Because the new stadium is being built directly beside the old one, entire parking lots have disappeared, and those spaces left are at a premium. Many spaces are reserved for season ticket holders and VIPs — and even if you can find a spot, you may balk at the $7 charge.

Your best bet is to park in one of MARTA's many free lots and take the train to the game. MARTA's stadium shuttle buses run from the West End station, but unless you really hate hoofing it, you can save time by taking MARTA to the Georgia State station and walking (about three blocks) to the stadium. After the game, the streets around the stadium will be swamped for an hour, and buses get snarled in the traffic, too. If you walk to Georgia State University and catch the train, you'll probably be back at your car while most fans are still inching their way out of the stadium area.

Football

Atlanta Falcons

The Falcons played their first game (a preseason match) before 26,072 fans in the new Atlanta-Fulton County Stadium on August 1, 1966. Like the Braves, the Falcons hosted a Pennsylvania team; unfortunately, also like the Braves, they were defeated (by Philadelphia, 9-7).

"Falcons" was a popular suggestion for the team name, for reasons best expressed by Griffin, Georgia, school teacher Julia Elliot: "The falcon is proud and dignified, with great courage and fight. It never drops its prey. It is deadly and has a great sporting tradition."

Following nine regular season losses and two wins on the road, the Falcons sealed their first home victory on December 11, 1966, beating St. Louis 16-10 before 57,169 fans. Linebacker Tommy Nobis became the first Falcon named to the AP all-pro team in December 1967.

On November 30, 1970, 30 million viewers watched the first nationally telecast Falcons game on ABC's "Monday Night Football" (a 20-7 loss to Miami). Almost exactly one year later, the team got its first nationally televised victory (28-21 against Green Bay, in Atlanta). In November 1973, a national audience watched again as the Falcons racked up their sixth straight win (20-14) against the previously undefeated Minnesota Vikings.

The birds got a big name when they drafted California All-America quarterback Steve Bartkowski in January 1975.

After holding training camps in a variety of locations around the South, the Falcons built their current camp northeast of Atlanta off I-85 in Suwanee in April 1978. In December 1980, the team earned its first-ever NFC Western Division title. In the playoff, victory seemed certain as Atlanta led 24-10 going into the fourth quarter — then 60,022 fans (a record) watched in shock as the Cowboys rallied to score 20 points. The final: Dallas 30, Atlanta 27.

The Falcons changed their team colors in 1990, adopting the black uniforms they wear today. In 1991, Falcon Deion Sanders signed to play with the Braves, becoming the first player in 30 years to play two pro sports in the same city.

TICKETS

All seats at all home Falcons games are $27. Single-game tickets are sold at the Georgia Dome ticket office (between gates A and D). To order by mail, write: Atlanta Falcons Ticket Office, 1 Georgia Dome Drive, Atlanta 30313. Tickets may be purchased at any TicketMaster retail outlet or charged by phone, 249-6400 or (800)326-4000. (See ticket information under Baseball for more details.) TicketMaster adds a service charge to all orders.

For season tickets, call the Falcons, 223-8444.

Falcons games are broadcast over a 55-station radio network: The local flagship is WSB AM-750.

THE GEORGIA DOME

The $214 million Georgia Dome is the world's largest cable-supported domed stadium. At its highest point, the roof is 275 feet — or 27 stories — above the playing field. The Teflon-coated Fiberglas roof weighs 68 tons and encloses 8.6 acres. When configured as an arena, the Dome's capacity expands to 80,000.

Planning for the Dome began back in June 1984. After considerable negotiations, it was decided in October 1988 that the state would build the Dome with help from the city and county.

In May 1990, the still-unbuilt Dome was selected to host Super Bowl XXVIII in 1994. Construction began the very next month. In September, Atlanta was awarded the 1996 Olympic Games, and the Dome was proposed as a venue for basketball and gymnastics.

By February 1992, the fabric roof was installed and made watertight. The 71,500 seats were in by June; the AstroTurf rolled out in July; in August the Falcons kicked

---

Insiders' Tips

You can save a small fortune by bringing your favorite (nonalcoholic) beverages and snacks to Braves games — in approved containers, of course.

off the action in the brand new Georgia Dome. Total construction time was 31 months. On August 23, 1992, 66,834 watched the Falcons play and win (20-10 over Philadelphia) the first football game in the brand new Georgia Dome.

An enormous Sony TV monitor hangs in each end zone; dozens of smaller Sonys are suspended from the ceiling throughout the complex. The four 1,250-ton air conditioners may work too well: Reports are that dome-goers complain more about being too cold than being too hot. The electricity used to power the Dome could light up a city of 13,000.

The Dome offers 183 executive suites and 5,600 executive club seats that are leased on a 10-year basis. Suite and club-seat members receive Falcons season tickets, one parking pass for every four seats and access to the private Executive Concourse and the private End Zone restaurant. Club seats (extra-wide cushioned armchairs with high backs) may be leased for $1,000 to $1,800 a year; the club section includes waiter service. Executive suites are $20,000 to $120,000 a year and come complete with custom furnishings (although leasees may bring in a decorator of their choice), cable-ready TVs, a wet bar and a private rest room. Suite- and club-seat holders get first option to buy tickets to any public Dome event.

DOME AMENITIES

Eight Dome Service Centers are located near the main entrance gates. These provide guests with various services, such as a check stand for items not allowed inside, a lost child location and a designated-driver program. For the hearing impaired, amplification devices are offered with the deposit of a picture ID. (The Dome also features hearing-aid compatible phones with volume control, TDD phones, flashing exit signs and visual fire alarms.)

A variety of food and drink is available at the Dome. There are two food courts on the upper and lower levels. Cocktails are also sold in the Dome, and you're allowed to take drinks to your seats. In fact, every seat comes with its own cupholder.

DOME RULES

Here are some policies to keep in mind when planning your day at the Dome.

• Fans are not allowed to bring in the following: food, beverages (including alcoholic beverages), coolers, cans, bottles and mechanical or compressed air noise makers.

• Smoking is not allowed, except where designated.

• No audio or video recording is allowed at Falcons games.

• Fans may use portable TVs and radios (with earphones only) providing they fit on one's lap and do not annoy other guests.

• Tickets are required for all children except infants occupying the same seat as their parent.

Bring binoculars to the Braves game! They're great for bringing the action up close — especially if you're in the outfield or the "nosebleed" seats high in the upper deck. And if the game gets boring, you can always use them to spy on your fellow fans!

Insiders' Tips

PARKING AND MARTA

Mass transit is a key component in the Dome's downtown location. Unlike Atlanta-Fulton County Stadium, which was built in the middle of acres and acres of parking lots, the Dome is closely surrounded by business and residential areas and the Georgia World Congress Center.

There are only about 3,260 parking spaces at the Georgia Dome, and these are reserved for suite-holders and media. Within walking distance are an additional 17,000 parking spaces in downtown lots, but all these together can only accommodate a fraction of the 71,500 fans at a sold-out Falcons game. Don't get any ideas about parking in the nearby Vine City neighborhood: Only residents with city-issued permits may park on Vine City streets during Dome events. Parking downtown can be a hassle at best; during Dome events it can be downright impossible.

Again, MARTA is the easy answer. The Dome is so huge that it's actually served by two MARTA stations on the east-west line: Vine City on the west side and Omni/Georgia Dome/ World Congress Center on the east side. If you're returning to a station on the north-south line after the game, you can avoid changing trains at Five Points by taking the special express shuttle bus to the Garnett station. These buses board on the Dome's south side.

During Dome events, MARTA runs a shuttle on a downtown loop route; it picks up passengers at downtown parking lots and takes them to the Dome. This shuttle runs every 5 minutes before and after events and every 25 minutes during events.

Peach Bowl

The Peach Bowl college football game has gained prestige since moving indoors to the Georgia Dome. The date varies slightly (between December 31 and January 2) to accommodate the TV schedule: it's cablecast on ESPN. For 1995 date and ticket information, call the Peach Bowl information line, 586-8500, or TicketMaster at 249-6400 or (800)326-4000; a service charge applies.

Heritage Bowl

The Heritage Bowl is played annually in Atlanta (also in the Georgia Dome, also around New Year's). Football teams from two historically African-American colleges compete (one from the Southwest Athletic Conference, one from the Mid-Eastern Athletic Conference).

For date and ticket information, call the Dome ticket office, 223-8427.

Basketball

Atlanta Hawks

The third jewel in Atlanta's pro sports crown was put into place in 1968 when the

Photo: MARTA

The MARTA rail system provides sports fans access to the Georgia Dome and the Omni.

St. Louis Hawks basketball team relocated to Atlanta. On October 15, Cincinnati beat Atlanta 125-110, and NBA excitement became a part of Atlanta life.

The Hawks battled to first-place central division finishes in 1969-70, 1979-80, 1986-87. In 1993-94, the Hawks tied a franchise record with 57 wins against 25 losses, winning the central division and earning the No. 1 seed in the playoff. After taking the first round three games to two, the Hawks were upset by Indiana, four games to two, in the second round. The Hawks wound up with the best record in the Eastern Conference.

For their first four seasons in Atlanta, the Hawks played in Georgia Tech's Alexander Memorial Coliseum before moving in 1972 to the brand new 16,510-seat Omni Coliseum.

Atlanta Hawks enshrined in the Basketball Hall of Fame include Walt Bellamy, Connie Hawkins and Pete Maravich.

TICKETS

Hawks tickets cost $30, $25, $20, $15 and $10 and are available at all TicketMaster retail locations and by phone: Call 249-6400 in Atlanta;

(800)326-4000 long distance; a service charge applies. For season tickets, call the Hawks directly at 827-DUNK.

You can watch the Hawks on SuperStation WTBS and the SportSouth cable network. You can listen to the games on the Atlanta Hawks Radio Network, whose flagship station is WGST 640 AM.

THE OMNI

Located downtown just west of Five Points, the Omni occupies 9.5 acres and has its own MARTA station. The 25 strange-looking "pods" on its distinctive roof allow for a column-free interior span of 360 feet in length and width.

The 337,000-square-foot Omni was the site of the 1988 Democratic National Convention, the 1980 U.S. Figure Skating Championship (more than 10 miles of refrigerant piping are buried beneath its concrete floor) and the 1977 NCAA Final Four.

OMNI RULES

No food or drink may be brought in from outside. Cameras are allowed at Hawks games but not at many other events.

PARKING AND MARTA

The Omni has a limited amount of parking, and there are additional lots in the surrounding area. To take it to the hoop without a lot of parking hassles, catch MARTA direct to the Omni/Dome/Georgia World Congress Center station via the east/west line.

Ice Hockey

Atlanta Knights

Professional ice hockey, absent from Atlanta since the Flames skated off to Calgary, returned in 1992. The Atlanta Knights play in the International Hockey League. In 1994, the Knights won the Turner Cup, the IHL championship.

The Knights play from October through April; the Omni is their home rink. Tickets are $16, $12, $10 and $8. For single or season tickets, call the Knights, 525-8900; TicketMaster, 249-6400 or (800)326-4000; a service charge applies.

Roller Hockey

Atlanta Fire Ants

Here's something different: a professional roller hockey team named for a fast-spreading and occasionally deadly pestilence!

For those unfamiliar with the sport (and who could blame you?), roller hockey is played on a smooth surface in regulation-size ice hockey rinks. The players zip around on in-line skates and use a special speed puck. Matches are played from June to August, with a two-week playoff period beginning in mid-August. Twenty-four North American cities have roller hockey teams.

The Fire Ants' home games are played in the Omni. Tickets are $10, $8 and $6. For tickets, call the anthill (we mean front office) at 521-ANTS; TicketMaster, 249-6400 or (800)326-4000; a service charge applies.

Golf

BellSouth Golf Classic

This $1 million PGA golf tournament is played in May at Atlanta Country Club, Atlanta Country Club Drive S.E., Marietta. Key rounds are typically telecast on network and/or cable TV.

Tickets (for all seven days) are $30 and are available from the tournament headquarters, 951-8777 or from TicketMaster, 249-6400 or (800)326-4000; a service charge applies.

Tennis

AT&T Tennis Challenge

1995 marks the 11th year of this competition, which has grown from an indoor exhibition at the Omni to a World Series event on the ATP tour. It attracted more than 80,000 spectators in 1994, as Michael Chang joined the star-studded roster of tournament champions including Andre Agassi, Boris Becker, Ivan Lendl and John McEnroe. One of only 18 official U.S. stops on the ATP tour, it's now the nation's largest clay court tournament.

The tournament is typically held the last week in April or the first week in May at the Atlanta Athletic Club in Duluth. Single tickets range from $5 to $36; series tickets are $237. Call TicketMaster at 249-6400 or (800)326-4000; a service charge applies. To reserve box seats or a champagne table, call ProServ at 395-3500.

Atlanta Thunder

Established by Billie Jean King, the World TeamTennis league is now in its 15th season. WTT's season is the month of July, between the Wimbledon and U.S. Open events. Atlanta's team, the Atlanta Thunder, took the league championship in 1991 and 1992 and the eastern division title in 1993.

The Thunder's home court is The Sporting Club at Windy Hill (from Atlanta take I-75 north to the Windy Hill Exit; turn right; the club is a half-mile down on the right).

Individual tickets ($20 to $35) are available from The Sporting Club, 953-1100, or from TicketMaster, 249-6400 or (800)326-4000; a service charge applies. For season tickets and the 1995 schedule of matches and players, call the Thunder at 881-8811.

Auto Racing

Road Atlanta is a 2.52-mile road racing track located about 30 minutes northeast of the Perimeter. From March through November, Road Atlanta offers an array of sports car, formula, motorcycle and go-kart races, as well as entertainment events. Policies vary somewhat with events, but in general, parking is free, as are in-field camping and admission for kids 12 and younger (accompanied by a ticketed adult). Ticket prices vary with events.

Purchase tickets from TicketMaster, 249-6400 or (800)326-4000; a service charge applies. Or, call Road Atlanta, 967-6143. From Atlanta, take I-85 north to Exit 49; turn left; follow the signs.

Atlanta Motor Speedway is an 870-acre racing complex located 30 miles south of downtown Atlanta in Hampton, Georgia; it features a 1.522-mile oval and a 2.5-mile road course. The short course is said to be the world's fastest true oval track.

The track hosts NASCAR Winston Cup events in March and November, plus an AutoFair in June. Call for a schedule of other events, including tours, 707-7970.

From Atlanta, take I-75 south to Exit 77, then take U.S. 19-41 south for 15 miles.

Tickets are available from the track: to charge by phone call 946-4211. Tickets are also available from TicketMaster, 249-6400 or (800)326-4000; a service charge applies.

Running

Peachtree Road Race

This annual event is as much a part of an Atlanta 4th of July as is smuggling fireworks in from South Carolina, Tennessee and Alabama. The Peachtree is the world's largest 10K road race: Its 25th running in 1994 drew 50,000 competitors. It also has the largest wheelchair division of any U.S. race.

The race starts at Lenox Square at 7:30 AM and runs down Peachtree Street, ending in Piedmont Park. Thousands of spectators (many fortified with eye-opening Bloody Marys) line the route to cheer the huffing throng. There are plenty of good places to watch the race; many bars and restaurants along the way open early for parties. Or, if you're really into suffering, pick out a spot along the slope known as "Heartbreak Hill": It begins around Peachtree Battle Shopping Center and crests — conveniently — right in front of Piedmont Hospital.

For information on how you can run in the Peachtree, call the Atlanta Track Club, 231-9065.

Cycling

First Union Grand Prix

Only in its fourth year, the First Union Grand Prix is already an Atlanta spring-time tradition. Thousands look on as more than 100 of the world's elite bicyclists whiz by Piedmont Park, Midtown and Virginia Highlands on a 120-mile race course. The start/finish area is located near Peachtree and 10th streets (at First Union Plaza), but the spread-out course makes for a great variety of vantage points for watching the action. Grab your lawn chair and your cooler, and stake out a good spot: This is a delightful way to pass a day outside on one of Atlanta's exquisite spring afternoons.

The race, of course, is free for spectators. Other "for fun" bike races and events are also held this weekend. Call 364-2060 for information.

Equestrian

Atlanta Steeplechase

Here's another Atlanta rite of spring: the annual running of the Atlanta Steeplechase. The 'chase is run at Seven Branches Farm in Cumming, less than an hour north of town. In the best Southern tradition, this is as much as cocktail party as it is a race; just as important as the handsome horses are the elaborate hats, outrageous finery, antique cars and sumptuous buffets. The seven-race steeplechase benefits the Atlanta Speech School.

Tickets are $12.50 per person; a parking pass (you'll need one for tailgating) is $15. Important: tickets are sold only in advance — not at the gate. To charge by phone, call 237-7436. Or write: Atlanta Steeplechase, 3160 Northside Parkway, Atlanta 30327. Tickets are limited; plan well in advance.

Georgia International Horse Park

The 1,269-acre Georgia International Horse Park is scheduled to open in September 1995 in Conyers, about 30 minutes east of Atlanta off I-20. During the 1996 Olympics, it will be the site of the equestrian events, mountain bike competition and the two final events of the modern pentathlon.

The development will include a 165-acre Nature Center, an 18-hole golf course, a 200-room hotel, a 205-acre pedestrian-friendly neighborhood, a steeplechase course and a covered training facility with seating for 2,000 spectators.

The central features of the park will be the 30,000-seat open Grand Prix stadium and an indoor coliseum with seating for 8,000 to 12,000.

In addition to horse shows and competitions, the facility plans to host a variety of events, such as dog shows, festivals,

Insiders' Tips

VIPs, such as team owner Ted Turner, his wife Jane Fonda and major Braves fans President and Mrs. Jimmy Carter, can often be seen watching the game from the field level seats directly behind the Braves dugout on the first-base side.

Photo: George Clark

Riders up! Cocktails up! The Atlanta Steeplechase is a springtime tradition — and it's as much a party as it is a horse race.

concerts and trade shows. For more information, contact the Georgia International Horse Park, P.O. Box 957, Conyers 30207; or call 785-6900.

Polo Club of Atlanta

Exciting polo matches are held each Sunday from May through the end of October at the Polo Golf and Country Club north of Atlanta. (Take Georgia 400 north to Exit 12; turn left and follow the signs.) Gates open at 12:30 PM, and the action gets under way at 2 PM; dress is casual; admission is $5 per person or $15 per vehicle. Barbecue and other concessions are available.

For more information, contact the Polo Club of Atlanta, 120 Perimeter Center West, Atlanta 30346; or call 396-9109.

Professional Wrestling

If gargantuan men in bizarre costumes threatening each other with grievous bodily harm is your idea of a big time, you've come to the right city. The sport known to Southerners as "Rasslin'" is perpetually popular with Atlanta fans of all ages.

World Championship Wrestling, a part of the Turner empire, is home to Hulk Hogan and many of the sport's biggest names. Every week, the heroes and villains of the WCW burst into the homes of America through 4 hours of cable programming on the TBS Superstation and 3 hours of syndicated shows that reach 90 percent of U.S. households.

In Atlanta, WCW matches are held at Center Stage and taped for broadcast. Tickets to the tapings are free! For information on upcoming events and where to obtain free tickets, call the WCW at 827-2066.

College Sports

If you're looking for high-powered college sports action, you'll find it in Atlanta. Call the number shown with each school's listing for information on schedules and tickets.

Georgia Tech, 894-5447, competes in the ACC. Tech fields teams in many sports, but football and basketball are the major ones. Tech's colors are old gold and white; the Yellow Jackets' arch-rivals are the Bulldogs of the University of Georgia in Athens.

Georgia State University, 561-2772, is best-known for its men's and women's basketball teams and its wrestling programs. The Panthers, whose colors are royal blue and white with crimson trim, compete in the NCAA's Division 1.

Three of the Atlanta University Center schools compete in football, basketball and other sports in the Southern Intercollegiate Athletic Conference. Call 220-0367 for information on the **Morris Brown College** Wolverines; 880-8123 for information on the **Clark Atlanta University** Panthers; and 215-2669 for information on the **Morehouse College** Tigers. The three schools, though all a part of the same university system, are nonetheless major rivals.

Oglethorpe University's Stormy Petrels take their name from a tough sea bird that flies right into storms. The birds compete in men's and women's soccer, cross-country, basketball and other sports in Division 3 of the Southern Collegiate Athletic Conference. Call 364-8422 for information.

The 1996 Olympics

To us — no lie — it was one of those moments when the course of history changes, and everyone knows it. On September 18, 1990, International Olympic Committee President Juan Antonio Samaranch stood before a packed Tokyo auditorium and made his announcement with deliberation:

"The International Olympic Committee . . . has awarded the 1996 Olympic Games . . . to the city of . . . Atlanta!"

Half a world away, pandemonium broke loose at Underground Atlanta, where thousands had gathered at the crack of dawn to await the announcement. The celebration continued for days. Kids got a break from school to attend the ticker-tape parade greeting the returning Atlanta Organizing Committee.

At first, all the work involved planning, conceptualizing and negotiating. The renamed Atlanta Committee for the Olympic Games (ACOG) introduced its mascot IZZY, and everyone weighed in with his or her opinion of the big-eyed, bright blue blob.

Then in the summer of 1993, the real action got under way as dignitaries gathered under the broiling July sun to break ground for the 85,000-seat Olympic stadium. In the summer and fall of 1994, more facilities began to rise out of the ground. Right now, construction of all new venues is scheduled to be complete by fall 1995; test events for all venues will take place this summer and fall.

The new facilities are spread throughout the Atlanta region: The Olympic Village and aquatics center are at Georgia Tech; the archery and cycling facilities and the tennis center are at Stone Mountain; basketball preliminaries will be held at a new gymnasium at Morehouse College; equestrian events will be at the

1,269-acre Georgia International Horse Park in Conyers; new field hockey facilities are at Morris Brown College and Clark Atlanta University; the rowing, canoeing and kayaking center is at Lake Lanier.

TICKETS

"Our pricing structure and the record number of tickets we have for sale means that these will be the most accessible Olympic Games in history," ACOG president and CEO Billy Payne announced when the Olympic ticket pricing structure was unveiled in the summer of 1994.

Talk about a range of prices: You can spend as little as $6 to attend a baseball preliminary — or as much as $600 for a seat at the opening or closing ceremonies. The average ticket price is $39.72, and 78 percent of tickets are priced at $45 or less. Every sport has at least one session for which tickets are $25 or less. And, for the first time, ticket prices include the cost of Olympic transportation during the Games.

Tickets will go on sale to the public in the spring of 1995. They will be sold first through the mail and then by phone. All tickets will be shipped to buyers in mid-1996.

To request complete information on ordering tickets to the 1996 Olympics, call 744-1996.

Inside
Daytrips

When the hustle of city life hits home, metro residents head for the hills, the seashore or the quiet charm of nearby countryside. As the largest state east of the Mississippi River, Georgia's boundaries extend from the Appalachian Mountains to the coastline of the Atlantic Ocean. That means a bounteous variety of experiences await you. And thanks to a good road system, it doesn't take long to refresh yourself with a different perspective.

The North Georgia Mountains

We'll begin with Atlanta's secret weapon against jagged nerves — escaping to the high country, the north Georgia mountains. For a natural tranquilizer, there's nothing like sparkling waterfalls (thousands of them), wide open spaces with blue skies above, silvery lakes and rising green vistas in the distance.

Georgia is home to 10 peaks of 4,000 feet or more. The southernmost portions of the Blue Ridge Mountains extend into north central and northeastern Georgia. The beloved 2,050-mile Appalachian Trail that passes through 15 states begins here at Springer Mountain just north of Atlanta in the Chattahoochee National Forest. In the northwest section near Tennessee, the land is predominantly a series of valleys and ridges. Below the mountains, the rolling land slopes gradually in a southeastern direction. The peaks and valleys of this region are said to be the oldest on the North American continent. Time has smoothed these massive yet inviting slopes covered by evergreens and wildflowers. You'll be glad you brought your camera.

Most areas north of Atlanta have their local interpretation of age-old traditions exhibited for visitors. You'll find colorful quilts, twig baskets, dulcimers, wooden games and toys. Carry home samples of the country handwoven wall hangings or perhaps some jars of mountain honey and apple butter. It's no exaggeration to say exploring the northern stretches of Georgia can easily fill your weekend calendars for many months.

Armed with a good map, you'll find many delightful mountain places within a few hours' drive of Atlanta. For specifics on locales not named in this sampling, call information for the local chambers of commerce, welcome centers or convention and visitors bureaus. Even the smallest hamlets have joined together to form associations dedicated to helping visitors partake of all this rolling terrain has to offer.

Please note: Unless otherwise noted, telephone numbers are within the 404 area code.

Dahlonega

Here's one mountain setting within a 90-minute drive of Atlanta. Head north on Ga. 400 out of Atlanta to Dahlonega (Dah LON a gah). Turn left off 400 at Ga. 60 and go 5 miles on a two-lane road that winds its way to this charming village. The Welcome Center, on the town square, has an extensive collection of brochures on the entire surrounding area.

You'll see evidence that Dahlonega's townspeople celebrate their past in many of the buildings listed on the National Register of Historic Places. Three dozen and more gift, jewelry and specialty shops make for a pleasant afternoon of browsing.

The Gold Museum, in the 150-year-old former courthouse, tells the tale of the nation's first gold rush. The discovery of gold near Dahlonega in 1828 encouraged the U.S. government to establish a branch mint here that operated from 1838 to 1861. Mining continues to this day, primarily in clays and limestone. Georgia is the leading producer of kaolin, a white clay found in vast pits in the mid-state areas and used in the manufacturing of aluminum, paper coating and ceramics.

Looking southwest from the museum, you can see the steeple of **Price Memorial Hall** (part of North Georgia College) covered in Dahlonega gold. If you feel gold fever overtaking you, head for **Consolidated Gold Mines**, inside the town's city limits. Tours of a gold mine, "gemstone grubbing" and panning for gold go on seven days a week. You'll see the mine as it was in the 1800s, learn the geology and techniques of the era and maybe find a nugget of your own.

Rest up from your labors with a ride through the countryside aboard a horse-drawn restored antique surrey built in 1890. Trips of 1 to 4 hours are available; for information, call (706)864-1266. You'll notice many eating places on or just off the square, one of which is **Park Place**, a family buffet-style restaurant open from 11 AM to 8 PM. In the evenings, you'll hear old favorites rendered on the electric organ. You may catch an impromptu accompanist "playing the spoons" by rapidly tapping the utensils against his knees in flawless rhythm.

Top off your meal with a visit to **The Fudge Factory** on the square. Choose from 12 types of homemade fudge and various other candies. Then walk off the calories with more browsing in such shops as **Mountain Christmas**, a two-story wonderland packed full of unusual ornaments and decorations.

Following U.S. 19 N. out of town to Ga. 60, you'll pass through the picturesque countryside near **Suches**. **Woody's Lake** tempts anglers to try their luck, and for a daily fee, it's yours. Even if you don't catch anything, the soul-soothing is reward enough. On the way there, you'll pass **Dockery Lake**, a spot to camp, fish or picnic; the **Chestatee Overlook**, part of the vast 750,000-acre Chattahoochee National Forest; and the **Woody Gap Picnic Area**'s panoramic view south toward Dahlonega.

Lake Sidney Lanier

Say you're ready for some aquatic adventures? En route to Dahlonega on Ga. 400, you'll pass signs directing you to **Lake Sidney Lanier**, a man-made lake about 45 miles northeast of Atlanta. Government operated by the nonprofit Lake Lanier Islands Authority, this recreational facility is said to be one of the most heavily visited of the entire U.S. Army Corps of Engineers projects.

When they dammed this part of the Chattahoochee River to supply electricity and make navigation possible on the river all the way to the ocean, the original communities were preserved beneath the lake that was created. Underwater divers can see remnants of life in the '50s: farmhouses, a golf course and churches. The tallest patches of land remain exposed to form the Lake Lanier Islands.

Whatever your pleasure, you're likely to find it here: a three-quarter mile beach, a water park with more than 2,600 feet of rapids and a water tube, picnic grounds, a sailing academy, boats of every type for rent, a special children's water playground with slides and more, riding stables, bike trails, an 18-hole golf course — need we say more? For information, call 945-6701.

Two nearby resorts offering excellent accommodations are the **Lake Lanier Islands Hilton Resort**, 7000 Holiday Road, 945-8787, or (800)768-5253; and the **Stouffer PineIsle Resort**, 9000 Holiday Road, 945-8921 or (800)468-3571. With golf and tennis facilities, and a full range of vacation activities for the whole family, both resorts receive our high rating.

Helen

Approximately 90 minutes north from Atlanta discover the town of Helen. Beginning back in 1969 and based on local artist John Kollock's memories of his Army days in Bavaria, Helen's stores and shops were given an Alpine-style facelift that now draws hundreds of thousands of visitors each year from every state and 50 foreign countries.

The flowering windowboxes, rooftop towers with steeples and beer halls with hearty German fare create a fairytale-like atmosphere. You may learn more on this Cinderella story, accomplished without government assistance, from the Alpine Helen/White County Convention & Visitors Bureau, (706)878-2181. Annual celebrations include the **Fasching Mardi Gras Festival** in January and February and the **Oktoberfests** in September and October.

Shopping ranges from inexpensive souvenirs to costly imported crystal (in the 150 import and craft shops) to bargains in the factory outlet mall's dozens of national shops.

You can get to Helen via Ga. 400, I-75 or I-85. The best way depends on which part of Atlanta you leave from. For directions, call the Convention & Visitors Bureau number listed above, or the Helen Welcome Center, (800)858-8027, on Chatahoochee Street in Helen.

CLEVELAND

Eight miles south of Helen in the town of Cleveland, visit **Babyland General Hospital**, the original home of the Cabbage Patch dolls.

Just one example of North Georgia's fine folk art is the work of the **Meaders**, a Cleveland family known through generations for their outstanding pottery work. A Meaders jug bought for $10 a decade ago now fetches $800. This family's work is turned out today with the same foot-treadle wheel used by John Milton Meaders in 1893. Among other national and international distinctions gained by this work is the honor of being displayed in the Smithsonian Institute. For more information, call the White County Chamber of Commerce, (706)865-5356.

Also near Helen on Ga. 75 is the **Storyland Petting Zoo and Castle of Dolls**, which features collectible dolls such as the Naber Kids, Barbies and McGuffies. For more information, call (706)865-2939.

CHATTAHOOCHEE NATIONAL FOREST

Northwest of Helen, the **Richard Russell-Brasstown Scenic Highway** is a beautiful mountain drive through the Chattahoochee National Forest. The drive is closed only by snow and is free to all. Within an hour of Helen is **Brasstown Bald**, the highest point in Georgia at 4,784 feet and deep in the heart of the **Chattahoochee National Forest**. After a winding, hairpin turn-filled drive off Ga. 180, you'll reach a plateau/parking area with picnic tables, a visitors center, a gallery and a bookstore. Board a shuttle bus that delivers you to the observation deck atop the peak, or walk the 930-yard trail to the top. The breathtaking, 360-degree panoramic view sweeps over four states: Tennessee, North Carolina, South Carolina and Georgia. Within the observation tower atop the summit, the U.S. Department of Agriculture's Forest Service offers exhibits on the region's human and natural history.

If your travels take you up to Blairsville, northwest of Brasstown Bald at the intersection of U.S. 76 and U.S. 19/129, stop by **The Baker's Curio Emporium and Toy Car Museum**, (706)745-9509, which sports an amazing display for more than 5,000 toy cars, plus other collectibles.

HIAWASSEE

Ten to 15 miles north of Brasstown Bald is **Hiawassee**, home of the 40-plus-year-old **Georgia Mountain Fair** held each August. The fair has been cited as one of the top 20 events in the Southeast. Observe the creation of fine mountain crafts. Or wander the giant midway, a flower show, a photography exhibit and the pioneer village where you'll see the making of soap and hominy. Singers, pickers and cloggers perform daily in this place that is recognized as the Georgia capital of country music.

Three miles west of Hiawassee on U.S. 76 is the elegant **Fieldstone Inn**, winner of a coveted listing in the *Great Inns of America* directory. Many of its 66 rooms overlook lovely Lake Chatuge. A restaurant, marina, pool and lighted tennis courts complete an inviting package. For information, call (800)545-3408; in Atlanta, call 446-1550.

Clarksville and Tallulah Falls

Two often-visited spots are Clarksville and Tallulah Falls, both northeast of Atlanta. To reach Clarksville, take I-85 north to I-985 to New Holland, where you will pick up U.S. 23. Near Mt. Airy, you'll see signs to U.S. 441, which you'll take north to Clarksville.

Clarksville is a charming little town to which, in days gone by, the wealthy folk from Savannah fled to escape the threat of malaria. Among the town's adorable bed and breakfasts are the **Glen-Ella Springs Inn**, 754-7295, whose 16 rooms and suites go for $80 to $150 per night. With much of its original flooring, walls and stone chimneys intact, it has earned a spot on the National Register of Historic Places. The **Burns-Sutton House**, 754-5565, with four-poster beds, stained-glass windows and guest-room fireplaces, also offers cozy accommodations in a gracious setting.

North of Clarksville on County Highway 197, you'll find an excellent display of local crafts at **Mark of The Potter**, (706)947-3440, a 25-year-old shop offering original, handmade wooden crafts, metal and ceramic jewelry, pottery, hand-blown glass and weavings. Housed in a restored mill building, it is a National Historic Site. Visitors can see and feed mountain trout in their natural habitat from the shop's porch over the Soque (the Cherokee word for pig) River.

Approximately 15 miles northeast of Clarksville on U.S. 441 is **Tallulah Falls**, which was a resort area known for its scenery and mountain climate as far back as the turn of century. The name derives from the Indian word meaning terrible or awesome. Local legend has it that Alabama-born actress Tallulah Bankhead's grandmother, and subsequently the actress herself, was named for the second meaning.

In the center of town, you'll see Tallulah Gorge State Park, (706)754-5103, with a 500-yard walking trail along the rim of Tallulah Gorge. This 1,000-foot-deep crevice is said to be oldest natural gorge in North America and second in depth only to the Grand Canyon. The great Karl Wallenda crossed the chasm on a two-inch-thick tightwire. Perhaps you'll remember seeing actor Jon Voight, in the movie *Deliverance*, climbing its sheer cliffs, splashed by the waterfalls spilling down its walls.

Several park pavilions offer information on local flora and fauna, as well as geologic formations. The visitors center, (706)754-3276, contains highlights of the area's history. Take a break on the hiking or wildflower trails and children's playground. A beach and camping ground are open seasonally.

Other sights include **Tallulah Falls School**, which owns a big part of the town, the **Tallulah Falls Gallery** (part of the school), the **King Tut Game Preserve** and **Terrora Park**, owned by Georgia Power. Tallulah Falls School, a coed boarding school sponsored by the Georgia Federation of Women's Clubs, was founded in 1909. At the Terrora Park and Visitors Center, open year round, you'll find mountain culture displays plus interactive video exhibits on the falls and the hydroelectric dam that reduced the once mighty river's roar to a relatively calm flow. Also provided for your pleasure are a 50-site campsite, a children's playground and swimming facilities. For more information, call (706)754-3276.

Amicalola Falls

Approximately 50 miles almost due north of Atlanta is Amicalola Falls, which got its name from the Cherokee word for tumbling waters. To get there from Atlanta, head north on U.S. 19 into Dahlonega, where you can pick up County Road 52 W. to the falls. Here, one of the highest falls in the eastern United States drops in several cascades some 729 feet. **Amicalola Falls State Park** encompasses 1,029 scenic acres. An 8-mile approach trail leads from the falls to **Springer Mountain**, the southern end of the 2,150-mile Appalachian Trail. Call the state park for directions, (706)265-2885, or the Dawsonville Chamber of Commerce, (706)265-6278.

Ellijay

Fifteen or so miles northwest of Amicalola Falls is Ellijay, Georgia's apple capital, nestled in the foothills of the verdant Appalachian Mountains. Each October brings Ellijay's **Apple Festival Arts and Crafts Fair**. The town offers one-of-a-kind antique and specialty shops with charming prizes such as apple-head dolls.

Ellijay's **Hillcrest Orchards**, open July to December, presents old-fashioned family fun with wagon rides through the orchard, a petting zoo with lambs and piglets, a working cider mill with free samples and more. The farm market overflows with apple peelers, stackers, cookbooks,

breads and, yes, pies. For information, call (706)273-3838.

Heading South

For a change of pace, come down out of the mountains and discover the charms of the regions south of Atlanta, such as Macon, Columbus, Warm Springs, Calloway Gardens and Pine Mountain. Each has special treasures to share with visitors.

Macon

Macon, the home of white columns and cherry blossoms, is in the heart of Georgia at the crossroads of two major interstates: I-75 (north-south) and I-16 (east-west). It's an easy trip from Atlanta, approximately 90 miles south on I-75. With the multitude of things to see and do, you may find yourself returning for a second chance to enjoy this hospitable setting.

It's a good thing Macon residents love their history because they're surrounded by it, from ancient Indian mounds to antebellum mansions. The Macon-Bibb County Convention & Visitors Bureau gives excellent assistance with information on Macon's pleasures — we present here a mere sample. You'll find the Macon CVB at 200 Cherry Street, (912)743-3401, (800)768-3401. Also, try the Welcome Center as you arrive on I-75, or call ahead, (912)745-2668.

When it comes to historic neighborhoods, Macon is unmatched, with more than 2,000 acres of neighborhoods listed on the National Register of Historic Places. Three specially designed walking tours will acquaint you with bygone days of the South.

The **Victorian Tour** covers some 17 sites of interest, including churches, Tuscan-Victorian homes and poet Sidney Lanier's Cottage. The **White Columns Tour** presents magnificently preserved mansions such as the **Hay House**, an 18,000-square-foot example of luxurious Italian Renaissance Revival that had indoor plumbing before the White House did. Other examples include the **1842 Inn**, now a bed and breakfast with adjoining Victorian cottages, and the **Cannonball House**, an authentic example of Greek Revival architecture built in 1853 and struck by a Union cannonball, becoming

Macon's only casualty during the Civil War. The **Downtown Walking Tour** includes homes, churches, government buildings and the elegantly restored Grand Opera House, built in 1883 and still in use. Sarah Bernhardt, Will Rogers and many other great stars performed here. You can still see the trap doors installed in the stage floor for The Great Houdini's mystifying escapes.

If you prefer to ride, costumed tour guides will escort you via "horseless carriage" or horse-drawn surrey for a behind-the-scenes tour of the downtown district. Practically all of Macon's downtown has been proclaimed a National Historic District, with 48 buildings and homes cited for architectural excellence.

Antique hounds will enjoy a newly forming travel loop called the **Antique Trail**. It links almost 100 vendors in nine central Georgia locations south from Atlanta, including Macon and nearby communities. You may receive information and a directory from the Macon CVB. Other landmarks include **Wesleyan College**, founded in 1836. Wesleyan was the first college in the world chartered to grant degrees to women. Among its well-known graduates is Madame Chiang Kaishek. Brick and marble structures grace the lovely, 240-acre campus at 476 Forsyth Road.

To go farther back in time, visit an ancient Indian community at the **Ocmulgee National Monument**. You may explore a ceremonial earthlodge; its clay floor dates back 1,000 years. A museum, prehistoric trenches, a funeral mound and several temple mounds provide tantalizing clues to the sequence of cultures that lived on the Macon Plateau. Centuries later, in 1540, Spanish explorer Hernando DeSoto is said to have recorded the first Christian baptism here on the banks of the Ocmulgee River. Open daily except Christmas and New Year's Day, the park has a visitors center complete with exhibits, a short film and other information. The park is on the eastern edge of Macon on U.S. 80 E. From I-75, exit on I-16 E. You may take either the first or second exit from I-16 and follow U.S. 80 a mile to the park.

Millions of years ago, the ocean covered what is now Macon. Prehistoric fossils, sand dollars and shark teeth are frequent finds here. The **Museum of Arts and Sciences and the Mark Smith Planetarium**, 4182 Forsyth Road, presents nature trails and a 40-million-year-old fossil skeleton unearthed near Macon. Call (912)477-3232 for hours of operation and information on the laser shows, art galleries and other events.

Macon's African-American history is rich with contributions to the arts, religious communities and leaders in education. The city's informative brochure, *Macon, Georgia: Black Heritage,* available from the Macon CVB, presents an **African-American Heritage Tour** and highlights such landmarks as the **Harriet Tubman Historical and Cultural Museum**, 340 Walnut Street, (912)743-8544. Here, past meets present in the works of local artists. For example, Wilfred Stroud's seven-panel mural "From Africa to America" visually traces a history filled with struggle and accomplishment.

While showing a deep respect for the past, the Macon of today marches to a modern tune. Its leaders guide the city to progress through several ventures. One is a $15 million expansion and renovation of the Macon Coliseum, a multiuse convention space. Plans are under way for a Sports Hall of Fame in a downtown location. And a venture about to bloom is the Georgia Music Hall of Fame, a $6.5

million investment in Georgia's cultural arts.

Scheduled to open in fall 1995 for Georgia Music Week, the **Georgia Music Hall of Fame** is adjacent to the historic Terminal Station in downtown Macon on Martin Luther King Jr. Boulevard. The three-story, 38,000-square-foot museum and more than 11,000-square-foot exhibition hall will focus on Georgia's rich and diverse musical heritage. The music and memorabilia of Georgia artists, such as Lena Horne, Otis Redding, the Allman Brothers and native son Little Richard Penniman, will be featured in a small village created in the exhibit hall. Visitors may enjoy music in a variety of vintage listening rooms where an audio program will intermix music, interviews and historical context. Video theaters will be satellite capable for current broadcasts.

Another special showcase is in Warner Robins, just 15 miles south of Macon and 7 miles from I-75. The **Museum of Aviation** presents more than 85 historic aircraft, from the Fairchild UC-119C Flying Boxcar to modern fighters such as the F-15 Eagle. Admission is free, though there's a small charge for two 30-minute films (*To Fly*

and *Flyers*) in a new 250-seat theater with wraparound sound and a 30-foot by 40-foot screen. The attached **Georgia Aviation Hall of Fame** honors notable pilots such as early women aviators, the first African-American military aviator and the founder of Delta Air Lines. For more information, call (912)926-6870.

If all that travel talk makes you hungry, two popular eateries are **Beall's 1860 House**, 315 College Street, a Macon landmark and restored 1850s era mansion with classic cuisine, and the **Green Jacket Restaurant**, 325 Fifth Street, for a primo salad bar (plus full menu).

In addition to special events scheduled year round in Macon, a particular highlight occurs each spring. The blooming of Macon's 170,000 flowering Yoshino cherry trees (more cherry trees than in any city in the world, including Washington, D.C., and cities in Japan) heralds the annual **Cherry Blossom Festival**. Events, performances and exhibits topped with Southern hospitality fill the calendar. This event begins on the third weekend of March and lasts one week. The festival even has its own outlet, **The Cherry Blossom Society Shop**, which sells all the goods associated with the event. The shop, open year-round, is in the Cherry Street Galleria, a gathering of boutiques listed on the National Register as a Historic Landmark and the main shopping area's focal point.

Warm Springs

From Atlanta, Warm Springs is about 80 miles south on I-85 to Alternate 27. Follow the signs to the peaceful place where Franklin Delano Roosevelt built the **Little White House**, (706)655-3511. In the home and adjacent museum, you'll find a sense of history in a naturally beautiful environment. Serene and slow-paced, the setting moves visitors with its low-keyed spirit of tribute.

Roosevelt, who suffered from polio-induced paralysis, had heard of the restorative powers attributed to the natural springs in this resort area. He began visiting Warm Springs in 1924, finding solace not only in the water but in the countryside's whispering pines and wooded ravines.

The President ordered a simple house built on the north slope of Pine Mountain. Filled with towering pines, hickories and oaks, the landscape's wild azaleas and dogwood bloomed everywhere, just as they do today. The six-room Little White House, maintained true to the era, is furnished with mementoes, paintings and personal items the President used while in residence. Even the leash for his dog, Fala, hangs in a cupboard near the door. A taped commentary accompanies your self-guided tour.

It's a short walk from the Little White House to the highly personal museum along an ornamental walkway flanked with state flags and native stones of the 50 states and the District of Columbia. Peruse at your own pace Roosevelt's walking cane collection, gifts from heads of state and exhibits depicting the life of this world leader. A 12-minute film memoir of his days here includes scenes of FDR and other polio patients in a rollicking game of water polo.

Housed nearby are FDR's two classic roadsters. One was equipped with hand controls, which allowed him to drive around the countryside, greeting local residents and flashing his famous grin. Roosevelt died at the Little White House in 1945 of a cerebral hemorrhage, having weathered four Presidential elections, a devastating economic depression and a global war.

As a fitting legacy, the **Roosevelt Warm Springs Institute for Rehabilitation**, which he founded with two-thirds of his personal fortune, provides medical and vocational rehabilitation for thousands of people each year. Ground was broken in 1994 for a 60,000-square-foot recreation building. The $9.6 million expansion will make the Institute's complex the first of its type in the Southeast completely designed for people with disabilities.

The nearby village of Warm Springs thrives with a cluster of 65 boutiques, restaurants and accommodations. Among them is Main Street's **Victorian Tea Room**, which is in an 83-year-old former general store. Spring Street's **Bulloch House**, built in 1892, sits on a hilltop surrounded by bird houses. Described as "country with class," the restaurant offers home-cooked Southern food with hospitality to match.

You'll find 14 overnight guest rooms in the **Warm Springs Hotel**, built in 1907. It's on Ga. 27-Alternate 41, the main thoroughfare of Warm Springs, also called Broad Street. For reservations and information, call (800)366-7616.

Revived by owners Geraldine and Lee Thompson into a charming bed and breakfast, the Warm Springs Hotel's history includes glory days when FDR's visits created much excitement. The style of bygone days remains alongside the welcome addition of modern conveniences such as individual heating/cooling units. The rooms feature either furniture made in a New York factory owned by Mrs. Roosevelt, which the owners call Eleanor furniture, or period antiques. All the rooms have private baths, some with clawfoot tubs. One room has an iron bed more than 100 years old (it belonged to Geraldine's grandmother).

Among famous guests documented in the hotel's books were the King and Queen of Mexico and the King and Queen of Spain. You'll see a picture of FDR and Bette Davis at breakfast following her stint entertaining the troops at Fort Benning in Columbus. Unfortunately, the original registration book was destroyed in an off-premises fire where the previous owner had stored it.

The Thompsons have added a honeymoon suite with a king-size bed, Victorian antiques and a red, heart-shaped Jacuzzi for two. Among extras available for wedding, anniversary or other special occasions are champagne, chocolates, strawberries and flowers. When you feel like venturing forth from your cozy nest, a full restaurant, ice cream parlor and gift shop await you on the property.

Another quality accommodation in the area is the **Mountain Top Inn**, on the top of Pine Mountain in the midst of beautiful mountain scenery surrounded by the 14,000-acre Roosevelt State Park. The Inn's location midway between Warm Springs and Callaway Gardens, just a 5-minute drive to either, is a special advantage. This facility offers lodging in three styles. House-size log cabins feature rock fireplaces, double-size Jacuzzi tubs, fully equipped kitchens, gas grills on the porch and all the comforts of home. These cabins, which have from one to seven bedrooms, usually are booked at least four to six weeks in advance. A second lodging style, built in the 1970s, is the Alpine-style chalet. These more rustic dwellings are popular for family reunions and religious retreats. They are in two-, three- and four-bedroom configurations.

Finally, an inn is situated in four buildings with five rooms in each. Each room is decorated in a nationality theme, so you can choose to wake up in Paris, Tokyo or some other exotic locale. Added in April 1994 is the 90-seat Log Wedding Chapel, with its bell tower, cathedral ceiling, oak pews, slate backdrop and nearby conference center for receptions.

To reach Mountain Top Inn from Warm Springs, turn right on Ga. 85. Go up the mountain on this road to Ga. 190. The inn is at the 7-mile marker.

Columbus

Journeying about an hour south, you'll find Columbus, Georgia's third-largest city. Columbus offers many attractions including a revived opera house and a riverwalk along the Chattahoochee. To reach Columbus, take I-85 S. from Atlanta to La Grange, then take I-185 to Columbus. Three museums, the **Confederate Naval Museum**, the **Infantry Museum** and the **Columbus Museum**, with its fine arts and historical displays, provide something for every interest and with a nice twist: They charge no admission.

Much of the city's historical architecture is showcased in a revitalized 28-block

National Historic District in "uptown" Columbus. Many of the homes on these brick-paved, wide avenues were relocated here to preserve them. One of the most intriguing is **The Folly**, an uncommon, double-octagonal design.

The grandest structure in Columbus seemed doomed until determined citizens took action. The **Springer Opera House**, built in 1871 and host to such stars as Lillie Langtry, Ethel Barrymore and Ruth Gordon, now shines resplendent and restored with year-round entertainment for the whole family. In 1971, then-governor Jimmy Carter declared the Springer as the State Theatre of Georgia; it has been a National Historic Landmark since 1975.

Golfers flock to the **Bull Creek Course**, which has been listed among the top 25 courses by *Golf Digest*.

Festivals, fairs and celebrations of all kinds take place throughout the year, from a **Cotton Pickin' Country Fair** in May to **Pine Mountain Heritage Festival** in October. For information on these attractions and more in the area, call the Columbus Convention and Visitors Bureau at (800)999-1613.

Pine Mountain

Rounding out our southward trips is Pine Mountain, home of the extraordinary four-star resort complex **Callaway Gardens**, as well as a whole host of other attractions.

Seventy miles south of Atlanta on I-85 and 30 miles north of Columbus on I-185, Callaway Gardens' 14,000 acres of natural beauty draws some 750,000 visitors each year. This floral wonderland was created in 1952 by the husband and wife team of Cason Callaway and Virginia Hand Callaway as a wholesome, family environment for relaxation and inspiration. The story of how the Callaways transformed hard-scrabble land into a visual feast has been told by John Wedda in his book *Gardens of the American South*.

You may visit Mr. Cason's Vegetable Garden, the Southern location of the PBS series *The Victory Garden* and the source of much of the good food served in the resort's restaurants. The Cecil B. Day Butterfly Center, billed as the largest glass-enclosed butterfly conservatory in the United States, houses approximately 1,000 free-flight butterflies from three continents. In the John A. Sibley Horticulture Center, a five-acre indoor/outdoor garden, you'll see unusual collections of native and exotic plants and flowers.

Callaway Gardens' most famous residents are found on the Azalea Trail, which has more than 700 varieties of this Southern charmer. Other flower trails include the Rhododendron and Holly Trails. Take special note of cofounder Virginia Callaway's favorite, the Wildflower Trail. Rest awhile in the solitude of the Ida Cason Callaway Memorial Chapel. Dr. Norman Vincent Peale officiated at the chapel's dedication. Then venture out to swim at Robin Lake Beach or watch Florida State University's "Flying High" Circus. Meander along the 7.5-

mile bike trail through breathtaking scenery.

As a guest of this premier resort, you can take advantage of tennis, fishing, sailing, water-ski championships, 63 holes of golf and a mountain-view course.

The resort offers a considerable variety of packages. Prices vary according to length of stay, type of accommodations, meal plans and activities accessed. For information on all Callaway Gardens attractions, call (800)282-8181.

Near Callaway is the **Pine Mountain Wild Animal Park**. Here you can drive your car or ride a safari bus through a 500-acre preserve where llamas, antelopes, camel and nearly 300 different animal species roam freely. Then visit **Old McDonald's Farm**, (800)367-2751, with a petting zoo, monkey house, snake house and alligator pit.

A perfect spot for antique buffs awaits 2 miles north of Callaway Gardens at 230 S. Main Street in the Pine Mountain Antique Mall. More than 100 dealer booths and lobby showcases present period furnishings, clocks, books and jewelry. For more information, call (800)638-9610.

Nature lovers will revel in Pine Mountain's 14,000-acre **Franklin Delano Roosevelt State Park**, approximately 12 miles from the Little White House on Ga. 190. This outstanding recreational facility offers camping, rental cabins, a mountain stone swimming pool and 23 miles of hiking trails. Lovely lakes for fishing and boating are surrounded by bountiful woodlands. For more information, call (706)663-4858.

To reach Pine Mountain from Atlanta, take I-85 S. to I-185 and continue south to Exit 14. Turn left on U.S. 27 and drive 11 miles to Callaway Gardens. For information about all the Pine Mountain attractions, call (800)441-3502.

Eastward, Ho!

An easterly direction outing from Atlanta is the combination of old world and new: Madison and Conyers. Conyers is the home of the Monastery of the Holy Spirit, where cloistered monks have lived for more than 50 years. Madison is called "Georgia's antebellum showcase," with almost 50 antebellum and Victorian homes that survived Union occupation.

Conyers

To reach Conyers, about a 25-minute drive from downtown Atlanta, take I-20 E. to the Ga. 138 Exit, head south to Ga. 212 and follow the signs.

The local monastery was founded in 1944 on this 2,000-acre site of open farmland and gardens. Inside the Abbey church, tranquility reigns beneath pink and blue stained-glass windows created by the monks. Outdoors, the placid blue lake is circled by snowy geese and ducks. Because self-sufficiency is the order's byword, all foods are grown or raised on the grounds, and all the buildings were constructed by the monks.

Parts of the complex are open to the public. A large assortment of succulents and rare bonsai trees are for sale. The greenhouse basement is a wonderland of some 600 sets of pots and trays, most of which were made in Japan or China and said to be the largest selection of pots in the United States. You'll find them glazed and unglazed; in earth tones and primary colors; round, hexagonal, free-form; ranging in price from $2.50 to a $558 luxury piece — in short, imagine a planting pot, and it's here. Books and tools to assist the bonsai gardener as well as fresh-baked bread and stained-glass designs (made by the monks) are also available. Mass is celebrated daily at the Abbey Church.

For more information, call 483-8705. Another helpful number is the Conyers-Rockdale Chamber of Commerce at 483-7049.

Madison

Madison, with its exquisitely restored homes, is about another 35 to 40 miles from Conyers. To get here, return to I-20 E. and continue on to Exit 51. Go to the Welcome Center on the town square (or call ahead for information, (706)342-4454). You'll be given a walking tour map highlighting the homes' histories and architectural detail. Twice a year, in spring and during the winter holidays, more than half of Madison's historic homes open their doors to visitors. The April event is accompanied by the annual blooming of dogwood, azaleas and wisteria. During December, all-white lights twinkle throughout the town as a tribute to the holidays.

Heritage Hall, one of the stately structures giving Madison its grand aura, is an 1825 Greek Revival design. The home's curving staircases, graciously proportioned rooms and white columns combine pleasingly for a journey back in time.

Visit the Madison-Morgan Cultural Center, host to a history museum, art exhibits and theatrical plays. The Center is a restored Romanesque Revival-style former schoolhouse, c. 1895. Among the exhibits are portions of a reconstructed log cabin from 1805-1820. Top off your visit with a sandwich and soda at the

Baldwin Pharmacy. This turn-of-the-century establishment joins other restaurants on the town square.

But Where's The Beach?

Well, it's true. Atlanta, with all its boosterism and bravado, hasn't been able to attract the Atlantic Ocean to its city limits.

Vacationers, never fear. If, despite the lakes and rivers abounding in the Atlanta area, nothing but the ocean will do, the interstates will get you to the beach in 5 or 6 hours.

You may head in either of two directions: due south to the Florida Panhandle or southeast to Georgia's Golden Isles. If Florida is your choice, the drive will take you to the Gulf of Mexico and **Panama City's** powdery beach. For information, call (800)PC-Beach. A slightly southwesterly direction from Atlanta takes you to **Pensacola**, in the northwest corner of Florida's Panhandle. Call the Pensacola Tourist Information Center, (904)434-1234 or (800)874-1234 for information. For detailed descriptions of all there is to see and do in Panama City and Pensacola read *The Insiders' Guide to Florida's Great Northwest*.

For our money, though, Georgia's beaches offer a unbeatable combination: environmentally unique settings, traditional oceanfront pleasures and historic sights.

Of the barrier islands protecting Georgia's coast, only four are accessible by car: Jekyll Island, Tybee Island, St.

Insiders' Tips

In Georgia, if your windshield wipers are on, you're required to turn your headlights on too.

Simons Island and Sea Island. The others are Wassaw Island, Ossabaw Island, St. Catherine's Island, Blackbeard Island, Sapelo Island, Little St. Simons Island and Cumberland Island.

Besides the broad beaches, the landscape features 300-year-old oak trees draped in moss, towering pines and fragrant magnolias. The area of these barrier islands encompasses 165,000 acres divided between marsh and dry land. Evidence of nature's influence is seen in the constantly changing shoreline, reshaped by winds, tides and the serpentine river channels snaking through the inlets.

To the untrained eye, the barrier islands' marshes look like a sea of dead grass. In reality, they are teeming with life, enormously productive and essential to Georgia's multimillion dollar seafood industry. Over the course of 25 years, one acre of marsh can produce a half billion dollars worth of shellfish alone. Wildlife, including alligators, snakes, birds, raccoons, minks and otters, live, breed and feed in these ecosystems. On any causeway near the marshland and tidal creeks, you may see the graceful Great Blue Herons or snow-white egrets.

Nearly half of the 165,000 acres are protected, with approximately 87,700 acres now developed, a somewhat remarkable ratio compared with other seashore areas. Since Georgia's seashore is the subject of entire books, let's narrow the focus for a closer look. Two islands, Jekyll and Tybee, will illustrate the diversity among these bits of land that dot the coast between Florida and South Carolina.

Tybee Island

Generations of Savannah families have escaped each summer to Tybee Island, one of America's earliest settlements where the laid-back atmosphere encourages utter relaxation. Funky beachfront shops and cafes line the wide sandy beach of this closest-to-Atlanta of the barrier islands. Lack of pretension is Tybee's religion, coupled with a certain vagabond flavor that keeps visitors coming back year after year.

Visit the **Tybee Lighthouse**, one of the first public structures in Georgia. The base of the existing lighthouse dates from 1773. A small museum nearby offers exhibits on the island's history. The lighthouse, museum and a keeper's cottage are open to the public. For more information, call (912)786-5801.

The **AAA Auto Club South**, (912)352-8222, can provide information on Tybee's motels and restaurants, as will the **Savannah Convention & Tourist Bureau**, (800)444-2427. Locals and tourists favor a bed and breakfast inn called **Hunter House,** 1701 Butler Avenue, (912)786-7515. Built one block from the ocean in 1910, it's been given a snazzy renovation complete with tastefully decorated dining rooms. Relax with appetizers on the wide front porch before ordering from the full dinner menu.

To reach Tybee Island, take I-75 S. from Atlanta, follow it to Macon where you'll take I-16 E. into Savannah. Take the 37th Street Exit off I-16, and turn right onto Abercorn Street. Follow Abercorn to Victory Drive (which turns into Ga. 80). Turn left onto Victory Drive and follow it for approximately 15 miles straight to the Atlantic and Tybee.

Jekyll Island

You'll find a different atmosphere on Jekyll Island, which began life as an upscale playground for the Rockefellers, Vanderbilts, Astors, Goodyears and

Pulitzers who migrated annually to the area. Some bought their own island, erecting incredible mansions with all the trappings of the good life.

At one time, the winter residents of Jekyll were said to control one-sixth of the world's wealth. Among significant events on Jekyll were the first interstate telephone calls, made from the president of AT&T to President Woodrow Wilson in Washington, D.C., and to Alexander Graham Bell in New York.

After World War II, skyrocketing taxes and other financial changes made the luxury level on Jekyll and its sister islands impractical, even for barons. This resulted in what's been called the real estate deal of the century. The State of Georgia bought Jekyll lock, stock and barrel for $675,000 — the price of building just one of the 20 opulent so-called cottages.

Nowadays Jeykll attracts families, honeymooners, retirees, conferences and the entire gamut of pleasure seekers to its 10-mile beach and expansive assortment of fun activities. Play tennis, cycle along some 20 miles of paved trails around the island or go surf fishing. Enjoy the picnic areas and campsites. You'll be challenged to take it all in.

Only **Cumberland Island**, a federally protected wilderness area off limits to motorized vehicles and all development, is more southern in the chain. To protect the unique environment, Georgia law specifies that no high-rises are allowed on Jekyll, and no more than one-third of the island can be developed.

If you want a bird's-eye-view of the coastal life, take part in Jekyll's nature walks offered each morning. On Mondays, the **Marsh Walk** covers the island's north end; Tuesday's walk explores the beach; Wednesdays you walk to the island's south end. Tours are a couple of hours long and are accompanied by a trained guide. The fee is around an amazingly low $2.50.

The famed riverfront **Jekyll Island Club Hotel**, after a $16 million facelift, once again offers Victorian charm in its 136 rooms with 14 different room plans. Other major motel chains as well as smaller lodgings are represented. A call to the **Jekyll Island Welcome Center**, (800)342-1042, on the Jekyll Island Causeway, will yield all the information you need to plan a trip.

Consider signing up for guided tours for an informed look at Jekyll's flora and fauna, as well as history. Visit the **Historic District Orientation Center** for a video presentation and tickets for a tram tour featuring the winter homes of millionaires. For more information, call (912)635-2762.

A livelier attraction is **Summer Waves**, (800)841-6586, a family aquatic theme park open daily with 11 acres of planned frivolity. Daring adventurers may brave the Hurricane Tornado and Force 3 rides; calmer spirits will gravitate toward the Pee Wee Puddle and the Slow Motion Ocean.

Jekyll is midway between Savannah and Jacksonville, Florida. To get there from

Atlanta, take I-75 to near Macon and pick up I-16. Follow I-16 S. to I-95 (about 80 miles). Take Exit 6 off I-95, and turn left on to U.S. 17. Travel 5 miles to Ga. 520, turn left and follow the Jekyll Island Causeway 6 miles. For in-depth information on this area and the entire state, check out *Georgia At Its Best,* by Jeanne Harman and Harry E. Harman III.

Nearby Major Destinations

One of Atlanta's happy advantages is the proximity and easy access to other major destinations. We'll take a quick look at two: Asheville and Athens.

Asheville

High up where the Great Smokies and the Blue Ridge Mountains meet is Asheville. The city's motto, "The Sky's the Limit" certainly suits its spectacular natural beauty.

Get started with a call to the **Asheville Travel and Tourism Office**, (800)257-1300, or if you're already in Asheville, stop by **Visitors Center**, 151 Haywood Street, (704)258-6100.

Asheville strains the imagination with a wondrous array of attractions and activities. For a complete guide to all that Asheville has to offer, read *The Insiders' Guide to North Carolina's Mountains.* Here, we mention a few attractions to whet your appetite.

First, begin with a few attractions right in the city, such as the home of well-known author Thomas Wolfe. Entering from Woodfin Street beside the Radisson Hotel, you'll wander through the Dixie boardinghouse depicted in his novel, *Look Homeward, Angel,* where furnishings, clothing and other memorabilia belonging to Wolfe are displayed. Call (704)253-8304 for more information.

Asheville's downtown historic district takes a back seat to no place, with an excellent collection of art deco design in the city's architecture, plus crafts and antiques shops, restaurants, festivals, walking tours and more.

Visit the combined **Antique Car Museum/North Carolina Homespun Museum**, open April through December. The museum is on the grounds adjacent to the **Grove Park Inn**, (704)252-2711, another must-see. Erected in 1913 and one of the South's oldest elegant resorts, the Inn is built of massive granite boulders in a remarkable feat of engineering. On Macon Avenue off Charlotte Street, just a few blocks from downtown, the inn overlooks Asheville's skyline and the mountains beyond.

Don't miss the **Botanical Gardens**, (704)252-5190. This 10-acre area of native plants is just off Broadway on Weaver Boulevard and is open during daylight hours.

Set aside an afternoon for **Pack Place**, (704)257-4500. Asheville's arts and sciences center, 2 South Pack Square in downtown. The $14-million complex includes the **Asheville Art Museum**, the **Colburn Gem & Mineral Museum**, a 520-seat performing arts theater and the historically rich African-American cultural center called **YMI** (Young Men's Institute).

The jewel in Asheville's crown has to be the 8,000-acre **Biltmore Estate**, billed as the largest private home in the United States. Designed by architect Richard Morris Hunt in the style of chateaux in France's Loire Valley, the mansion took five years to build and was completed in 1895. Its original 250 rooms were filled with treasures owner George Vanderbilt collected during his world travels. Works by Albrecht Dürer, John Singer Sargent and Pierre August Renoir grace the walls. Wedgewood china, Oriental rugs and the finest furnishings fill each room.

Guests of the Vanderbilts had a choice of 32 bedrooms. For entertainment, they chose from the billiard room, the winter garden, countless sitting rooms, an indoor pool, a bowling alley and a gymnasium. Vanderbilt equipped his home with luxuries unbelievable in that era — central heat, indoor bathrooms, mechanical refrigeration and electric lights and appliances. Presently, 60 rooms are open for your self-guided tour. (Vanderbilt commissioned Frederick Law Olmstead, designer of New York's Central Park, to create this living work of art.) A 75-acre-garden, filled with blooming flowers, offsets the manicured grounds and adjoining forest lands.

The Biltmore Estate Winery offers complimentary wine tastings in what were originally the estate's dairy barns. A 3,000-square-foot wine shop displays a wide assortment of gourmet foods, giftware and a sampling of Biltmore wines. Three restaurants provide dining for visitors made hungry by all the exploring. Browse through the half-dozen gift shops for candles, Victorian accessories and unique toys.

The Biltmore Estate is on U.S. 25 just north of Exit 50 or 50B off I-40 in Asheville. The estate is open daily except Thanksgiving, Christmas and New Year's Days. Adult tickets are $24.95; youngsters from 10 to 15 are charged $18.75; children 9 and younger are admitted free with a paying parent. A $1 increase is added to each ticket from November 12 throughout the holidays. A special behind-the-scenes tour is offered for an additional charge. For more information, call (800)543-2961, or write Biltmore Estate, One North Pack Square, Asheville, North Carolina 28801.

From Asheville

Take a short drive from Asheville, approximately 17 miles, and travel back in time to **Black Mountain**, a well-known vacation spot with bountiful antique shops and major conference centers. Capturing the true spirit of mountain life, you can hike the great Blue Ridge, revel in the spray of waterfalls and frolic in the 1,500 varieties of wildflowers that thrive here. For information, call (704)669-2300. Or stop by the visitors center, off I-40 at Exit 64.

The **Great Smoky Mountain National Park and Railway**, the **Cherokee Indian Reservation**, **Chimney Rock Park** and the incomparable scenery along the **Blue Ridge Parkway** are just a few more of the many pleasures that await you here.

Athens

Athens is home of University of Georgia (UGA) and a whole lot more that makes it well worth visiting. From north Atlanta, take I-85 N. to Ga. 316 to Athens. From east Atlanta and Gwinnett County, take U.S. 78 E. to Athens. Gen-

erally, it's a 75-mile trip of approximately 90 minutes. For leisurely touring, avoid football weekends or you'll be surrounded by thousands of barking, howling UGA Bulldogs fans cheering on their team.

Athens presents a fascinating split personality. The center of Georgia's bona fide Southern heritage in its historic heartland launched rock greats the B-52's and R.E.M. Graciously restored antebellum mansions co-exist with an 1863 double-barreled cannon poised on City Hall's lawn and pointed north, as the natives say, just in case.

Begin your visit at the 175-year-old **Church-Waddel-Brumby House**, 280 E. Doughtery Street, the city's oldest structure. Open as a house museum, this fine example of Federal-style architecture is home to the **Athens Welcome Center** (706)353-1820. Or call the **Athens Convention and Visitors Bureau**, (706)546-1805, for information on guide services for group tours as well as all attractions.

Established in 1785, the University of Georgia campus offers many diversions to visitors as well as to its 28,000 students. You'll see the campus trademark, rounded-globe gaslights trimmed in black wrought iron, shining down on wide streets shaded by towering trees.

You may make an appointment to visit the **University of Georgia's President's Home**, c. 1857, which is surrounded by giant columns, Corinthian around the front and sides, Doric on the back. Tour the permanent collection to see more than 5,000 works of art. **Butts-Mehre Heritage Hall**, the university's sports museum, honors Heisman Trophy-winner and U.S. Winter Olympian Herschel Walker; Teresa Edwards, three-time member of the U.S. Women's Olympic Basketball Team; and Katrina McClain, winner of Olympic gold and bronze medals in basketball.

Athens' music/club scene ranges from country to new wave. Likewise, you'll find fine dining and every ethnic cuisine represented. Feast on Mexican or vegetarian dishes at the **Mean Bean**, 184 College Avenue, or sample homestyle Southern cooking at **Lu Lu's Normaltown Cafe**, 1344 Prince Avenue.

Visit **Morton Theatre**, a living monument of Athens' African-American community, at the intersection of Washington and Hull streets once called "the Hot Corner." Built, owned and operated by African Americans in 1910, the structure is listed on the National Register of Historic Places. Monroe "Pink" Morton's 550-seat performing arts center plus the adjoining shops and offices formed the heart of the community's business district. The offices were occupied by professionals such as Dr. Ida Mae Johnson, Georgia's first licensed female African-American dentist. Legendary performers, including Bessie Smith and Cab Calloway, played the Morton. Thanks to efforts of preservationists, the theater is once again thriving.

Follow the scenic tour signs through Athens' historic districts and residential areas to view a diversity of architectural styles. Take note of the 13 towering Doric columns of the Greek Revival-style **Taylor-Grady House**, built in 1840.

As befits the birthplace of America's first established Ladies Garden Club (1891), Athens is home to the **State Botanical Garden of Georgia**. The 313-acre horticultural preserve is set aside by the University as a living laboratory for the study and enjoyment of plants and nature. The garden is 3 miles from the UGA campus at 2450 S. Milledge Avenue, (706)542-1244. Georgia's state flower, the Cherokee Rose, is among the flowering plants and wishing ponds that grace the walking trails along the scenic riverfront.

We've barely scratched the surface of scenic destinations close to Atlanta; for a broader perspective, you may wish to contact the Georgia Department of Industry, Trade and Tourism, 656-3590 or (800)VISIT GA, P. O. Box 1776, Atlanta 30301.

Inside
Green Atlanta

Two aspects of Atlanta often puzzle first-time visitors, whether they arrive by air or car. From a bird's-eye view, the speck that is downtown pops up out of a mass of green. Likewise, on many sections of the interstates, deep woods line both sides of the road. Isn't Atlanta supposed to be big? So where is the rest of it?

Unanimity is hard to come by; yet if you ask most Atlantans, old-timers or newcomers what it is they like most about their city, chances are the answer will be "the trees." In fact, a 1989 *New York Times* article quoted then-mayor Maynard Jackson as saying the word that best describes Atlanta is trees. According to city arborist Susan Newell, as quoted in the Atlanta *Journal-Constitution,* "The function of trees in an urban condition is vital not only to our breathing and our health, but our sanity and our aesthetics."

This city's love affair with trees bursts forth in springtime's Dogwood Festival, where people spotlight their best trees for a lighted tree tour, much like a Christmas decoration tour.

The heated battle in 1994 that arose when some healthy treetops were lopped off to improve the view of billboards filled the newspapers and airwaves for weeks.

Atlanta's government is very serious about protecting the tree canopy the city's residents cherish. Under the Atlanta Tree Ordinance that went into effect on January 1, 1994, city approval is required prior to the removal of any living tree from private or public property. Trees can be removed when necessary as part of an approved construction project, but under the law, trees that are removed must be replaced. Only trees that are clearly hazardous may be removed without a permit. For more

Photo: Georgia Tourist Division

Atlanta — the city of trees.

Photo: Georgia Tourist Division

Atlanta's Midtown skyline.

information, contact the city arborist, 817-6814.

Swarms of cars pass leisurely through Atlanta's well-off neighborhoods such as Habersham in the Buckhead area and Lullwater Road in Druid Hills. They come to view the blooming of lush plantings — the dogwood, the forsythia, the Bradford pear, the azaleas. At times, the riot of color has lured many a gawking motorist off the road. At one home, 3018 Habersham, you're welcome to get out, politely take pictures and make notes of the landscaping. Continuing a 40-year tradition begun by the previous owners, the Goddard family graciously allows a close-up look at their dazzling display of tulips, daffodils and other springtime beauties.

Atlantans' enchantment with the natural beauty surrounding them dates back to the original design of major city landmarks. Frederick Law Olmsted, the foremost American landscape architect who designed New York's Central Park, Boston's Back Bay, the grounds of the Biltmore House in Asheville and the Capitol grounds in Washington, played a central role in how Atlanta looks today.

Olmsted visited Atlanta at the invitation of developer Joel Hurt, for whom one downtown park is named. This pocket park affords downtown workers a place to sit and watch the passing parade of humanity. Olmsted's visit led to the initial plans for Piedmont Park and his design for the elegant beautifully landscaped neighborhood of Druid Hills. He designed the strip of parks along one of Atlanta's major east-west thoroughfares, Ponce de Leon Avenue. This strip of greenery, nearly 2 miles long, softens a busy area. Among Olmsted's national projects was the landscaping of the rolling hills surrounding Emory University in Atlanta.

The U.S. Forest Service calls Atlanta the most heavily wooded urban area in the nation. It has long been known as the city in a forest. During 1993, Georgia's Department of Transportation planted 98,500 trees alongside interstates 75 and 85 on the route from Hartsfield Airport into the city. The same department placed 38,000 trees along the Ga. 400 extension from I-285 to I-85.

Support for the planting and preservation of trees comes from all sectors of the community. When Georgia Power decided to lend sprucing-up efforts to its neighbor, the Atlanta Civic Center, the company asked employees to volunteer to plant 80 crape myrtles, dogwoods, maple and other species. The volunteers who turned out outnumbered the trees.

But Atlanta has not been spared the downside of its phenomenal growth over the past 20 years. According to Trees Atlanta, between 1975 and 1985, a 16-percent decrease in forest cover occurred, most noticeably in the downtown area. Trees Atlanta is the hard-driving advocate behind tree conservation and planting. This non-profit volunteer organization has planted more than 12,000 trees alongside Atlanta's downtown streets and in parking lots since 1991. (See Resources at end of this chapter for more information.)

Now lets take in some green delights spread throughout the metro area that make visiting or living here such a pleasure any season of the year.

Gardens

ATLANTA BOTANICAL GARDEN

1345 Piedmont Ave.	876-5859
Plant Hotline	888-GROW

Three miles from downtown stands a living museum to nature and gardening, which is more passion than pastime for a great many Atlantans. ABG's three main components — the outdoor gardens, the Fuqua Conservatory and the Storza Woods — are spread over 60 acres of Piedmont Park, which ABG leases from the city. The outdoor gardens, a showcase for plants that thrive in the north Georgia climate, encompass 15 acres with more than 3,000 ornamental plants. Special gardens devoted to roses, herbs, ferns, summer bulbs and rocks display innovative landscape designs. There's even a vegetable garden for urban farmers and a fragrance garden to delight the senses.

Lily ponds, a native aquatic plant pond with blossoms swaying in the breeze and a fountain spraying crystal droplets create a lovely setting for cultural and social events taking place year round. Many a bride and groom have pledged eternal vows beneath the verdant tree canopy.

The fabulous **Dorothy Chapman**

Fuqua Conservatory is a $5.5 million glass-roofed wonderland of endangered and valuable plants. Just a few steps will take you from the Mediterranean to the desert to the tropics. Each section is climate controlled by computer.

It's said that Dorothy and J. B. Fuqua traveled for two years to study 15 conservatories around the world before building the setting for this worldwide collection. Tiny, colorful birds flit among the trees and dart beneath a waterfall. The visual feast, from blooming orchids and unusual bromeliads to sprawling cacti and succulents, is well worth a visit.

The **Storza Woods** is a 15-acre hardwood forest, one of the few remaining in the city. When you stroll along the walking trails in this cool, sheltered setting, the looming office towers of nearby Midtown seem a world away. A ceramic waterfall created by Atlanta artist Christine Sibley combines human artistry with nature's elements. Blossoms both familiar and exotic bloom everywhere.

Atlanta Botanical Garden was established in 1977 for the purposes of display, education, research, enjoyment and conservation. This private, nonprofit organization gets its main support from corporations and individual donations from its more than 10,000 members. Overseen by a board of trustees, the gardens are cared for by 50 full-time employees and a loyal group of 250 volunteers. And ABG does a lot more than look pretty. Among its programs is Gardens for Connoisseurs. Held each May, visits to several private gardens around the city give an eye-opening look at local gardening possibilities. Its visitors center offers programs, scheduled speakers, woodland tours, ongoing classes and workshops for ABG members and nonmembers. For information on ABG classes and tours, call 641-2818.

If you're a new resident and are seeking fellow rose gardening enthusiasts, ABG will refer you to an appropriate group, perhaps in the area where you reside. Many of the hundreds of garden clubs and specialty societies meet regularly at ABG, with exhibits and competitions scheduled year round. For instance, the Southeast Flower Show, held in late February, presents an entire range of garden related events such as artistic design displays, children's activities and more. This show benefits ABG.

If you have questions about a particular plant or gardening method, call the Plant Hotline. Leave a message, and a volunteer horticulturist or master gardener will return your call.

The **Sheffield Botanical Library** stocks some 2,000 books and 80 periodicals. These are offered for on-site library research only.

The **Garden House Gift Shop** is filled with unexpected finds for yourself or the gardeners on your gift list. From April through October, you can lunch on sandwiches, salads and desserts on the Lanier Terrace overlooking the Rose Garden.

The Atlanta Botanical Garden is in the northwest corner of Piedmont Park. The entrance is on Piedmont Road between 14th Street and Monroe Drive. Accessible to disabled persons, the garden allows strollers everywhere but in the Conservatory. Limited parking is available. For public transportation, take MARTA to the Arts Center Station where you may transfer to the No. 36 North Decatur bus. On Sunday, take the No. 31 Lindbergh bus from MARTA's Lindbergh or Five Points stations.

We recommend you allow at least an hour to tour the garden. Facilities are closed on Thanksgiving, Christmas and New Year's Day. Admission is adults, $6; seniors older than 65, $4.75; children ages 6 to 12 and students with I.D., $2.25; children younger than 6 and Atlanta Botanical Gardens' members, free. After 4 PM each Thursday admission is free to all.

Hours of operation are Tuesday through Sunday 9 AM to 6 PM in the winter, 9 AM to 7 PM in the summer. It's closed Monday. Hours of the Fuqua Conservatory and the gift shop are 10 AM to 6 PM.

THE CARTER PRESIDENTIAL CENTER GARDENS

One Copenhill Ave. N.E.   *331-3900*

Lovely garden spots abound at the Carter Presidential Center, which is easy to reach via the Freedom Parkway. The circle of flags at the center's entrance includes seasonal flowers that are changed twice yearly. The terraced overlook to the Jimmy Carter Library contains seasonal color beds that are also changed twice annually. The 2,500-square-foot rose garden has 400 plants in 80 varieties. Four species of wildflowers enliven a meadow. The three-acre native oak forest affords views of the Japanese gardens across the lake.

The Japanese gardens were designed by master gardener Kinsaku Nakane and

Insiders' Tips

Tune in gardeners — to two local radio shows, aired on Saturdays, that encourage listeners to call in for gardening advice. *The Kathy Henderson Show* airs on WQXI-AM from 6 to 10 AM. You'll hear Walter Reeves' *Lawn and Garden Show* on WSB-AM 750, from 6 to 10 AM.

contain azaleas, rhododendrons, camellias and more. The large waterfall symbolizes President Carter; the smaller waterfall represents Rosalynn Carter.

Thousands of bulbs and plants in the flower garden produce the flowers that beautify the Carter Center's many meetings and social events. Twenty-four cherry trees at the property's northwest corner were planted in 1993.

The Carter Presidential Center has plenty of free parking and can be easily reached via the Freedom Parkway from the 75/85 connector, Ponce de Leon Avenue and Moreland Avenue.

Parks

Whether you want to go for a hike or a stroll, the metro area provides a gorgeous setting. You can wander through wooded hills or along flowing streams.

Following we give a sample of some of Atlanta's premiere parks. For more information call the parks and recreation department nearest you. See our Recreational Sports chapter for a complete listing of parks and recreation departments and their phone numbers.

WOODRUFF MEMORIAL PARK
Peachtree St. and Park Pl.   *No phone*

In the heart of downtown Atlanta, this green space was closed in late 1994 for major renovations in preparation for the 1996 Olympics. A favorite spot for lunchtime relaxation, the park is named for Robert W. Woodruff, Coca-Cola magnate and major-league city philanthropist. The park is scheduled to reopen by the spring of '96, in time for the Olympics.

GEORGIA'S STONE MOUNTAIN PARK
U.S. 78, Stone Mountain   *498-5701*

If you've read our Attractions chapter, you already know about all the man-made amusements in Stone Mountain Park. And, yes, this is the same park that will be an official site for the 1996 Summer Olympics events of canoeing, rowing, archery, cycling and tennis.

Described as Atlanta's primitive campground, this 3,200-acre park with picnic and hiking trails features more than 400 campsites. Limited reservations are taken subject to availability; you must be 18 or older to rent a campsite. Recreational vehicles are accepted year round; electricity and county water are available. Partial and full hookups and tent sites are available March through October; call to verify specific dates. Parking permits must be validated at the campground office for park re-entry during your stay.

Ten miles of trails provide hiking for all levels of fitness. Many people enjoy the 1.3-mile walk to the top of the mountain.

Admission to Georgia's Stone Mountain Park is charged per vehicle: $5 per car. An annual pass costs $20.

FERNBANK FOREST
150 Heaton Park Dr. N.E.   *378-4311*

After touring the wonder of the Fernbank Science Center (see our Kidstuff chapter), spend a pleasant afternoon on a paved 2-mile trail that meanders through this amazing 65-acre stretch of virgin forest, said to be one of the largest remaining in any metropolitan area in the Southeast. Maps are available at the gate. Grounds are open from 2 to 5 PM on weekdays, from 10 AM to 5 PM on Saturday and Sunday. Fernbank Forest is about 6 miles east of downtown. Take Ponce de Leon Avenue and turn north at Heaton Park Drive.

ALEXANDER PARK
East Wesley Rd. N.E.   *No phone*

Smack in the heart of Garden Hills, a

*Only 3 miles from downtown, the Atlanta Botanical Garden
is a living museum to nature and gardening.*

pleasant residential community off Peachtree Road, you'll find a small 11-acre wooded park with an enjoyable trail. Alexander is simply a nice place to stroll. Within walking distance, virtually connected to Alexander Park, are the Garden Hills Parks at East Wesley and Rumsom Road. These parks are virtually connected to each other. Here you'll find a swimming pool, a playground and a community center on 3.6 acres of land.

ELWYN JONES WILDLIFE SANCTUARY
Holly Ln., Decatur   *No phone*

A haven amidst hectic city life, this several-acre site in DeKalb County is overseen by the Atlanta Audubon Society. Several nature trails weave through the acreage.

From the N. Druid Hills Exit off I-85, head east on Druid Hills Road. Just after you pass the Briarcliff High School you'll see Holly Lane on your right. Follow Holly Lane to a dirt road leading to the sanctuary.

PANOLA MOUNTAIN STATE PARK
2600 Hwy. 155, Stockbridge   *474-2914*

Special programs are held throughout the year in this DeKalb County park, which is managed by the Georgia Department of Natural Resources. Besides self-guided tours, 2- and 3-hour guided hikes to the top of the mountain and along the lake are conducted on scheduled dates; call for exact times. You'll observe interesting aspects of nature, such as how natural forces weather rock and the growth stages of simple organisms. Take I-20 E. to Wesley Chapel Road Exit, go right on Wesley Chapel. Turn left at the first traffic light, Snapfinger Road. Continue 10 miles on Snapfinger Road to the park, which will be on your left.

KENNESAW MOUNTAIN NATIONAL BATTLEFIELD PARK
Old U. S. Hwy. 41 N.W.
Kennesaw   *427-4686*

A visitors center in this National Park displays relics from this bloody battle of

Photo: Georgia Tourist Division

the Atlanta Campaign, one in which the Confederate forces had the upper hand. The 2,884-acre park has 16 miles of wooded hiking trails.

Take I-75 N. to the Kennesaw Park Exit and follow signs to the park.

See our Attractions chapter for more information.

WILDWOOD PARK
South Cobb Dr. and Barclay Cr.
Marietta   *No phone*

For a great chance to commune with nature, come to this 28-acre site with 2.5 miles of hiking and nature trails. Outdoor programs are available from the Marietta Parks and Recreation Department; call 492-4211 for a complete listing. In addition to programs for adults, several "kids only" programs include a challenge-adventure course and map reading.

PIEDMONT PARK
Piedmont Ave. and 14th St.   *817-6785*

Atlanta's largest park and home of the Atlanta Botanical Garden, Piedmont Park is the site of numerous fairs, festivals, Atlanta Symphony Orchestra concerts and much more.

In this 185-acre setting, you'll find a paved 3-mile jogging trail plus other trails for walking, cycling and skating. Football and baseball games are commonplace, and softball leagues use the park's athletic fields for spring and summer competitions. Even the massive Peachtree Road Race, held each July 4, ends in Piedmont Park near the 10th Street entrance.

Piedmont Park's outdoor hillside concerts have long been a favorite Atlanta tradition. The park is home to the annual Arts Festival of Atlanta held each September, another generation-spanning tradition since its beginnings in 1954 (see

our Annual Events and Festivals chapter for more information). Special year-round programs for senior citizens at the Outings in the Park Clubhouse are popular.

A children's play environment called Playscapes creates special diversion for little ones. This playground is the work of famed sculptor Isamu Noguchi and is next to the park's 12th Street entrance. The park has four formal entrances, all dating to 1927: the stone archway at 12th and Piedmont streets; the stone archway at 10th Street and Charles Allen Drive; the Park Place Bridge, a red brick and concrete structure listed in the American Historic Engineering Survey; and the stone entranceway at Piedmont Avenue at the Prado.

Piedmont's current happenings in no way outshine its colorful history. The land on which Piedmont Park stands was originally part of the Gentlemen's Driving Club (later the Piedmont Driving Club), a group whose members were the force behind Atlanta's progressive development at the end of the 1800s. This private club's building, constructed in 1887, still stands today north of 14th Street on Piedmont Avenue.

As part of his modernity-embracing "New South" philosophy, *Constitution* editor Henry Grady lobbied for the staging of large industrial expositions to establish Atlanta as a regional leader and to attract new investment capital. The first fair, held in 1881 on a 19-acre site near the Western & Atlantic track on the city's west side, was a big success, drawing 300,000 visitors during its three-month run.

Even bigger plans were made for the next exposition, which was held on the site of the present Piedmont Park. The city leased land from the Gentlemen's Driving Club, which owned a 200-acre tract. Twenty thousand thronged to the first day of the fair; President and Mrs. Grover Cleveland attended. When the 12-day event closed, it had made a profit of $9,746.

In 1895, six years after Grady's death at age 39, the city launched its most ambitious expo ever, again on the site of Piedmont Park. The Cotton States and International Exposition of 1895 ended up costing almost $3 million to produce, but it was wildly successful at bringing Atlanta national attention. In Washington on September 18, President Grover Cleveland pressed a button that set the exposition's machinery in motion. Twenty-five thousand rushed the fair on opening day as a band played Victor Herbert's new piece "Salute to Atlanta." John Philip Sousa's band premiered "King Cotton," a march written especially for the event.

Reflecting the city's progressive outlook, special pavilions celebrated the progress and achievements of women and African Americans; Booker T. Washington attended and delivered an important speech on race relations. Its thesis — that blacks should accept political disenfranchisement as the price of educational and employment opportunities — became known as the Atlanta Compromise.

For insightful perspective on events surrounding the expositions, we recommend a book called *Atlanta, A City for the World* by Diane C. Thomas. Published in 1988, the book provides fascinating detail as well as many fine pictures of Atlanta landmarks.

After the expositions, an 1898 reunion of Confederate veterans camped on the grounds. The park was home to the Atlanta Crackers baseball team until their move, following the 1904 season, to Ponce de Leon Park, which was opposite the present City Hall East. In their day, these players were heroes and won 17 pennants, more than any pro team except the Yankees.

Piedmont Park became a public park in 1904 when the city agreed to buy the park for $98,000; later, certain rights were sold back to the adjacent Driving Club for $5,000. So, Atlanta paid $93,000 for the park's 185 acres. A solemn unveiling of the Peace Monument at the 14th Street entrance drew respectful crowds. This work of New York sculptor Allan Newman represents the growth of peace and reconciliation between the North and the South. It is said to have been built from funds collected mostly from Northern states.

A citizens' support group called the Piedmont Park Conservancy was formed in 1989 to support and conserve the park's natural assets through citizen volunteer efforts. This nonprofit, private-membership group sponsors guided walking tours each Saturday at 11 AM and each Sunday at 2 PM at the 12th Street entrance to the park. The group schedules regular work parties to clean and repair features of the park. For more information on the work of this group, write to 1155 Peachtree Street N.E., or call 875-7274. Another source of information on Piedmont Park happenings is the Atlanta Parks, Recreation and Cultural Affairs Office, 658-6691.

A favorite spot with strollers, the park provides slightly hilly terrain with lots of shade trees where you can stretch out to rest your weary bones. A loop trail through the park will give you a chance to take in all the scenery.

Parking around the park is limited, and during some events, it's completely prohibited. Make it easy on yourself and leave your car behind. MARTA's Midtown station is on 10th Street between Peachtree and West Peachtree. The Arts Center station is on 15th Street behind the Arts Center. There's regular bus service along Piedmont Avenue on the No. 36 North Decatur bus, that travels from the Arts Center station and the Decatur station.

CHASTAIN PARK
City of Atlanta
Parks and Recreation Dept.   *817-6785*

About 8 miles north of downtown, the irregularly shaped Chastain is bounded by three main roads: West Wieuca Road, Powers Ferry Road and Lake Forrest Drive. To reach the park, take Peachtree Road to Roswell Road, then turn left on Powers Ferry Road. Or exit I-285 at Powers Ferry and go south approximately 4 miles.

For more than 40 years, this multi-purpose park has provided respite from city life. To really take in the park's features, consider joining a Southern Bicycle League ride through the park. This group sponsors rides of varying lengths through the park (see our Recreational Sports chapter). These open-to-the-public rides are regularly listed in area newspapers. Call the league, 594-8350, for more information. Also try out Chastain's 3.5 mile jogging trail.

A description of Chastain's facilities sounds like a one-stop vacation destination. You'll find a gym plus athletic fields for softball, soccer, football and baseball. Chastain's riding stables host many equestrian events and provide boarding space for horses. A special program called the Crawford Center for Therapeutic Learning teaches life skills to handicapped children through horseback riding.

But wait, there's more, including picnic and playground areas plus a swimming pool. Chastain's crafts center and art gallery hold exhibits and workshops regularly. The tennis facilities are the site of Atlanta Lawn Tennis Association tournaments. And the public golf course remains a popular draw.

The amphitheater seats more than 6,000 patrons. Here Atlantans revel in various entertainments, from symphony concerts to theater productions. Pops concerts by the Atlanta Symphony Orchestra and guest performers fill the amphitheater during summer months.

Parking lots are near the ballfields and the amphitheater. Some street parking is permitted along W. Wieuca Road. Or you can leave your car and take the No. 38 Chastain Park bus from the Lindbergh MARTA station.

GRANT PARK
Georgia and Cherokees Aves.   *658-6374*

Atlanta's oldest park is about 2 miles southeast of downtown. Take I-20, get off at the Boulevard Exit and head south to Georgia Avenue where you'll turn right. Turn right again on Cherokee Avenue to the parking lot on your right next to Cyclorama and the Zoo.

Loaded with history, Grant Park was once home to Creek Indians. Confederate artillery troops lined the park's eastern perimeter during the Battle of Atlanta.

The park was named for Lemuel Grant, a 19-century philanthropist and former Confederate engineer whose designs shored up Atlanta's defenses against Union troops. Col. Grant donated land for the park from his sizable estate.

Grant Park's features — athletic fields and pavilions — make it a popular relaxation spot. Various amateur leagues for football, softball and other sports use the park's athletic facilities. Perhaps its prime attractions are the Atlanta Zoo and Cyclorama (see our Attractions chapter for more information). Other nearby attractions are the Sweet Auburn Historic District (see Attractions) and Oakland Cemetery, a burial ground of famous figures such as Margaret Mitchell, author of *Gone With the Wind*, and golfing great Bobby Jones. The area abounds in lovely old Victorian homes. Some reflect the splendor of that era; others are in various states of restoration. Every September the Grant Park Tour of Homes draws crowds to view these reminders of bygone days. A highlight of December is the Christmas Candlelight Tour. Much of the area is on the National Register of Historic Places.

You can take MARTA to here from several stations: Five Points, Peachtree Center and Lindbergh. Then connect with the No. 31 Grant Park/Lindbergh bus to the park.

PROVIDENCE OUTDOOR RECREATION CENTER

13440 Providence Park Dr.
Alpharetta   740-2419

Here's where you can get a good start on adventures in nature. Courses in basic map and compass reading, rock climbing, rappelling, backpacking and canoeing are taught by staff naturalists. Some of the classes last all day; others are overnight. Charges range from $15 to $45.

Special events held at Providence Center include the Summer's End River Clean-Up and a Community Volunteer Work Day. CPR and first aid classes are offered. Various groups, such as the North Fulton Bass Club and scout troops, hold their meetings at the center.

CHATTAHOOCHEE OUTDOOR CENTER

1990 Island Ford Pkwy.   395-6851

The Chattahoochee Outdoor Center is on the banks of the river with put-in facilities at Johnson Ferry and Powers Island. Take-out facilities are at Powers Island and Paces Mill. Take a ride down the river by raft, canoe or kayak, all of which are available for rent. Classes in these sports are offered too.

The center is open from 9 AM to 8 PM on weekends and from 10 AM to 8 PM on weekdays. Call for more information about boat ramps, marinas, camping areas and picnic facilities.

OUTDOOR ACTIVITY CENTER

1442 Richland Rd. S.W.   752-5385

A surprise just 3 miles southwest of downtown Atlanta, this 26-acre forest has a designated National Recreation Trail, which allows foot-traffic only, running through it.

The area is part of a mature piedmont forest, a band of gently rolling hills that distinguish it from Georgia's coastal plains. The region's granite rock base means hikers will see different tree life here. You'll also enjoy a live animal display area and a natural science research library. The center is open Monday through Friday from 9 AM to 4 PM. Admission is $3.

Gardening/Outdoors Resources

COOL COMMUNITIES PROGRAM

255-2950

This is a national project of the American Forestry Association with demonstration bases across the country. The project compares the electricity usage of houses with trees nearby to those without. The aim is to measure trees' capacity to reduce heat and promote energy conservation. Georgia Power Company is a partner in this project. Call the coordinator at the number listed to become involved.

GEORGIA STATE
DEPARTMENT OF AGRICULTURE
19 Martin Luther King Jr. Dr.   656-3685

Take advantage of a free, biweekly publication called the *Farmers and Consumers Market Bulletin*. This unusual and helpful source of information gives a variety of advice to gardeners seeking specialty items. You may also call the Agriculture Consumer Line for assistance, 656-3645, (800)282-5852.

PARK PRIDE ATLANTA
675 Ponce de Leon Ave.   607-7714

Established to encourage park renovation, Park Pride offers community environment workshops so volunteers can learn how to maintain and improve parks. Classes are designed to increase neighborhood awareness of local environmental issues.

The organization provides tools and materials. Among the subjects covered are soil erosion, planting and pruning techniques, composting and xeriscaping. The classes are offered to neighborhoods on request. Park Pride was responsible for the planting of nearly 90 trees in Grant Park that helped restore the park to its original 1912 design.

THE PATH FOUNDATION
P.O. Box 14327
Atlanta 30324   355-6438

An admirable partnering of abilities, individuals, businesses, engineers and city and county planners, PATH is a nonprofit group committed to building nearly 112 miles of trails throughout Atlanta. PATH has drawn support from more than 1,000 volunteers who have cleared hiking/biking/skating trails, on- and off-street. The off-street trails are essentially linear parks 10 to 12 feet wide. Among the benefits of these trails are better connections between neighborhoods and a cleaner form of commuting. Construction of trails is ongoing and has been accepted in the city's Comprehensive Development Plan, an indication of city support.

Besides a trail in Chastain Park, three others are under study or construction: the 18-mile Stone Mountain-Atlanta Trail, the 9-mile Chattahoochee River Trail and the 2.3-mile Freedom Parkway Trail. A fourth, the 2-mile Lionel Hampton Trail is completed.

PATHWAYS OF GOLD
7 Gilbert Tr.   *No phone*

The Garden Club of Georgia's pre-Olympic program to help beautify the metro area is called Pathways of Gold. You can get free seeds for a black-eyed Susan that blooms June through August by sending a stamped, self-addressed envelope to Pathways of Gold, Kathy Henderson's Garden, WQXI-AM, 3350 Peachtree Road N.E., Atlanta 30326. This plant is a two-foot reseeding annual. (Gold and yellow are meant to symbolize the Olympic gold medal.)

TREES ATLANTA
96 Poplar St. N.W.   522-4097

The main goals of this organization are advocacy and protection of existing trees, implementing large urban street plantings in the downtown area and planting smaller trees through the volunteer program throughout the metro area. Formed in 1984, Trees Atlanta relies on a solid volunteer base to accomplish its many projects. Some of these are highway and gateway tree planting, street tree planting and the Olympic Tree Planting Project.

USDA FOREST SERVICE
Southern Region
1720 Peachtree Rd. N.W.   347-1647

Opportunities abound for volunteers here. The USDA Forest Service provides technical assistance and materials to citizens. The USDA Forest Service lectures to neighborhood groups on developing tree ordinances and how to inventory local trees. This organization works with researchers and generally acts as a conduit for information between people at the grass roots level and those at the more technical level. A $6 million grant program assists small-town and neighborhood groups in planning efforts and other needs.

GEORGIA TREES COALITION
Rm. 810, Floyd Bldg., West Tower
200 Piedmont Ave. 656-3204

An umbrella group formed by Georgia Forestry Commission Director John Mixon, the GTC coordinates the groups actively involved in Olympic tree plantings. The coalition is a partnership of municipal, state and federal agencies, green industry representatives, the Georgia Urban Forest Council, the Olympic committee and nonprofit tree action groups. In civic support, Georgia Power Company donates the printing of the coalition's monthly newsletter. Volunteers are welcome to help with tree planting projects, especially during the spring planting season.

COBB COUNTY EXTENSION SERVICE
Horticulture/Natural Resources 528-2445

Home gardeners in Cobb County rely on this county facility for information about what to plant and when to plant it. Acting as a resource center, the department offers referral services, such as water quality testing and rentals of nuisance animal traps. Cobb County Extension has a very active master gardener program, with projects in hospitals and other settings. As volunteers, residents take the master gardener training, then help

throughout the county in answering questions for other gardeners.

Additional services include programs and lectures for the public. A call to the Cobb Extension Service will get your name on the mailing list for the quarterly publication called *Lifestyle,* which includes upcoming events. Announcements of events also are made in the *Marietta Daily Journal.*

DEKALB COUNTY EXTENSION SERVICE
Main Office 371-2821

This office provides literature on specifics about plant materials and related matters, such as weed control, composting, landscaping and property maintenance.

When you have a question about an insect, your soil or a plant disease, here's the place to turn for advice. The service presents public seminars on a quarterly schedule and a free newsletter. Just call the above number to get on the mailing list.

This extension office also does consultations for groups, such as homeowners and condo associations, and provides training for professional groundskeepers and master gardeners. Volunteers help in various ways, such as sponsorship of urban garden programs in low income areas.

FULTON COUNTY EXTENSION SERVICE
Urban Garden 762-4077

This extension service handles calls from urban gardeners on a wide range of issues, including pest, soil and growing problems. This extension service works with communities and schools to provide teaching assistance and to show how to grow vegetables on small tracts of land.

In addition to the standard helpful services and advice, the department has launched a program called Leadership

Training that draws attention from across the country. The program focuses on low income and public housing groups, using gardening as a basis for teaching leadership training. Participants learn how to organize a garden club and how to deal with conflict resolution.

Another major project involves growing vegetables for the homeless. For Thanksgiving of 1994, residents in public housing and substance-abuse centers grew and delivered enough greens to feed 500 people staying in shelters.

GWINNETT COUNTY EXTENSION SERVICE
Agricultural/Natural Resources   822-7700

This extension service provides unbiased, research-based information for do-it-yourselfers who need answers. This service offers advice on water testing, safe pesticide use and pest control in the garden. It furnishes gardening-related publications and tips on how to get started in gardening. Call for a quarterly schedule of seminars.

Inside
Neighborhoods and Real Estate

Occasionally — just once in a blue moon — we hear someone express a negative impression after a visit to Atlanta. Upon investigation, the visitor making the remark nearly always turns out to be a business person whose short stay was spent only in the airport and downtown. Yet we rarely hear a complaint about Atlanta from those who come here to visit friends. These visitors are more likely to return home raving about Atlanta and vowing to return. What accounts for the different opinions?

Though we Atlantans point with pride to our exciting skyline, the plain truth is that very few of us live downtown. The visitor who only sees downtown, then, may remember Atlanta as a city populated entirely by out-of-towners.

Atlanta is a city of many different neighborhoods connected by a web of roads and rails. It is in these neighborhoods, more so than in any central district, that Atlantans make their lives and pass their time.

In a metro area that sprawls across 20 counties and more than 6,000 square miles, neighborhoods help Atlantans keep their lives in perspective. Your neighborhood is more than just a place to hang your hat and pick up the mail. It provides a refined sense of focus, bringing a manageable, human scale to urban life. To be one person among 3 million in a 6,000-square-mile region is overwhelming; to

be one among a few thousand in a friendly neighborhood is to feel a sense of community.

Because so much of Atlanta life is organized around communities, you don't have to be a new resident to benefit from knowledge of the city's neighborhoods. In this chapter, we'll explain some of the parts of town you'll likely hear people talking about everyday. Some of them have funny names — you can be forgiven if you snicker the first time you hear someone talking about Buckhead or Cabbagetown. Some — like Inman Park, Grant Park and Ansley Park — have names that honor the futuristic pioneers who helped make Atlanta a great city.

In your conversations with Atlantans, you'll no doubt hear much discussion about the relative advantages and disadvantages of life in various neighborhoods. You may hear diehard in-towners speak disparagingly of life beyond the I-285 Perimeter; you may also hear suburbanites discussing in-town Atlanta as if it were an outlaw zone or a mysterious foreign land. And you'll find many Atlantans playfully but unabashedly chauvinistic about where they live. Perhaps you'll see a resident of laid-back Little Five Points sporting a T-shirt reading "30307: It's not just a ZIP code — it's a way of life"; or you may hear a trendy northsider quote the mantra "Buckhead is a state of mind."

The happy truth is that whether you

The Virginia-Highland neighborhood was first developed in 1916.

prefer to live in a high-rise condo or a walled compound, a downtown loft or a lavish mansion, you'll find what you're looking for in Atlanta if you're willing to be persistent and flexible.

As you begin to look for an Atlanta address, the first question to answer is a basic one: Do you prefer to live inside or outside I-285? Your answer to this question will be determined by your lifestyle and goals, where you work and play and the kind of people you want to live around. Do you want to make your home far from the noise and hustle or the city — or right in the thick of everything?

In this chapter, we'll look first at some of the best-known residential areas inside I-285, then we'll give you some basic facts about the 20 counties that make up the metro Atlanta area. Space permits us to offer only an overview of Atlanta's neighborhoods, so we'll also suggest several ideas to aid you in further research.

Birth and Rebirth

Atlanta's city seal bears two dates: 1847, when the city was chartered, and 1865, when it began to rise from the ashes of the Civil War. In the same way, the story of many Atlanta neighborhoods is a fascinating one that unfolds in several acts: a story of birth, decline and renewal.

In the 1960s and '70s, Atlanta was widely perceived to be in big trouble. Once-proud areas, such as Inman Park, had badly declined. Peachtree Street in Midtown gained national attention as a hippie hangout where drugs were sold openly. Adult bookstores and movie theaters were abundant. Shocked visitors returned from the city describing it as something like the Sodom of the South. Charging that the "sorry, no good, cowardly" city government was not able to control lawbreakers, segregationist Gov. Lester Maddox threatened in 1969 to call out state troopers to restore order.

And there was the matter of race. Blacks long accounted for a very large minority of the city's residents. Many slaves who had been brought to Atlanta to build the city's fortifications before the Civil War returned afterward to make their lives here as free citizens.

Then came the race riot of 1906, in which white mobs, enraged by inflammatory newspaper accounts of black "outrages" against white women, went on a rampage that lasted nearly a week, murdering blacks in the streets of downtown and burning black homes. Image-conscious Atlanta got some very bad publicity as the riot was reported across the globe. And in the wake of it, the progressive city passed some very unprogressive legislation. In 1910, the city council passed a law requiring all restaurants to serve one race only. In 1913, Atlanta became the first city in Georgia to legislate segregation in residential areas.

During the Civil Rights era, Atlanta integrated without much of the violence and rancor that tore apart many other Southern cities. Atlantans understood the importance of living up to Mayor William B. Hartsfield's famous remark, when he proudly dubbed it "the city too busy to hate." But beneath the veneer of cooperation, Atlanta was in turmoil. The end of residential segregation sent many affluent whites fleeing to the suburbs north of Atlanta and beyond. Newspaper articles warned of the creation of an all-black city surrounded by all-white suburbs. In 1975, the Atlanta *Journal & Constitution* published a mournful series of articles decrying Atlanta as a "City in Crisis."

Although this complete racial polarization did not come about, the white flight of the 1960s and '70s left Atlanta with a solid black majority. Today, African Americans, who account for only 25 percent of the metro area's population, comprise 67 percent of the city's residents. This pattern of population migration has had a predictable effect on politics in the Atlanta region. Just as Atlanta has a major street and a MARTA station named after Dr. Martin Luther King Jr., Cobb County christened a stretch of I-75 to honor its late Congressman Larry McDonald, an ul-

traconservative who was killed when the Soviet Union shot down Korean Air Lines flight 007 in 1983. In the 1992 Presidential election, 15 of Atlanta's 20 counties voted for Bush; three, Clayton, Newton and Pickens went for Clinton by slim margins; and two, Fulton and DeKalb, went lopsidely for Clinton.

But even as many once-fashionable areas spiraled into seemingly endless decline, something remarkable happened. Atlanta began to attract new residents who were eager to live in an integrated city. When these visionaries looked at the dusty old mansions and rundown bungalows along Atlanta's tree-lined streets, they saw not inevitable decay but tremendous opportunity. One by one, Atlanta's historic neighborhoods began to awaken as if from a dream. Freed from the backward and Draconian practices of segregation, Atlantans — whose city had always been multiracial — now began to integrate it, block by block and street by street.

This is not to say that Atlanta is entirely integrated: Segregated housing patterns are still quite evident today. The southside remains home to more blacks than whites; the northside, to more whites than blacks. But there are blacks who live on the northside, just as there are whites who live on the southside. And in the intown areas where the two halves of the city come together, black and white Atlantans, as well as those of other races and nationalities, live, work, play and worship together with an ease that would have been thought impossible just a few decades ago.

And now, with the 1996 Olympics on the horizon, some of Atlanta's poorer neighborhoods — such as Summerhill and Vine City— are hoping to experience the same type of rebirth that better-known neighborhoods — such as Midtown and Inman Park — have been undergoing for years.

In this chapter, we'll discuss neighborhoods in the northeast, northwest, southwest and southeast sections of town. On the northside, Peachtree Street, Peachtree Road and Roswell Road divide east and west; on the southside, Capitol Avenue divides east and west. On the eastside, Edgewood Avenue and Boulevard Drive divide north and south; on the westside, Martin Luther King Jr. Drive divides north and south.

As you read about Atlanta's neighborhoods, keep the following points in mind. Neighborhoods are somewhat intangible: Most lack traditional signage to let you know precisely when you're leaving one and entering another. It's not uncommon for one street to be claimed informally by two different neighborhoods, which can be a little confusing. Also, the same name may be used for a neighborhood and for its primary park. For example, Candler Park is the name of a city park, the neighborhood around it and the area's MARTA station. Many neighborhoods are served by a nearby MARTA station; those without a rail station are served by MARTA buses.

Following is a brief roundup of some of the interesting neighborhoods inside I-285. For more in-depth information, we recommend these excellent books: *Atlanta — A City of Neighborhoods* by Joseph F. Thompson and Robert Isbell, and *Atlanta Walks*, by Ren and Helen Davis. Let's begin in the northeast section with Atlanta's oldest planned suburb: Inman Park.

Northeast Atlanta

Joel Hurt was a civil engineer, a developer and a visionary. In 1887, Hurt hired James Forsyth Johnson to design Atlanta's first garden suburb after the fashion of famed landscape architect Frederick Law Olmsted. Inman Park's name honors civic leader Samuel M. Inman. Since **Inman Park** was 2 miles east of Five Points, an important part of Hurt's plan was the building of the city's first electric trolley line, which ran from downtown to 963 Edgewood Avenue. The restored original Trolley Barn, 521-2308, at that address is now a popular rental hall for weddings and other events. The trolley line went into service on August 22, 1889.

Inman Park's plan included broad streets along which were planted coastal Georgia live oak trees. Though such trees had never been known to survive in Atlanta, many of these giants still tower over the neighborhood today. Many prominent Atlantans lived in Inman Park, including Coca-Cola founder Asa Candler, whose Callan Castle stands at the corner of Euclid Avenue and Elizabeth Street, and Hurt himself, who lived at 167 Elizabeth Street.

Inman Park peaked as a fashionable address around the turn of the century. Shortly after, it began to lose rich residents to other, more opulent developments such as Druid Hills and Ansley Park. The neighborhood declined in prestige and was considered little better than a slum by the 1960s. The amazing transformation symbolized by the neighborhood's logo (a butterfly) began in the late '60s and continues to this day. Determined Atlantans moved in to revitalize the area; in the process, helping halt an expressway through the district that would have destroyed many homes.

Today, Inman Park is listed on the National Register of Historic Places and is home to Atlanta's Mayor Bill Campbell.

Homes in Inman Park range from bungalows in need of lots of work to fully restored Victorian mansions. The district's annual springtime festival draws thousands of visitors and is one of the most popular of Atlanta's many neighborhood festivals. Lively Little Five Points, the eclectic shopping district between Inman Park and Candler Park, helps nearby areas attract new residents as well as visitors. The Inman Park/Reynoldstown MARTA station serves this area.

East of Little Five Points is **Candler Park**, which was once part of the independent town known as Edgewood. The neighborhood's centerpiece is Candler Park, a hilly park with a public golf course; it's named for Asa Candler, who donated the land for recreation. In the early days of the automobile, the area gained popularity as a residence for Atlanta commuters. Though Candler Park lacks the grand Victorian mansions that grace Inman Park, the area has many pleasant homes both large and small.

Similar homes may be found in **Lake Claire**, which is just east of Candler Park and Clifton Road along McLendon Avenue. (And no, despite those whimsical "Ski Lake Claire" bumper stickers you may observe, there is not a lake here.) In general, the blocks north of McLendon are further along in their revitalization than those south of McLendon. If you're lucky enough to be here in the springtime, take a drive up steep, dogwood-lined Claire Drive, a much-photographed example of Atlanta's floral glory. Candler Park and Lake Claire are served by the Edgewood/Candler Park MARTA station.

Throughout much of the 1980s, neighbors in Lake Claire, Candler Park and Inman Park waged a fierce battle — in the courts, in the media and sometimes through bulldozer-blocking direct action — to prevent construction of the Presidential Parkway. The roadway was to have linked Ponce de Leon Avenue with the downtown connector via the Carter Presidential Center, but residents protested the big road's impact on the area's cherished parks and laid-back lifestyle. This was a case of "you *can* fight city hall"— though the huge pylons that were to have held the big road were already built, residents prevailed. The renamed Freedom Parkway has a 35 mph speed limit and bike and jogging trails — and it stops at Moreland Avenue, instead of crossing the neighborhood to join Ponce.

Directly north of Candler Park along Ponce de Leon Avenue is one of Atlanta's most famous neighborhoods, 1,400-acre **Druid Hills**. Fresh from developing Inman Park, Joel Hurt hired renowned landscape architect Frederick Law Olmsted, designer of New York's Central Park, who was then in Asheville designing the grounds of the Vanderbilts' Biltmore Estate, to lay out the neighborhood. Olmsted worked on preliminary plans but died before he could finish them. He left it to his sons Frederick Jr. and John Charles to complete his work. Olmsted's plans placed six elegant linear parks like a string of pearls along winding Ponce de Leon. (These parks too would have been severely impacted by the original Presidential Parkway.)

Druid Hills' many beautiful homes preside over broad lawns that are ablaze with seasonal colors in the spring and fall. The present St. John's Melkite Catholic Church, 1428 Ponce de Leon Avenue N.E., was once the home of Asa Candler. Druid Hills' location beside Emory University helped preserve it even in the face of Atlanta's turbulent growth. The Druid Hills Historic District is listed on the National Register of Historic Places.

Druid Hills' most famous resident never actually existed — but her house does. Jessica Tandy won an Oscar for her portrayal of the feisty Druid Hills widow who is the title character in *Driving Miss Daisy*. The house used as the setting for the movie is at 822 Lullwater Road.

While we're on the east side of town, we'll touch on lovely **Decatur**, 6 miles east of downtown Atlanta. Decatur is an independent city more than a decade older than Atlanta with its own fascinating history. It's home to Agnes Scott College and to Columbia Theological Seminary.

Ponce de Leon Avenue passes through the center of Decatur, becoming East Ponce de Leon. Another major east/west thoroughfare is College Avenue. Clairmont Road and Columbia Drive are big north/south routes. Decatur has areas of poverty and wealth as well as numerous transitional areas, and home values vary accordingly. In general, pricier housing is more likely to be found north of College Avenue than south of it. The south side, however, has many pleasant streets and areas, such as Winnona Park, that attract young homeowners looking for houses to improve. Decatur is served by the East Lake, Decatur and Avondale MARTA stations.

One mile east of Decatur is another independent city, **Avondale Estates**. In the early 1920s, patent medicine millionaire George F. Willis' idea for a totally self-contained residential development attracted national attention. Willis bought an existing small community, Ingleside, and over a period of four years transformed it into a world of its own, with parks, clubhouses, a lake and a pool.

While he worked on the giant carving at Stone Mountain, sculptor Gutzon Borglum, who was a friend of Willis, lived in a house here.

In 1926, the Georgia Legislature designated Avondale Estates an independent city with its own mayor, city council, police and sanitation departments. The district's commercial buildings are in a Tudor style that suggests an English village, but most of the houses are of more conventional architecture and varying sizes. Avondale Estates is listed on the National Register of Historic Places. MARTA's Avondale and Kensington Stations serve this area.

Now let's swing back west. As you travel north on Peachtree from Five Points, the first substantial residential area you encounter is **Midtown**. Like Inman Park, it's about 2 miles from Five Points. And, like Inman Park, it was the brainchild of a streetcar builder. Developer Richard Peters bought up the area's more than 400 acres in the early 1880s with the idea of building a neighborhood and operating a streetcar line to it. Building in the district continued for nearly 50 years, and there is a commensurate range in architecture, from simple bungalows to showy Victorian mansions.

But after World War II Midtown lost many residents to the suburbs, and some fine homes were converted to apartments and boarding houses. In the late '60s and early '70s, Midtown went hippie in a big way; more conservative people shunned the area and neighboring Piedmont Park, which was the site of numerous anti-Vietnam War protests.

By the mid-'70s, Midtown, like some other city neighborhoods, was turning a corner. Its solidly built homes, tree-lined streets and convenient location convinced adventurous buyers of the area's Wren's lying value. Gays, singles and yuppie couples were drawn by Midtown's tolerance and urban charm and settled there by the thousands, many as homeowners who greatly improved their properties. Midtown property values and rents have climbed dramatically over the years, but some more moderate properties remain. As you drive across Midtown from the Ponce side (near Third Street) to the park side (bordering 10th Street), you'll generally notice the quality of the neighborhood going up along with the street numbers. Midtown is served by the Midtown and North Avenue MARTA stations.

Between Midtown and Druid Hills, **Virginia-Highland** grew and took its name from its central intersection: Virginia and N. Highland avenues. When it was first developed in 1916 as North Boulevard Park, the subdivision was another "streetcar" community, with a line that ran down N. Highland to Ponce. Many of the houses are solid brick Craftsman structures with porches.

Virginia-Highland was damaged in the 1960s and '70s when the state tried to build an expressway, I-485, through the neighborhood. The road was eventually halted but not before homes were condemned and the community was disrupted. After that experience, Virginia-Highlanders took to jealously guarding their neighborhood against too much change. They keep a watchful eye, for example, on growth in the popular N. Highland Avenue commercial district, whose restaurants and bars attract visitors from all over town.

North of Virginia-Highland is the **Morningside/Lenox Park** section. Similar in many ways to Virginia-Highland, this area's residents also had to battle the state of Georgia over plans to build the I-485 Expressway. Morningside dates from the post-World War I years; a former farming community, it was purchased and developed by M.S. Rankin and James R. Smith. Lenox Park got under way in 1932, the product of the architectural firm Ivey and Crook.

Many Lenox Park homes are built of stone and brick in Tudor and English Country styles. Morningside's homes are in a variety of styles, reflecting the influence of neighboring districts Virginia-Highland and Ansley Park. Some area homes make good use of a narrow lot by cleverly stacking a screened porch on top of the attached garage beside the house. Morningside Elementary is one of the city's most highly regarded public schools.

North of Midtown is another of Atlanta's most famous neighborhoods: **Ansley Park**. Edwin Ansley launched this development in 1904. Unlike other early Atlanta neighborhoods, Ansley Park was designed as a community for automobile, not streetcar, commuters. The development was laid out by Solon Zachary Ruff, who had worked with the Olmsted firm in creating Druid Hills.

Ansley spent more than $500,000 to drain swamps and otherwise whip the section's more than 230 acres into shape. Six hundred home lots of varying sizes and numerous small parks were planned in the district. Many Ansley Park homes sit atop hills with broad lawns descending to the street. In several sections, houses that might have sat directly across from each other are instead separated by parallel streets flanking a hilly park. As a result, Ansley Park — though it is bordered by two of Atlanta's busiest streets (Peachtree and Piedmont) — is a district of almost pastoral beauty. It's listed on the National Register of Historic Places.

Homes of various sizes are to be found here, including many fashionable mansions by famous architects, such as Philip Shutze, Neel Reid, Walter Downing and Henry Hornbostel, whose signature designs made an indelible mark on Atlanta's architecture. From 1924 to 1967, the Georgia Governor's mansion was at 205 The Prado. Margaret Mitchell and John Marsh lived for a time in the apartments (now condos) at One South Prado and Piedmont Avenue. The Robert W. Woodruff Arts Center is nearby, as are the Colony Square complex and the Arts Center MARTA station.

North of Ansley Park is another neighborhood that traces its origins to post-World War I enthusiasm and the growing popularity of the automobile: **Brookwood Hills**, developed by B.F. Burdette. The land, which was once owned by the Collier family, was the site of the fierce Battle of Peachtree Creek during the Atlanta Campaign. Brookwood Hills has tennis courts, a community swimming pool and many shade trees. It's listed on the National Register of Historic Places.

Peachtree Hills is north of Brookwood Hills. It was established after the Depression; most houses are of brick and frame bungalow-style construction. The neighborhood has many apartments and a pleasant community commercial district at Peachtree Hills Avenue and Virginia Place.

North of Peachtree Hills is **Garden Hills**, another pleasant neighborhood of tree-lined streets and solid homes, most of which were built in the 1920s and '30s. Developer Philip McDuffie laid out the area in accordance with the popular Frederick Law Olmsted aesthetics. To creat more of a self-contained village, he called for two schools, a small commercial district and some multi-family housing.

Home styles in Garden Hills include American Colonial, Tudor, English Cottage, Georgian and more. The southern part of the district was developed by Eurith

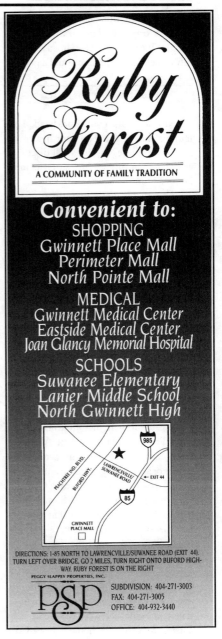

Rivers (who became Georgia's Governor) and was originally known as Peachtree Heights East. Garden Hills has a community center with a clubhouse and a pool.

Northwest Atlanta

Now let's talk about **Buckhead**. This famous district has both northeast and northwest addresses, but we'll discuss it as a whole in this section, since its most famous homes are west of Peachtree.

This is an area where districts and neighborhoods overlap. As we just discussed, Brookwood Hills, Peachtree Hills and Garden Hills are each distinct neighborhoods — but they are all claimed by Buckhead, as are Peachtree Heights and Collier Hills, which we'll discuss in a moment. As defined by the Buckhead Coalition leadership group, Buckhead comprises all of Atlanta north of I-75, I-85 and Peachtree Creek to Cobb County in the west, the city limits in the north and DeKalb County in the east.

Buckhead residences can sell for from less than $100,000 to several million dollars. But when most people envision Buckhead real estate, they think of W. Paces Ferry Road and Tuxedo Park. Along W. Paces and the streets turning off it are homes of astonishing elegance and beauty. This area is home to the Georgia Governor's Mansion and the Swan House, the opulent 1928 mansion that presides over the Atlanta History Center's grounds. Philip Shutze designed the Swan House and other area homes; Neel Reid also designed fabulous mansions in the area. Anne Cox Chambers of the Cox media empire, one of the world's wealthiest women, has a stately mansion here. Windcrofte at 3640 Tuxedo Road was the home of Coca-Cola president Robert Woodruff.

Northwest of central Buckhead and about 8 miles north of downtown is Chastain Park, named for former Fulton County Commissioner Troy G. Chastain. The popular park has a golf course, athletic fields, a crafts center and an art gallery. Its most well-known feature is the outdoor amphitheater that holds nearly 6,500 people and presents some 60 popular and classical concerts between the spring and fall. The streets surrounding the park feature many fine homes.

Still on the west side, let's head back down Peachtree to **Peachtree Heights**, about 5 miles north of downtown. This neighborhood was developed in the 1910s and '20s by Eurith Rivers and W.P. Andrews. It boasts many lovely trees and homes by leading architects of the day. Special attractions here are the Bobby Jones Golf Course, named for the famous Atlanta golfer who is buried at Oakland Cemetery, and the Bitsy Grant Tennis Center, named in honor of the Atlantan who was a tennis champion. Peachtree Heights is listed on the National Register of Historic Places.

Immediately south of Peachtree Heights is **Collier Hills**, which, along with Brookwood Hills on the other side of Peachtree, was the site of the bloody Battle of Peachtree Creek. Most of the houses here are in the traditional styles of the 1940s and '50s. Just south of Collier Hills is **Loring Heights**, some of whose houses along Deering Road and elsewhere enjoy views of the Atlanta skyline.

West of Peachtree and south of 14th Street is **Home Park**, a working-class neighborhood whose modest homes and sleepy streets have been attracting new interest in recent years. Rental properties here are popular with students at nearby Georgia Tech.

Southwest Atlanta

Vine City is bisected by Martin Luther King Jr. Drive, where the addresses change from northwest to southwest. The district takes its name from Vine Street.

Vine City is home to the six historically black colleges that make up Atlanta University Center, the nation's largest center of African-American higher education. It was also home to black millionaire Alonzo Herndon, who built a stunning Beaux-Arts mansion at 587 University Place N.W. Until his assassination, Dr. Martin Luther King Jr. lived with his family in the house at 234 Sunset Street N.W. Vine City has middle-class as well as poor areas; the area underwent much upheaval with the construction of the Georgia Dome. The district is served by the Vine City, Ashby and Garnett MARTA stations.

West of Vine City is **Mozley Park**, which was the site of the Battle of Ezra Church during the Atlanta Campaign. A former Rebel soldier, Hiram Mozley, settled in the area after the war, became a doctor and invented a patent medicine. Following his death, his estate was divided into various home lots and sold. The neighborhood grew up around the city park named for Mozley. In 1949 a black clergyman and his family braved the color barrier, and by the late 1950s the area was home to more minority residents than whites.

Southwest of Mozley Park and bordering I-285 is **Cascade Heights**. This beautifully wooded area of rolling hills is home to many of Atlanta's middle-class and upper-income African Americans and to some of the city's leading black citizens, like the Rev. Dr. Joseph P. Lowery. Black Atlantans began moving into the area in the 1960s and '70s and eventually became the majority.

South of Mozley Park is **West End**. It was here, on the corner of Lee and Gordon streets, that Charner Humphries opened his roadside Whitehall Tavern in 1835, two years before railroad surveyors drove in the "zero milepost" that marked the center of what became Atlanta. The area largely escaped destruction in the Civil War.

After the war, Col. George Washington Adair christened the area West End after the famous district in London. Adair ran a line of mule-drawn streetcars between West End and the present location of Midtown. Train service was also avail-

Homes in Inman Park range from bungalows to fully restored mansions.

Photo: Chuck Morgan

able to the central district, making the section a popular address for those employed downtown. West End's best-known resident was Joel Chandler Harris, the journalist who penned the Uncle Remus stories. His restored home, the Wren's Nest, is a National Landmark. West End is also home to Hammonds House, a pre-Civil War home that is now a museum of African-American fine art.

West End was adversely affected by the construction of I-20 and lost many residents to other neighborhoods but remains a vibrant community. The area's historic homes and churches help provide stability. West End's annual neighborhood festival was established in 1975. The West End MARTA station serves the area.

East of West End, **Adair Park** is named for Col. George Washington Adair, who was, in addition to being a real estate developer and streetcar builder, a newspaper publisher, a train conductor and a wholesale grocer. Adair went bankrupt in 1873 and again in 1877; however, upon his death in 1899, he left his sons a vast real estate empire. Today this integrated residential district is served by the West End and Oakland City MARTA stations.

Southeast Atlanta

Just east of Capitol Avenue, the **Summerhill** section is keeping its fingers crossed. Once a thriving neighborhood populated principally by African Americans and Jews, Summerhill was decimated by the construction of I-20 in the 1950s. The exodus from the neighborhood was only exacerbated when a big section of it was condemned to make way for Atlanta Fulton County Stadium. Now, with construction of the Olympic Stadium under way, Atlanta knows that the world will soon be coming to Summerhill's front yard, and

plans are in process to help the neighborhood modernize.

Bordering Summerhill to the east is **Grant Park**. Col. Lemuel P. Grant, a civil engineer who moved to the South to help build the Western & Atlantic railroad and who also designed the Civil War fortifications around Atlanta, donated 100 acres of his land to the city in 1882 for use as a park. Grant Park became a favorite playground for Atlantans, and a lovely Victorian neighborhood grew up around it. Grant Park faltered following World War II due to suburban migration and the construction of I-20 through the area. As in many other intown neighborhoods, however, discounted property values and the area's charming homes began bringing people back. Today Grant Park residents continue to restore the district, which contains small, moderate-sized and imposing homes.

One Grant Park man, Woodrow Mankin, is undertaking a truly massive project: the restoration of Col. Grant's own crumbling 20-room mansion at 327 St. Paul Avenue. Many years ago, Margaret Mitchell bought the house, determined to save one of the city's few surviving antebellum homes. In a court fight, however, she lost the house to its caretaker, an eccentric who lived there for decades until his death. Several owners later, Mankin plans to restore the mansion and use part of it as the headquarters for the Georgia Decorative Arts Society.

Directly east of Grant Park is **Ormewood**. It's one of the few remaining in-town areas with low-priced attractive housing for those who have been priced out of more established neighborhoods such as Midtown and Virginia-Highland. The Burns Club of Atlanta, a private social club, meets at 988 Alloway Place S.E. in a cottage that is a replica of poet Robert Burns' home in Scotland.

Atlanta's Libraries

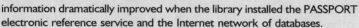

Following passage of a $38 million bond referendum in 1985, Atlanta embarked on one of the nation's largest library-building programs. The construction program added more than 170,000 square feet, doubling the amount of branch space.

The Atlanta-Fulton Public Library System houses some 3.5 million items, 1.8 million of which are in circulation. Access to information dramatically improved when the library installed the PASSPORT electronic reference service and the Internet network of databases.

Library cards are free to all residents of Atlanta and Fulton County; proof of residency, such as a driver's license or utility bill, is required.

The library presents educational programming around-the-clock everyday on The Library Channel, Atlanta cable channel 16. Using the Tele-Librarian feature, 730-1860, patrons may renew regular 28-day materials for another 28-day period. The helpful research specialists in the library's telephone reference office, 730-4636, can help locate answers to questions ranging from complex to whimsical.

Here are a several points of special interest in the library system:

On the main floor of the **Central Library**, Peachtree and Forsyth streets at Carnegie Way, 730-1700, is a permanent Margaret Mitchell exhibit, including the author's typewriter, manuscript and movie script pages, a brick from the Lowe's Grand Theatre (site of *Gone With the Wind's* premiere) and other items.

The **Buckhead branch** at 269 Buckhead Avenue, 814-3500, features a strikingly modern design by the Atlanta architectural firm Scogin, Elam and Bray.

In 1994 the system opened the new 50,000-square-foot **Auburn Avenue Research Library on African-American Culture and History**, Auburn Avenue at Courtland Street, 730-4001. This non-circulating reference facility houses a wealth of data in many formats, including video and audio recordings as well as CD-ROM materials. Special features are the electronic textbook *The African-American Experience: A History*, the Ethnic NewsWatch article retrieval service, Compton's Interactive Encyclopedia and a videodisc presentation of the PBS civil rights documentary *Eyes on the Prize*, narrated by former Atlantan Julian Bond.

Directly north of Grant Park and across I-20, historic Oakland Cemetery stands serenely, a Victorian time capsule surrounded by a modern metropolis. Just east of Oakland on the other side of Boulevard is another reminder of days gone by: the Fulton Bag and Cotton Mill. The mill's 2,600 workers and their families, many of whom came to Atlanta from Appalachia, lived in the adjacent mill village. Developer George Adair originally named the development Pearl Park, in honor of his daughter, but over the years it gained, and retained, a less poetic name: **Cabbagetown**.

The mill closed in 1976, but many of its residents remained in their neighborhood and found other work in Atlanta. Winter Properties Inc. of Atlanta has an ambitious $32 million plan to renovate the giant mill structure into lofts, offices and retail space before the 1996 Olympics. Cabbagetown's streets are narrow, and its modest houses are set close together. Here, as in other parts of town, good bargains on in-town homes have lured buyers. The King Memorial MARTA station serves this district.

Before we leave in-town Atlanta and head out to the surrounding areas, we'll touch briefly on **downtown Atlanta**. It's no secret that the simple presence of people going about their lives can often do more than anything else to make an area safe. And people — in the form of full-time residents — are a resource that downtown Atlanta badly needs. Other than a few high-rises and some renovated loft space, downtown Atlanta does not have the quality residential space and services needed to convince office workers to forego the commute and live where they work. With 24,000 students, Georgia State University is the second-largest institution of higher learning in the state and the largest urban university in the Southeast — but all of its students must commute, since it has no dormitories.

This picture is changing for the better. An $85.2 million complex being built at Techwood Drive and North Avenue to house 4,000 Olympic athletes in 1996 will become a dormitory for 2,000 GSU students after the Olympics. And the University's president Dr. Carl Patton, an urban planner by background, is spearheading a revitalization program of the 23-block Fairlie-Poplar district downtown. Part of the program is the renovation of the former Rialto movie theater into a concert hall for the university's performing arts groups. Dr. Patton has even proposed that the university's president's residence should be located downtown.

West of Five Points, former industrial complexes have been revitalized as the Nexus and King Plow arts centers, which include studio and residential space for artists. And the city council has formed a loft development task force to facilitate the renovation of old downtown properties into modern living and working spaces.

All this takes time, of course. Downtown Atlanta was dealt a severe blow by the closing of Rich's flagship store in 1991, not to mention the loss of other stores and businesses. But downtown, the place where the city got its start, is still dear to many Atlantans. And the tenacious spirit that prompted Atlantans to resettle and restore other historic parts of town, is still alive and well. Watch for some big improvements in downtown Atlanta as 1996 draws closer.

Atlanta County by County

Although both authors of this book live in town, we understand that city life may not be for everyone. Whether you prefer to live in the center of everything or far from the madding crowd, you'll find a wealth of options around Atlanta.

In the 1890s, the advent of streetcars made it possible for people to live some distance from where they worked. In the 1900s, the automobile accelerated that process, making more distant areas convenient to the downtown business district. After World War II, the advent of the interstate highway system created by President Dwight D. Eisenhower made it possible for Atlanta workers to commute from remote areas, some so remote they were a long day's buggy ride away in the previous century. This process, as we have seen, led to the virtual abandonment of some of Atlanta's original neighborhoods, most of which are now again attracting residents.

In this section, we'll briefly discuss the 20 counties that make up the Atlanta metropolitan region. The real estate data shown were provided by Magellan Information Services and represent home sales through the third quarter of 1994.

Fulton County

North Fulton — Principal cities/towns/communities: Alpharetta, Mountain Park, Roswell, Sandy Springs.

New homes sold: 1,891. Average price: $232,367.

Resale homes sold: 6,452; Average price: $151,627.

(1994 sales through third quarter.)

South Fulton — Principal cities/towns/communities: College Park, East Point, Fairburn, Hapeville, Palmetto, Union City.

New homes sold: 330. Average price: $109,907.

Resale homes sold: 2,765; Average price: $47,537.

(1994 sales through third quarter.)

Fulton, which contains almost all of the City of Atlanta, is Georgia's most populous county. The city divides the county into northern and southern halves whose farthest reaches are 173 miles apart.

Major north Fulton businesses include Digital Equipment Corp., Equifax, American Honda and AT&T, which employs 2,500 workers in 1 million square feet of office space. Ninety percent of North Fulton students take the SAT, and almost that many continue their education after high school. Housing opportunities range from apartments and condos to private estates and golf/tennis communities such as the Country Club of the South. Ga. 400 provides north Fulton with fast, easy access to downtown, the interstate highways and the airport.

South Fulton County's proximity to Hartsfield International Airport and its railroad infrastructure have made it a natural for commercial development: It has 12 industrial parks, the headquarters of Delta Air Lines and Chick-fil-A, a Ford plant and the facilities of many other major companies. It's also home to the internationally renowned private school Woodward Academy in College Park. The 40,000-square-foot Georgia Convention and Trade Center near the airport can accommodate groups of up to 5,000. The Southeast's only velodrome in East Point is every cyclist's dream. Homes available in this 109-square-mile district are in every category, including farm houses, luxury condos, apartments and planned communities.

DeKalb County

Principal cities/towns/communities: Avondale Estates, Chamblee, Clarkston, Decatur, Doraville, Lithonia, Stone Mountain, Pine Lake.

New homes sold: 1,065. Average price: $136,411.

Resale homes sold: 6,812; Average price: $81,322.

(1994 sales through third quarter.)

The easternmost parts of Atlanta's city limits stretch into DeKalb County; it's named for Baron de Kalb, a German nobleman who fought alongside the Americans in the Revolution. DeKalb is home to the state's largest school system and claims the lowest dropout rate; it also pays teachers the highest starting and average salaries in the state. DeKalb is home to Emory University, the U.S. Centers

A peaceful Lake Claire setting makes for a pleasant place to live.

for Disease Control and the American Cancer Society's national headquarters. DeKalb is part of the MARTA system, affording its citizens dependable transportation all around the county and Atlanta. DeKalb's housing opportunities range from inexpensive apartments to the luxury of Druid Hills estates to country living in the shadow of Stone Mountain.

shoppers northeast of Atlanta, who once faced a long drive to reach major malls in Atlanta. More than 94 percent of Gwinnett's kids achieve a high school diploma, and more than 70 percent go on to post-secondary education. The Gwinnett Civic and Cultural Center, which includes a 1,200-seat performing arts theater, opened in 1992.

Gwinnett County

Principal cities/towns/communities: Buford, Grayson, Dacula, Duluth, Lawrenceville, Lilburn, Norcross, Suwanee, Snellville.

New homes sold: 3,485. Average price: $143,917.

Resale homes sold: 7,961; Average price: $69,922.

(1994 sales through third quarter.)

This county's water towers beside I-85 have long crowed "Gwinnett is Great"— turns out they weren't joking. For some years, Gwinnett has been one of the fastest-growing counties in the United States. The giant GwinnettPlace Mall has been hugely popular with

Forsyth County

Principal cities/towns/communities: Cumming

New homes sold: 996. Average price: $178,462.

Resale homes sold: 2,221; Average price: $68,970.

(1994 sales through third quarter.)

North of Gwinnett, Forsyth County lies along the western side of Lake Lanier. The county has six interchanges on Ga. 400, which gives it great access to the city and the interstate system to the south and to the mountains in the north. The highly rated educational system includes seven elementary schools, three middle schools, two high schools and one private school.

Forsyth is home to 21 industrial parks. Housing opportunities range from apartments to lavish mansions on the hilly shores of Lake Lanier.

Barrow County

Principal cities/towns/communities: Auburn, Bethlehem, Carl, Russell, Statham, Winder.

New homes sold: 225. Average price: $87,033.

Resale homes sold: 739; Average price: $42,394.

(1994 sales through third quarter.)

Northeast of Gwinnett is Barrow County, which saw its population increase by 38 percent during the 1980s. Agriculture remains big business in Barrow: 421 farms, at an average size of 94 acres each, produce an annual economic impact of $62 million. Barrow attractions include the exotic Chateau Élan Resort and Winery in Braselton (the town that became famous when actress Kim Bassinger bought it) and the 1,850-acre Fort Yargo State Park, second in popularity only to Georgia's Stone Mountain Park among the state's parks.

Walton County

Principal cities/towns/communities: Between, Good Hope, Jersey, Loganville, Monroe, Social Circle, Walnut Grove.

New homes sold: 195. Average price: $105,621.

Resale homes sold: 967; Average price: $42,636.

(1994 sales through third quarter.)

Walton County, south of Barrow, traces its roots to 1818. Seven Walton County citizens served as Georgia's governor; two also served as U.S. senators.

Alonzo Herndon, born a slave in Social Circle, went on to found Atlanta Life Insurance Co. and become Atlanta's first African-American millionaire. There are two public schools systems (Walton County and Social Circle City), plus the 21-acre private George Walton Academy. Walton County is about 45 minutes from downtown Atlanta.

Newton County

Principal cities/towns/communities: Covington, Mansfield, Newbern, Oxford, Porterdale, Social Circle.

New homes sold: 226. Average price: $84,383.

Resale homes sold: 1,110; Average price: $43,572.

(1994 sales through third quarter.)

South of Walton, Newton County is bisected by I-20, which helps it attract big corporate players such as Mobil Chemical, Stanley Tools and Bridgestone. Eight thousand students attend Newton's one high school, two middle schools and eight elementary schools; there are also three nearby private schools. Newton was founded in 1821 and has 85 churches.

Rockdale County

Principal cities/towns/communities: Conyers, Milstead.

New homes sold: 179. Average price: $146,026.

Resale homes sold: 868; Average price: $68,091.

(1994 sales through third quarter.)

East of Newton, Rockdale County is also bisected by I-20, which makes it just a 30-minute commute to downtown Atlanta. The county's population mushroomed by 54 percent during the 1980s.

Rockdale has four major industrial parks and has attracted many international — particularly Japanese — companies: It's home to Maxell, which donated the cherry trees whose annual springtime display sparks a large festival in Conyers. Major U.S. firms here include John Deere and AT&T. The new Georgia International Horse Park in Conyers will host equestrian events during the 1996 Olympics.

Henry County

Principal cities/towns/communities: Hampton, Locust Grove, McDonough, Stockbridge.

New homes sold: 884. Average price: $117,456.

Resale homes sold: 2,194; Average price: $42,536.

(1994 sales through third quarter.)

Henry County is southeast of Rockdale and has seven interchanges on I-75. The county saw its population double in the 1980s; it has also attracted such businesses as NEC Technologies and BellSouth. Housing opportunities range from modest starter homes to lush country club communities. Henry's school system is among the state's top five in terms of increased enrollment. Henry and Clayton are the only two south metro counties with arts councils.

Clayton County

Principal cities/towns/communities: College Park, Forest Park, Jonesboro, Lake City, Lovejoy, Morrow, Riverdale.

New homes sold: 666. Average price: $103,663.

Resale homes sold: 2,767; Average price: $47,804.

(1994 sales through third quarter.)

Clayton County, northeast of Henry, is home to Hartsfield Atlanta International Airport; it's also the fictional site of the mythical plantations Tara and Twelve Oaks in *Gone With the Wind*. Houses in Clayton range from modest starters to elegant homes in planned communities and on the shores of Lake Spivey. Spivey Recital Hall on the campus of Clayton State College has been lauded as a world-class venue and hosts a performance series featuring many greats in the fields of classical music, opera and jazz. There are 26 elementary, 10 middle and seven high schools and eight private schools.

Spalding County

Principal cities/towns/communities: Experiment, Griffin, Orchard Hill, Pomona, Rover, Sunny Side, Vaughn, Zetella.

New homes sold: 70. Average price: $74,420.

Resale homes sold: 848; Average price: $38,881.

(1994 sales through third quarter.)

Below Clayton on the southern edge of the metro area is Spalding County, which offers apartments, starter homes and upscale houses. The consolidated city/county school system has 13 elementary schools, a junior high and a high school. Spalding is home to the Cherokee Rose Shooting Resort, a world-class shooting facility.

Fayette County

Principal cities/towns/communities: Brooks, Fayetteville, Peachtree City, Tyrone.

New homes sold: 522. Average price: $181,185.

Resale homes sold: 1,637; Average price: $88,814.

(1994 sales through third quarter.)

Northwest of Spalding, Fayette County's per-capita income was the highest in Georgia from 1980 to 1990. Priding itself on a balance of progress and preservation, the county has developed a master plan to direct growth well into the next century. The planned community of Peachtree City, incorporated in 1959, is home to 20,000 residents and has 40 miles of pathways for golf carts (a favored local mode of transportation) and jogging. I-85 gets commuters to downtown Atlanta with ease.

Coweta County

Principal cities/towns/communities: Corinth, Grantville, Haralson, Madras, Moreland, Newnan, Palmetto, Sargent, Senoia, Sharpsburg, Turin.

New homes sold: 663. Average price: $107,717.

Resale homes sold: 1,813; Average price: $42,746.

(1994 sales through third quarter.)

Coweta is west of Fayette in the southwestern corner of the metro area. The county saw its population increase by 37 percent during the 1980s. Newnan has many antebellum homes that survived the Civil War and has often been used as the location for movies and TV shows, particularly *I'll Fly Away*. The 2,500-acre Shenandoah Industrial and Business Park is home to a Kmart distribution center and many other companies.

Carroll County

Principal cities/towns/communities: Bowdon, Carrollton, Mt. Zion, Roopville, Temple, Villa Rica, Whitesburg.

(No sales or average price information available.)

Carroll County sits northwest of Coweta on I-20. It's home to more than 100 manufacturing firms, including Southwire, which provides jobs for 3,000. The 21 schools tout their 17.5-to-1 student-teacher ratio; there are also two private schools. Some 67 parks provide plenty of room to play.

Douglas County

Principal cities/towns/communities: Douglasville, Fairplay, Lithia Springs, Winston.

New homes sold: 363. Average price: $120,960.

Resale homes sold: 1,599; Average price: $47,139.

(1994 sales through third quarter.)

Douglas County, northeast of Carroll, is bisected by I-20; its residents can make it to downtown in just 20 minutes. There are 166 acres of county parks, 50 acres of Douglasville city parks and the 2,000-acre Sweetwater Creek State Park. The county operates 13 elementary schools, five middle schools and three high schools. Two acute-care hospitals serve residents. Douglas was recently named one of the 50 fastest growing counties in the nation.

Paulding County

Principal cities/towns/communities: Dallas, Hiram.

New homes sold: 718. Average price: $93,576.

Resale homes sold: 1,217; Average price: $37,440.

(1994 sales through third quarter.)

North of Douglas is Paulding County, which is 20 miles from Atlanta on its east side and 40 miles away on its west side.

Seventy percent of residents came here from elsewhere, and, though the county has more than 200 subdivisions, 70 percent of its land remains undeveloped. Paulding is home to the concrete manufacturer Metromont and to Shaw Industries, the world's largest carpet maker. It was recently listed as the nation's 14th fastest-growing county.

Bartow County

Principal cities/towns/communities: Adairsville, Cartersville.

(No sales or average price information available.)

Bartow is the most northwestern of the counties in the Atlanta region; it's about 50 minutes from downtown via I-75. In addition to its convenience to both the city and the nearby Blue Ridge Mountains, the county touts its cost of living (6 percent below the national average) and its educational system. Its schools boast a 17-to-1 student-teacher ratio; its students score better than the average on SAT tests; and about 70 percent of high school grads go on to seek further education. Major employers include Lever Brothers and Anheuser-Busch.

Pickens County

Principal cities/towns/communities: Jasper, Nelson, Talking Rock.

(No sales or average home price information available.)

Pickens County, the northernmost of metro Atlanta's counties, was only added to the Atlanta MSA by the Census Bureau in 1993. Its population grew by an impressive 24 percent during the 1980s. Marble has been mined here for more than 100 years. Community leaders have

recently drafted a long-range plan to manage the county's continuing growth. The major resorts Bent Tree and Big Canoe are located here. The high school and middle school offer the Industrial Technology Education Program — two of only 25 Georgia schools that offer the advanced, futuristic course of study.

Cherokee County

Principal cities/towns/communities: Ball Ground, Canton, Holly Springs, Nelson, Woodstock, Waleska.

New homes sold: 1,074. Average price: $151,424.

Resale homes sold: 2,978; Average price: $62,504.

(1994 sales through third quarter.)

South of Pickens County, Cherokee takes its name from the Native Americans who once called the area home. Sixty percent of county residents commute to work in metro Atlanta, most via I-575 and I-75. Homes are available at a wide range of prices. Canton is the site of a large marble finishing plant. The school district has 18 elementary, three middle and three high schools and a special education facility; there are also several private schools.

Cobb County

Principal cities/towns/communities: Acworth, Austell, Kennesaw, Marietta, Powder Springs, Smyrna.

New homes sold: 2,679. Average price: $160,676.

Resale homes sold: 8,383; Average price: $93,590.

(1994 sales through third quarter.)

We'll wrap up our whirlwind tour of 20 counties and 6,000 square miles with

Cobb County, Atlanta's big, powerful neighbor to the northwest. Cobb saw its population increase by 50 percent in the 1980s. It's home to more than 500 manufacturing firms including Lockheed Aeronautical Systems Co., the state's largest industry, which employs 12,000, and to Dobbins Air Force base, where *Air Force One* lands whenever America's chief executive visits Atlanta. Cobb boasts an array of attractions, including Six Flags Over Georgia, White Water and the Kennesaw Mountain National Battlefield Park. An additional boost to business is the new Cobb County Galleria Convention Centre. Two public school systems and several private schools educate the county's youth. Thanks to organizations such as the ground-breaking Theatre in the Square in Marietta, the arts are booming in Cobb.

Apartment Living

The metro area has thousands of apartments for rent at nearly every price level. Some areas, such as the Buford Highway in northeast Atlanta and the Chattahoochee River area in Cobb, have large concentrations of apartments. But you can also find apartments in areas such as Midtown and Garden Hills, which are best known for their single-family homes. In addition to the ads in the Atlanta *Journal and Constitution* and the *Marietta Daily Journal*, there are several other publications to help you find the right place to rent.

Publications

Besides the local newspaper's weekend classified section, the following publications are good sources for checking current apartment availability. Also see the Media chapter for further suggestions.

THE ATLANTA APARTMENT BOOK

1975 Century Blvd., Ste. 5   315-9998

Widely available in area grocery stores and other retail establishments, this free guide lists apartments by area with full color pictures and maps, prices and amenities. It's published quarterly.

ATLANTA APARTMENT GUIDE

3139 Campus Dr. N.W.
Norcross   417-1717

Call for your free copy of this publication that lists locations, prices, photos, maps and the special features of a broad range of rental properties.

CREATIVE LOAFING

750 Willoughby Way N.E.   688-5623

Published weekly, *CL's* cheaper classified rates attract lots of advertisers, especially for the non-complex, smaller rental sites in-town. For suburban choices, check the suburban editions: *Gwinnett Loaf* and *Topside Loaf*. Because of the affordable ad rates, the *Loafer's* ads sometimes offer more detailed descriptions. You will find these free publications in racks near groceries, drug stores, restaurants and many other retail establishments.

Apartment Locator Services

While these aren't all the apartment locator firms in Atlanta, they will give you an overview of services. Besides these locators, a free information service from Southern Bell, called the Real Consumer Tips, can be helpful. There are brief messages on how to make good use of apartment locating services, renter's insurance and apartment management services. Call 633-3336 for assistance.

APARTMENT SELECTOR
552-9255

In business since 1959, this national company has several metro offices. Offering properties of all sizes in all areas, the company provides free transportation for your apartment search seven days a week. All services are paid for by the property owner. For out-of-state rental information, call (800) 569-7368.

APARTMENTS TODAY
11285 Elkins Rd., Roswell   664-4957

For free assistance in finding your new home, this company seeks short-or long-term rentals and represents the major rental communities. Fees are paid by the owner.

FREE HOME FINDER
3652 N. Peachtree Rd.   455-1781

This firm will drive you to view properties of your choice. A free roommate match service and a newcomer kit are available. They will even pick you up at MARTA stations. All prices and sizes, furnished and unfurnished apartments are offered.

PROMOVE
3620 Piedmont Rd. N.E.   842-0042

For our money, these are the champs. Personal experience has verified the staff's high level of professionalism and helpfulness. Promove will help you narrow your choice range to focus on what's really important to you, provide you with returnable color pictures of the selected properties and answer a vast number of questions about any aspect of living in the metro area. The firm's data base is thoroughly up to the minute. The staff

here is dedicated to helping people through the significant, and somewhat stressful, experience of relocation.

Realtors

"The Atlanta real estate market remains very strong," says Maya Hahn, GRI, CRS, of the firm RE/MAX Metro Atlanta Inc. "Home prices here are below those of many other major metro areas. And with the wide range of houses on the market in many desirable neighborhoods, a great many people can afford a single-family home in Atlanta," says Hahn, a specialist in in-town properties who's eager to help you find a home in Atlanta — call 321-3123.

Like most major cities, Atlanta has a thriving real estate community with thousands of informed agents who are eager to assist you. In the Yellow Pages, 21 pages detail real estate services including appraisals, home inspections and sales. Virtually all the brokers will mail to you relocation packages, which are loaded with maps, statistics, listings of homes and lots of other useful information. Here are just a few firms among the larger real estate brokerages.

CENTURY 21 CROSS CREEK REALTY
2072 Defoors Ferry Rd. N.W.   355-2833

This is the Buckhead location from among the 40 affiliated offices in this independently owned and operated network. Virtually every section of the metro area, its suburbs and outlying counties are served by this real estate giant. Both home purchase and rental needs are handled as part of the Century 21 residential package. The core services remain the same throughout the network, while individual offices provide a variety of services including foreign language assistance.

NORTHSIDE REALTY
6065 Roswell Rd., Ste. 600 255-6937
(800)241-2540

With 850 sales associates in 23 residential branch offices, it's easy to see why many Atlantans think of Northside for their real estate needs. Georgia's largest independent real estate broker, Northside is among the top independent brokerages in the United States based on number of homes sold. In 1985, Northside was the first Atlanta real estate firm to sell more than $1 billion in residential real estate. That track record continues, with an estimated $3 million in sales each day throughout the larger metro area and surrounding counties. Solid marketing information and devotion to service are Northside hallmarks. NR Hotline, 843-1800, open round the clock every day of the week, allows you to enter a five-digit access number shown on a property's yard sign and get detailed information on the property being considered. Talk with a sales associate at any time by pressing the star (*) key. Northside's Relocation Division's services include group move assistance and personalized area tours. The corporate office listed above will direct you to the Northside office nearest you.

BUCKHEAD BROKERS
3650 Habersham Rd. N.W. 237-5227

Despite the name, this firm covers the entire metro area with nine offices. Its beginnings were in the Buckhead area, which is the office number listed above. The firm offers all real estate services, including a home rental division. The relocation office's number is 252-7030; the toll-free number is (800)989-7733. A call to the number listed in the header will direct you to the regional office serving the area of your choice.

JENNY PRUITT & ASSOCIATES REALTORS
990 Hammond Dr. 394-5400

Another multi-location presence, this firm has four offices that serve the entire metro area and are in Buckhead, Cobb County and Dunwoody and Sandy Springs. Special divisions for rental, relocation and new homes are provided. The corporate office, listed above, will put you in touch with the specific office you need.

HARRY NORMAN REALTORS
5229 Roswell Rd. N.E. 255-7505

Thirteen sales offices covering the entire northern metro area have grown from this firm's beginnings in 1930, when Harry Norman's mother started the company. Relocation is one of the firm's specialties. This service includes picking you up at the airport, making your hotel reservations and other helpful assistance.

SANFORD REALTY COMPANY
4118 Snapfinger Woods Dr. 289-8989

With 40 associates and one office location in DeKalb County, Sanford offers personalized service and a full package of real estate services. The firm provides free market analysis and property management. HUD foreclosures are one of the firm's many specialties. Acreage plus residential and commercial properties are available through Sanford's listings.

PRUDENTIAL ATLANTA REALTY
868 Buford Rd., Cumming 887-8542

Beautiful, wooded Lake Lanier is less than an hour from Atlanta. If you're looking for a home in this area, call Realtor Yvonne Godwin, a relocation specialist in business since 1986, who concentrates on properties in the Lake Lanier area.

PEGGY SLAPPEY PROPERTIES INC.

3374 Buford Dr., Buford   *932-3440*

Realtor Peggy Slappey's firm specializes in marketing new home communities. The company handles new and resale homes, primarily in the subdivisions of north Gwinnett.

Builders

BENCHMARK HOMES

2266 Fairburn Rd.
Douglasville   *949-3006*

Building homes in a wide price range, from the mid-$70s to the $300s, Benchmark is active in Cobb, South Fulton and Douglas counties. Operating since 1971, this locally owned company builds homes with a 10-year warranty. Benchmark participates in Georgia Power's Good Cents Homes Program, an energy-saving effort.

BOCK HOMES

743 Washington Ave.
Marietta   *499-1188*

Owner David Bock was named Builder of the Year in 1993 by the Greater Atlanta Home Builders Association. Active in Cobb and Cherokee counties, the company builds homes for the market from the $70s to the low $100s. Bock homes meet Georgia Power's Good Cents requirements and offer homes in carefully planned settings. As a third-generation Atlantan, David Bock puts emphasis on value teamed with affordable pricing.

JOHN WIELAND HOMES

1950 Sullivan Rd.   *497-1122*

For 24 years, this company has built fine homes in the metro Atlanta area. Prices range from the low $100s to the $400s. A transferable 10-year warranty program helps provide peace of mind for buyers. More than 30 communities in Fulton, Clayton, Fayette, Gwinnett, Forsyth, DeKalb and Cobb counties are the sites of John Wieland homes.

MACAULEY PROPERTIES UNLIMITED

2759 Delk Rd., Ste. 107
Marietta   *951-8108*

Family owned and operated, this company has built homes in 17 communities in Cobb, North Fulton and Forsyth counties since 1979. Prices range from the $100s to $300s. Macauley has won many awards, among them a national award for Best Community of the Year in the eastern region. Environmental concerns and fine architectural styling are among the company's foremost goals.

Inside
Education

Atlanta's students have powerful incentives to succeed in elementary and secondary school, and when they finish, they may choose to attend some of the nation's top universities without leaving the Atlanta area.

In addition to an overview of the four counties' public school systems, we present a look at private elementary and secondary schools, schools for special students and institutions of higher education in this chapter.

Public School Systems

The state's schools have seen significant improvement since the state passed the Quality Basic Education Act in 1986. The QBE Act established statewide standards of accountability for schools, school systems, teachers and students. It guarantees that each child will receive proper educational opportunities regardless of economics within individual local school systems. State government officials have declared education as priority No. 1 for the next decade and beyond.

If you are enrolling a child in Georgia public schools, be aware that the law requires a child to be 5 years old by September 1 to enroll in kindergarten and 6 years old by September 1 for first grade. Children below these ages who move into Georgia having attended a public or accredited private school may present proof of enrollment and previous residency for consideration.

During enrollment, parents must provide the most recent report card and/or school withdrawal documents; certification of immunizations; proof of eye, ear and dental screenings; an official copy of birth certificate; a Social Security num-

Photo: Chuck Morgan

Atlanta is home to the Georgia Institute of Technology which will host the 1996 Olympic aquatic events.

ber; and proof of residency. Immunization and health certificates must be signed by a Georgia physician or by an authorized official at a Georgia health center.

The Majority-to-Minority Program in Atlanta area schools is a viable tool for furthering integration. It allows students to transfer from a school where the student's race is in the majority to a school where his or her race is in the minority.

For a comprehensive review of Atlanta's public and private schools, call the school board of the area in which you are interested. A helpful publication, from the Atlanta Chamber of Commerce, is the *Greater Atlanta Newcomer's Guide* with some 25 pages devoted to specific school characteristics. For the Georgia Department of Education's information on other educational benefits, call 656-2800.

Here's an overview of the City of Atlanta and its surrounding four-county area, with details on each county's school system.

ATLANTA BOARD OF EDUCATION
210 Pryor St. S.W.   *827-8000*

The City of Atlanta system includes 81 elementary schools with a pupil-teacher ratio of 22-to-1, 14 middle schools with a ratio of 25-to-1, and 15 high schools with a ratio of 23-to-1.

Atlanta city schools benefit from intense community support. Business and education partnerships now exist in virtually every public school system in the metro area. One such program is the Atlanta Partnership of Business and Education. The Atlanta Chamber of Commerce takes an active role in school board elections, in creating corporate volunteer programs and in supplying expertise for school system needs.

Other support programs include Adopt-A-School and the Atlanta Collaborative on Dropout Prevention.

Besides these programs, the City of Atlanta schools are enriched by the support of the Atlanta Council of PTAs and the Mayor's Task Force on Public Education. Through combined efforts, Atlanta's public schools have made significant progress toward academic excellence. In 1989, the system had eight National Merit finalists, 14 National Achievement Finalists, 18 winners of Excellence in Scholarship Awards and four recipients of Mayor's Scholarships.

The Atlanta Magnet School Program is an impressive model for schools nationwide. The system offers some 15 four-year programs for concentration in specific fields of study. Some include on-the-job training and other work-related experiences.

The magnet schools focus on a significant range of occupation areas, such as the performing arts, international studies, communications, science and mathematics, financial services and information processing and decision-making. Other subject areas include transportation, educational careers, engineering and applied technology, language studies, fashion retailing, entrepreneurship and health care professions.

Two other programs are good examples of community support for Atlanta city schools: the Atlanta Partnership of Business & Education and Apple Corps, Inc. The Atlanta Partnership is a shining example of the pairing of businesses and schools that exists in most of the city's public schools. This joint venture between the Atlanta Chamber of Commerce and the public schools is based on two principles: one, that human beings are the primary asset in any business, industry or community organization and two, that quality education is a necessary foundation for the future. Apple Corps stands for Atlanta Parent and Public Linked for Education and is a support group focused on finding solutions to educational needs in the city's system.

COBB COUNTY PUBLIC SCHOOLS
514 Glover St., Marietta   *426-3300*

This fast-growing suburban area across the Chattahoochee River from Atlanta is the third-largest county in Georgia. With approximately 475,000 residents, Cobb County encompasses six cities and 346 square miles of territory. As the second-largest school system in Georgia, Cobb has more than 77,000 students in 55 elementary schools, 19 middle schools and 14 high schools. Cobb County is an acknowledged leader in middle school development.

All Cobb County schools are accredited by the Southern Association of Colleges and Schools. They meet or exceed standards of pupil-teacher ratio, adequacy of facilities, qualification and certification of personnel, comprehensiveness of course offerings and availability of materials. All Cobb schools also meet standards set by the Georgia Board of Education.

The pupil-teacher ratio varies by grade level and specific activity. In general, the ratio ranges from one teacher per 20 students to one teacher per 27 students. The expenditure per pupil in 1992-'93 was $4,098.

In SAT (Scholastic Assessment Test) and basic skills tests, Cobb County's public school students have exceeded state averages and compare well with national averages. The system's students also score well above average in advanced placement tests. Seventy percent of Cobb's graduates continue their education after high school graduation.

The Cobb County system is one of only 12 among 16,000 systems nationwide to have one or more schools designated as National Schools of Excellence. Cobb has six schools so designated, as well as 11 schools named as Georgia Schools of Excellence. A magnet school for the performing arts is open to all students by audition. The community school program in Cobb County offers 3,000 enrichment, recreational, vocational, special classes and activities in six school clusters.

The Special Education Department administers a full range of programs for all exceptional students, including gifted. Cobb County, along with the Marietta City Schools and the Cobb Chamber of Commerce, participates in Partners in Education, which matches businesses with schools to provide enrichment and incentives to students.

Cobb County schools garner a significant share of special honors. A few are the National Teacher of the Year in Marketing award, the Georgia Literary Meet Champions, the Georgia Academic Bowl Champions and the Georgia Geography and Spelling Bee Champions.

DEKALB COUNTY SCHOOL SYSTEM
3770 N. Decatur Rd., Decatur   297-1244

DeKalb's school district encompasses an area of 258 square miles with an enrollment of approximately 82,300 students. DeKalb's 77 elementary schools, 18 high schools and seven junior highs make it the largest school operation in Georgia.

DeKalb's median household income of $40,466 is one of the highest in the metro Atlanta area and exceeds averages for the state, the seven-state Southeast area and the United States. The level of affluence trickles down to the school system, where per-pupil expenditures rose to $5,019 for the 1993-'94 school year.

The Georgia Lottery

The subject of a lottery had been kicked around in the Georgia Legislature for years, but it only got off the ground in 1992. That November, after a tough campaign by pro- and anti-lottery forces, voters narrowly approved the lottery in a statewide referendum. The first "scratch-off" game tickets went on sale on June 29, 1993; first-day sales were an enormous $13 million. First-week sales topped $52 million.

In August 1993, the "Ca$h 3" daily numbers game debuted; then, in September, Georgians finally got a shot at the big bucks when the long-awaited Lotto Georgia "pick six" game went on-line.

In its first year, Lotto Georgia had 30 jackpot winners who claimed more than $135 million in prizes. Another 5.4 million players won a share of $57.5 million.

Georgia Lottery's proceeds are invested in education. In the first 18 months of play, the lottery's contribution to education was $221 million ahead of the General Assembly's projections. By early 1995, the Georgia Lottery Corp. had contributed more than $600 million to education.

The following is presented only as an informal introduction to the games of the Georgia Lottery. For the official rules and claims procedures, see the back of your playslip or game card. A few instant games cost $2 per ticket, otherwise, tickets for all Georgia Lottery games are $1 each; there is no sales tax on lottery tickets. Only persons 18 or older may buy Georgia Lottery tickets.

There are two basic types of Georgia Lottery games:

Instant games — These "scratch-off" tickets are sold under a variety of names, such as "Holiday Surprise" and "Instant Fun." Just tell the lottery retailer which game you want and how many tickets. The ticket's instructions will explain how to win; scratch off the covering from the gray area and see if this is your lucky day. Instant games are sold wherever you see the "Georgia Lottery" sign.

On-line games — These are "the numbers" games. Only retailers with the "Lotto Georgia" sign have the computer that prints tickets for these three games:

Lotto Georgia — Following the instructions on the back of the playslip, pick six numbers between 1 and 46 by placing a heavy vertical mark over each number you select. You may use pencil or pen but not red ink. You can play up to five different number combinations on a single playslip; if you'd like to play the same numbers for several weeks in a row, mark the "multi-draw" option on the playslip. If you make a mistake, mark the "void" box at the bottom of the panel; do not erase. Give your playslip to the retailer, whose computer will then print your ticket.

The Lotto Georgia jackpot for picking all six numbers is always at least $2 million; lesser pay-outs (determined by a pari-mutuel formula) go to winners who pick three, four or five of the six numbers. Jackpot winners receive their money in the form of a check each year for 20 years.

The Lotto Georgia drawing is held every Saturday night at 10:59 and is broadcast live from Atlanta on WSB-TV 2.

Fantasy 5 — This game is similar to Lotto Georgia, with the following differences: You pick five numbers (instead of six) from 1 through 35 (instead of 46). You can win by picking three or more numbers correctly; again, a pari-mutuel formula determines how much. The prize for picking all five is tens of thousands of dollars to $100,000 or more, depending on how many players win, and it's paid in a single jaw-dropping check.

The Fantasy 5 drawing is held every Tuesday and Friday night at 10:59 and is broadcast live from Atlanta on WSB-TV 2.

Ca$h 3 — In this game, you pick three numbers from 0 to 9. Bets are placed on whether you think your numbers will come up in the exact order (a "straight" bet) or in another order (a "box" bet). You may fill out a Ca$h 3 playslip, write your numbers on a piece of paper or tell the retailer the numbers you want to play. The Georgia Lottery's brochure on Ca$h 3 explains the different bets and pay-outs. The maximum pay-out is $500.

The Ca$h 3 drawing is held every night at 6:59 PM and broadcast live from Atlanta on WSB-TV 2.

You can let the computer pick your numbers for any on-line game: Just ask for a Quik Pik and tell the retailer which game you're playing (if you don't specify, he or she will likely assume you're playing "big lotto," as the weekly game is sometimes called).

In all on-line games, your playslip is of no value; only your computer-printed ticket is valid; if you lose a winning ticket, anyone who finds it can legally claim the prize unless you've signed the back. Prizes of up to $599 may be claimed at any on-line lottery retailer; see the back of the playslip for how to claim prizes of $600 and more.

Good luck, and remember: If you don't play, you can't win!

Statistics from the school years 1987 to 1993 showed DeKalb's per-pupil expenditures as consistently higher than the state average. Eighty-two percent of DeKalb students continue their education past high school.

All DeKalb schools meet standards of the state board of education and are accredited by the Southern Association of Colleges and Schools. In the DeKalb system, elementary schools for the most part extend through the 7th grade, with high schools serving grades 8 through 12. The county is moving to a junior high system, with seven junior high schools operating in 1994-'95. There is full-day kindergarten in every DeKalb elementary school.

An additional component in DeKalb County's system is the DeKalb Technical Institute, which provides education, training and job placement for 25,000 adults in more than 55 technical careers as the largest public post-secondary training center in Georgia.

Students in DeKalb enjoy a student-teacher ratio that ranges from 21- or 26-to-1, depending on enrollment and grade level. A majority of teachers and administrators hold a master's degree or doctorate.

DeKalb's magnet school program for students with special interests and abilities offers bountiful opportunities. There are schools for high achievers, math, science and technology, computer education, the performing arts, a writing academy and more than a half dozen foreign languages, including Russian, Japanese and Chinese.

A special feature operated by the county school system is Fernbank Science Center. This museum, classroom and woodland complex is on 65 acres of old-growth forest. It houses the nation's third-largest planetarium. The telescope in its observatory is the largest in the world dedicated primarily to public education. Each year, the STT Program (Scientific Tools and Techniques) gives nearly 200 9th- and 10th-grade students the opportunity for independent study in science and math. In 1992 Fernback drew almost 850,000 visitors from 51 Georgia counties, 50 states and 48 countries and provinces. (For more information on Fernbank, see our Kidstuff chapter.)

Special education classes serve approximately 8,500 children with special needs in specific areas, including learning disabilities, hearing, vision, speech and emotional disorders. Unique in the Southeast, and one of a handful in the country, is DeKalb's International Center. Established in 1985, the Center acts as liaison between schools and minority language students and their families. Sixty-five percent of the student population is black; 34 percent is white. The remainder is from races and ethnic groups representing 138 countries and 66 language groups.

FULTON COUNTY SCHOOLS
786 Cleveland Ave. S.W.   763-6830

Besides Atlanta, the county seat, nine other incorporated cities lie within Fulton's boundaries: Alpharetta, Roswell, Mountain Park, College Park, Hapeville, East Point, Fairburn, Palmetto and Union City. Fulton County, divided into North Fulton and South Fulton, serves all students who live in the county consisting of 420 square miles outside Atlanta's city limits.

Approximately 50,000 students attend 31 elementary schools, 11 middle schools, 11 high schools and one career/technology center. Average student-teacher ratios are from 23- or 27-to-1, depending on the grade level. Fulton County's students come from diverse backgrounds. The communities represented include rural, suburban and urban; students have the opportunity to interact with and develop understanding of a variety of people.

All Fulton County schools are accredited by the Southern Association of Colleges and Schools. All Fulton high schools have at least one business partner. One school, College Park, is the first in Georgia to offer a year-round school calendar. Kindergarten classes are part of each school. Specialized services for certain disabled students are available beginning at age 3. A limited number of schools offer half-day preschool programs for 4-year-

Insiders' Tips

Did your numbers hit? Find out by calling the Georgia Lottery's free results line: Dial GA-LUCKY. Outside the Atlanta calling area, dial the nationwide toll-free number, (800)GA-LUCKY.

olds meeting criteria. Head Start programs exist in six schools.

The system provides comprehensive programs for exceptional children with a wide range of needs including those with mental and behavior disorders, high academic talent, physical limitations and learning disabilities. School counselors implement developmental guidance programs to help students maximize their potential.

Students in the system consistently score at or above the national average on comprehensive tests and have garnered an impressive list of national and statewide competitive awards. Between 70 and 80 percent continue their education after high school.

Fulton's honors include: Georgia English Teacher of the Year, Georgia Music Educator of the Year and Presidential Award Winner for Excellence in Science Teaching. The Georgia Department of Education has named five Fulton schools as Schools of Excellence. Among many other honors, Dolvin Elementary was named a Blue Ribbon School by the U.S. Department of Education, and S. L. Lewis Elementary is named a School of Excellence by the Minnesota Educational Computer Corporation. The school system's Media Services Department has been named National Library Media Program of the Year. Banneker High School is a National School of Excellence; two other Fulton County high schools are state Schools of Excellence.

Magnet school programs in Fulton County include international studies, mathematics/science and performing arts.

GWINNETT COUNTY PUBLIC SCHOOLS
52 Gwinnett Dr., Lawrenceville   822-6508

More than 75,000 students from kindergarten to 12th grade attend 64 schools in Gwinnett County Public Schools (GCPS). As one of the fastest-growing systems, in a fast-growing county, GCPS student enrollment is projected to reach 100,000 by the year 2000. Since 1990, the school system has received the highest bond rating a governmental body can earn, according to Moody's Investors Services.

Gwinnett provides educational opportunities through its vocational education center, special education center, community schools program and the Gwinnett Technical Institute, the state's largest vocational/technical school. With approximately 8,000 employees, the school district is the largest employer in the county. Each year, GCPS receives more than 4,000 teacher applications, eventually selecting some 400 to meet its needs. The school system aims to match teachers with an increasingly diverse student population. A minority recruiter hired in 1991 has helped increase the pool of minority applicants.

The student-teacher ratio averages 25-to-1. Currently, 50 percent of Gwinnett's teachers have post graduate degrees. Teachers have an average of 10 years experience. The per-pupil expenditure in Gwinnett is more than $4,000. The system's dropout rate is 3.2 percent. Gwinnett's 1993 seniors scored above the national average on ACT tests.

Gwinnett's students and educators are recognized regularly for outstanding achievement. Eleven Gwinnett schools have been named as National Schools of Excellence; 24 as Georgia Schools of Excellence. Seventeen GCPS educators were recently honored at the national level and 35 at the state level.

GCPS graduates in the class of 1994 earned nearly $17 million in scholarships. About 80 percent continue education beyond high school. All high schools offer

Photo: Spelman College

Spelman is one of the nation's top female colleges and the oldest U.S. institution dedicated to the education of African-American women.

advanced placement courses, joint enrollment with area colleges and work/study programs.

Special programs, such as gifted education, at all grade levels in all schools are an integral part of Gwinnett's educational plan. Special education for learning disabled students and those with a wide range of mental, physical and emotional disabilities is provided. A preschool physically disabled program is offered for 3- and 4-year-olds. Full-day kindergarten is part of all elementary schools.

Many enrichment programs in art, music, foreign language, drama and debate are available. Numerous extracurricular activities centering on sports, service clubs, social clubs and intellectual stimulation are part of GCPS programs.

Active parental and community involvement are achieved through local PTAs, local school advisory committees and the business-minded Partners in Education program.

Resources

GEORGIA DEPT. OF EDUCATION
Public Information/Publications Division
2052 Twin Towers East   656-2476

SOUTHERN ASSOCIATION OF COLLEGES AND SCHOOLS
1888 Southern Ln., Decatur   329-6500

U.S. DEPT. OF EDUCATION
Secretary's Regional Representative
P.O. Box 1777, Atlanta 30301   331-2502

Private Schools

This section addresses the sizeable number of educational facilities in the metro Atlanta area that flourish apart from the public school system. They take many forms: residential preparatory, church-affiliated, Montessori, international schools and schools for students with special needs. As of 1990, the Catholic Church operated some 12 elementary schools, two high schools and one special education facility.

Curricula range from traditional liberal arts programs to those designed for the gifted or the learning disabled. Tuitions generally range anywhere from $1,000 to $30,000. Evaluating the metro area's many private schools, somewhere in the neighborhood of 150, could fill this entire book. As with the public schools, space permits only an overview. The Atlanta Chamber's *Education* booklet provides extensive information on these schools. Be assured whatever your child's needs — academically gifted, learning disabled, developmentally delayed and all shades in between — the Atlanta area schools stand ready with an appropriate program.

The Atlanta Area Association of Independent Schools publishes a complete directory of schools belonging to the association; call the association at 923-9230, for a rundown. For more information on Catholic schools, call the Catholic Archdiocese of Atlanta, 888-7833.

The Southern Association of Independent Schools Executive Director Tom Redmond may be reached at 458-7300. The Georgia Independent School Association's Executive Director Morvis Johnson may be reached in Griffin, Georgia, at 227-3456. The Bureau of Jewish Education's office number is 873-1248.

Experienced teachers and parents offer a few tips when checking out a school. Talk with the principal and inspect the school. Ask your neighbors or business associates if they have knowledge of a school's reputation. And ask to speak with a few parents of children in the school being considered.

One recommended source of information is *The Atlanta Area Independent School Directory* by Jan Cleveland. It's published by Resource Publications Inc., P. O. Box 532, Morrow, Georgia 30260. This helpful book is quite comprehensive and offers a wealth of information for parents seeking excellence in education.

A second source is the *Bunting and Lyon Blue Book: Private Independent Schools 1994*. This 47th annual guide to U.S. elementary and secondary schools is published by Bunting and Lyon Inc., 238 N. Main Street, Wallingford, Connecticut 06492; (203)269-3333. (Most likely it's available in your public library.)

In this overview we present a sampling of schools by county.

Cobb County

COBB ACADEMY
2871 Cherokee St. N.W., Kennesaw 943-7038

An independent, interdenominational school founded in 1985, Cobb Academy serves a Montessori preschool through grade 10. Cobb Academy encourages a strong parent-school relationship. Its Montessori curriculum includes intensive phonics in a strong liberal arts program in small classes. After-school care is offered until 5:30 PM.

LA PETITE ACADEMY
1100 Mt. Bethel Dr.
Marietta   977-8892

This school was established in 1970 to serve children from 6 weeks to 12 years old. As part of a nationwide educational chain, La Petite has many locations throughout the metro area. The curriculum is called Learning for Living, which the school says is a modified Montessori method. After-school care is given until 6:30 PM.

SHREINER SCHOOL
1340 Terrell Mill Rd.
Marietta   953-1340

Employing a curriculum expressly designed for the school, this facility was founded in 1980 for preschool through grade 6. It's said to have one of the largest preschools in Georgia. Traditional class structure is enhanced by foreign language and computer instruction, among many other offerings.

THE WALKER SCHOOL
700 Allgood Rd., Marietta   427-2689

Since its inception in 1957, this independent day school has focused on a college prep program for its students. The students served are from 4-year-old kindergarten through grade 12. Three science labs, a large gym/auditorium and two libraries are campus features. After-school care is available.

DeKalb County

DEKALB CHRISTIAN ACADEMY
1985 LaVista Rd. N.E.   325-8540

Since 1959, this academy has offered a combination of traditional class structure and special programs for students from kindergarten through grade 12. Eight buildings are set on the school's 25-acre site. The academy's philosophy

is "to provide a quality education with eternal perspective."

HEBREW ACADEMY
5200 Northland Dr.   634-7388

Founded in 1953, the Hebrew Academy offers a child-centered traditional approach in a curriculum specially designed for the school. Students attend classes in pre-kindergarten through 8th grade. Science and computer labs, music and art centers accompany classes in Hebrew.

ST. MARTIN'S EPISCOPAL SCHOOL
3110-A Ashford-Dunwoody Rd.   237-4260

Academic excellence with a Christian orientation characterizes this school, founded in 1959 for preschool to 6th grade students. The school enjoys an adopt-a-school relationship with Oglethorpe University (Atlanta), which provides many enrichment programs for the students. After-school care is offered until 6 PM.

ST. PIUS X CATHOLIC HIGH SCHOOL
2674 Johnson Rd. N.E.   636-3023

Based on faith and religious belief, this 37-year-old school offers three levels of instruction: accelerated, college prep and remedial. The philosophy is to help students develop individual potential, build the community and foster service to others. A traditional class structure serves students in grades 9 through 12.

MARIST SCHOOL
3790 Ashford-Dunwoody Rd. N.E. 457-7201

This Catholic college prep school educates boys and girls in grades 7 through 12. Founded in 1901 in downtown Atlanta, the school moved to its present 57-acre campus in 1962. Marist is owned and operated by the Marist Society of Georgia, a nonprofit corporation. While the majority of students are Catholic, the school accepts and welcomes qualifying students of any race, creed or national origin.

The staff includes approximately 90 full-time teachers plus about a dozen administrators, more than three-quarters of whom hold master's degrees. Advanced placement classes are offered.

Fulton County

GALLOWAY SCHOOL
215 W. Wieuca Rd.   *252-8389*

Galloway was founded in 1969 by Elliott Galloway on the principle that children need to learn the values of common decency and dignity along with the arts, physical fitness, problem solving and collaborative skills. Serving students from pre-kindergarten through grade 12, the school sits on a hill overlooking Chastain Park in the Buckhead section of north Atlanta. Within the past several years, almost all the interior spaces in the original hand-hewn brick main building were extensively renovated. Additionally, a new 24-classroom building was constructed.

THE HEISKELL SCHOOL
3260 Northside Dr.   *262-2233*

This nondenominational Christian school was founded in 1949 with a traditional class structure. The school is based on the belief that a child's home, church and school should complement each other. Students served are from 2 years old to 7th grade. Academic excellence is stressed as are learning responsibility and the history of the United States.

LOVETT SCHOOL
4075 Paces Ferry Rd. N.W.   *262-3032*

On a picturesque 100-acre setting, Lovett aims to develop the whole child in all aspects of its programs. This college prep school was founded in 1926 and serves students from 4-year-old kindergarten through grade 12. Total development of each child, in academic, moral and spiritual training, is offered in a supportive atmosphere. After-school care is available.

PACE ACADEMY
966 W. Paces Ferry Rd.   *262-1345*

Pace Academy, established in 1958 for students in kindergarten through 12th grade, emphasizes an atmosphere of caring and personalized attention. The school's stated philosophy is "to have the courage to strive for excellence." The traditional college prep curriculum includes advanced placement classes and honors classes. An extensive service program fosters good citizenship.

TRINITY SCHOOL
3254 Northside Pkwy. N.W.   *237-9286*

In an atmosphere that fosters self esteem, this academic preschool and elementary school offers experiential learning. Founded in 1951, Trinity has a literary-based reading program. Programs are designed for children from age 2 to grade 6. After-school care is available.

WESTMINSTER SCHOOLS
1424 W. Paces Ferry Rd. N.W.   *355-8673*

Founded in 1951, the schools challenge students from kindergarten through 12th grade with a rigorous academic program based on Christian philosophy. Divided by age groups, Westminster is situated on a 180-acre campus with tennis courts, a pool, a gym, playing fields and more. The traditional curriculum is college preparatory, while the school's philosophy aims to develop the whole person for college and life through excellent education.

WOODWARD ACADEMY

1662 Rugby Ave., College Park   765-8262

Woodward was founded in 1900 by Col. John Charles Woodward as Georgia Military Academy. In the mid-1960s the school dropped the military focus, went coeducational and was renamed in honor of the founder. The curriculum is college prep with a traditional structure.

The diverse student population of 1,800 studies on three campuses, two of which are in south Fulton County (one for kindergarten through grade 12, the other for pre-kindergarten through grade 6) and a third in north Fulton County for grades pre-kindergarten through grade 6.

Woodward has third generation students from some Atlanta families and about 30 alumni employed on campus. Day and boarding students are accepted. Woodward operates nearly 20 bus routes daily, transporting some 700 students.

YESHIVA HIGH SCHOOL OF ATLANTA

3130 Raymond Dr.   451-5299

This school was recognized as exemplary by the United States Department of Education. The traditional class structure is offered in dual curriculum, half-day in Judaic/Hebraic studies and half-day in general studies. The 50,000-square-foot facility sits on a 10-acre site. The students served are in grades 8 through 12.

Gwinnett County

CORNERSTONE CHRISTIAN SCHOOL

4102 U.S. 78, Lilburn   488-2157

This Christian day school was founded in 1982 to serve students from 4-year-old kindergarten through grade 12. Cornerstone offers a traditional class structure. After-school care is available.

COUNTRY BROOK MONTESSORI SCHOOL

2164 Norcross-Tucker Rd.
Norcross   446-2397

An academic preschool and grade school founded in 1983, the facility serves children from age 2 to 9. As just one of the Montessori schools in the metro area, Country Brook also offers after-school care. The teachers are trained in the Montessori curriculum, which supports full development of children in all aspects.

GREATER ATLANTA CHRISTIAN SCHOOL

1575 Indian Trail School
Norcross   923-9230

Founded in 1968 for children pre-kindergarten through grade 12, this four-campus school system offers a traditional class structure. It has campus locations on McGarrity Road; McDonough, south of Atlanta; Fairburn, southwest of the city; and Smyrna, northwest of the city. The Norcross campus is northeast of Atlanta. After-school care is available for preschoolers and elementary students.

Special Schools

Approximately 40 institutions exist for students with special needs beyond the public school system or private school programs. These needs encompass a wide range of physical, mental and emotional needs. For more information, call United Way of Metropolitan Atlanta, 527-7200, or a local county school board for referral. A multitude of Atlanta agencies and organizations exist to lend assistance.

CEREBRAL PALSY CENTER - CHILDREN'S REHABILITATION CENTER OF ATLANTA

1815 Ponce de Leon Ave. N.E.   377-3836

Services for children from birth to 6 years are designed for moderate to severely developmentally delayed, those with multiple handicaps and those with neuromuscular and musculoskeletal disorders. This center serves Fulton and DeKalb counties.

EASTER SEAL
CHILD DEVELOPMENT CENTER
55 Coca Cola Pl.   *589-3586*

This special school helps to ready disabled children from age 6 months to 5 years for mainstream schools. Therapy services are provided as needed.

EASTER SEAL OF ATLANTA
2030 Powers Ferry Rd. N.W., Ste. 140 980-1744

This organization provides integrated multidisciplinary treatment programs for infants and preschoolers with disabilities.

GEORGIA ASSOCIATION FOR CHILDREN
AND ADULTS WITH LEARNING DISABILITIES
2779-G Clairmont R. N.E.   633-1236

This organization offers services to assist those diagnosed with slight to severe learning disabilities.

GEORGIA CENTER
FOR THE MULTI-HANDICAPPED
542 Church St., Decatur   378-5433

This school offers comprehensive psycho-educational and medical evaluations and planning for children from birth to age 21. Admission is through review by a screening committee to determine eligibility, appropriateness and need. Educational evaluation is made through a fully equipped diagnostic classroom. Evaluations are made in the areas of occupational therapy, general medicine, psychology and speech therapy as well as others.

GEORGIA EASTER SEAL SOCIETY
1900 Emery St. N.W., Ste. 106 351-6551

This school offers comprehensive services for disabled children from birth to age 5. Equipment is available for loan. A summer program and family camp weekend are special features.

Special Needs Resources

ASSOCIATION FOR
RETARDED CITIZENS OF GEORGIA
1851 Ram Runway, Ste. 104
College Park   761-3150

AUTISM SOCIETY OF
AMERICA, GEORGIA CHAPTER
2830 Clearview Pl.   451-0954

RETARDED CITIZENS/ATLANTA
1687 Tullie Cr., Ste. 110   321-0877

THE PSYCHOLOGICAL CENTER
(TESTING CENTER)
Dept. of Psychology
Emory University   727-7451

Colleges and Universities

Atlanta's richly varied colleges and universities make it a magnet for students and teachers from around the world. Here are institutions specializing in a wide range of studies from engineering, law and medicine to religion, art and fashion design.

Beyond their own academic programs, Atlanta's colleges and universities give their students the broader benefits associated with life in a major city that is home to people from every culture. The Atlanta environment yields great possibilities for enhancing education — through arts and cultural events, interaction with the business world, the resources of other area schools and daily exposure to people from all walks of life.

Among major U.S. cities, Atlanta ranks sixth in the percentage (26.9) of citizens with four or more years of college. Some 95,700 students are currently pursuing more than 350 programs of study in metro area colleges and universities.

Following is a brief look at some of Atlanta's institutions of higher learning.

AGNES SCOTT COLLEGE
141 E. College Ave., Decatur   371-6285

Six miles east of downtown Atlanta, Agnes Scott College is a private, four-year liberal arts college for women. Founded in 1889 by Decatur Presbyterian Church, it was named for the mother of industrialist and developer Col. G.W. Scott; his $112,000 gift to the school was the largest contribution to education ever made in Georgia at that time. In 1907, Agnes Scott became the first of Georgia's colleges and universities to be accredited.

Today Agnes Scott's 600 students come from 28 states and 18 countries. The college boasts an 8-to-1 student-faculty ratio; the average class size is 13; 97 percent of the faculty hold doctorates. About 16 percent of students are adult women returning to college to complete degree work. The library maintains extensive collections relating to Robert Frost, who vis-

ited the college 20 times, and Catherine Marshall, alumna, class of '36.

A $23 million renovation program marked the college's centennial year in 1989. ASC's many fine Gothic- and Victorian-style buildings are situated on a 100-acre campus distinguished by broad lawns, old trees and winding brick walks. Portions of 17 movies and TV shows have been filmed here, including *A Man Called Peter*, *Fried Green Tomatoes* and *I'll Fly Away*.

THE ART INSTITUTE OF ATLANTA
3376 Peachtree Rd. N.E.   266-1341

The Art Institute of Atlanta was founded in 1972 and includes The Fashion Institute of Atlanta, The Music Business Institute and The School of Culinary Arts. The institute offers associate of arts degrees in culinary arts, fashion marketing, interior design, music entertainment management, photographic imaging and visual communications. Diploma programs are offered in advertising design, commercial photography and residential interiors.

This five-story Peachtree Road facility houses The Art Institute of Atlanta, which includes The Fashion Institute of Atlanta, The Music Business Institute and The School of Culinary Arts.

The institute's facilities include IBM and Macintosh computer labs, a 24-track recording studio with twin control rooms, a multi-camera video studio, audio and video editing suites, photography studios and labs.

ATLANTA COLLEGE OF ART

1280 Peachtree St. N.E.   898-1163

Founded in 1928, Atlanta College of Art offers a four-year program leading to a bachelor of fine arts degree. As a founding member of the Woodruff Arts Center, ACA is the only art college in the United States that shares a campus with three major arts organizations: the High Museum of Art, the Alliance Theatre and the Atlanta Symphony Orchestra. Woodruff Arts Center is in Midtown and is served by the Arts Center MARTA station.

Of ACA's 437 students, about 120 are housed on-campus in the six-story Lombardy Hall. The college has 23 full-time and 50 adjunct professors; the student-faculty ratio is 12-to-1. The college's 88,000 square feet of space includes studios, darkrooms, a sculpture building with a woodshop and foundry, a 400-seat auditorium and a 3,850-square-foot gallery.

ATLANTA METROPOLITAN COLLEGE

1630 Stewart Ave. S.W.   756-4440

A coeducational, nonresidential institution, Atlanta Metropolitan College was founded in 1974 and today has more than 1,800 students. The college's 83-acre campus includes wooded areas and a lake; additional facilities are planned for future development.

AMC offers programs leading to associate's degrees in arts, science and applied science. The college offers extensive developmental studies programs for students requiring help with basic English, math and reading skills, and it has a cooperative program with Atlanta Area Technical School.

BAUDER COLLEGE

Phipps Plaza
3500 Peachtree Rd. N.E.   237-7573

A college in a mall? It sounds too good to be true, but Bauder's "campus" is also home to Saks Fifth Avenue, Lord & Taylor, Parisian and (opening in 1996) Bloomingdale's. The college was founded in 1964 and offers associate of arts degrees in fashion merchandising, fashion design, interior design and an optional program in finishing and modeling. Theoretical knowledge and applied skills are emphasized and provided through a variety of teaching techniques.

Atlanta itself is an important part of the students' education: their college is at one of the Southeast's leading fashion malls in a city that's a regional design and wholesale center — home to the Atlanta Apparel Mart, the Atlanta Merchandise Mart and the Atlanta Decorative Arts Center, the second-largest freestanding design center in the nation.

Bauder has dormitory apartments, for female students only, two blocks from the college.

COLUMBIA THEOLOGICAL SEMINARY

701 Columbia Dr., Decatur   378-8821

Founded in South Carolina in 1828, Columbia Theological Seminary relocated in 1927 to a 57-acre campus in Decatur. Affiliated with the Presbyterian Church (USA), Columbia has 640 students working toward master's (divinity, theological studies, theology) and doctoral (ministry, theology) degrees.

The school also attracts clergy and lay persons from across the nation to its seminars, retreats and continuing education programs. Its center for Asian ministries provides exchange programs and educational opportunities for Korean-American churches.

DEKALB COLLEGE

3251 Panthersville Rd., Decatur   244-5090

DeKalb College's 16,349 students are divided among its four campuses: Decatur, Clarkston, Lawrenceville and Dunwoody. They work toward two-year associate's degrees in arts, science and applied science.

The average age of the students is 25; under the college's flexible schedule, classes are offered in the day, evening and on Saturdays, allowing students to earn their degree while fulfilling their responsibilities of work and family. A special College on TV program lets participating students view classes and earn credits with a minimal number of visits to a campus.

Two-thirds of students work more than 20 hours a week and attend college part-time. Since DeKalb College first held classes at its original Clarkston campus in 1964, more than a half-million students have passed through the system. DeKalb is the third-largest college in the University System of Georgia.

DEVRY INSTITUTE OF TECHNOLOGY

250 N. Arcadia Ave., Decatur   292-7900

DeVry/Atlanta, established in 1969, moved to its own 22-acre campus in 1985 and now has more than 2,800 students. The age of the average student is 26; 20 percent receive military benefits.

The institute confers bachelor's degrees in accounting, business operations, computer information systems, electronics engineering technology, science of technology management and an associate's degree in applied science in electronics. The school boasts a student-to-computer ratio of 7-to-1 and reports that 85 percent of a recent term's graduates found work in their chosen field within six months of graduation.

EMORY UNIVERSITY

1380 S. Oxford Rd. N.E.   727-6123

Emory had just 15 students when it began back in 1836; today more than 10,000 (representing all 50 states) are enrolled there. In addition to the 631-acre Atlanta campus, Emory has a two-year division, Oxford College, in Covington, Georgia, 38 miles east of Atlanta.

Emory is made up of the 49-major undergraduate liberal arts Emory College and the schools of medicine, nursing, theology, law, business, arts and sciences and public health. The undergraduate student-faculty ratio is 10-to-1. Emory's seven libraries house 2.2 million volumes.

In 1980, Emory received the assets of the Emily and Ernest Woodruff Fund; the $105 million gift was the largest ever given to a philanthropically supported institution up to that time. The value of the fund had grown to $560 million by 1992. Since 1987, Emory has increased the size of its physical plant by 25 percent, building or acquiring more than 1.4 million square feet. Especially notable is the Michael C. Carlos Museum on campus (designed by famous architect Michael Graves). Emory University Hospital is a nationally known medical facility (and a favorite of ailing celebrities).

GEORGIA STATE UNIVERSITY

University Plaza   651-2000

In downtown Atlanta just east of Five Points, GSU is the second-largest institution of higher learning in Georgia and the largest urban university in the Southeast. GSU has its own MARTA rail station, used daily by about 10,000 students, faculty and staff. The university has a total of 24,000 students.

There are 50 academic departments at GSU, divided among six colleges: arts and sciences, business administration, education, health sciences, law and public and urban affairs. There are 125 student organizations on campus, an award-winning student newspaper (*The Signal*) and a popular 100,000-watt student radio station (WRAS 88.5-FM).

As GSU has no dormitories, all its students must commute — but that's about to change. An $85.2 million complex being built to house 4,000 Olympic athletes will be converted after the Games into permanent dorm facilities for 2,000 students. GSU's physical education complex will be remodeled to host the Olympic badminton competition. And the university is raising money to renovate the Rialto Theater, a former downtown movie theater, as a concert hall for performing arts groups.

GEORGIA TECH
GEORGIA INSTITUTE OF TECHNOLOGY
225 North Ave. N.W.   *894-2000*

Georgia Tech's reputation extends light years beyond its 330-acre campus west of the Downtown Connector near Midtown. In a recent ranking, *U.S. News and World Report* named Tech No. 1 in the industrial and manufacturing programs and praised its schools of mechanical engineering, ranked seventh nationally; aerospace engineering, ranked fifth nationally; and civil engineering, ranked ninth nationally.

During the 1996 Games, Tech will be known to people around the world as the Olympic Village. It will also be the site of an aquatics center, the venue for swimming, diving, synchronized swimming and water polo. The village's population will include about 16,000 athletes and officials. Immediately after the Olympics, Tech will host the 1996 Paralympic Games for physically challenged athletes, using many of the same facilities the Olympics used.

Georgia Tech was established in 1885 and has fared especially well in the past 20 years. Its nearly 13,000 students are enrolled in five colleges: architecture, computing, engineering, sciences, management, policy and international affairs.

Tech's student radio station is WREK 91.1-FM; its mascot is the Yellow Jacket; its nemesis is Bulldog of the University of Georgia, Athens; and its unofficial dining room is the Varsity, the world's largest drive-in, conveniently located just across the North Avenue bridge from campus.

JOHN MARSHALL LAW SCHOOL
805 Peachtree St., Ste. 400   *872-3593*

In Midtown, John Marshall Law School was founded in 1933. The school has five full-time faculty members as well as a full-time librarian and assistant librarian. Day and night classes are offered. The number of John Marshall students who pass the Georgia Bar Exam the first time they take it has risen from 20 percent to 60 percent in the last three years. The school has 460 students and confers the doctor of jurisprudence degree.

KELLER GRADUATE
SCHOOL OF MANAGEMENT
250 N. Arcadia Ave., Decatur   *298-9942*

Founded in Chicago in 1973, Keller's MBA program has grown to become one of the largest and most successful in the country. In 1987, Keller acquired the DeVry Institute system. Keller's Atlanta center opened in 1993; today the school operates 17 centers in six states.

In addition to the MBA, Keller offers master of human resource management and master of project management programs. The programs are geared toward working adults, who often find it easy to continue their studies at another Keller center if they are transferred to another city. In addition to the main campus, Keller has a northside facility at Perimeter Center.

KENNESAW STATE COLLEGE
3455 Frey Lake Rd. N.W.
Kennesaw   *423-6000*

More than 12,000 students attend classes at Kennesaw State, which was founded in 1964. Today, it's nationally recognized as an innovative, teaching-oriented college, offering a wide variety of undergraduate studies in the arts, sciences, education and business, as well as graduate degrees in business, education, accounting and public administration.

Off I-75 10 miles north of Marietta, Kennesaw State's enrollment includes many traditional and nontraditional students: The average student age is 27.

LIFE COLLEGE
1269 Barclay Cr., Marietta   *424-0554*

Founded with 22 students in 1974, Life College is now the single-largest chiropractic college in the world and has the world's largest chiropractic library. It has 15 buildings, almost 3,500 students and more than 180 faculty members.

Life confers the degrees doctor of chiropractic, bachelor of business administration, bachelor of science in nutrition for the chiropractic sciences and master of sports health science. The college has more than 50 service, social and fraternal clubs and many sports teams, including a nationally ranked rugby team.

MERCER UNIVERSITY
Cecil B. Day Campus
3001 Mercer University Dr.   *986-3419*

The second-largest Baptist-affiliated institution in the world, Mercer University was founded in 1833 and is based in Macon, Georgia. It was rated one of the

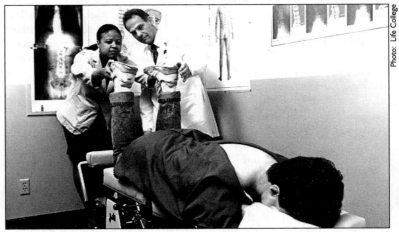

Photo: Life College

Ten percent of all the world's chiropractors are graduates of Life College in Marietta, the largest chiropractic college in the world.

top-six universities in the South by *U.S. News and World Report* in 1994. The Cecil B. Day Campus in Atlanta is known as Mercer's Graduate and Professional Center, although it also offers undergraduate programs.

Mercer's 971 full-time and 745 part-time students at the Atlanta campus study programs including pharmacy, business and economics, graduate teacher education and engineering. University College, Mercer's continuing education department, serves about 1,800 students at six centers throughout central Georgia and metro Atlanta.

OGLETHORPE UNIVERSITY
4484 Peachtree Rd.   *261-1441*

Named for the founder of Georgia, James Edward Oglethorpe, Oglethorpe University was founded in 1835 by Georgia Presbyterians to train ministers. It was originally located near Milledgeville, at that time the capital city of Georgia. During the Civil War, the university's students became soldiers, its buildings became barracks and hospitals, and its endowment became worthless Confederate bonds. The college closed in 1862 and tried unsuccessfully to reorganize in Atlanta during Reconstruction.

Oglethorpe University was rechartered in 1913; two years later the cornerstone was laid for the present 118-acre campus, whose layout and Gothic Revival architecture were inspired by Corpus Christi College, Oxford, England, the honorary alma mater of James Oglethorpe.

The university's 1,215 students hail from 31 states and 32 nations. The student-faculty ratio is 13-to-1; 96 percent of faculty members hold terminal degrees. Internships are available in all of the school's 27 academic majors

Atlanta University Center

Atlanta University Center is a consortium of six historically black colleges in southwest Atlanta. Together, the six colleges form the largest predominantly African-American private institute of higher learning in the nation.

Although the six institutions share a library and cooperate in many areas, they remain distinct from one another. Following is a look at Atlanta University Center's six member colleges.

CLARK ATLANTA UNIVERSITY
James P. Brawley Dr. and Fair St.   *880-8000*

Clark Atlanta University was formed in 1988 through the consolidation of Atlanta University, founded in 1865, and Clark College, founded in 1869. CAU is one of only two private, comprehensive, historically black universities in the nation offering programs of instruction and research from bachelor to doctorate degrees.

CAU's 4,480-member student body is 68 percent female. The university provides on-campus housing for 1,600 students. The student-faculty ratio is 16-to-1. Several of CAU's dormitories provided the setting for Spike Lee's movie *School Daze*. CAU operates the all-jazz radio station WCLK 91.9-FM.

INTERDENOMINATIONAL THEOLOGICAL SEMINARY
671 Beckwith St. S.W.   *527-7700*

Established in 1958, the Interdenominational Theological Seminary is made up of six separate seminaries: Gammon Theological Seminary, United Methodist, founded in 1872; Charles H. Mason Theological Seminary, Church of God in Christ, founded in 1970; Morehouse School of Religion, Baptist, founded in

1867; Phillips School of Theology, Christian Methodist Episcopal, founded in 1944; Johnson C. Smith Theological Seminary, Presbyterian Church USA, founded in 1867; and Turner Theological Seminary, African Methodist Episcopal, founded in 1885.

ITC's 331 students come from 27 states and seven nations. ITC offers master's (divinity, Christian education, and church music) and doctoral (ministry, sacred theology) degrees.

Since its formation in 1958, ITC has graduated more than 35 percent of all trained black ministers in the world.

MOREHOUSE COLLEGE
830 Westview Dr. S.W.   *681-2800*

Established as Augusta Institute in Augusta, Georgia, in 1867, this college relocated to Atlanta in 1879, where it was first known as Atlanta Baptist College and then, in 1913, as Morehouse College.

Today Morehouse is the nation's only predominantly African-American, all-male liberal arts college. Its 2,990 students represent 43 states and 11 foreign countries; more than half graduate high school in the top 20 percent of their class. Of its 150 faculty members, 74 percent hold terminal degrees. Morehouse confers bachelor of arts, bachelor of science and interdisciplinary bachelor of science degrees in 36 major areas of study.

Morehouse's most famous alumnus was Nobel laureate Dr. Martin Luther King Jr.; Morehouse is also where filmmaker Spike Lee spent his "School Daze." Fourteen Morehouse men have gone on to serve as president of a college or university.

MOREHOUSE SCHOOL OF MEDICINE
720 Westview Dr. S.W.   *752-1500*

Morehouse School of Medicine began with 24 students in 1975; today it has 160 students and a faculty of 176. MSM confers the four-year doctor of medicine degree and the Ph.D. degree in biomedical sciences.

Residency programs have been established in family medicine, internal medicine, preventive medicine, psychiatry and surgery. In conjunction with testing services to be performed, the Atlanta Committee for the Olympic Games is providing $1 million to help MSM establish a research laboratory to study sports performance-enhancing drugs.

MORRIS BROWN COLLEGE
643 Martin Luther King Jr. Dr. N.W.   220-0270

In 1885, Morris Brown College first held classes for 107 students in a wooden building at the corner of Boulevard and Houston, today known as John Wesley Dobbs Avenue. Its name honors the memory of the second consecrated bishop in the African Methodist Episcopal Church; the college was founded through the generosity of the members of Big Bethel AME on Auburn Avenue.

For the past 47 years, Morris Brown College has been fully and continuously accredited by the Southern Association of Colleges and Schools. Its faculty members take pride in motivating not only average and better than average students but also those considered to be high risk. Today MBC's 1,750 students are pursuing degrees in more than 40 areas of study.

SPELMAN COLLEGE
350 Spelman Ln. S.W.   *681-3643*

Founded in 1881, Spelman College is the oldest U.S. institution with the education of African-American women as its primary mission. Recent years have brought new recognition to the long-respected school: Spelman was listed

Quality
live-in child care...

with a special European *flair*.

- carefully screened European au pairs
- about $170/week for any size family
- AuPairCare counselors in your area

800-4-AUPAIR

AuPairCare

among the top 10 U.S. women's colleges and the top 10 Southeast colleges in *Money* magazine's list of college "best buys." Applications for admission increased by 92 percent between 1986 and 1991. In 1993, Spelman received 3,713 applications for 450 freshman openings. Dr. Johnetta B. Cole declined an offer to serve as U.S. secretary of education in the incoming Clinton administration in order to remain as Spelman's president.

Spelman has 1,943 students and a student-faculty ratio of 15-to-1. More than 81 percent of full-time faculty have doc-torate or other terminal degrees. Nearly half the students are engaged in some form of community service; 37 percent major in math or the natural sciences. Upon graduation, 45 percent of Spelman women continue their studies.

This year, 1995, marks a new milestone for Spelman, whose first class for 11 students was held in the basement of Friendship Baptist Church: The college will celebrate the opening of a new 92,000-square-foot academic center made possible by a $20 million grant from entertainer Bill Cosby and his wife Camille.

Inside
Medical Care

If you have to get sick or injured, you've come to the right place. As a regional center for health care, the Atlanta area offers a rare combination of top-quality health care with enviable accessibility.

According to the Georgia Hospital Association, anywhere in the 20-county radius surrounding the city is within a 15- to 20-minute drive of a major acute care hospital. Further, Georgia has one doctor for every 510 people, a ratio that is 26 percent above the national average.

The wealth of good doctors and medical facilities says a lot about the desirability of the Atlanta area as a place to live. It also reflects the steady stream of new doctors, nurses and allied health professionals graduating from the many training centers in the metro and surrounding areas.

Medical students train at Emory University's School of Medicine and Morehouse School of Medicine, while future pharmacists study at Mercer University's Southern School of Pharmacy. Nursing programs are offered at Clayton State College, DeKalb College, Emory University, Georgia State University, Kennesaw State College, Morris Brown College and Oglethorpe University.

Programs leading to careers as hospital administrators, licensed practical nurses, medical technologists, laboratory technicians and occupational, physical, respiratory and speech therapists find their place in the curricula of many schools. Within driving distance of Atlanta are the Medical College of Georgia Schools of Medicine and Nursing and the Mercer College of Medicine in Macon.

Health-related research at these schools benefits Atlantans as well as thousands of health care seekers from all parts of the United States and the world. Because Atlanta is a national center in medical research, residents have the opportunity to participate in many clinical research trials that evaluate new treatments.

Since there are 50 or so medical facilities of varying sizes within the four-county area we focus on, and dozens more within close range, we can't do justice to their multispeciality programs in one chapter. We are, instead, providing an overview. Consider our thumbnail sketches the tip of the iceberg, and know that whatever your medical need, there are skilled and dedicated health care professionals in the Atlanta area ready to serve you.

As with the rest of this book, we present hospitals within the perimeter of I-285 as being in the city of Atlanta and list those outside the perimeter by county. All these institutions are within the area code (404), which is one of the largest in the nation. In some locations, it may be necessary for you to dial the area code before the actual phone number, depending on the distances involved.

For urgent care, many hospitals have established walk-in clinics with procedures that quickly funnel more difficult cases to their major facility. A sampling of these are included at the end of this chapter, along with information about hospice care.

Numbers to Call

When an emergency arises or you need general information and direction to community resources, refer to this list for assistance.

For emergencies requiring ambulance, police or fire departments   911

Aging Helpline	248-7998
AID Atlanta	872-0600
American Hospital Association	936-0331
Atlanta Healthcare Alliance	350-4300
Georgia Dental Association	636-7553
Georgia Hospital Association	955-0324
Georgia Psychological Association	876-7535
Georgia Poison Center	589-4400
Georgia Registry for Interpreters for the Deaf	299-9500
Medical Association of Atlanta Information and Referral Service	881-1714
Medical Association of Georgia	876-7535
Mental Health Association of Georgia	634-2850
Mental Health Association of Metropolitan Atlanta	527-7175

Hospitals

As this book is being printed, many area hospitals are realigning themselves into systems designed to better use their resources. In most cases, there will be no name changes, and services will likely not change in any drastic way.

At press time, three major metro hospital systems had joined to form an alliance called Promina Health System, the largest nonprofit hospital system in Georgia. Promina Health System has 10 hospitals. The Columbia/HCA Healthcare Corporation has eight metro hospitals under its wing. Industry expectations are that additional alliances will be made in the future.

At present, the metro members of the Promina Health System are the six-hospital Northwest Georgia Health System based in Cobb County, Piedmont Hospital in Atlanta's Buckhead district and Gwinnett Health System in Gwinnett County.

The metropolitan Atlanta area has 11 strategically located trauma centers, listed below. A rating of Level I trauma care indicates the hospital offers the most extensive, immediate and round-the-clock services for emergency, life-threatening needs. A Level II rating indicates 24-hour capability for surgery and specialty care. A Level III rating means these services, surgery and specialty care, are usually available within 30 minutes to 1 hour.

If your interest is in improving your state of health, a wealth of wellness programs awaits you in Atlanta. Virtually every metro-area hospital offers a barrage of programs designed to promote good health and fitness. A call to the facility's help/referral line will yield answers to your request.

Amidst Atlanta's towering trees and rolling landscape, thousands of well-trained professionals toil around the clock to provide an excellent standard of health care for visitors and residents alike. Rest assured that whatever your health care need, from childbirth to geriatric medicine, from disease prevention to treatment for chronic illness, you can find the right assistance at the right time.

Atlanta

CRAWFORD LONG
HOSPITAL OF EMORY UNIVERSITY
555 Peachtree St. N.E.   **686-4411**

Crawford Long is designated as host hospital for the 1966 Olympic Games by the Atlanta Olympic Organizing Committee. As part of the Emory University System of Health Care, this 583-bed hospital is staffed by EU School of Medicine faculty as well as community physicians.

A wide spectrum of services is offered, including four 12-bed adult intensive care units, a Level III neonatal intensive care unit and a two-chamber hyperbaric oxygen unit. Extensive women's services are a specialty, as is family-centered maternal and infant care. The hospital's nursery is based on the developmental model for premature and ill babies.

Crawford Long was one of the first facilities in Georgia to have a cancer program approved by the American College of Surgeons. The hospital pioneered a treatment for prostate cancer called cryosurgery, which offers a shorter recovery period than traditional methods.

DEKALB MEDICAL CENTER
2701 N. Decatur Rd.
Decatur   **501-1000**

Offering a medical staff of more than 600 physicians in 42 specialty areas, this 525-bed general acute care hospital is owned by DeKalb County Hospital Au-

thority. Some 2,400 employees tend patients in this not-for-profit facility.

Among DeKalb Medical Center's special services are a diabetes center, an arthritis care center, a cancer center and a wellness center. For sudden cardiac problems, the Chest Pain Emergency Center provides quick assistance. It has a Level III Trauma Center.

Located in an industrial park, the hospital's WorksWell Occupational Health Services Center designs individual treatment plans for each worker's needs. Opened in 1993, the 107,000-square-foot Surgery and Maternity Center is part of the hospital's TenderCare Maternity Services. This new center has transformed DeKalb's obstetrical and surgical facilities into one of the area's premier programs.

EGLESTON CHILDREN'S
HOSPITAL AT EMORY UNIVERSITY
1405 Clifton Rd. N.E.   **325-6000**

Founded in 1916, Egleston Children's Hospital, a 235-bed facility, is the heart of Georgia's largest children's health care system, Egleston Children's Health Care System. More than 100,000 children each year are treated at the hospital and in 10 neighborhood centers by 130 of the top pediatricians throughout metro Atlanta. As a major referral center for the Southeast, the system has several nationally recognized programs, including the Childhood Cancer Center and the Emory Egleston Children's Heart Center.

The hospital provides comprehensive pediatric care ranging from the diagnosis and treatment of ear infections to complex diseases including heart surgery and organ transplants. Its affiliation with Emory University and its location on the Emory campus give it distinct advantages. As a clinical, teaching and research institution, the hospital offers all subspecialities in medical care. It enjoys a Level I rating for trauma care.

Egleston excels in several areas, including treatment of cystic fibrosis, transplants and care for brain tumors, orthopedics, medical-psychiatry patients and premature infants. Among Egleston's technological innovations are the high-frequency ventilators for newborns that can breathe for a baby at a 600 to 900 breaths per minute (instead of a baby's usual 40 to 60) to help immature lungs heal faster.

Each year, more than 500 heart surgeries are performed at Egleston Children's Hospital. It is the state's only pediatric facility to perform a full range of pediatric transplants.

Outpatient services and treatment for minor injuries or illnesses are part of the hospital's pediatric network. With satellite clinics located in Gwinnett, Cobb, Fulton and DeKalb counties, Egleston's excellent services are within easy range of many metro residents.

EMORY UNIVERSITY HOSPITAL
1364 Clifton Rd. N.E. 727-4881

From its roots in 1905, Emory University Hospital has grown in reputation and excellence with each decade. For the second time in a row, the hospital has ranked ninth in the nation in cardiology care, according to an annual list compiled by *U.S. News & World Report*. On this list of the country's best hospitals, Emory was 34th in orthopedics and 41st in urology. The ratings, published July 1994, ranked the nation's 1,488 hospitals affiliated with research and teaching institutions.

The university-owned, not-for-profit institution has 604 beds, including 491 beds in the main facility, 56 in the Center for Rehabilitation Medicine, 47 beds for psychiatric treatment in the Uppergate Pavilion and a number of beds for research purposes. Thirteen percent of the total beds are dedicated to intensive care. The hospital staff numbers nearly 3,000 employees, with more than 400 physicians and scientific professionals holding staff privileges.

Emory provides the full range of specialized care characteristic. Besides cardiology, the notable specialities include multiple organ, tissue and bone marrow transplants, oncology, hematology and neurosurgery.

Emory Hospital, part of the Emory University System of Health Care (EUSHC), is a division of the Robert W. Woodruff Health Sciences Center of Emory University. The Center consists of six divisions: Emory Hospital; the schools of medicine, nursing and public health; Crawford Long Hospital; and the Yerkes Regional Primate Research Center.

The Emory Clinic is the setting for patient care and group practices of the more than 600 physicians who teach at Emory's schools of medicine and public health. EUSHC has affiliations with private community hospitals throughout Georgia.

GEORGIA BAPTIST MEDICAL CENTER
300 Boulevard N.E. 653-4000

From its 93-year heritage, Georgia Baptist has grown to more than 500 beds and approximately 2,500 employees. The facility's nursing school, established in 1902, now offers a four-year degree program that meets nurses' more demanding roles in today's health care field.

The not-for-profit, general acute care institution has several centers of excellence, including heart, cancer, orthopaedics and maternal-child care. Georgia Baptist's Cancer Center is based on a multidisciplinary approach to cancer care, employing a team of

Photo: Georgia Baptist Medical Center

The nursing school at Georgia Baptist Medical Center was established in 1902.

social workers, psychologists, psychiatrists and chaplains.

Georgia Baptist offers such highly technical services as cardiothoracic surgery with technology capable of sustaining the heart through critical surgery. Physical, occupational and speech rehabilitation therapies are comprehensive.

Atlanta's first and only hospital-based aeromedical service is based at Georgia Baptist. The LifeFlight program travels a 100-mile radius and is fully staffed for extreme emergencies. The hospital's five satellite facilities are located in the outlying areas of Morrow, Fayetteville, Palmetto, Stockbridge and Cumming.

GRADY MEMORIAL HOSPITAL
80 Butler St. S.E.   *616-4307*

This 1,100-bed hospital is named for Henry Grady, the editor of the *Atlanta Constitution* newspaper who inspired Atlantans with a vision of a "New South" following the Civil War. Grady Memorial is located in heart of downtown Atlanta. With more than 4,500 employees, the general and acute care facility is owned by the Fulton County Hospital Authority.

Grady is a teaching hospital for Emory University and Morehouse Schools of Medicine. The facility is undergoing a massive renovation to further extend its scope of available services.

The hospital's excellence has drawn recognition from many national publications, such as *Reader's Digest* and *USA Today,* for its position as one of the nation's best emergency and trauma care centers. In meeting the most stringent requirements as a Level I Trauma Center, Grady provides round-the-clock care in surgery, anesthesia and specialized services such as neurosurgery and obstetrical surgery. Physicians treat more than 750 cases daily among Grady's five emergency clinics. With annual averages of more than 55,000 admissions and 900,000 outpatient visits, Grady qualifies as one of the busiest trauma units in the nation.

A full range of services includes a regional perinatal center for high-risk mothers and babies, a diagnostic imaging center and a radiation therapy center. The hospital is a designated regional burn center and offers a 388-bed long-term care facility, neonatal intensive care nursery, diabetes detection and control center, sickle cell center and a rape crisis center. The Grady Health System infectious disease program has set national standards in providing comprehensive health care for HIV-positive and AIDS patients.

HUGHES SPALDING PEDIATRIC HOSPITAL
35 Butler St. 616-4307

In 1992, a century after its medical mission began at Grady Hospital, the facilities for children's care moved to a freestanding facility near Grady. Hughes Spalding provides excellent care for a full range of children's medical needs.

It is the site of Georgia Poison Control Center. Staff of this center provide emergency advice by phone to almost 10,000 parents and medical professionals per month through this state-supported program. More than two-thirds of the lives saved through these efforts are of children younger than 6.

METROPOLITAN HOSPITAL
3223 Howell Mill Rd. N.W. 351-0500

Metropolitan Hospital is a community hospital offering a variety of medical services combined with in-town convenience. Surgery procedures span a wide range, including general surgery, endoscopic/video surgery and cosmetic surgery. Among the hospital's specialties is treatment for impotence.

An orthopaedic/sports medicine clinic offers comprehensive services. Specialty areas include Women's Services, a Sinus Center, an Eye Care Center and treatment for urological problems.

NORTHSIDE HOSPITAL
1000 Johnson Ferry Rd. N.E. 851-8000

More than 1,000 staff physicians deliver more than 8,300 babies a year in Northside's 19 labor/delivery rooms.

Thus it has earned the nickname "the Baby Factory" and ranks as one of the top 25 hospitals in the nation for deliveries. The hospital provides a diagnostic center for high-risk pregnancies.

Northside's Institute for Cancer Control diagnoses more than 1,000 new cancer patients each year, which puts it in the top 15 percent of community hospitals nationwide. The hospital's ScreenAtlanta program uses a mobile van with diagnostic equipment and a professional medical staff to bring low-or no-cost cancer screening and education to the metro area.

Among ScreenAtlanta services are screenings for colorectal; oral and skin cancer; mammograms; self exam instruction for breast and testicular cancer; and cancer risk assessments. Northside's blood pressure, diabetes and cholesterol screenings have been awarded recognition from the American Cancer Society. Care for mental disorders includes three outpatient mental health centers and a fully accredited sleep disorders center.

PIEDMONT HOSPITAL
1968 Peachtree Rd. N.W. 605-5000

Throughout most of this century, Piedmont Hospital has mirrored the growth of the Buckhead district in which it is located. Beginning with a 10-bed sanatorium in 1905, it now has a 458-bed acute care and a 42-bed extended care/skilled nursing care facility on its 26-acre site on Peachtree Road. More than 2,000 employees and a medical staff of 750 physicians offer care in every major category of medicine in this private, not-for-profit, non-tax-supported hospital.

Situated on a ridge nicknamed "Heartbreak Hill" by the approximately 50,000 runners in the annual Peachtree Road Race, Piedmont is known for its centers of excellence. These include obstetrics and women's services, ophthalmology, diagnostic services, microsurgery, neuroscience and cardiology. Newly opened, The Heart Center at Piedmont centralizes all cardiac care, including catheterization, angioplasty, open heart surgery and prevention programs.

Because of staff expertise in orthopaedics and sports medicine, the facility's physicians are the team doctors for the Braves, the Hawks and the Falcons. The hospital's Level III 24-hour Emergency Department has a helipad atop the building.

With 18,000 inpatient admissions and 93,000 outpatient visits annually, Piedmont Hospital qualifies to serve as a clinical rotation site for nursing students from Emory University, Georgia State University and Kennesaw College School of Nursing, as well as residents from Emory University School of Medicine and Mercer University Southern School of Pharmacy.

SAINT JOSEPH'S HOSPITAL
5665 Peachtree Dunwoody Rd. N.E.   851-7001

This is Atlanta's first hospital, established in 1880 by the Sisters of Mercy. A private, not-for-profit, 364-bed facility, it counts cardiac care, cancer care and orthopaedic care as three speciality areas. Medical staff includes more than 700 physicians.

Well established as a regional referral hospital, Saint Joseph's provides outreach health care through two mobile testing units. Good Moves is a mobile mammography program that visits corporate sites as well as homeless shelters. Mercy Mobile provides economically disadvantaged Atlantans with general health screenings.

Saint Joseph's has scored a number of firsts in cardiac care: first in the Southeast to perform open-heart surgery, to de-

velop a comprehensive cardiac catheterization lab and to open a pacemaker clinic. It performs more than 1,000 vascular procedures annually and more cardiac procedures than most medical facilities in the country.

In 1993, the hospital began taking part in the National Cancer Institute's prostate cancer prevention study. Currently the hospital offers more than 90 clinical trials investigating various therapies for cancer and cancer prevention. The hospital's orthopaedic program provides such specialized treatment as bone fracture realignments, knee ligament repairs, joint replacements, joint and cartilage transplantations, as well as the treatment of penetrating bone infections and soft tissue injuries.

SCOTTISH RITE
CHILDREN'S MEDICAL CENTER
1001 Johnson Ferry Rd. N.E.   256-5252

This north Atlanta multispeciality pediatric center has received national attention for its orthopedic advances and is gaining a reputation for excellence in plastic and reconstructive surgery, especially of craniofacial disorders and skin discolorations.

Since its founding in 1915, Scottish Rite has grown to 165 beds and 1,400 employees. The hospital provides general pediatric services as well as advanced subspecialty care in some 40 specialties, retaining more than 500 doctors and dentists. The hospital offers 27 single-specialty clinics, 13 multispeciality clinics and 10 surgical suites in which 10,500 surgical procedures are performed annually.

Board-certified pediatricians staff Scottish Rite's 24-hour pediatric Level I emergency/trauma center. Each year, 43,000 emergency/trauma center visits are logged.

With satellite clinics located in Gwinnett and Cobb counties, Scottish

Photo: Chuck Morgan

Founded in 1915, Scottish Rite provides pediatric care through more than 500 doctors and dentists.

Rite is part of the Pediatric Emergency Network that provides crisis intervention nearby where a child lives or was injured.

SOUTH FULTON MEDICAL CENTER
1170 Cleveland Ave.
East Point 305-4533

For more than 25 years, South Fulton has provided a wide spectrum of medical services to the Atlanta area. It is located conveniently between downtown Atlanta and Hartsfield Airport.

The 388-bed hospital employs more than 1,000 people to care for patients in its various specialty clinics. A full-service cardiology department and the Community Cancer Center provide comprehensive treatment.

Among other areas of concentration are the Small Wonders Newborn Center, a new Diagnostic Imaging Laboratory and a center for rehabilitation. A newly renovated Outpatient Surgery Area offers patients up-to-the-minute health care with added efficiency. South Fulton also offers vascular laboratory and renal dialysis services.

Plans are under way for expanded women's services. The hospital's Health Advancement Clinic is augmented by an array of support groups and screenings to promote wellness.

SOUTHWEST HOSPITAL AND MEDICAL CENTER
501 Fairburn Rd. S.W. 699-1111

Southwest dates back to 1943, when the Society of Catholic Medical Mission Sisters established the Catholic Colored Clinic in response to a lack of adequate medical care in south Atlanta. By 1974, governance of the hospital had passed to a Board of Trustees with an official name being bestowed in 1975. Southwest proudly proclaims its status as one of only 10 institutions of its kind in the nation that is owned, governed and managed by African Americans.

The 125-bed acute care hospital's medical staff includes more than 200 physicians. In 1981, Southwest formed an affiliation with Morehouse School of Medicine for clinical training and services. The facility's Primary Care Center specializes in the treatment of children and adolescents. The full range of inpatient and outpatient services includes laparoscopic surgery and maternity care.

Southwest's cardiopulmonary department offers respiratory therapy, EKG and EEG testing, rehabilitation and physical therapy. A program for asthma intervention and education helps patients cope with that illness.

A first phase of new equipment acquisitions gained a state-of-the-art cysto table essential to endourological surgery for the department of urology. Recent construction on the campus is the $8.5 million Fulton County Department of Family and Children's Services. This facility is designed to provide health care and social services to Medicaid and Medicare clients as well as to those who receive public assistance.

V.A. MEDICAL CENTER-ATLANTA
1670 Clairmont Rd.
Decatur   *321-6111*

For our visitors and new residents who are veterans, this federally owned hospital provides general acute care in addition to a wide range of other services. With nearly 600 beds and more than 2,000 employees, the VA Hospital, as it is commonly called, is well prepared to provide patients with quality medical care.

Special services include cardiac catheterization, open heart surgery and a special team devoted to amputations. The VA Hospital offers prosthetics programs for veterans with complex amputations. Other specialities are designed for rehabilitation; eye, ear, nose and throat ailments; psychiatric needs; and alcohol and substance abuse.

WESLEY WOODS GERIATRIC HOSPITAL
1821 Clifton Rd. N.E.   *728-6200*

Wesley Woods Geriatric Hospital is a not-for-profit teaching and research hospital located in the lovely, old, Druid Hills section of Atlanta. The site is close to Emory University School of Medicine, with which the hospital is affiliated. The 100-bed outpatient and acute care hospital is staffed by board-certified internists and geriatricians, among whom are Emory faculty physicians and community physicians.

Its outpatient services include geriatric primary care, neurology, ophthalmology and dentistry, as well as other major specialities. A geriatric evaluation and management service is designed to help patients handle the activities of daily living. Rehabilitation programs encourage increased energy and strength.

Evaluation of patterns and management of Alzheimer's disease takes place in Wesley Woods' Memory Assessment Clinic. The Movement Disorders Services specializes in care and treatment of Parkinson's and Huntington's diseases.

In addition to the hospital, Wesley Woods offers three residential programs: The Towers Apartments, Budd Terrace for intermediate nursing care and The Health Center for those requiring 24-hour nursing services.

WEST PACES MEDICAL CENTER
3200 Howell Mill Rd. N.W.   *351-0351*

With approximately 300 beds and more than 800 employees, West Paces offers a substantial array of medical care. This includes general acute care, psychiatric, rehabilitation and alcohol and substance abuse programs.

The Cancer Center at West Paces offers comprehensive care for patients from diagnosis to all stages of treatment. The center is affiliated with the University of Alabama, Birmingham, to provide the most progressive programs available.

Patients may avail themselves of a wide spectrum of surgical procedures at the West Paces Georgia Laser Center.

At the Diabetes Center, advanced insulin therapy is given via insulin pumps and a treatment known as the Glucommander.

The hospital's Center for Mental Health offers many programs designed to reduce stress and alleviate anxiety. The Center for Women, the Wound Care Center and corporate health services are additional areas of focus. The hospital's Greater Atlanta Sports Medicine program offers education and research, orthopaedic evaluation, treatment and rehabilitation.

Atlanta Specialty Hospitals

CPC PARKWOOD
1999 Cliff Valley Way N.E.   *633-8431*

CPC Parkwood is a 152-bed psychiatric and chemical dependency facility with specialized programs for children, adolescents and adults. Separate programs are offered for each age group.

The hospital provides flexibility for patients' needs. The CPC Parkwood continuum offers acute inpatient treatment, intermediate treatment care, partial hospitalization, evening partial hospitalization and aftercare.

Treatment for a variety of problems, including sexual or physical abuse, anxiety and depression, takes place on a relaxed campus setting. A 24-hour helpline is available, as is assistance with transportation when needed.

HILLSIDE PSYCHIATRIC HOSPITAL
690 Courtenay Dr. N.E.   *875-4551*

From its origins in 1888, Hillside is Atlanta's oldest social service agency. Its various roles demonstrate great flexibility in responding to the changing needs of the community.

Originally founded as a home for needy children, today Hillside is a licensed psychiatric hospital serving children and adolescents from ages 10 to 18. The 61-bed facility offers individualized psychotherapy, as well as group and family therapy.

Hillside's licensed special education program enables youngsters to continue their schooling. Diagnostic services for severely emotionally disturbed patients are available. With both open and closed facilities, Hillside provides the appropriate setting for a wide range of needs.

The hospital's excellent programs are designed to return the whole child to a well state. Activity therapy, art therapy, speech and language therapy, administered by members of Hillside's 100-employee staff, contribute to a child's progress. Twenty-four hour nursing and an extensive aftercare program are part of Hillside's comprehensive treatment.

LAUREL HEIGHTS HOSPITAL
934 Briarcliff Rd.   *888-7860*

This licensed psychiatric hospital has more than 100 beds and approximately 150 employees on staff. Laurel Heights offers intensive residential care for children and adolescents, ages 5 to 17, and their families.

The hospital provides psychiatric care on specific tracks appropriate for the patient's needs. Among them are a dual-diagnosis chemical dependency track, a sexual abuse track, a substance abuse track and a track for children who are firesetters.

Year-round schooling is offered so patients can continue their education. Laurel Heights' progressive treatment includes an Experiential Challenge Program, which is a ropes course that fosters self esteem and independence. Family programs are an integral part of the facility's services.

MIDTOWN HOSPITAL
144 Ponce De Leon Ave. N.E.   875-3411

Midtown Hospital is a speciality hospital for women. It is recognized for providing personalized treatment for women's concerns, such as pregnancy, abortions and contraception.

The 21-bed facility is staffed by 48 employees. General gynecology services are available to patients, in addition to such surgical procedures as tubal ligations. Patients may take part in genetic studies and receive consultation on the results.

PSYCHIATRIC INSTITUTE OF ATLANTA
811 Juniper St. N.E.   881-5800

Part of the Brawner Health Care System, P. I. Atlanta, as it is commonly referred to, is a 40-bed psychiatric and rehabilitation facility. This private speciality hospital provides both inpatient and outpatient care for adults experiencing acute or chronic disorders.

P. I. Atlanta is founded on the philosophy of combining the latest advances in treatment with a safe, caring and therapeutic setting. The programs are supported by a staff of 70 employees.

Free assessments are offered 24 hours a day, seven days a week. Both day and evening outpatient programs ease coordination of patients' schedules. Among P. I. Atlanta's programs are those designed to assist with alcohol and substance abuse, anxiety and depression.

SHEPHERD CENTER
2020 Peachtree Rd. N.W.   352-2020

This hospital is the largest facility in the United States dedicated exclusively to the care of patients with paralyzing spinal cord injuries and neuromuscular diseases. It is one of 13 hospitals designated by the U.S. Department of Education as a Model Spinal Cord Injury System Program.

Founded in August 1975, the 100-bed facility has an eight-bed intensive care unit for patients with traumatic injuries. In May 1992, a $23 million expansion was opened to provide expanded outpatient facilities. Also added were an aquatics center with a 25-yard pool, a fully equipped fitness center and a 20-bed unit for younger patients.

Among Shepherd's inpatient and outpatient services are a comprehensive Multiple Sclerosis Center, a special program for ventilator-dependent patients, a Fertility Clinic that makes fatherhood possible for paralyzed men and a career planning/placement program to assist patients in employment.

Multiple community-based programs, such as a seating clinic for expert consultation on wheelchair and other mobility devices, round out Shepherd's whole-person approach.

VENCOR HOSPITAL ATLANTA
705 Juniper St.   873-2871

Vencor Hospital is a licensed long-term acute care hospital specializing in extended care for the medically complex

Photo: Egleston Children's Health Care System

Egleston Children's Health Care System treats more than 100,000 children each year.

patient. Particular focus is on pulmonary services for the ventilator-dependent patient. Most of Vencor's patients transfer from other acute care hospitals' intensive care units.

A full range of medical services is available to Vencor patients, including renal dialysis, orthopedic care and diagnostic radiology. Psychiatric treatment and support groups address the psychological needs of patients.

A regional referral center, Vencor Atlanta patients come from a five-state area. One-hundred and seventy-five employees staff this 72-bed hospital.

Fulton County

CHARTER PEACHFORD HOSPITAL
2151 Peachford Rd.   *455-3200*

Charter Peachford's mission is the care of psychiatric illnesses and addictive disease in adults, adolescents and children. More than 19,000 patients have been served at the facility since it opened in 1973.

Comprehensive programs for the treatment of alcohol and substance abuse are offered. The hospital's programs are available for inpatients, those who are partially hospitalized and for outpatients in the day and evening.

Charter Peachford has specialized plans for patients with dual diagnoses, chronic pain and eating disorders. Specific orientation programs are part of the hospital's spectrum — for example,

women's issues, geriatric patients and those with codependency issues.

Charter Peachford has a 24-hour admission policy. Intervention services are offered, and counselors are available 24 hours a day.

NORTH FULTON REGIONAL HOSPITAL
3000 Hospital Blvd.
Roswell   *751-2500*

As a Level II Trauma Center, North Fulton Regional provides seven-day, 24-hour in-house anesthesia and operating room coverage. For more than a decade, the 168-bed hospital has offered general acute care to the rapidly growing areas north of metro Atlanta, including the townships of Roswell and Alpharetta.

Nearly 900 employees provide support to patients in this full-service medical/surgical community hospital. Treatment for major illnesses, such as cancer and heart problems, are part of North Fulton's programs. The hospital provides care in the areas of nuclear medicine, women's services (including obstetrics), orthopaedic services, diagnostic radiology and renal dialysis.

Individualized treatment in The Renaissance Rehabilitation Center focuses on progressive care that enables patients to return to normal life quickly. A neonatal care unit tends to the needs of infants born preterm. Special sports medicine programs and a sleep disorder center are available.

North Fulton offers outpatient surgery procedures in addition to a fully staffed emergency room. The hospital's ongoing series of health education pro-

---

Take part in special opportunities to volunteer in area hospices.

Insiders' Tips

grams is designed to raise the level of health awareness in the community. These are augmented by periodic screening programs and support groups.

Cobb County

BRAWNER PSYCHIATRIC INSTITUTE
3180 S. Atlanta Rd.
Smyrna   436-0081

Brawner Psychiatric Institute is a fully accredited hospital that has offered psychiatric and substance abuse treatment for adolescents and adults since 1910. The 108-bed hospital occupies 32 wooded acres in Smyrna. Treatment space and administrative offices are joined by a dining hall, school gymnasium, indoor pool and outside recreation areas. A recovery residence also is available, providing a halfway house setting during transitions.

Brawner's progressive programs are available to inpatients, outpatients and partial hospitalization patients. Adult treatment programs include those focused on eating disorders and the trauma of sexual abuse. Adolescents at Brawner continue their education at the campus Brookside School, with teachers certified by the Georgia Department of Education.

Brawner offers a summer partial-hospitalization day program for children ages 6 to 12 with Attention Deficit Hyperactivity Disorder (ADHD).

A new service called intensive 23-hour stabilization serves patients in acute crisis with immediate intensive treatment to prevent full hospitalization. The 23-hour category also helps meet certain restrictions of insurance coverage.

COBB HOSPITAL AND MEDICAL CENTER
3950 Austell Rd.
Austell   732-4000

Located in south central Cobb County, this 322-bed hospital creates a baby boom of its own in its innovative service called The Family Birthplace. A prime example of family-centered care, the Birthplace enables mother and baby to be cared for in one private birth suite from admission to discharge. The convenience of flexible visitation hours is an added bonus. For babies with special needs, Cobb offers advanced care in its Level II nursery.

As part of an alliance called Northwest Georgia Health Systems and the overall Promina system, Cobb Hospital enjoys the advantages of sharing advanced medical services and equipment with its sister hospitals. With more than 1,000 employees providing care to patients, Cobb Hospital is a full-service facility conveniently located near metro Atlanta as well as Cobb County.

PROMINA KENNESTONE HOSPITAL
677 Church St.
Marietta   793-5000

As a Level II Adult Trauma Center, Kennestone Hospital serves a vital need for high-level medical expertise. Located near the Kennesaw Mountain National Battlefield Park, the Hospital has 539 beds and more than 3,000 employees.

This general acute care hospital is also a part of the alliance called Northwest Georgia Health Systems, which gives its access to a shared pool of resources. Its full range of comprehensive services provides medical care for Cobb County residents, as well as those in the surrounding areas.

THE PROMINA WINDY HILL HOSPITAL
2540 Windy Hill Rd.
Marietta   644-1000

Another member of Northwest Georgia Health Systems, Kennestone Hospital at Windy Hill is a 115-bed hospital for general acute care. Three hundred employees make up a well-trained and caring staff.

Kennestone at Windy Hill offers a wide range of medical services. Among these are extensive women's programs in such areas as low-dose mammography and breast ultrasound. Treatment for substance abuse takes place through an intervention unit and a combined medical/psychiatric program. Comprehensive care is available through Kennestone at Windy Hill's pain management program, occupational health clinic, headache clinic and rehabilitation/evaluation program. The hospital's chronic pain management program is nationally accredited.

RIDGEVIEW INSTITUTE

3995 S. Cobb Dr.
Smyrna 434-4567

Ridgeview Institute, a private, nonprofit psychiatric hospital, was established in 1976. Ridgeview offers treatment for a broad range of mental health and addiction problems, with specialty programs designed for children, adolescents and adults of all ages.

The hospital's comprehensive continuum-of-care philosophy operates through various stages: inpatient, partial hospitalization, outpatient and continuing care. Overall, Ridgeview's streamlined programs keep costs down and promote a prompt return to job, family and community.

One of a minority of hospitals in the country not owned or managed by a healthcare corporation, Ridgeview has treated more than 25,000 patients from all 50 states and several foreign countries. The ACTION program for chemical dependence is an intensive partial hospitalization program for adolescents. The New Life Christian Treatment Programs for adolescents and adults are offered. These programs are designed to promote both spiritual and emotional growth by integrating Biblical principles with the highest quality clinical care and treatment methods.

In the past year, Ridgeview has added two new elements: the Older Adults Partial Hospitalization Program and provision of home healthcare for the emotionally disturbed through an association with Catholic Social Services.

The Women's Center at Ridgeview offers sophisticated treatment for eating disorders and survival of trauma such as sexual abuse. Ridgeview's 24-hour assessment program, available on call to local hospitals lacking a psychiatric unit, features a mobile assessment team with a clinician available around the clock.

SMYRNA HOSPITAL

2049 S. Cobb Dr.
Smyrna 434-9710

Providing general acute care, Smyrna Hospital is a 100-bed facility with 400 employees. Cobb County residents in need of cardiac care saw progress in the opening of The Emory Heart Center at Smyrna. The heart center's relationship with Emory University Hospital and Crawford Long Hospital is one in a series of cooperative ventures between Smyrna Hospital and other medical institutions.

Located next to Smyrna Hospital, this new center offers patients the expertise for which Emory cardiologists are known throughout the South. The Emory physicians are available round the clock through the hospital's emergency center. The new service enables cardiac patients to keep the same doctor should they need to go outside Cobb County for cardiac services not yet available in their home county.

In another collaboration, three Emory otolaryngologists have associated with Smyna Hospital's Sinus Center. This team offers expanded treatment of all conditions of the ear, nose, throat and neck, as well as acute and chronic sinus disorders and audiology services.

Smyrna Hospital's Foot and Ankle Center is staffed by a team of specialists from throughout metro Atlanta to offer state-of-the-art medical care. Heel pain syndrome is one of the special needs treated in this center. Plans are under way for a Pain Center at Smyrna Hospital. This center will offer comprehensive treatment for chronic pain and provide all services needed for pain management.

DeKalb County

DECATUR HOSPITAL
450 N. Candler St.
Decatur   377-0221

This 120-bed hospital, supported by a well-trained staff of nearly 200 employees, offers high level medical technology for general acute care. It is located in the picturesque town of Decatur, the DeKalb County seat that proudly traces its origins to predate Atlanta's by some 20 years.

Decatur Hospital is considered a leader in laser surgery, using four types of lasers in various procedures including those for the eye, general surgery and gynecological problems. A comprehensive adult alcohol and chemical dependency program is offered. The hospital's program for eating disorders is a specialty.

NORTHLAKE REGIONAL MEDICAL CENTER
1455 Montreal Rd.
Tucker   270-3000

Offering general acute care in a broad range of medical services, Northlake Regional is also known as HCA Northlake Regional (as part of the Hospital Corporation of America). The 120-bed hospital's special services include maternity care,

oncology, cardiology, orthopaedics and podiatry.

Maternity care takes place in The Birthplace, which has private labor/delivery/recovery/postpartum suites. Northlake's childbirth education program, called "Birthsense," helps prepare parents for their baby's arrival. A newborn intensive care unit stands ready to assist babies in need of special care.

From the spectrum of surgical procedures available are general surgery, neurosurgery, podiatric reconstructive surgery, plastic reconstructive surgery, vascular and orthopaedic surgery. Same Day outpatient surgery services are offered.

Northlake's extensive rehabilitative programs include physical therapy, respiratory therapy and occupational and speech therapy. For diagnoses of illness, the hospital uses the latest technology, such as nuclear medicine, magnetic resonance imaging, ultrasound, EKG and EEG. For women, the Womancare Breast Diagnostic Center provides comprehensive care.

The hospital is home to the Advanced Georgia Laser Center, a diabetes treatment center and an industrial medicine program. Northlake Regional's 24-hour emergency department is staffed with board-certified doctors.

DUNWOODY MEDICAL CENTER
4575 N. Shallowford Rd.   454-2000

Formerly called Shallowford Hospital, Dunwoody Medical Center provides surgical services, an intensive care unit, a coronary care unit, a gastroenterology lab and a cardiac catheterization lab. The 24-hour Level III Emergency Services offer cardiac monitoring, radiology services, advanced cardiac life support and advanced trauma support.

The recently completed Women's Pavilion features 10 labor/delivery/recovery suites and a Mother-Baby Unit with 28 well-appointed private rooms. Accommodations for fathers or significant others are provided. An aspect of the family-centered care at Dunwoody Medical Center is encouragement of unlimited sibling visits to the new mother and infant. The hospital's Neonatal Intensive Unit is under the supervision of a board-certified neonatologist.

Doctors certified in all the major medical specialties, including neurosurgery and cardiology, are on staff. Childbirth classes, a Women's Resource Center and educational series offer education to area residents.

Gwinnett County

Founded in 1959, the Gwinnett Hospital System (GHS) was established as a not-for-profit healthcare organization to provide high quality medical care to its neighbors.

Among many collaborative ventures involving several support organizations is the Care-a-Van, a mobile health unit providing on-site education and screening for business, industry and the community at large, including the underserved population. In 1994, GHS launched its Parish Nurse Program, which places a nurse in local churches to provide health education, referral information and counseling on health matters. New projects include a major outpatient services center in nearby Duluth.

In 1993, GHS began an affiliation with Emory University Hospital for Emory resident physicians working under full-time Emory faculty physicians to staff the GHS Prenatal Clinic, a joint venture with the Gwinnett Health Department.

Approximately 1,900 companies with more than 155,000 employees are enrolled in the system's Healthy Business Program, which provides such services as physical exams, immunizations, employee assistance programs and worksite health education. Call the hospital of your choice to find out more about specific programs.

GWINNETT MEDICAL CENTER OF LAWRENCEVILLE
1000 Medical Center Blvd. N.W.
Lawrenceville 995-4321

Officially opened in 1984, the Medical Center is a 190-bed acute care hospital offering all general medical, surgical and diagnostic services. Centrally located in the county, it also houses a Level III 24-hour Emergency Department that is the trauma triage center for Gwinnett County. Gwinnett Medical Center also provides cardiac catheterization, lithotripsy and magnetic resonance imaging services.

Also located on the Gwinnett Medical Center campus is Gwinnett DaySurgery, which houses the GHS Laser Institute. This facility specializes in some of the most advanced outpatient laparoscopic and laser surgeries available regionally and is the site of national physician and nurse training.

The Scottish Rite Children's Emergency Center at Gwinnett Medical serves pediatric emergency cases.

GWINNETT WOMEN'S PAVILION
700 Medical Center Blvd. N.W.
Lawrenceville 995-3600

The 34-bed Gwinnett Women's Pavilion is situated on the 120-acre Gwinnett Medical Center campus. It opened in 1991 as metro Atlanta's first freestanding hospital for women.

Gwinnett Women's offers maternity, diagnostic and educational services to women of all ages. The diagnostic center provides mammography, ultrasound and osteoporosis screenings. A 16-bed neonatal intensive care unit is staffed by experienced health care professionals.

JOAN GLANCY MEMORIAL HOSPITAL
3215 McClure Bridge Rd.
Duluth   497-4800

This 90-bed general hospital offers medical, surgical, diagnostic and 24-hour emergency services. Twenty of the hospital's beds are dedicated to the Glancy Rehabilitation Center, established in 1988.

At the Rehab Center, accident and stroke patients get the training and therapy needed for independence. Outpatient services are offered through the Glancy Outpatient Rehabilitation Center. Expanded services are planned with the opening in 1995 of the Glancy Outpatient Services Center on Pleasant Hill Road.

SUMMITRIDGE
250 Scenic Hwy.
Lawrenceville   822-2222

Gwinnett Hospital System's newest addition is SummitRidge, a 76-bed facility. The hospital provides psychiatric and chemical dependency treatment for adults and adolescents.

Services are available for inpatient, partial hospitalization and outpatient care as well as aftercare programs. Supported by a free, confidential assessment, assistance is provided 24 hours a day.

SummitRidge's community services include education programs for schools and other groups, seminars and support groups. Additional outpatient services are offered at the Outpatient Recovery Center in Peachtree Corners, also located in Gwinnett County.

Walk-In Clinics

In the Atlanta metro area, some but not all urgent care centers are affiliated with hospitals. All offer immediate care for a wide variety of needs, often with extended hours, some as late as 9 PM seven days a week. If the situation requires, patients are quickly transported to the hospital's main facility. We list a sample of these; for more, see Emergency or Clinics in the phone book's yellow pages.

The Centers for Disease Control and Prevention, known as the CDC, conducts research at its Atlanta headquarters.

Atlanta Medical Immediate Care Center
100-10th St. N.W.   897-6800

FamilyCare Centers
(Affiliated with DeKalb Medical Center)
6038 Covington Hwy.
Decatur   501-2270

5019 LaVista Rd.
Tucker   501-3270

1045 Sycamore Dr.
Decatur   501-4270

The Family Physician Center
(Affiliated with Smyrna Hospital)
1225 Powder Springs Rd. S. W.
Marietta   426-6088

Med-Plus Centers
Duluth Center
4075 Pleasant Hill Rd. N.W.
Duluth   623-1331

Lilburn Center
4025 Lawrenceville Hwy.
Lilburn   925-0600

Roswell Center
900 Holcomb Bridge Rd.
Roswell   998-0605

Johnson Ferry Minor Emergency Center
1230 Johnson Ferry Rd. N.E.
Marietta   971-2776

Old National Family Care
5536 Old National Hwy.   763-0886

Peachtree Corners Medical Center
6920 Jimmy Carter Blvd.
Norcross   449-0990

Piedmont Health Center
1830 Piedmont Rd. N.E., Ste. C   874-1111

Piedmont Hospital Medical Care-Brookhaven
(Affiliated with Piedmont Hospital)
4062 Peachtree Rd. N.E.   231-4231

Research Centers

Some major centers of research here are: the Centers for Disease Control and Prevention (CDC); the American Cancer Society national headquarters; Arthritis Foundation national headquarters; Yerkes Regional Primate Research Center; Emory University; Georgia Institute of Technology Research Institute, one of the country's premier bioengineering programs producing advances in prosthetics and engineered assistance for the disabled; Advanced Technology Development Center at Georgia Tech; Georgia Research Consortium, which applies engineering to medical problems such as heart and vascular disease; Georgia Biomedical Partnership; and Carter Center of Emory University, which has focused on international public health programs and is now turning its attention to urban health problems.

Centers for Disease Control and Prevention
1600 Clifton Rd. N.E.   639-3534

For almost half a century, the massive institution called the Centers for Disease Control has fought against disease. In 1992, the name was changed to the Centers for Disease Control and Prevention. It remains known by the acronym CDC.

The mission of the CDC is to promote the health and quality of life by preventing and controlling disease, injury and disability. As the agency of the government's Public Health Service, its responsibilities have expanded from prevention of diseases such as malaria, polio and smallpox to contemporary threats such as environmental and occupational hazards, behavioral risks and chronic diseases.

One of the CDC's most important efforts is research. This work takes place in the agency's Atlanta headquarters, as well

Physician Referral Services

Virtually every hospital has a phone service, usually nurse staffed, to provide physician referrals or to give general health information. You'll probably choose a physician based on your needs, your location and, in some cases, your health insurance policy requirements. Below is a sample of the help lines available.

Atlanta Medical Associates
897-6882

Crawford Long Hospital
248-7744

Cobb Hospital and Medical Center
732-3627

Decatur Hospital Med-Match
373-0590

DeKalb Medical Center
501-9355 (WELL)

Dunwoody Medical Center Call for Health
454-2005

Egleston Physician Referral
325-9700

Emory University Hospital
248-7744

Georgia Baptist
653-3627

Gwinnett Hospital System
995-4444

Henry General Hospital
389-2242

Joan Glancy Memorial Hospital
995-4444

Kennestone Hospital
793-7000

Kennestone Hospital at Windy Hill
429-5999

Metropolitan Hospital
351-0500

North Fulton Regional Hospital
751-2600

Northlake Regional Medical Center
633-2255

Northside Hospital Doctor Matching
851-8817

Piedmont Hospital Physician Finder
605-3556

St. Joseph's Hospital Physician Referral Service
851-7312

Scottish Rite Children's Medical Center
250-5437

South Fulton Medical Center
305-3000

Southwest Hospital and Medical Center
505-5695

Vencor Hospital Atlanta (pulmonary services)
(800)634-2856

Wesley Woods Aging Helpline
728-4999

West Paces Medical Center
633-2255

Photo: Chuck Morgan

Grady Memorial Hospital is named for an editor of the Atlanta Constitution.

as in field stations, health departments and other facilities throughout the nation and abroad.

Eleven separate centers or officially designated programs span every aspect of health concerns: the National Center for Chronic Disease Prevention and Health Promotion, the National Center for Environmental Health, the National Center for Health Statistics, the National Center for Infectious Disease, the National Center for Injury Prevention and Control, the National Center for Prevention Services, the National Institute for Occupational Safety and Health, the Epidemiology Program Office, the International Health Program Office, the National Immunization Program and the Public Health Practice Program Office.

Supporting the cause of research, the CDC also funds grants and state programs to aggressively pursue eradication of such health hazards as smoking, violence and high-risk sexual behavior, in addition to known diseases and environmental hazards. In 1988, the CDC established a Minority Health office to improve the health of African Americans, Hispanic Americans, Native Americans, Asian Americans and other minority groups. The agency researches causes of infant mortality; issues bulletins relied on by medical authorities to forecast outbreaks of specific illness; and oversees the CDC toll-free National AIDS Hotline, (available in English, (800)342-AIDS, Spanish, (800)344-SIDA and for the hearing impaired, (800)AIDS-TTY), which is called by more than 1 million people a year.

Mental Health

When you need assistance with mental health concerns, Atlanta's facilities are ready and waiting. Nine hospitals with close to 1,000 beds are dedicated to emotional or chemical dependency needs. The programs are designed for all ages, from children to elderly citizens. Many of the general acute care hospitals also have extensive programs for the treatment of psychiatric disorders, substance abuse, eating disorders and other related problems. Below we've listed several facilities' free phone lines, through which you can gain necessary information or referral assistance.

Anchor Hospital (for problems with alcohol)
(800)252-6465

CPC Parkwood   633-8431

Laurel Heights Hospital (psychiatric)
888-7868

Hillside Psychiatric Hospital   875-4551

Ridgeview Institute 24-hour helpline
434-4567

SummitRidge   822-2222

Hospice Care

Atlanta is blessed with a number of facilities offering alternatives in cases of life-limiting illness. Counseling services for the patient and family in bereavement are helpful. The services offered vary from hospice to hospice. Here are some points you may want to consider when selecting a hospice.

Ask if the institution is Medicare/Medicaid certified and if it accepts private insurance. Many hospices have a 24-hour emergency service line. Inquire about a specific hospice's membership in national certifying organizations as well as the types of licenses it holds.

CENTRAL HOSPICE CARE
6666 Powers Ferry Rd. N.W.   988-8662

HAVEN HOUSE AT MIDTOWN
250-14th St. N.E.   874-8313

HOSPICE ATLANTA
133 Luckie St.   527-0740

METRO HOSPICE
2045 Peachtree Rd. N.E.   355-3134

NORTHSIDE HOSPICE
5825 Glenridge Dr.   851-6300

Inside
Media

Evidence clearly indicates Atlanta's status as a communication hub for the Southeast and beyond. Consider the growing number of national news bureaus, major magazines and newspapers represented here. Many of them reside on or near Atlanta's famed Peachtree Street.

ABC, NBC and, of course, Ted Turner's whole CNN operation are in Atlanta. On the print side, *Time, Life, Newsweek, Fortune, U.S. News & World Report* and *Business Week* cover the booming Southeast region from Georgia's capital city. The *Wall Street Journal, The New York Times, USA Today* and the *Los Angeles Times* are among the larger newspapers surveying the news from here. Further enlivening the scene are the bureaus of smaller Southeastern newspapers and two major news services, the Associated Press and Reuters. The Georgia Press Association calls Atlanta its home base from offices on Mercer University Drive.

Printing and publishing is the largest single category among Georgia's top-10 manufacturing industries. In the communications field the names of the players, owners or even format can change overnight. For the most part, we've avoided naming specific personalities, opting for a panoramic sweep of Atlanta's information brokers.

Newspapers

Deep as well as broad-based, Atlanta's newspaper scene includes at least four publications established in the 19th century. For instance, *Marietta Daily Journal* began in 1867. The Atlanta *Constitution* has roots in 1868, while the Atlanta *Journal* harkens back to 1883. The *Fulton County Daily Report* started publishing in 1890.

New publications crop up with regularity to serve special interests and new communities. Here are most of the players — to really get the picture, spend an afternoon browsing newsstands loaded with local publications.

Dailies

ATLANTA CONSTITUTION
72 Marietta St.   526-5151

Col. Cary Styles founded the *Constitution* in 1868. Eight years later, a momentous addition arrived — the energetic and farsighted Henry W. Grady. Within four years, Grady became managing editor. His courageous leadership till his death in 1889 left a lasting legacy. Grady is credited with promoting "the New South," a politically and economically progressive philosophy that encouraged looking forward rather than living in the past. You'll see Grady's statue downtown just a block from the present-day headquarters of the paper.

In early summer of 1950, the *Consitution* merged with the *Journal*, the *Constitution* publishing mornings and the *Journal* in the evenings. They maintain separate editorial policies to this day. The papers combine for the Saturday and Sunday editions and on holidays. Extra editions are published for Clayton/South Fulton, North Fulton and Cobb, DeKalb, Fayette and Gwinnett counties. Special sections of the *Constitution* include the "Weekend Preview," a healthy section devoted to the arts, dining out, concerts, exhibits, movies and interviews with notables. "City Life," a special section appearing each Thursday, divides the city into neighborhoods and focuses on residents' special interests.

Among a long roster of memorable staffers are Joel Chandler Harris, author of the Uncle Remus stories, who was associate editor for 24 years. The Pulitzer Prize-winning publisher Ralph McGill helped lead the community to a pro-integration stand in the late 1950s.

Though steeped in history, the papers nonetheless travel today's information highway. For example, Access Atlanta, a computer on-line service furnished by the newspaper company and Prodigy, brings Atlantans a dazzling array of information for less than $10 a month. A flea market bulletin board, movie listings, classifieds and a pay-per-call news service, Find-It 511, are among the offerings. Major malls have displays in department or computer stores demonstrating how Access Atlanta works.

ATLANTA JOURNAL
72 Marietta St.   526-5151

The Atlanta *Journal* "covers Dixie like the dew" — just as its banner proclaims.

The *Journal* and its sister morning publication, the Atlanta *Constitution*, have long provided coverage of events both near and far for Georgians. Back in 1883, Col. E. F. Hoge, a Confederate veteran and prominent lawyer, founded the *Evening Journal*. Building circulation and credibility through the decades, the paper succeeded in attracting readers. In 1912 the *Journal* became the first Southern paper to publish its own magazine, which appeared for more than four decades under the editorial guidance of Angus Perkins and Medora Field Perkerson.

An impressive list of outstanding journalists and editors including *Gone With the Wind* author Margaret Mitchell, football great Grantland Rice and Harold Ross of *The New Yorker* helped the *Journal* forge its way. The staff brought home Pulitzer Prizes, Georgia Press Association awards and other honors on a regular basis.

Evening Journal was eventually sold for a figure in $3 million to the Cox family of Ohio.

The Atlanta *Journal*, published in the evening, has a circulation of approximately 146,000. The paper covers local, statewide, national and international news.

Aimed at a delivery time of no later than 5:30 PM, the *Journal* draws an audience that wants to read about what's happened while they were at work. The later deadline allows reporting on news that broke too late for coverage in the morning papers.

ATLANTA DAILY WORLD
145 Auburn Ave.   659-1110

Publishing since 1928, the *Atlanta Daily World* lays claim to title of Atlanta's oldest African-American newspaper. Its circulation falls in the range of 16,000 to

18,000. In addition to extensive coverage of local news, the paper also carries national news briefs.

FULTON COUNTY DAILY REPORT
190 Pryor St.   *521-1227*

Established in 1890, this organ for Fulton County court notices has a circulation of approximately 5,500. The tabloid-size publication carries the court calendar and editorial geared to the legal community. Average issues include 40 pages.

MARIETTA DAILY JOURNAL
580 Fairground St., Marietta   *428-9411*

From prosperous Cobb County, the *Marietta Daily Journal* serves residents with local news plus full coverage of state and national news. The paper was established in 1867 and has a current circulation of approximately 30,000. With inclusion of news on business, education and sports, its average issue contains 36 pages.

WORLD JOURNAL
5151 Buford Hwy., Doraville   *451-4509*

This daily covers local and national news in Chinese for Atlanta's Chinese community as well as for Chinese readers in six other states. In business for 12 years, *World Journal* has a circulation of more than 10,000.

Weekly Newspapers

Atlanta's weeklies enjoy spirited formats and healthy circulations. We present a selection to portray the variety available.

ATLANTA BUSINESS CHRONICLE
1801 Peachtree St. N.E.   *249-1000*

Published each Friday, this paper presents Atlanta's bustling business scene with a specialist's eye for detail and significance. A readership of 28,000 paid circulation includes executives, managers and professionals in all aspects of business. The paper was established in 1978. Issues range from 62 to 100 pages. *Atlanta Business Chronicle* is distributed in a five-county metro area and beyond.

CREATIVE LOAFING
750 Willoughby Way N.E.   *688-5623*

Creative Loafing is a lively and opinionated alternative that tackles sacred cows and pretentious food palaces with equal gusto. News, public issues, arts and entertainment are reported "from across the political and social spectrum." Subscriptions are available, but the paper is widely distributed free of charge at bookstores and many retail establishments.

In-depth food criticism, theater and movie reviews, music/club scene reports and a sizeable calendar of events great and small make the hefty 150-page plus tabloid a habit with Atlanta readers.

Two regional editions are published. *Topside Loaf,* 642-9774, focuses on the towns just north of Atlanta: Roswell, Alpharetta, Marietta and Dunwoody. *Gwinnett Loaf,* 923-7181, covers the scene in fast-growing Gwinnett County.

ATLANTA TRIBUNE
875 Old Roswell Rd., Roswell   *587-0501*

This biweekly newsmagazine covers seven metro Atlanta counties. With a readership of affluent African-American professionals and entrepreneurs, *Atlanta Tribune* bills itself as "your pulse on Atlanta and the Southeast's leading minority newsmagazine." In addition to supporting a corporate and entrepreneurial business community, the publication presents readers with progressive cultural and

Photo: Chuck Morgan

Ted Turner's CNN operation calls Atlanta home.

entertainment events. Established in 1987, it has a subscription of 32,000 with additional pass-along readership. *Atlanta Tribune* appears the first and the 15th of each month.

EL NUEVO DIA

3754 Buford Hwy. N.E., Ste. A-4   320-7766

Although this paper is a biweekly, we include it in the weekly section due to its influence. In the words of editor Glen Winberg, of Hispanic heritage on his mother's side, the paper was established "to build bridges between communities." Billed as Georgia's only bilingual Hispanic paper, *El Nuevo Dia* has a circulation of about 30,000 readers.

Eighty percent of the editorial is in Spanish, with twin front pages in Spanish and English. *El Nuevo Dia's* coverage of local and national news represents all 26 countries that comprise Latin America.

NEIGHBOR NEWSPAPERS, INC.

580 Fairground St. S.E.
Marietta   428-9411

This company publishes some 25 neighborhood-specific newspapers to keep residents alert to goings-on near the homefront. Besides Fulton, Cobb and Gwinnett county papers, the company has established itself in several adjacent counties. Local news and extensive calendars of noteworthy events are a highlight.

Ethnic Newspapers

The Atlanta metro area supports a varied list of special-interest publications.

The Atlanta Jewish Times, 352-2400, has been serving readers since 1925. It covers local, national and international news of interest to the Jewish community. Available by subscription, the paper is distributed all over the United States and abroad. Present circulation stands at about 10,000. *The Jewish Civic Press*, 231-2194, is a monthly publication geared toward the same community.

Atlanta's Korean community is served by a handful of papers. One of these is *Southeast Journal*, 454-9655, a daily paper that covers local news of interest to Koreans throughout the entire southeastern United States. Established in 1989, the paper currently has a circulation of about 10,000. It is available in both Korean and English.

Additional publications for the Korean community include *Joong Ang Daily News*, 458-7001, covering local news; *The Korean Journal*, 451-6946, a daily with local and Southeastern coverage; *The Korea Times*, 458-5060, a weekly newspaper delivering local and Korean community news; and *Sae Kye Times*, 478-5497, a daily publication of national news for Korean readers.

The Hispanic community is served by such publications as *El Nuevo Dia* (see our weekly section) and *Mundo Hispanico*, 881-0441, a monthly publication covering local Hispanic news.

Newsstands

Newcomers who need a fix from their hometown paper head for a number of well-stocked newsstands. **Eastern Newsstand Corp.** operates more than a half-dozen strategic shops on major thoroughfares such as Peachtree and Piedmont Avenue. A call to the main store at 231 Peachtree Street N.E., 659-5670, will help you locate the newsstand nearest you.

Oxford Books, 360 Pharr Road N.E., 262-3333, is an excellent source. So is **Borders Book Shop**, 3655 Roswell Road N.E., 237-0707, with some 60 out-of-town papers. The **Tower Lobby Shops'** several locations can be learned by calling their main office, 804-9151.

U.S. News Inc. has two Peachtree locations: 1100 Peachtree Street N.E., 892-5171, and 1201 Peachtree Street N.E., 874-9721. Same-day delivery of *The New York Times,* (800)631-2500, to specific zip codes and of *The Wall Street Journal,* (800)568-7625, requires only a phone call.

Magazines

Atlanta publishing offices issue more than 100 periodicals in all shapes, sizes and formats. Many circulate nationally, some are trade or association publications for designated audiences.

One of only a few such statewide organizations, the Magazine Association of Georgia actively promotes excellence and professionalism among its more than 300 members. Among the works produced by these pros are magazines for children and teenagers, Jewish, African-American and Hispanic residents. Claiming their own turf are retirees, food service employees, socialites, real estate seekers, health nuts, investors, weekend athletes, classic car addicts — you name it.

Take some time to browse the local bookstores and newsstands for a satisfying breadth of titles. Here's a sampling of general-interest Atlanta publications.

ACCENT ON ATLANTA
4940 Peachtree Industrial Blvd., Ste. 330
Norcross   242-1800

This monthly newcomer and lifestyle magazine offers calendars of events, a dining guide, coverage of the performing arts, historical articles and more in its aim of "exploring the spirit of the New South."

ATLANTA MAGAZINE
Two Midtown Plaza
1360 Peachtree St.   872-3100

Atlanta, the award-winning and widely read city/lifestyle publication, light-heartedly pinpoints what makes Atlantans tick, as well as what ticks them off. The latest redesign further enhanced this publication's tricky combination of sophistication with down-home awareness.

In 1994, the magazine's panache level rose when it was used as the setting for a new book by bestselling novelist Anne Rivers Siddons. Called *Downtown* and set in the '60s, Siddons' 10th book emerged from memories of the writer's early years as an *Atlanta* magazine staffer. At an Oxford Books signing event, long-time Atlantans lined the sidewalk to get Siddon's autograph while scanning their copy for real life characters.

ATLANTA NOW
233 Peachtree St., Ste. 2000   521-6600,
                                (800)ATLANTA

This is the official visitors guide of the Atlanta Convention & Visitors Bureau. The bimonthly guide presents hotels, restaurants, attractions, sporting events, nightclubs, upcoming festivals, shows and exhibits.

ETCETERA MAGAZINE
P.O. Box 8916, Atlanta 30306   525-3821

Established in 1985, *Etcetera* is a free weekly magazine that offers news and entertainment features for Atlanta's large and politically powerful gay and lesbian community. It's available through bars and other businesses and from street boxes around town. Beyond Atlanta, *Etcetera's* distribution network takes it to many cities across the South.

ATLANTA SINGLES
180 Allen Rd., Ste. 304-N   256-9411

Atlanta Singles features personal ads plus articles of interest to single adults. Each issue includes a comprehensive listing of singles' activities.

GEORGIA TREND
1770 Indian Trail Lilburn Rd. N.W.
Norcross   806-6700

The well-respected *Georgia Trend* puts statewide business matters into focus for wheeler-dealers and wannabes. Profiles of business leaders and in-depth industry reports are part of the magazine's stock in trade. Many consider this award winner must reading.

KEY MAGAZINE ATLANTA
550 Pharr Rd. N.E.   233-2299

This is a weekly newcomer's guide to entertainment, events and happenings of all kinds.

KNOW ATLANTA
7840 Roswell Rd., Dunwoody   512-0016

This quarterly guide in a slick magazine format presents comprehensive information on neighborhoods, schools and other aspects that concern both newcomers and long-term residents.

PEACHTREE MAGAZINE
120 E. Interstate North Pkwy. N.W. 956-1207

Presenting lifestyle with a Southern accent, *Peachtree Magazine's* glossy and colorful look accents the positive with stories of movers and shakers, local celebs and more.

PRESENTING THE SEASON
P.O. Box 420133
Marietta 30342   565-1499

The beautiful people are alive and well in Atlanta. This presentation of social affairs demonstrates the art of gracious living. A calendar filled with charity balls and philanthropic endeavors portrays a lively scene with events to suit the most discerning taste.

SOUTHERN VOICE
P.O. Box 18215, Atlanta 30316   876-1819

News and events of interest to the lesbian and gay community are the focus of the free weekly magazine *Southern Voice*. Established in 1988, it is widely distributed around in-town neighborhoods through businesses and from street boxes. Gay-friendly businesses beyond Atlanta help *SoVo* reach interested readers throughout the South.

WHERE MAGAZINE
1293 Peachtree St. N.E.   876-5566

Published on a monthly basis, this newcomer's guide includes bountiful information about who to see, where to go and how to get there.

WINSOME WAY
Holcomb Bridge Station
P.O. Box 769282, 30076   377-4541

Winsome Way calls itself the only activity magazine in the United States for children of color from age 5 to 12 years of age. It was established to provide positive reinforcement and solutions for real-life problems in an entertaining format. The magazine's African-American superhero (in cartoon form) addresses the issues many children face today, such as violence, gangs and drugs.

YOUNG HORIZONS INDIGO
2897 Bradmoor Ct., Decatur   241-5003

Published for the parents and teachers of African-American children, this publication aims to have a positive influence on youth.

Special Interest Publications

The lively and competitive publishing scene in Atlanta produces still more narrowly focused information. Whether you're seeking a new home, a new mate or a challenging golf course, someone has designed a magazine just for your need.

The Atlanta Apartment Book, 237-7213, is a quarterly guide to apartments. *Atlanta Homes & Lifestyle*, 252-6670, offers a look at residents' homes for your inspiration. *Communities Magazine*, 438-3030, features homes, condos and townhomes for sale, while *For Rent Magazine*, 988-0870, is a guide to rental property. *Metro Atlanta Apartment Guide*, 457-1301, (800)929-5812, offers monthly advice on apartment living. *Target Directories by PMI*, 255-5603 or (800)875-0778, is a relocation guide organized according to metro regions.

Atlanta Happenings, 303-8608, guides you through the entertainment scene and provides discounts to local businesses. *Tafrija Magazine*, 938-0267, centers on entertainment of special interest to African Americans. *Guide to Georgia*, 892-0961, is published monthly as a source to entertainment and the arts for visitors, residents and newcomers. *Atlanta Parent*, 454-7599, is full of helpful tips, as is *Our Kids*, 438-1400.

Atlanta Small Business Monthly, 446-5434, targets the entrepreneurs among us.

The following publications' titles provide their reason for being: *Atlanta Sports and Fitness*, 842-0359; *Car Collector & Car Classics*, 442-1952; *Georgia Golf on My Mind*, 512-0016; *Senior News*, 921-6756.

Television

The major networks plus independents number nearly a dozen stations in Atlanta, including Ted Turner's TBS Network. For cable devotees, some 30 cable channels beam into the metro area, with everything from Disney and Discovery to MTV and ESPN. The statewide association office of the ever-present electronic media, the **Georgia Association of Broadcasters**, is at 8010 Roswell Road, Suite 260, 395-7200.

The association appears to breed an independent lot. In 1994, Johnny Beckman, a decades-long weather forecaster on local TV, blasted national TV policy in a 1994 letter to an alternative paper, *Creative Loafing*. Other media representatives privately agreed with Beckman's charge that the industry's coverage of local news avoids real controversy to focus on sex and violence. As of press time, Beckman, a Harley rider who has been called "Sam Elliot without the moustache" had joined WGNX/Channel 46 (CBS).

A major change for television stations, the realignment of the CBS and Fox networks, occurred in 1994. WAGA/Channel 5 announced plans to drop its CBS connection to become a Fox affiliate. Speculation flared that Ted Turner would renew efforts to buy CBS and convert his Atlanta broadcast station, WTBS/Channel 17, to the new CBS affiliate. After much jockeying for position and a period of months when Atlanta's television profile was up for grabs, CBS announced it would move to WGNX/Channel 46, formerly an independent station. WGNX is now the CBS affiliate in Atlanta.

At the same time, a new company called Quest Broadcasting bought WATL/Channel 36 for a reported $150 million. Pending FCC approval, the deal involves celebs as minority owners: Quincy Jones, composer/publisher/producer; Geraldo Rivera, talk-show host; Don Cornelius, TV personality; and Willie Davis, businessman and former Green Bay Packers player.

Visitors flock to **CNN Center** in downtown Atlanta to watch writers, producers, technicians and on-air journalists in action. This headquarters for Ted Turner's history-making ventures houses the Omni Sports Arena, the renowned Omni Hotel, CNN Cinema 6 and many restaurants and retail shops.

Insiders' Tips

The *Atlanta Business Chronicle* reports that on January 1, 1995, Atlanta became the 10th largest television market in the United States according to Nielsen TV rating service. With a total of 1,567,300 TV households, Atlanta, formerly the 11th largest market, overtook Houston to move into the top 10.

Turner's CNN and Headline News, the two 24-hour all-news networks, revolutionized television's coverage of news events. CNN is the largest television newsgathering organization in the United States, reaching more than 60 million U.S. households, according to *International Atlanta*. CNN International, the world's first global news network, reaches an additional 70 million homes in more than 200 countries and territories.

CNN's latest innovation in programming is *Talkback Live*, a live, 1-hour show seen as a national town hall meeting. Aired on weekdays at 1 PM EST from a studio in the CNN atrium, the show's "stars" are made up of an off-the-street audience of 150, phone call-ins, faxes and on-line computer exchanges. CNN anchor Susan Rook fields questions and views on current topics, ending the show with a mystery guest of national standing.

Free audience tickets are available at 23 Drug Emporium locations, 26 local hotels, CNN Center's Turner Store and by mail. Write to: Talkback Live Tickets, CNN Center, Box 105366, Atlanta 30348. For group tickets, call 827-0623 or 827-3969. Arrival by 11:30 AM is recommended; for more information, call (800)410-4CNN. To participate from home, by phone, call (800)310-4266; by fax, dial (800)310-4329; by computer, use Compuserve, see "Talkback" command on message board.

CNN tours highlighting Turner's extensive communications empire are offered Monday through Sunday from 9 AM to 5 PM for the following charges: adults, $6; seniors 65 and older, $4; children 12 and younger $3.50. The tour lasts approximately 45 minutes. For reservations, call 827-2300. Advanced reservations are accepted; same-day tickets are available on a first-come, first-served basis. Advanced reservations for groups of 35 or more receive a special rate of $4 per person.

Television Stations

NATIONAL AFFILIATES
ABC - WSB/Channel 2
CBS - WGNX/Channel 46
NBC - WXIA/Channel 11
PBS - WGTV/Channel 8 (Georgia public television)
PBS - WPBA/Channel 30 (Atlanta public television)
Fox - WAGA/Channel 5
Warner Bros. - WATL/Channel 36

Local Independent Broadcast Channels

WTBS/Channel 17
WTLK/Channel 14
WVEU/Channel 69
WHSG/Channel 63

INTERNATIONAL TELEVISION SHOWS
Japan CableVision (JCV)
Higgins Inc.
WVEU-TV 69
Mon. through Fri. 7 to 7:30 AM

Latin Atlanta
Sun. (WPBA TV30) 8:30 to 9 AM

Radio

Whatever your mood, punch a button. You'll find a station with the tunes to set your toes a-tapping or maybe a zippy talk show to clear your mental cobwebs.

Tune into an Atlanta fave, Super Consumer Man Clark Howard. On WSB 750 AM, from 2 to 5 PM, Monday through Friday, Howard responds to callers' questions as if the money involved were his own. For information on travel, appliances and service contracts, he's your bottom-line guy.

Due to reception irregularities, not all stations are available throughout the metro area.

CHRISTIAN FORMAT

WAEC - 860 AM	355-8600
WAFS - 920 AM	889-0920
WDCY - 1520 AM	920-1520
WFOM - 1230 AM	419-0935
WFTD - 1080 AM	424-9850
WDUN - 550 AM	584-5815
WNIV - 970 AM	365-0970
WSSA - 1570 AM	361-8843
WWEV - 91.5 FM, 1420 AM	577-9150

NEWS/TALK/SPORTS

WSB - 750 AM	897-7500
WGST - 640 AM, 105.7 FM	233-0640
WGUN - 1010 AM	491-1010
WIGO - 1340 AM	752-5460
WCNN - 680 AM	688-0068

ROCK/CONTEMPORARY

WKLS - 96.1 FM	
Album Rock	325-0960
WPCH - 94.0 FM	
Light Rock	261-9500
WNNX - 99.7 FM	
New Rock	266-0997
WRAS - 88.5 FM	
College Rock (Georgia State U.)	651-2240
WZGC - 92.9 FM	
Classic Rock	851-9393
WSB - 98.5 FM	
Adult Contemporary	897-7500
WSTR - 94.1 FM	
Top 40	261-2970

HISPANIC

WAOS - 1600 AM	944-0900
WXEM - 1460 AM	944-0900
WAZX - 1550 AM	436-6171

COUNTRY

WCHK - 1290 AM	
Country/Gospel	524-5316
WHNE - 1170 AM	
Country/Gospel	577-5998
WKHX - 590 AM, 101.5 FM	955-0101
WPLO - 610 AM	962-4848
WYAY - 106.7 FM	
Country	955-0106

GOSPEL

WTJH - 1260 AM	344-2233
WXLL - 1310 AM	
Gospel/Talk	288-3200
WYZE - 1480 AM	622-4444
WAOK - 1380 AM	
Gospel/Talk Radio	898-8900
WPBS - 1050 AM	483-1000

OTHER FORMATS

WABE - 90.1 FM	
W300AB - 107.9 FM	827-8900
NPR/Classical/News	
WJVF - 104.1	
Jazz	897-7500
WALR - 104.7 FM	
Urban Oldies and Hits	688-0068
WVEE - 103.3 FM	
Urban Contemporary/Top 40	898-8900
WCLK - 91.9 FM	
Jazz/Soul (Clark Atlanta U.)	880-8273
WFOX - 97.1 FM	
Oldies	953-9369
WGKA - 1190 AM	
Classical	231-1190
WKKP - 1410 AM	
Adult Contemporary	957-0208
WLKQ - 102.3 FM	
Oldies ('50s-'60s)	945-9953
WMKJ - 96.7 FM	
Adult Contemporary	577-4850
WREK - 91 FM	
Diversified (Georgia Tech)	894-2468
WRFG - 89.3 FM	
Rock/Blues/Afro-pop	523-3471
WQXI - 790 AM	
Nostalgia/Talk	261-2970

Inside
Places of Worship

You'd be hard-pressed to leave Atlanta unfulfilled no matter what kind of worship service you seek. Coexisting comfortably with its Bible Belt origins is a great diversity of religious communities, which is a powerful demonstration of the city's growing internationalism.

Local publications have put the number of churches at 2,000. By actual count, subheadings in the Atlanta phone book show 121 separate subdivisions of denominations. These listings include all those conventionally represented in most cities and then some. The Baptist denomination alone has nine categories. You'll also notice Baha'i, Eckankar, Hindu, Islamic, Jehovah Witness, Krishna Consciousness, Latter-Day Saints, Mennonite, Metaphysical Science, Moravian, Mormon, Nazarene, Quaker, Religious Science and Swedenborgian congregations.

Atlanta's proclivity for the graceful melding of cultures displays itself in churches for Vietnamese Catholics, Spanish Seventh-day Adventists, Chinese Baptists and Korean Presbyterians. The city is home to a number of mosques and Buddhist and Hindu temples. A major mosque, Al-Sarooq Masjid, is on 14th Street near Northside Drive. Near Grant Park is a Vietnamese Buddhist Temple. In the DeKalb County town of Lithonia, construction is under way on a Korean Buddhist Temple where as many as 200 monks will live, work and study on a 11-acre site.

A cluster of Russian Orthodox, Eastern Orthodox and Coptic churches give their members an opportunity to practice traditions and rituals common to their forebears in other lands.

Various polls conducted over the years consistently show many Southerners

Photo: Chuck Morgan

Second Ponce de Leon Baptist Church is one of Atlanta's larger congregations.

within the Bible Belt to be faithful church-goers and Scripture readers. Moreover, in the traditional Southern life, church is more than a place to visit once a week. Atlantans are no exception to this profile, sometimes naming their businesses as testimony. On downtown's Marietta Street, you can buy a pastry at the Heavenly Father's, Jesus' and Our Bake Shop. Shop for shag at the By Faith Carpet Enterprises on Memorial Drive. Dine at the House of Prayer Rib Shack on Edgewood Avenue.

Community efforts toward interfaith action are commonplace. Three downtown churches continue a tradition begun long ago and jointly celebrate Easter with a procession of members bearing colorful banners and palms, accompanied by hymns and music from all three liturgies. These churches, Trinity Methodist, Central Presbyterian and Atlanta's oldest church, The Shrine of the Immaculate Conception, shared salvation from Gen. Sherman's torches, due to the persuasive powers of Father Thomas O'Reilly, the shrine's pastor.

Ecumenical efforts among Atlanta's synagogues, temples and churches include building community centers, operating homeless shelters and working to promote harmony among Atlanta's citizens.

Take, for example, the week-long event sponsored by the Peachtree Corridor Congregations, an association of 11 Midtown and downtown churches, and the Midtown Ministerial Association. Called the Summer 1994 Arts in Worship, the celebration began with dedication of a **Psalm Wall**, made of 16 door panels painted with a participating congregation's interpretation of a psalm. The panels are housed at Peachtree Christian Church, 1580 Peachtree Street N.W., 876-5535 (you need to call the church office in advance to view the panels). Following the dedication of the wall, each congregation hosted an event featuring some combination of organ and choral music, visual arts, dance, drama and architecture or garden tours. The event used the arts to demonstrate the commonalities among all denominations.

To experience the role of church life here, take a leisurely Sunday morning stroll down Peachtree Street. Clustered in bunches either on or close to this path through the heart of Atlanta, clear out past Buckhead, are churches of every denomination. In the section known as the **Peachtree Corridor**, from downtown to midtown, are Baptist, Catholic, Lutheran, Jewish, Episcopal, Christian, Presbyterian, Christian Scientist, Unitarian and Methodist churches.

From a visual standpoint, there's much to see, such as the cobblestone floors of **St. Luke's Episcopal Church**, 435 Peachtree Street N.E. The area's best-known synagogue, **The Temple**, 1589 Peachtree Street, plays an established role in local Jewish life. The Temple is recognized from its appearance in the movie *Driving Miss Daisy*. Other prominent temples in the metro area are the **Abavath Achim Synagogue**, **Temple Sinai** and **Temple Emanu-el**.

Farther up Peachtree is the "holy point" in Buckhead, where Andrews Drive meets this serpentine street. Here, three of the city's most prominent churches beckon worshippers inward: the **Cathedral of St. Philip**, Episcopal Diocese of Atlanta, on a majestic rise above the roadway; the **Cathedral of Christ the King**, Catholic Archdiocese of Atlanta; and **Second Ponce de Leon Baptist Church**, one of Atlanta's largest Baptist congregations. A few blocks on, **Peachtree Road United Methodist Church** houses a sizeable congregation at 3180 Peachtree Road N.E.

Splendid houses of worship are found in all parts of the metro area. Many travel to see the priceless Tiffany stained-glass windows in **All Saints Episcopal Church** on North Avenue.

Besides the renowned **Ebenezer Baptist Church,** home to Martin Luther King Jr., other influential predominately African-American churches gather near world-famous Auburn Avenue, the setting of thriving entrepreneurship among African Americans. Churches in this area include the **Wheat Street Baptist Church, Big Bethel AME Church** and many others.

Music is the quintessential soul of religion in the South, and Atlanta's churches showcase vocal talents second to none. The choirs are a vital force in worship services. For instance, at Ebenezer Baptist, 150 voices in four choirs sing praises for Sunday services.

Churches are an integral part of Southern culture. They continue to pass on traditions and beliefs, supported by the labors of their parishioners. We present just an overview; many more await your discovery.

EBENEZER BAPTIST CHURCH
407 Auburn Ave. N.E.   *688-7263*

From its founding in 1886, Ebenezer Baptist Church has stood as a beacon of progress in civil rights and justice for all Americans. The church has enjoyed outstanding pastoral leadership throughout its history in several locations. The present structure in downtown Atlanta was completed in 1922.

During 44 years of leadership under the Rev. Martin Luther King Sr., the church grew in size and influence. King became the church's third pastor in 1931. He led his congregation and the community to progressive stands on human rights issues. He fought for equal pay for public school teachers of all races and helped black citizens register to vote. Under King, the church made considerable improvements to its facility and fiscal administration. He oversaw the creation of Christian education programs and buildings in which to house them.

Ebenezer's first co-pastor, the Reverend Dr. Martin Luther King Jr., served the church from 1960 until his assassination in 1968. Dr. King is credited with instilling in Ebenezer Baptist an ecumenical spirit. During his time at Ebenezer, Dr. King was honored with the Nobel peace prize in recognition of his outstanding leadership of the Civil Rights Movement. Tens of thousands of visitors from all over the world each year visit Ebenezer Baptist as part of their pilgrimage to Atlanta's Martin Luther King, Jr. Center for Nonviolent Social Change, adjacent to the church. It is listed on the National Register of Historic Places. Several books have been written about the church, reflecting the enduring faith and sacrifices of its congregation.

The year after King's death, his brother, Rev. Alfred Daniel Williams King was installed as Ebenezer's second co-pastor. Serving until his death in 1970, he initiated a Sunday morning television ministry and established a committee to serve the needy, among many other projects.

THE TEMPLE
1589 Peachtree St. N.E.   *873-1731*

The Temple is the third home to the Hebrew Benevolent Society, founded in 1860 to serve religious needs for the growing number of German-Jewish immigrants. Known for activism in the community, the congregation founded the English-German-Hebrew Academy in 1869. This school became the forerunner of the Atlanta public school system. Efforts to abolish child labor and establish an 8-hour work day were led by the Council of Jewish Women. Early in this century, an annual Thanksgiving interfaith service became a tradition.

The Temple was completed in 1931 and designed by well-known architect Philip T. Shutze. Its neoclassical style features rich interiors with intricate plaster relief work.

Because the congregation, under the leadership of Rabbi Jacob Rothschild, acted in the civil rights movement, The Temple was bombed in 1958. It has since been restored to its former beauty and is entered on the National Register of Historic Places.

PEACHTREE CHRISTIAN CHURCH
1580 Peachtree St. N.W.   *876-5535*

Peachtree Christian Church is a replica of Melrose Abbey, a church outside London that was destroyed by bombs in World War II.

Completed in 1928, the 15th-century Gothic-style edifice was designed by English-born architect Charles Hopson, known for his ecclesiastical projects. The exterior features brick and other local materials rather than the original model's stone, which was predominant in medieval times.

Among Peachtree Christian's adornments are a large number of stained-glass windows, handmade by the London firm of William Glasby.

THE CHURCH OF THE SACRED HEART OF JESUS
353 Peachtree St. N.E.   *875-0431*

The Church of the Sacred Heart of Jesus on Peachtree Street in downtown is home to a Catholic parish that began in 1880. When the first wooden structure, 12 blocks from the present site, became too small, the Marist Fathers commissioned well-known Atlanta architect W. T. Downing to build a church of French Romanesque style. At the time, some said the new location was too far out of town to survive.

Rich in history and architectural detail, Sacred Heart's pressed brick and terra cotta exterior features twin octagonal towers rising 137 feet above street level, once the tallest points in the Peachtree neighborhood. Its 28 stained-glass windows from the Mayer Studio in Munich were installed in 1902. Fourteen windows adorning the walls of the nave depict episodes in the life of Christ, including the Sermon on the Mount. The seven pairs of narrow windows following the curve of the apse above the sanctuary portray miraculous appearances, such as an angel appearing to Christ in Gethsemane. A thriving congregation today supports ongoing preservation efforts of their church, which is on the National Register of Historic Places.

NORTH AVENUE PRESBYTERIAN CHURCH
Corner of Peachtree St. and
North Ave.   *875-0431*

On the busy Midtown corner of Peachtree Street and North Avenue, this church is made of granite from Atlanta's Stone Mountain. Listed on the National Register of Historic Places, the fortress-like structure was organized in 1895. Its large congregation began with charter members from as far away as Athens, Georgia.

Insiders' Tips

Avoid the far right lane of traffic on Peachtree during Sunday morning hours as it officially becomes a parking lane for the overflow crowds from the clusters of churches on this main thoroughfare.

Photo: Chuck Morgan

The Cathedral Church of Christ the King was chosen the most beautiful building in Atlanta by Architectural Record in 1939.

FIRST CONGREGATIONAL CHURCH OF ATLANTA

105 Courtland St. N.E.   *659-6255*

This church had its start in 1867 as a mission led by the Reverend and Mrs. Frederick Ayer of Wisconsin. It grew from The Storr's School, a pioneering facility to educate black freedmen and their children. Seven of the church's original members were black, and three were white.

From 1894 to 1919, under Dr. Henry U. Proctor, the church became the largest black Congregationalist church in the nation and introduced extensive community social welfare programs.

The present church was built in 1908 in the Renaissance Revival style. A rose window in the rear of the church bears a dedication to Edmund Asa Ware, who set up an educational center for freed slaves after the Emancipation Proclamation was signed by President Lincoln. The church has had many prominent members, among them Atlanta Life Insurance Co. founder Alonzo F. Herndon, former Atlanta mayor Andrew Young and noted educators Horace and Julia Bond. Long a meeting place for black and white community leaders, First Congregational is listed on the National Register of Historic Places.

BUTLER STREET C. M. E. CHURCH

23 Butler St. S.E.   *659-8745*

This downtown Atlanta church, another edifice honored by being on the National Register of Historic Places, was organized in 1882 by the Reverend S. E. Poe. The present church was built in 1920.

The neo-gothic style church was built on land donated by Atlanta developer John Grant to honor his former slaves. A dedication of the church was made to Bishop Luscious H. Holsey, a prominent minister who established many churches in Georgia.

Today, the congregation feeds the needy through the Open Door Community program.

SHRINE OF THE IMMACULATE CONCEPTION

48 Martin Luther King Jr. Dr. S.W.521-1866

Atlanta is home to several cathedrals, one of which is the Shrine of the Immaculate Conception in downtown. Its congregation formed in 1846, making it Atlanta's oldest church.

When Gen. Sherman's troops captured the city in 1864 and threatened to set fire to the shrine, Pastor Father Thomas O'Reilly pleaded that his church, five neighboring churches, the City Hall, the courthouse and several residences be spared. Some of these structures were acting as hospitals for the wounded of both armies. Sherman conceded to O'Reilly's request.

The shrine's history has been dotted by adversity. The Depression and, later, population shifts toward suburban living caused a decline in church membership. In 1982, the shrine, once saved from Union soldiers, fell prey to fire and burned to a shell, leaving few remains behind. One of these was O'Reilly's crypt. Successful rebuilding efforts began almost immediately. In 1985 the church was rededicated and now resides on the National Register of Historic Places.

ST. JAMES UNITED METHODIST CHURCH

4400 Peachtree Dunwoody Rd. N.E.   *261-3121*

This church presents "the Message of the Windows" in its carefully planned and executed series of stained-glass windows. A pattern for living a holy life, the windows begin with Old Testament scenes looking forward to Christ's coming. Glass in the chancel depicts the life, death and resurrection of the Lord. The south aisle's windows present scenes of the apostles, worship and social service. The balcony windows encourage churchgoers to go forth and do good in the world and to care especially for the poor and physically handicapped.

Dr. John R. Brokhoff, professor of homiletics at Candler School of Theology, Emory University, consulted with the St. James building committee on the project's iconography. The Willet Stained Glass Studio of Philadelphia designed and produced the windows.

CATHEDRAL OF CHRIST THE KING
2699 Peachtree Rd. N.E.   233-2145

Bishop Gerald P. O'Hara blessed and laid the cornerstone for the building of the Cathedral of Christ the King in 1937. The Philadelphia firm of Henry D. Dagit designed the structure, which echoed a design used earlier by the firm in a smaller version for Rosemont College in Pennsylvania. Fratelli Ruggati of Padua, Italy, built the cathedral's 3,000-pipe organ.

The Catholic cathedral's 65 stained-glass windows were designed and executed by Henry Lee Willet of Willet Stained Glass Studio in Philadelphia. They present "an instructive chronological history of the great beliefs of the Church," says Cathedral's 15th anniversary memorial booklet. All windows are made from the finest hand-blown pot metal glasses and Norman slabs, using the same processes as the craftsmen of the Middle Ages. The 22 principal windows and 43 smaller windows contain more than 200 references to Scripture and present 200 persons in pictorial history. Each window tells its own story. In 1939, *Architectural Record* chose the cathedral as the most beautiful building in Atlanta.

An interesting note: The church's cornerstone was laid the same year Margaret Mitchell won the Pulitzer Prize for *Gone With the Wind*. The story goes that Mitchell penned a hasty note to the Bishop Gerald P. O'Hara in apology for unintentionally using his name for Scarlett's father in her novel. She explained the book was set in type before she discovered the coincidence.

CATHEDRAL OF ST. PHILIP
2744 Peachtree Rd. N.W.   365-1000

This community dates back to 1847, when five people met to organize Atlanta's first Episcopal church. A small frame building at the corner of Hunter and Washington streets first served the parish; that was followed by a larger brick structure on the same site near what is now the State Capitol. A move to north Atlanta came in 1933, when Bishop Henry Judah Mikell, Bishop of Atlanta from 1917-1942, dedicated the new church at the corner of Peachtree Road and Andrews Drive. Many items were brought from the original church, including pews, the eagle lectern, stained-glass windows, the pulpit, the communion rail and the altar. Some of these items are still in use today in St. Mary's Chapel beneath the apse of the cathedral itself.

On Easter Day in 1962, the congregation joined for services in a new church building on the same site, the current cathedral. Among the cathedral's many architectural treasures is the Mikell Memorial Chapel, named for Bishop Mikell. A popular setting for weddings, the 100-seat chapel's aisle windows portray various Biblical parables in lessons of faith. The nave of the cathedral itself stretches 217 feet from the entrance leading to the high altar. The freestanding altar is made of green and white Italian marble. Nearby are needlepoint kneelers and benches made by the Cathedral Daughters of the King. Each section of the cathedral contains multihued stained-glass windows depicting significant elements of the Episcopalian faith.

CATHEDRAL OF THE ANNUNCIATION
2500 Clairmont Rd. N.E.   633-5870

This Greek Orthodox church is the foundation for Atlanta's vigorous Greek-American community. Filled with religious statuary and artifacts, the cathedral is renown for the mosaic created on its dome. This artwork is said to be one of the largest dome mosaics in the world.

Each fall, the church stages an elaborate festival. This celebration of Greek culture, food, music and fable is a fund-raiser that supports church activities.

Inside
Service Directory

When you come to a new place, for a visit or to stay, you can predict there will be a host of mundane matters to attend to along with unexpected dilemmas. In this chapter, we present some sources of information that will help answer questions or pull you out of a jam. While the people at these local services may not be able to solve all your problems, you can expect them to do their best. If they can't help you, at least they may be able to refer you to someone who can.

Automobiles

Auto Registration and Driver's Licenses

You are required to get both a Georgia driver's license and a car tag within 30 days of establishing residency. The Georgia state driver's license fee is $15, payable in cash or money order only. Persons with valid out-of-state licenses are required to pass written and vision tests.

The minimum driving age in Georgia is 16. A learner's permit costs $10, also payable in cash or money order only. For the location of the driver's license office closest to you, call 657-9300.

Getting your driver's license need not be a hassle. Besides its regional offices, the Georgia State Patrol operates a mobile service that provides many services. These include renewals, applications for lost licenses, handicapped parking permits, identification cards and written tests for the commercial driver's license. For

information on scheduled locations, call 657-9300.

To get your Georgia license tag, take with you to the county office representing the jurisdiction in which you live: a copy of your current registration; your car title or name and address of lien holder or a copy of lease agreement; an emission certificate to prove any post-1980 car has passed the state-approved test; proof of insurance (no-fault insurance is required by Georgia law); and proof of residency. An ad valorem tax establishes the fee for tag renewal.

Here are the county license tag offices for the metro area covered in this book. We strongly recommend you call ahead for any additional documents needed, as they may vary. Also ask what form of payment is acceptable and for the current hours of operation.

FULTON COUNTY TAGS & TITLE
141 Pryor St. S.W.   730-6160

COBB COUNTY AUTO TAG OFFICE
1738 County Farm Rd. S.W.
Marietta   528-4020

DEKALB COUNTY MOTOR VEHICLE OFFICE
120 W. Trinity Pl., Decatur   371-TAGS

GWINNETT COUNTY MOTOR VEHICLE OFFICE
75 Langley Dr., Lawrenceville   822-8801

Citizenship

To register to vote, call these numbers listed for your respective county. Citizens are required to register to vote at least 30 days prior to an election. Many counties have several voter registration sites. To find the one nearest you, call the office of your county of residence.

Cobb County	528-2300
DeKalb County	371-2241
Fulton County	730-7072
Gwinnett County	822-8787

Consulates

As of spring 1994, 49 countries have official representation in Atlanta, 25 of which are career consulates. Eighteen honorary consulates, 23 trade and tourism offices and 22 foreign-American Chambers of Commerce round out the picture steeped in internationalism.

These offices perform a number of duties. They issue tourist and business visas, renew passports, legalize documents and provide assistance to United States importers, exporters and investors. Many of them also provide general tourist information for visitors. For more information, call the Atlanta Chamber of Commerce International Department, 586-8460; fax line, 586-8464. For information about translation services, see our International Visitors section later in this chapter.

Thanks to the Atlanta Chamber of Commerce for compiling this listing.

CONSULATE OF ARGENTINA
229 Peachtree St. N.E., Ste. 1401   880-0805

AUSTRALIAN TRADE COMMISSION AND CONSULATE GENERAL
303 Peachtree St. N.E., Ste. 2920   880-1700

CONSULATE OF AUSTRIA
10 N. Parkway Sq.
4200 Northside Pkwy. N.W.   264-9858

HONORARY CONSULATE OF BARBADOS
3935 Flowerland Dr.   454-0355

CONSULATE GENERAL OF BELGIUM
225 Peachtree St. N.E., Ste. 800
South Tower   659-2150

CANADIAN CONSULATE GENERAL
One CNN Center, Ste. 400
South Tower   577-6810

HONORARY CONSULATE OF CHILE
5573 Martina Way   804-9067

CONSULATE GENERAL OF COLOMBIA
3379 Peachtree Rd., Ste. 220   237-1045

CONSULATE GENERAL OF COSTA RICA
315 W. Ponce de Leon Ave., Ste. 455   370-0555

HONORARY CONSULATE OF THE REPUBLIC OF CYPRUS
895 Somerset Dr.   941-3764

HONORARY CONSULATE OF DENMARK
225 Peachtree St. N.E., Ste. 201   614-5207

HONORARY CONSULATE OF ECUADOR
2058 Walton Woods Cr.
Tucker   491-6026

HONORARY CONSULATE OF FINLAND
9240 Huntcliff Trace   993-6696

CONSULATE GENERAL OF FRANCE
285 Peachtree Center Ave.
Marquis Two, Ste. 2800   522-4226

CONSULATE GENERAL OF THE FEDERAL REPUBLIC OF GERMANY
285 Peachtree Center Ave. N.E.
Marquis Two Tower, Ste. 901   659-4760

CONSULATE OF GREECE
3340 Peachtree Rd. N.E.
Tower Place, Ste. 167   261-3313

HONORARY CONSULATE OF GUATEMALA
4772 E. Conway Dr. N.W.   255-7019

HONORARY CONSULATE OF HAITI
P. O. Box 80340, Atlanta 30366   847-0709

HONORARY CONSULATE OF THE REPUBLIC OF HONDURAS
3091 Chaparral Pl., Lithonia   482-1332

HONORARY CONSULATE GENERAL OF ICELAND
1677 Tullie Cr. N.E., Ste. 118   321-0777

CONSULATE GENERAL OF ISRAEL
1100 Spring St. N.W., Ste. 440   875-7851

HONORARY CONSULATE OF ITALY
755 Mount Vernon Hwy.   355-0771

HONORARY CONSULATE OF JAMAICA
6721 Covington Hwy.
Lithonia   593-1500

CONSULATE GENERAL OF JAPAN
100 Colony Sq., Ste. 2000   892-2700

CONSULATE GENERAL OF THE REPUBLIC OF KOREA
229 Peachtree St.
Ste. 500, Cain Tower   522-1611

HONORARY CONSULATE OF LIBERIA
2265 Cascade Rd. S.W.   753-4753

CONSULATE GENERAL OF MEXICO
3220 Peachtree Rd. N.E.   266-2233

CONSULATE OF THE NETHERLANDS
133 Peachtree St., Ste. 2500   525-4513

ROYAL NORWEGIAN CONSULATE
3715 Northside Pkwy.
399 Northcreek, Ste. 650   239-0885

CONSULATE GENERAL OF PANAMA
260 Peachtree St. N.W., Ste. 1760   525-2772

Currency Exchange

Outside major cities in the United States, exchanging funds from foreign currencies is difficult. Some of Atlanta's larger hotels offer this service to registered guests.

RUESCH INTERNATIONAL
191 Peachtree St.
Lobby Level   222-9300, (800)448-4685

Offering many of the same services as Thomas Cook, Ruesch buys and sells any freely traded currency and offers an exchange rate better than hotels and banks. It is next to the downtown Ritz-Carlton Hotel.

THOMAS COOK FOREIGN EXCHANGE
245 Peachtree Center Ave., Marquis One Tower
Gallery Level   681-9700, (800)582-4496

This firm offers a wide range of services in more than 100 currencies. Among them are commission-free traveler's checks, drafts and wire transfers and check collections. Their rates are considered competitive and their service very good. Two other locations will serve you: one at Hartsfield International (see next entry) and the other on the second level at Peachtree Battle Shopping Center, 2385 Peachtree Battle. Hours for the Peachtree Battle office are 9 AM to 6 PM.

HARTSFIELD INTERNATIONAL AIRPORT

Two currency exchange centers are available to assist travelers. One is in the Main (North) Terminal and is open from 11 AM to 7 PM. The other is in Concourse E, open from 7 AM to 8 PM. Call 761-6331 for more information.

Domestic Services

Whether you're visiting or new to town, the time may come when you need a helping hand. You'll find many enterprising companies ready and willing to pitch in with services such as child care, home maintenance, errands, pet care and more. Ask about references and bonding of employees. As an alternative to commercial services, try calling a few of the churches in your area. Some of them may have a list of church members who make themselves available for child care. Whatever route you take, be sure to check references thoroughly, interview the sitter personally and assure yourself of the highest level of security.

A FRIEND OF THE FAMILY
895 Mt. Vernon Hwy.   *255-2848*

For 10 years, this firm has provided bonded caregivers for a variety of in-home, or in-hotel, services. All the staff members have references. You can arrange care to suit your needs for day, night or overnight care, as well as permanent live-in or live-out situations. Office hours are Monday through Friday, 7 AM to 10 PM; Saturdays, 8 AM to 8 PM; Sundays and holidays on an on-call basis.

TLC OF ATLANTA
1262 Concord Rd., Smyrna   *435-6250*

TLC screens the references of its bonded employees, who are required to undergo the extra precaution of finger-printing. The company offers a full range of services on a customized basis. If you need a party helper or assistance with your church or convention event, the folks at TLC will do their best to meet your needs.

ATLANTA METRO SITTERS SERVICE INC.
1381 E. Carnegie Ave.   *766-6016*

Metro Sitters has been serving the Atlanta area since 1967 with licensed caregivers for children, the elderly and the disabled. Spanish-speaking employees are among the company's staff.

Emergencies

Dial **911** for all emergencies. Throughout the Atlanta metro area, a 911 call will bring prompt help in emergency situations.

You'll find the names, addresses and phone numbers of the major hospitals with emergency rooms in our Medical Care chapter.

House Call Doctors provides doctors available round the clock to provide treatment in your hotel room or home. Whether it's a minor ailment or a prescription problem, call 681-3200. Credit cards are accepted.

Traveler's Aid Society, 40 Pryor Street S.W., 527-7400, will likely help if trouble has intruded on your vacation. This 24-hour number will connect you with emergency services for travelers in distress. Part of a national, nonprofit social service agency, the Society has several locations in the metro area: at Hartsfield International Airport, 766-4511; at the Greyhound Bus Terminal, 81 International Boulevard, 527-7411; and in the Cobb County town of Marietta, 377 Henry Drive, 428-1883.

Information Sources

As a place that draws more than 16.5 million guests each year, Atlanta is well equipped to supply visitors and newcomers with the information they need. In this section you'll find some of the larger sources of information.

For statewide information, call the **Georgia Department of Industry, Trade and Tourism**, 656-3590.

Convention and Visitors Bureaus

ATLANTA CONVENTION & VISITORS BUREAU

233 Peachtree Street N.E., Ste. 2000
Harris Tower (main office)   521-6688
Peachtree Center Mall, 231 Peachtree St. N.E.
Lenox Square Center, 3393 Peachtree Rd.
Underground Atlanta, 65 Upper Alabama St.

You'll find a slew of information through this bureau. If you call or write in advance, you can get a copy of *Atlanta Now* visitors' guide, a map and a two-month calendar of events free.

When you're in town, visit the Peachtree Center Mall, Lenox Square and Underground Atlanta centers for an impressive selection of printed materials. Often those staffing the centers can provide you with time- and effort-saving answers.

COBB COUNTY CONVENTION & VISITOR BUREAU

1100 Circle 75 Pkwy., Ste. 125   933-7228

DEKALB COUNTY CONVENTION & VISITORS BUREAU

750 Commerce Dr., Decatur   378-2525

GWINNETT COUNTY CONVENTION & VISITORS BUREAU

6400 Sugarloaf Pkwy., Duluth   623-8793

HALL COUNTY CONVENTION & VISITORS BUREAU

830 Green St.   536-5209

Chambers of Commerce

The chambers of commerce are prime sources of information on businesses, schools, housing and other facts on their locales. You'll find quite an assortment of booklets and brochures, many of which are free. These offices have done all the homework for you, so take advantage of their expertise.

ATLANTA CHAMBER OF COMMERCE

235 International Blvd. N.W.   880-9000

COBB COUNTY CHAMBER OF COMMERCE

P.O. Box COBB
Marietta 30067   980-2000

DEKALB COUNTY CHAMBER OF COMMERCE

750 Commerce Dr., Ste. 201
Decatur   378-8000

GWINNETT CHAMBER OF COMMERCE

P.O. Box 1245
Lawrenceville 30246   963-4887

NORTH FULTON CHAMBER OF COMMERCE

1024 Old Roswell Rd., Ste. 101
Roswell   303-8880

SOUTH FULTON CHAMBER OF COMMERCE

6400 Shannon Pkwy., Union City 964-1984

International Visitors

Southern hospitality in Atlanta extends in special measure to those from other countries. The agencies and services listed here make every effort to anticipate the specific needs of our foreign visitors. Also see the sections titled Currency Exchange and Consulates for assistance.

Several entities have joined in a cooperative effort called **Language Visitors Assistance**. Multilingual visitors services representatives are jointly sponsored by the City of Atlanta and the U.S. Travel and Tourism Administration. They meet all arriving international flights to assist passengers with translation and other needs.

The new International Terminal at Hartsfield Airport also offers an **International Calling Assistance Center** that displays important calling information in six languages. This is the first computerized system of its kind to assist travelers.

THE GEORGIA COUNCIL FOR INTERNATIONAL VISITORS

999 Peachtree St. N.E. 873-6170

This volunteer-staffed multilingual language bank acts as a referral center for those seeking language assistance. Basically it is a liaison to interpreters and translators. The Council recommends a free source of information called the *Multi-Lingual Guide*, which is available at most hotels. You may obtain a copy by calling 299-7742.

GEORGIA STATE UNIVERSITY TRANSLATORS AND INTERPRETERS SERVICE

Language Dept.
University Plaza 651-2265

The university maintains a current roster of skilled professionals who translate and interpret a number of languages. Dr. Steven DuPouy is director of the graduate degree program involved with this service.

LANGUAGE SERVICES

2256 Northlake Pkwy., Tucker 939-6400

This company offers a broad range of professional translation and interpretation services. Language Services' staff also teaches foreign languages and provides city tours.

ATLANTA ASSOCIATION OF INTERPRETERS & TRANSLATORS

P. O. Box 12172, Atlanta 30355 587-4884

Accredited interpreters and translators provide services in close to 40 languages. The association publishes a membership directory for frequent users of their services.

These services are often used in court cases, business situations and now for the needs of Olympics planners. Dr. Jeannine Normand, director, stresses the importance of accreditation for services in the critical area of communication.

LATIN AMERICAN BUSINESS SERVICES

1401 Johnson Ferry Rd.
Ste. 328-B-7
919-0991

Avail yourself of an array of services for the Spanish-speaking business persons. These include translating, interpreting and an aide-de-camp for conventions.

M. T. TOURS

211 Fernwood Ct., Alpharetta 524-7127

A staff of translators, interpreters and tour guides offers their services to assist you. The company is familiar with local events, entertainment and hotels.

VISITOR INFORMATION NETWORK

3393 Peachtree Rd. N.E. 239-6600

This new information channel is offered in selected metro area hotels. Information on dining, shopping and sights to see are augmented with historical background on Atlanta.

CITIINFO

5988 Peachtree Corners E.
Norcross 447-6469

For multilingual tourist information, look for these multimedia information centers in hotels and other locations throughout the city.

Insiders' Tips

If you're younger than 16, you must wear a helmet when riding a bicycle.

INTERNATIONAL FRIENDSHIP FORCE
522-9490

This unique extension of Southern hospitality was founded by Wayne Smith in 1977. Since the Friendship Force was announced by President Jimmy Carter, more than 1.5 million volunteer ambassadors and hosts from all countries have donated their skills to practice the art of citizen diplomacy. Launched to promote world peace and eliminate barriers between peoples, the Force is funded by private sources including a major grant from Japanese philanthropist Ryoichi Sasakawa.

SISTER CITIES PROGRAM
2349 Fair Oaks Rd.
Decatur   894-4590

Another example of Atlanta's growth toward internationalism is the Sister City programs in the following locations: Brussels, Belgium; Rio de Janeiro, Brazil; Newcastle-Upon-Tyne, England; Montego Bay, Jamaica; Lagos, Nigeria; Port-of-Spain, Trinidad; Toulouse, France; and Tbilisi, Georgia, of the former Soviet Union. In addition, other cities in the metro area take part in the Sister Cities Program. Multiple pairings are in place for Decatur, Marietta and many more cities in the region surrounding Atlanta.

Library Services

For big-time fun on a budget, count on the library system to provide something for everyone. Each county in the metro area operates an extensive system of branches with many educational and enjoyable services and activities. Call the main information lines, listed here by county, for the location of the branch nearest you.

ATLANTA FULTON PUBLIC LIBRARY
One Margaret Mitchell Sq.   730-1700

At Forsyth and Carnegie Way downtown, this is the Atlanta-Fulton County central branch. The library makes available a considerable inventory, including a large collection of African-American books, records and photos. Two special sights are the permanent exhibit on Margaret Mitchell and an extensive collection of first and rare editions of *Gone With the Wind*.

Hours at the central branch are Monday through Thursday from 9 AM to 9 PM; Friday and Saturday from 9 AM to 6 PM; and Sunday from 2 PM to 6 PM.

A full range of programs, including storytelling, art exhibits, classes, films and more is offered. Records, tapes, foreign language publications and framed prints are available for checkout with a library card.

You may obtain a library card by showing two pieces of identification with your current address. A driver's license, voting registration card and a printed bank check are among acceptable forms of identification. Children may obtain a card via a parent's identification plus their own Social Security number.

There are 32 branch libraries through-

You can get the time and temperature free any hour of the day or night by calling 603-3333 or 455-7141.

out the metro area. You'll find a complete list in the blue pages in back of the phone directory's business volume, under Fulton County.

The adjoining counties' library systems also offer extensive services and programs. For the DeKalb County Library system, call the Decatur branch 370-3070. For libraries in Gwinnett County, call 822-4522. In Cobb County, the central headquarters' number is 528-2320.

Moving Time

Right up near the top of the stress scale ranks the experience of relocating. If you're contemplating that big step, take heart, for you have lots of company in Atlanta. The U-Haul Corporation announced in 1993 that more people used their trucks to move here than to any other city in the United States.

Savvy home-seekers get the Sunday newspaper early to get a jump on the competition for that perfect nesting spot. Many area grocery stores and convenience stores have the first edition of the Sunday paper as early as Saturday morning.

One happy result of this constant stream of newcomers is the bounty of companies offering services to make your transition smoother. This sampling will give you an idea of the help that awaits you.

ACCESS ATLANTA TOURS
231 Peachtree St.   *523-1326*

Relocation tours are the specialty of this company. They will show you the city's finest neighborhoods and point out advantages to each location. Tours are offered either one-on-one or in small groups.

BLACK ATLANTA TRANSPLANTS
219 Hermer Cr. N.W.   *696-3571*

Since 1987, Black Atlanta Transplants has been extending a warm welcome to new residents. The company publishes the monthly "Atlanta in the Black" calendar of events.

PROMOVE
3620 Piedmont Ave.   *842-0042*
(800)950-6683

There are many good apartment-locating services in the metro area. ProMove is one we can recommend from personal experience, although other companies offer similar features.

ProMove's well-trained staff uses a specialized computer service to pinpoint properties with the features you want. You can scan color pictures before heading out to inspect the place. Call ahead for an appointment.

If you decide to use an apartment locator company, be sure to determine whether you or the property owner pays for the service.

Pet Care

For exercise service, call **A Friend of the Family**, 643-3000. And for grooming needs, how about a mobile dog salon? **AAA Port-A-Pet Grooming Salon on Wheels**, 288-1293, will come to your rescue.

LOVING TOUCH ANIMAL CENTER
1975 Glenn Club Dr.
Stone Mountain   *498-5956*

At Loving Touch, veterinarian Michelle Tilghman, D.V.M., will perform acupuncture and chiropractic care for your animals. Chinese herbal remedies are part of her treatment services.

UNIVERSITY OF GEORGIA
Veterinary Teaching Hospital
Athens   *(706)542-8343*

Suspect the ailment might be emotional in nature rather than physical? Call Sharon Crowell-Davis, D.V.M., Ph.D., who is a animal behaviorist. She will treat your pet on referral from a regular vet.

Kennels

When you must be away, here are a few examples of places offering good care to your pets.

CLOUD 9 PET RESORT
651 Ward Rd., Ellenwood   981-9512

East of downtown near the intersection of I-285 and I-20, this kennel has been catering to pets since 1961. Their services — supervised individual play, a nine-acre site and extra activities — make you wonder if you could register yourself as a guest. Cloud 9 accepts all kinds of pets. The kennel also offers obedience and protective training.

LAKEVIEW KENNELS
595 Hwy. 120, Roswell   993-2224

Since 1976, Lakeview has offered professional grooming and boarding for all breeds. Other services include obedience training and separate cat boarding facilities. Large-size indoor and outdoor runs ensure your pet's exercise needs are filled.

Varied and Sundry

The following are a variety of services that defy placement in a category. They're included to demonstrate that no matter how unusual your need, some enterprising Atlantan has probably launched a business to serve you.

LAWN LAFFS
P.O. Box 361
Avondale Estates 30002   373-LAFF

This wacky company will plot with you for a prize-winning surprise gift. How about 50 fake pink flamingos flown in between midnight and 6 AM and deposited around a personalized sign in the front yard of your unsuspecting giftee? If flamingos aren't your thing, Lawn Laffs will conspire with you for other suitable images — maybe cows, pigs or heart shapes. Call for additional bright ideas.

CREATIVE TABLES
408 S. Atlanta St., Ste. 140,
Roswell   992-1113, (800)992-1105

On the more elegant side of life, Creative Tables solves entertaining dilemmas with a fine selection of specialty rental linens. The company promises uncompromising attention, from design to installation.

L'ECOLE DE L'ART DE VIVRE
440 Kentbrook Dr. N.W.   843-8647

What if it's not the table setting but your own decorum you want to improve? Atlanta's answer to Miss Manners, Anne Oliver, hosts courses on the art of graceful living. This instruction is part of what has been called a finishing school for adults.

Subjects include an informative look at the etiquette of at-home entertaining for those whose busy lives may have precluded such attentions. For more information, call Ms. Oliver. And remember to say please and thank you.

Special Interests and Late-night Services

Say you're seeking a club to join or fellow hobbyists? For special interest groups, see the daily newspaper calendars. A really extensive list appears each week in *Creative Loafing,* where you'll find everything from theater auditions to health activists and environmental groups. The newspaper is available in racks near many restaurants and in bookstores.

Looking for specific facts? Try the Atlanta *Journal-Constitution's* **News Search line**. For a fee, they can provide you with information on a wide array of topics such as business trends, your competitors, travel destinations and long-lost recipes. Call 222-8899.

When your schedule is full to overflowing, Atlanta's services help you keep up the pace. If you need an all-night grocery store, most of the stores in the Kroger chain are open 24 hours a day. Many have pharmacies that stay open till at least 9 PM.

A 24-hour **postal station** is at 3900 Crown Road in Hapeville. The Sandy Springs Post Office, on Boylston Drive in north Fulton County, is open till 11 PM.

Bibliography

The Campaign for Atlanta. Conshohocken, Penn.: Eastern Acorn Press, 1986.

Davis, Ren and Helen. *Atlanta's Urban Trails, Vols. 1 and 2*. Atlanta: Susan Hunter Publishing, 1988.

Edwards, Anne. *Road to Tara: The Life of Margaret Mitchell*. New Haven and New York: Ticknor & Fields, 1983.

Garrett, Franklin M. *Atlanta and its Environs*, Vol. 1 and Vol. 2. Athens: University of Georgia Press, 1954.

Gleason, David King and Don O'Bryant. *Atlanta*. Baton Rouge and London: Louisiana State University Press, 1994.

Greater Atlanta Newcomer's Guide 1994-95. Atlanta Chamber of Commerce, 1994.

Key, William. *The Battle of Atlanta*. Atlanta: Peachtree Publishers Ltd., 1958.

Martin, Harold M. *Atlanta and its Environs*, Vol. 3. Athens: University of Georgia Press, 1987.

Martin Luther King, Jr. 1929-1968: An Ebony Picture Biography. Chicago: Johnson Publishing Co., 1968.

McBath, Robert Luttrell Jr. and J.O. Baylen. *"Oh, The Patriots, The Patriots!": Oscar Wilde, Georgia, and the Fourth of July*. The Atlanta Historical Journal: Spring, 1980.

McCarley, J. Britt. *The Atlanta Campaign: A Civil War Driving Tour of Atlanta-Area Battlefields*. Atlanta: Cherokee Publishing Co., 1984.

Mitchell, Margaret. *Gone With the Wind*. New York: Macmillan, 1936.

Shavin, Norman and Bruce Galphin. *Atlanta: Triumph of a People*. Atlanta: Capricorn Corp., 1985.

Shavin, Norman and Martin Shartar. *The Million Dollar Legends: Margaret Mitchell and Gone With the Wind*. Atlanta: Capricorn Corp., 1974.

Sweet Auburn: Street of Pride — A Pictorial History. Atlanta: African-American Panoramic Experience, 1988.

Thompson, Joseph F. and Robert Isbell. *Atlanta: A City of Neighborhoods*. Columbia, S.C.: University of South Carolina Press, 1994.

Urban, Wayne J. *Black Scholar: Horace Mann Bond 1904-1972*. Athens, Ga., and London: University of Georgia Press, 1992

Williams, Roger M. *The Bonds: An American Family*. New York: Atheneum, 1971.

Index of Advertisers

ORDER FORM
Fast and Simple!

Mail to:
Insiders Guides®, Inc.
P.O. Drawer 2057
Manteo, NC 27954

Or:
for VISA or
Mastercard orders call
1-800-765-BOOK

Name _____

Address _____

City/State/Zip _____

Qty.	Title/Price	Shipping	Amount
	Insiders' Guide to Richmond/$12.95	$3.00	
	Insiders' Guide to Williamsburg/$14.95	$3.00	
	Insiders' Guide to Virginia's Blue Ridge/$12.95	$3.00	
	Insiders' Guide to Virginia's Chesapeake Bay/$12.95	$3.00	
	Insiders' Guide to Washington, DC/$12.95	$3.00	
	Insiders' Guide to North Carolina's Outer Banks/$12.95	$3.00	
	Insiders' Guide to Wilmington, NC/$12.95	$3.00	
	Insiders' Guide to North Carolina's Crystal Coast/$12.95	$3.00	
	Insiders' Guide to Charleston, SC/$12.95	$3.00	
	Insiders' Guide to Myrtle Beach/$12.95	$3.00	
	Insiders' Guide to Mississippi/$12.95	$3.00	
	Insiders' Guide to Boca Raton & the Palm Beaches/$14.95 (8/95)	$3.00	
	Insiders' Guide to Sarasota/Bradenton/$12.95	$3.00	
	Insiders' Guide to Northwest Florida/$12.95	$3.00	
	Insiders' Guide to Lexington, KY/$12.95	$3.00	
	Insiders' Guide to Louisville/$14.95	$3.00	
	Insiders' Guide to the Twin Cities/$12.95	$3.00	
	Insiders' Guide to Boulder/$12.95	$3.00	
	Insiders' Guide to Denver/$12.95	$3.00	
	Insiders' Guide to The Civil War (Eastern Theater)/$14.95	$3.00	
	Insiders' Guide to North Carolina's Mountains/$14.95	$3.00	
	Insiders' Guide to Atlanta/$14.95 (4/95)	$3.00	
	Insiders' Guide to Branson/$14.95 (12/95)	$3.00	
	Insiders' Guide to Cincinnati/$14.95 (9/95)	$3.00	
	Insiders' Guide to Tampa/St. Petersburg/$14.95 (9/95)	$3.00	

Payment in full (check or money order) must
accompany this order form.
Please allow 2 weeks for delivery.

N.C. residents add 6% sales tax _____

Total _____

Who you are
and what you think
is important to us.

**Fill out the coupon and we'll give you
an Insiders' Guide® for half price ($6.48 off)**

Which book(s) did you buy? _____

Where do you live? _____

In what city did you buy your book? _____

Where did you buy your book? ❑ catalog ❑ bookstore ❑ newspaper ad
❑ retail shop ❑ other _____

How often do you travel? ❑ yearly ❑ bi-annually ❑ quarterly
❑ more than quarterly

Did you buy your book because you were ❑ moving ❑ vacationing
❑ wanted to know more about your home town ❑ other _____

_____

Will the book be used by ❑ family ❑ couple ❑ individual ❑ group

What is you annual household income? ❑ under $25,000 ❑ $25,000 to $35,000
❑ $35,000 to $50,000 ❑ $50,000 to $75,000 ❑ over $75,000

How old are you? ❑ under 25 ❑ 25-35 ❑ 36-50 ❑ 51-65 ❑ over 65

Did you use the book before you left for your destination? ❑ yes ❑ no

Did you use the book while at your destination? ❑ yes ❑ no

On average per month, how many times do you refer to your book? ❑ 1-3 ❑ 4-7
❑ 8-11 ❑ 12-15 ❑ 16 and up

On average, how many other people use your book? ❑ no others ❑ 1 ❑ 2
❑ 3 ❑ 4 or more

Is there anything you would like to tell us about Insiders' Guides? _____
_____

_____

Name _____ Address _____

City _____ State _____ Zip _____

**We'll send you a voucher for $6.48 off any Insiders' Guide© and a list of available
titles as soon as we get this card from you. Thanks for being an Insider!**